Fundamentals of CRM with Dynamics 365 and Power Platform

Enhance your customer relationship management by extending Dynamics 365 using a no-code approach

Nicolae Tarla

BIRMINGHAM - MUMBAI

Fundamentals of CRM with Dynamics 365 and Power Platform

Commissioning Editor: Richa Tripathi
Acquisition Editor: Denim Pinto
Content Development Editor: Digvijay Bagul
Senior Editor: Storm Mann
Technical Editor: Gaurav Gala
Copy Editor: Safis Editing
Project Coordinator: Francy Puthiry
Proofreader: Safis Editing
Indexer: Pratik Shirodkar
Production Designer: Joshua Misquitta

First published: December 2014
Second edition: May 2016
Third edition: October 2020

Production reference: 1011020

Published by Packt Publishing Ltd.
Livery Place
35 Livery Street
Birmingham
B3 2PB, UK.

ISBN 978-1-78995-024-3

www.packt.com

Packt‹›

Packt.com

Subscribe to our online digital library for full access to over 7,000 books and videos, as well as industry leading tools to help you plan your personal development and advance your career. For more information, please visit our website.

Why subscribe?

- Spend less time learning and more time coding with practical eBooks and Videos from over 4,000 industry professionals

- Improve your learning with Skill Plans built especially for you

- Get a free eBook or video every month

- Fully searchable for easy access to vital information

- Copy and paste, print, and bookmark content

Did you know that Packt offers eBook versions of every book published, with PDF and ePub files available? You can upgrade to the eBook version at www.packt.com and as a print book customer, you are entitled to a discount on the eBook copy. Get in touch with us at customercare@packtpub.com for more details.

At www.packt.com, you can also read a collection of free technical articles, sign up for a range of free newsletters, and receive exclusive discounts and offers on Packt books and eBooks.

Contributors

About the author

Nicolae Tarla is an Independent Consultant focused on business transformation, enterprise architecture, and digital transformation. He has architected and implemented business solutions for over 15 years for private and public sectors, at both enterprise and SMB level. With a passion for CRM, he has touched multiple platforms during his career and continues to recommend the best business solutions for clients. He was awarded the Microsoft MVP for four consecutive years. He is actively involved with the leadership team for the local D365UG and participates in organizing the local D365 Saturday events. He continues to share his knowledge through his personal blog and other channels. His Twitter handle is `@niktuk`.

> *I would like to thank my family for the support provided during this time. Without your encouragement, I would never have embarked on this project, yet I'm glad I did. Also, a big thumbs up to the Dynamics teams at Microsoft and the Community. Keep on creating, keep on rocking!*

About the reviewer

Danilo Capuano is a Microsoft Dynamics 365 CE technical manager and Microsoft certified trainer with over 13 years' experience in IT, having been involved in all phases of ALM. Currently, Danilo works for AGIC Technology, a Microsoft Gold partner, in the role of Microsoft Dynamics 365 CE technical delivery manager and Naples delivery center head. He is involved in the CRM service line and manages and leads both technical resources and projects' technical phases, dealing with everything from Microsoft DevOps methodology to delivering innovative solutions that help customers' digital transformation.

Packt is searching for authors like you

If you're interested in becoming an author for Packt, please visit authors.packtpub.com and apply today. We have worked with thousands of developers and tech professionals, just like you, to help them share their insight with the global tech community. You can make a general application, apply for a specific hot topic that we are recruiting an author for, or submit your own idea.

Table of Contents

Preface

This book presents an overview of the Dynamics 365 core capabilities, the solutions available out of the box, as well as the underlying platform powering this suite of solutions. The book takes you on a journey through the basics of the platform, looking at each functional app and its capabilities. In this book, in the later chapters, we will look at the basic configuration options and integration capabilities, and conclude with an overview of the administration capabilities.

Who this book is for

This book is for those who are looking for comprehensive guidance on the latest Dynamics 365 and Power Platform features in terms of configuration and customization. This book will also introduce you to the core concepts for Microsoft Dynamics certifications. You can find the basics to get you going on your journey to obtaining certifications such as the MB-200 series and the MB-901 series.

This title primarily targets new users to this platform, as well as functional consultants looking to expand their knowledge. It focuses on a no-code approach to configuring and extending the platform capabilities to suit your specific business needs.

What this book covers

Chapter 1, *Getting Started with Dynamics 365*, presents you with an introduction to the platform, an overview of the cloud offering model, and the steps to create your first free trial instance.

Chapter 2, *Dynamics 365 Platform Structure*, delves into the platform structure and core capabilities and introduces you to the core concepts around finding your way through the various functional applications.

Chapter 3, *Dynamics 365 Sales Application*, introduces you to the Sales application and its available features.

Chapter 4, *Dynamics 365 Customer Service*, moves on to the Customer Service application, introducing you to its intended purpose.

Chapter 5, *Dynamics 365 Field Service*, looks at the Field Service application and its set of services available to users.

Chapter 6, *Dynamics 365 Project Service Automation*, tackles the **Project Service Automation (PSA)** application and feature set.

Chapter 7, *Dynamics 365 Marketing*, presents the application and features released with the new Marketing offering.

Chapter 8, *Dynamics 365 Customer Engagement and Power Platform*, looks at how the Power Platform powers the core functionality for the various Dynamics 365 applications.

Chapter 9, *Customizing Dynamics 365*, assumes that once you are familiar with the existing applications offered, you will want to either extend these applications to fit your specific business needs or create entirely new applications.

Chapter 10, *Building Better Business Functionality*, builds on the concepts learned so far, and looks at automating business needs, making for better user experience and closer alignment with existing business processes.

Chapter 11, *Out-of-the Box Integration Capabilities*, looks at the configurable integration options. The platform leverages a set of adjacent services for extended features and functionality.

Chapter 12, *Custom Integration Capabilities*, builds on the concept that a well-integrated platform presents more value. It looks at various integration options, allowing direct integration with other external and third-party solutions.

Chapter 13, *Core Administration Concepts*, presents an overview of the most common administrative options available for a well-tuned solution.

To get the most out of this book

To follow along, you will need a computer connected to the internet. The solution is presented as a web application that is primarily cloud-hosted.

Certain features will require you to have the local Microsoft Office applications installed. We touch on using Microsoft Word for templates, as well as Microsoft Excel for working with tabular data. While you could use the online versions of these applications, you will have a better experience with the locally installed applications.

In addition to that, we touch on the mobile application that is available. This will require a mobile device with a recent mobile OS version. Both Android and iOS are supported.

Software/hardware covered in the book	OS requirements
Computer with an internet connection	Windows or macOS
Office suite	Microsoft Word and Microsoft Excel
Mobile device	Android or iOS

Download the color images

We also provide a PDF file that has color images of the screenshots/diagrams used in this book. You can download it here: `https://static.packt-cdn.com/downloads/9781789950243_ColorImages.pdf`

Conventions used

There are a number of text conventions used throughout this book.

`CodeInText`: Indicates code words in text, database table names, folder names, filenames, file extensions, pathnames, dummy URLs, user input, and Twitter handles. Here is an example: "Navigate to your OneDrive, create a folder called `PowerApps`, and create a new Excel file. We'll call this file `Customers.xlsx`."

Bold: Indicates a new term, an important word. Here is an example: The extensibility model leverages the **Common Data Model (CDM)** along with the **Common Data Service (CDS)** for apps, which is also an integral part of the Power Platform.

Screen text: Indicates words that you see onscreen. For example, words in menus or dialog boxes appear in the text like this. Here is an example: "In the **User name** area, click on the **Get a new email address** link to create a new address."

 Warnings or important notes appear like this.

 Tips and tricks appear like this.

Get in touch

Feedback from our readers is always welcome.

General feedback: If you have questions about any aspect of this book, mention the book title in the subject of your message and email us at customercare@packtpub.com.

Errata: Although we have taken every care to ensure the accuracy of our content, mistakes do happen. If you have found a mistake in this book, we would be grateful if you would report this to us. Please visit www.packtpub.com/support/errata, selecting your book, clicking on the Errata Submission Form link, and entering the details.

Piracy: If you come across any illegal copies of our works in any form on the Internet, we would be grateful if you would provide us with the location address or website name. Please contact us at copyright@packt.com with a link to the material.

If you are interested in becoming an author: If there is a topic that you have expertise in and you are interested in either writing or contributing to a book, please visit authors.packtpub.com.

Reviews

Please leave a review. Once you have read and used this book, why not leave a review on the site that you purchased it from? Potential readers can then see and use your unbiased opinion to make purchase decisions, we at Packt can understand what you think about our products, and our authors can see your feedback on their book. Thank you!

For more information about Packt, please visit packt.com.

Section 1 - Platform Structure and Extensibility Capabilities

In this section, you will gain the necessary platform understanding around deployment models, data centers, platform modular structure, and extensibility options.

This section comprises the following chapters:

- Chapter 1, *Getting Started with Dynamics 365*
- Chapter 2, *Dynamics 365 Platform Structure*

Getting Started with Dynamics 365

1

Industries have seen **customer relationship management (CRM)** become one of the most essential tools for business growth. Businesses have an interest in tracking their regular customers from the very beginning, offering them a better experience and attracting new customers. This interest led to the birth of the traditional CRM system.

Add to that the need to track vendors and partners, determine where the best relationships are in place, and find out what the most efficient way to collaborate with these other businesses is, and you can see how CRM becomes a rather complex endeavor.

Over time, it turned out that having such platforms hosted in house, while absolutely providing increased value, encountered new challenges when faced with a mobile workforce. The cloud was there to support this sorely needed expansion.

The next logical evolution happened somewhat in parallel with the move to the cloud. Organizations are recognizing that a simple system, on its own, cannot provide the value needed for the business to gain an edge over its competitors. As such, the tools evolved again, integrating with other essential tools in the organization, as well as with various social channels.

The last few years have seen a merger of the core **enterprise resource planning (ERP)** platforms with the classic customer relationship management platform. This results in better end-to-end processes across the entire organization, and better visibility into where the biggest issues are within an organization. The end results provide better customer experience and a faster and better service, while adapting to the customers' growing online presence.

Dynamics 365, now joining under its umbrella with both CRM and ERP functionality, is Microsoft's response to a growing trend. It is a set of robust business applications, with a long history and presence in the market, all brought together to maximize an organization's performance and homogenize its data.

This book focuses on the functionality, which was formerly part of the CRM platform. While at times we might touch on some of the newer offerings, we'll be spending most of our time focusing on the revamped modules for Sales, Customer Service, Field Service, Project Service, and Marketing. We'll also be looking at the new paradigm and features offered through the Power Platform. As the new kid on the block, the Power Platform quickly gained popularity by not being entirely dependent on the typical CRM functionality, but rather by allowing us to build brand new functionality for the organization in a much simpler and rapid manner.

The following topics will be covered in this chapter:

- What is Dynamics 365 really?
- Global data center locations for Dynamics CRM Online
- What do you need to customize Dynamics CRM?
- Opening a free 30-day trial of Dynamics 365 for Sales
- Configuring a domain name for your environment
- Integrating with Office 365 E3 trial services

In this chapter, we will first look at what environment we need to complete the examples presented in this book. We will create a new environment based on a Microsoft Dynamics 365 Online 30-day trial. This approach will give us the means to experiment with a trial environment for free.

Let's get started!

Understanding what Dynamics 365 really is

Dynamics 365 is an *umbrella marketing term* describing several platforms and functional products. The various applications under this branding include the following:

- Sales
- Customer Service
- Field Service
- Human Resources
- Finance and Operations
- Retail
- Project Service Automation

- Marketing
- Artificial Intelligence
- Mixed Reality
- Business Central

A detailed look at these applications will show that, at their core, these are the next evolution of the Dynamics CRM, Dynamics AX, and Dynamics NAV platforms. Some have organically evolved into what they are now, while others have received a major update with the move under the Dynamics 365 umbrella.

As mentioned before, the focus of this book is centered around the former Dynamics CRM platform, and how the separate modules evolved from it, becoming the following:

- Dynamics 365 for Sales
- Dynamics 365 for Customer Service
- Dynamics 365 for Field Service
- Dynamics 365 for Project Service Automation
- Dynamics 365 for Marketing

Whereas before, you were buying a package that included most of these, now you have the flexibility to select only the modules you need when choosing the cloud SaaS offering. This allows your organization to start with, let's say, Sales, and later expand into Customer Service.

Note that if you still choose to purchase the on-premise deployment option, which continues to be available, you will continue to get the same model that we've all seen in Dynamics CRM, with modules for Sales, Service, and Marketing. But the real value is in the cloud offering, where additional services and functionality are abundant.

Along with the standard platform functionality provided, we have a wide range of customization options, allowing us to extend and further customize solutions to satisfy a large range of other business scenarios. In addition, we can integrate this platform with other applications and create a seamless solution spanning across multiple platforms.

While it is by no means the only available platform on the market today, Microsoft's Dynamics 365 is one of the fastest-growing platforms and is gaining large acceptance at all levels (from small to mid-size to enterprise-level organizations). This is because of a multitude of reasons, some of which include the following:

- The variety of deployment options
- The scalability
- The extensibility
- The ease of integration with other systems
- The ease of use

Deployment options include the SaaS (cloud) offering, which provides the most advanced functionality, the classical on-premise deployment, and (not as common anymore) a third-party hosted solution, which is just another model of an on-premise deployment.

 For the purpose of this book, we're looking at the SaaS model and we're leveraging a 30-day trial. Once you have a trial in place, you can turn this into a paid subscription when you're ready to move to production.

A recent development gives us the ability to host a virtual Dynamics 365 (CRM) environment in Azure. This offloads the cost of maintaining the local infrastructure in a fashion similar to a third-party hosted solution, but takes advantage of the scalability and performance of a large cloud solution maintained and fully supported by Microsoft.

 The white paper released by Microsoft (which you can read at `http://www.microsoft.com/en-us/download/details.aspx?id=49193`) describes the deployment model using Azure Virtual Machines.

In the next sections, we will look at some of the benefits that Dynamics 365 provides.

Scalability

Dynamics 365 can scale over a wide range of deployment options—from a single box deployment (used mostly for development) to a cloud offering that can span over a large number of servers and host a large number of environments. The same base solution can handle all the scenarios in between with ease.

Let's now see some of the extensibility features.

Extensibility

Dynamics 365 is a rapid-development platform. While the base offering comes in prepackaged functionality for Sales, Customer Service, Field Service, Project Service, and Marketing, a large variety of solutions can be built on top of the Dynamics 365 platform. The extensibility model leverages the **Common Data Model (CDM)** along with the **Common Data Service (CDS)** for apps, which is also an integral part of the Power Platform. This allows power users, nondevelopers, and developers alike to build custom solutions to handle various other business scenarios or integrate with other third-party platforms.

Microsoft AppSource is a great example of such solutions that have been built to extend the core platform, and is offered for sale by various companies. These companies are called **independent software vendors (ISVs)**, and they play a very important role in the ecosystem created by Microsoft. In time, and with enough experience, some of them become the *go-to partners* for various implementations.

If nothing else, AppSource is a cool place to look at some of the solutions created and search for specific applications. The idea of the marketplace became public sometime around 2010 and was integrated into Dynamics CRM in 2011. At launch, it was designed as a searchable repository of solutions. It is a win-win for both solution providers and customers alike. Solutions can also be rated, thus giving customers better community feedback before they commit to purchasing and implementing a foreign solution into their organization.

 AppSource can be found at `https://appsource.microsoft.com/`.

When navigating to the AppSource home page, you will be presented with a search option right at the top of the screen, as shown in the following screenshot:

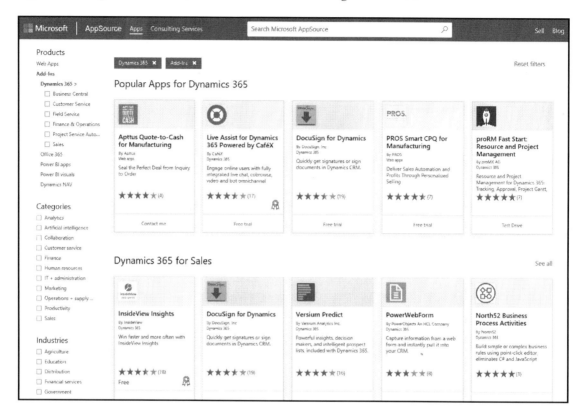

Now you have the option to filter your results by platform/product, standard categories, or industries. In addition, you can easily search for a specific solution using keywords or the name of the solution or ISV.

When searching for a solution provider, all solutions from that provider are listed, and you can further drill down by using the choices in the sidebar.

As mentioned previously, the community rating is clearly visible and provides the necessary feedback that you should consider when evaluating new solutions.

In addition to third-party and ISV solutions, starting with Dynamics 365, your organization might now choose to create a specific line of business applications and make them available to specific user groups. You can access these by extending the Dynamics 365 dropdown from the top-most navigation bar. This will bring up the left pane, which lists the standard Microsoft solutions and any other custom solution provided by the enterprise, as follows:

Microsoft recognized early on that a disparate system does not hold as much value as an integrated one. As such, various capabilities have been provided for better integration. In addition, some of the partners in the ecosystem have also provided their own solutions. Let's look at some of these capabilities in the next section.

Ability to integrate with other systems

There is a large variety of integration options available when working with Dynamics 365. In addition, various deployment options offer more or fewer integration features. With the Dynamics 365 Online (SaaS) model, you get more configurable integration options with cloud services, while the on-premise solution typically requires a more intensive effort to achieve integration. Here is where third-party tools shine.

You can use specific connectors provided by either Microsoft or other third-party providers for integration with specific solutions. This again varies depending on the deployment model and the integration service or tools used.

Microsoft provides services such as Power Automate Flows or Logic Apps. These services provide a large variety of prebuilt connectors and facilitate a user-friendly experience when designing and implementing integrations with external systems.

When the aforementioned connector options are not available, you can still integrate with other solutions using a third-party integration tool. This allows real-time integration with legacy systems. Some of the most popular tools used for integration include the following:

- **Kingsway Software**: https://www.kingswaysoft.com/
- **Scribe**: http://www.scribesoft.com/
- **BizTalk**: http://www.microsoft.com/en-us/server-cloud/products/biztalk/

Let's look at some of the features that were introduced for better user experience in the next section.

Ease of use

Dynamics 365 offers users a variety of options to interact with the system. You can access Dynamics 365 through a browser (now with support for all recent versions of the major browsers).

In addition, a user can interact with the system directly from the very familiar interface of Outlook, or through the App for Outlook if you're using the web version. The Dynamics 365 connector for Outlook allows users to get access to all of the system data and features from within Outlook. In addition, a set of functions built specifically for Outlook allows users to track and interact with emails, tasks, and events from within Outlook. Similar functionality is now built into the App for Outlook.

Offline support still remains the biggest benefit of using the Outlook client. Data can be taken offline, work can be done while you are disconnected, and then the data can be synchronized back into the system when connectivity becomes available again.

For mobile users, Dynamics 365 can be accessed from mobile devices and tablets. Dynamics 365 provides a standard web-based interface for most mobile devices, as well as specific applications for various platforms, including Windows-based tablets, iPads, and Android tablets. With these apps, you can also take a limited sub-set of cached data offline, create new records, and then synchronize them back to the platform the next time you go online. The quality of these mobile offerings has increased exponentially over the last few versions, and new features are being added with each new release.

In addition, third-party providers have also built mobile solutions for Dynamics CRM. Resco, for example, is leading the pack with a very robust mobile client for Field Service with full offline support.

With the ability to build additional apps leveraging the unified interface, users can now also have a specific line of business application built for their mobile clients that is controlled at the enterprise level. For the most part, these apps can be built through configuration alone, and are an easy way for organizations to provide only specialized functionality to mobile clients, thereby removing clutter and making life easier for the user.

Global data center locations for Dynamics CRM Online

Dynamics CRM Online is hosted at various locations around the world. Preview organizations can be created in all available locations, but features and updates are typically rolled out on a schedule, which is faster in some locations than others.

The format of the Dynamics CRM Online Organization URL describes the data center location. As such, the standard format is `https://OrganizationName.crm[x].dynamics.com`.

The `OrganizationName` phrase is the *name you have selected* for your online organization. This is customizable and is validated for uniqueness within the respective data center.

The `[x]` represents a *number*. At the time of writing, this number can be anywhere between *2, 4, 5, 6, 7, 9, or no number at all*. This describes the global data center that is used to host your organization.

Microsoft has chosen to disclose the locations of data centers used on the Office 365 site. The following screenshot shows the available locations at the time of writing:

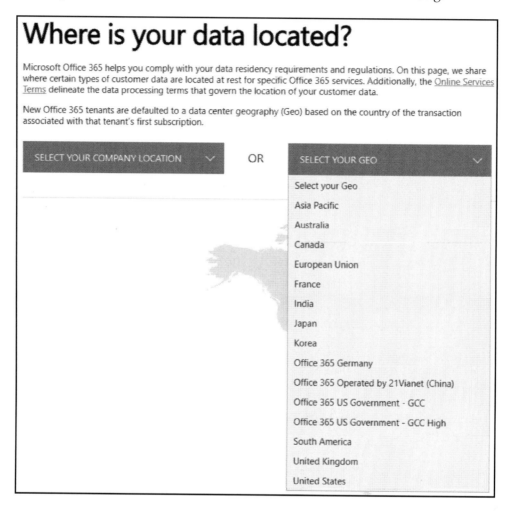

New data centers are being added on a regular basis. Some of the drivers behind adding these new data centers revolve around not only performance improvements, as a data center located closer to a customer will theoretically provide a better performance, but also a need for privacy and localization of data. Strict legislation around data residency has a great impact on the selection of the deployment model by customers who are bound to store all data locally to the country of operation.

These data centers share services between Dynamics 365 Online and other services, such as Azure and Office 365.

Advantages of choosing Dynamics 365 Online

The decision to select one hosting model over another for Dynamics 365 is typically driven by a multitude of factors, including, but not limited to, the following:

- The better feature set
- Financially backed uptime guarantee
- Extended compliance
- Scalability
- Time to market
- Integration with other online services

Over the last few years, there has been a huge increase in reliance on the cloud. Microsoft has been very focused on enhancing its Online offering and has continued to devote more functionality and more resources to support the cloud model. As such, Dynamics 365 Online has become a force to reckon with. It is hosted on a very modern and high-performing infrastructure. Microsoft has invested literally billions of dollars in new data centers and infrastructure. This allows new customers to forego the necessary expenses for infrastructure associated with an on-premise deployment.

Along with investments in infrastructure, the **service-level agreement (SLA)** offered by Dynamics 365 Online is financially backed by Microsoft. Depending on the service selected, the uptime is guaranteed and backed financially. Application and infrastructure are automatically handled for you by Microsoft, so you don't have to retain staff to handle these functions. This translates to much lower upfront costs, as well as reduced costs for ongoing maintenance and upgrades.

The Dynamics 365 Online offering is also compliant with various regulatory requirements and backed and verified through various third-party tests. Rules, regulations, and policies in various locales are validated and certified by global and local organizations. Some of the various compliance policies that are evaluated include, but are not limited to, the following:

- Data privacy and confidentiality policies
- Data classification
- Information security
- Privacy
- Data stewardship
- Secure infrastructure
- Identity and access control

All these compliance requirements conform to regulations stipulated by the **International Standard Organization** (**ISO**) and other international and local standards. Independent auditors validate standards compliance. Microsoft is ISO 27001 certified.

 The Microsoft Trust Center website is located at `http://www.microsoft.com/en-us/trustcenter/CloudServices/Dynamics`. This website provides additional information on compliance, responsibilities, and warranties. Whenever the platform is updated to comply with new regulations, you can find the information at this website. Take GDPR as one of the most recent examples of regulations with a potentially global impact. This site has an entire section dedicated to this topic and guides the reader through what's needed for an organization to remain compliant.

Furthermore, choosing the cloud over a standard on-premises deployment offers other advantages around scalability, faster time to market, and higher value proposition.

In addition to the standard benefits of an Online deployment, one other great advantage is the ability to *spin-up a 30-day trial* instance of Dynamics 365 Online and convert it to a paid instance only when you are ready to go to production. This allows customizers and companies to get started and customize their solution in a free environment, with no additional costs attached. The 30-day trial instance gives us a 25-day license instance that allows us to not only customize the Organization, but also test various roles and restrictions.

In the next section, we will learn about the prerequisites needed to customize Dynamics CRM.

Customizing Dynamics 365

First and foremost, in order to follow through with the information presented in this book, you will need an instance of Dynamics 365 Online. The following sections will describe in detail how you can obtain a 30-day trial instance.

In addition, in order to subscribe to a 30-day trial, you will need a Microsoft account (formerly called a **Live account**) or an existing Office 365 account if you will be associating this trial with your organization. You can obtain a Microsoft account by going to `https://signup.live.com/`.

The **Create account** page presents you with a sign-up form. In the username area, click on the **Get a new email address** link to create a new address:

At the time of writing, you have a choice of `outlook.com` or `hotmail.com` for your newly created email address. The selected username is validated, as it must be *unique*.

Once your account is created, you will be logged into your new account and will see the welcome email. At this point, you can use this account to create your 30-day trial for Dynamics 365 Online.

 If you do have an existing Microsoft account, you do not need to create a new one. You can create multiple trials for both Dynamics 365 Online and Office 365.

While this book will not provide step-by-step instructions to be followed, it is strongly recommended that you have an environment available to supplement the material you will be reading and to familiarize yourself with the platform. In order to minimize the footprint and allow everybody to start quickly, I have opted to present all the topics based on a Dynamics 365 for Sales Online 30-day trial organization in the next section.

Opening a free 30-day trial of Dynamics 365 for Sales

In order to open your 30-day trial of Microsoft Dynamics 365 for Sales, you will need to go through a wizard-driven process that we will learn about in the following subsections.

Note that for partners, you can also use the demos site to create new trial instances. This is accessible at `https://demos.microsoft.com`. But for the purpose of this book, I will assume that you are not associated with an existing partner, which means that instead, you should navigate to `https://dynamics.microsoft.com/`.

Let's now proceed with provisioning a new 30-day trial.

Trial provisioning

Let's look at the steps to create a new instance:

1. From the **Applications** dropdown at the top, expand **Sales**, and then select **Overview**.
2. Review the features. Toward the bottom of the page, you will find a **Get Started** button. Note that, as the platform evolves, so does the home site; this link could be moved to another location on the page by the time this book reaches its audience. Regardless of its current location, you will still find a link to trigger the process to create your trial on the home site.
3. Next, you will be presented with an option to either sign up for a free trial or request a callback. The second option involves receiving support from Microsoft, but the process is so simple that we will do it ourselves. Select **Sign up for a free trial**.
4. You will then be directed to `https://trials.dynamics.com/`.

It's true that you could have just started from this link, but if at a later time Microsoft decides to shuffle things around on the site, know that you will always find your way to a trial from the main platform page.

At the time of this writing, the trials page looks like the following screenshot:

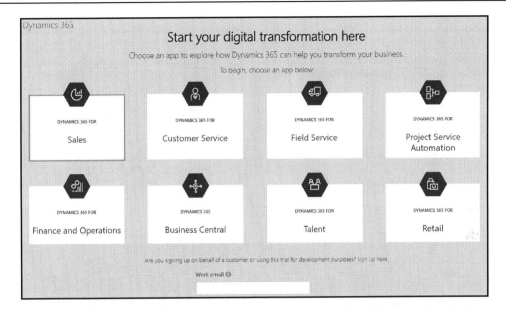

5. Now, you could associate this trial with your existing Office 365 subscription tenant by logging in with an Office 365 account. Instead, we're going to find the **Sign up here** link right above the login area and click it. This will allow us to use a personal account that is not associated with a partner. In the pop-up window, select **No, continue signing up**. This will put us in the trial creation workflow:

Note that the country cannot be changed once assigned. This determines the global data center in which your instance is provisioned. I suggest you choose a location close to where you or your client/employer are located if you are building this for a client.

6. Next, you will be prompted to create your organization and its first user:

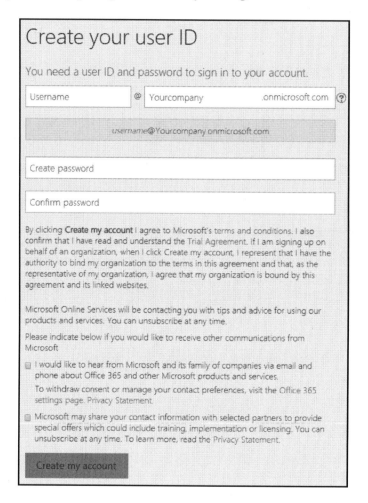

7. Once you fill in the organization name in the **Yourcompany** field, this name will be validated for uniqueness. If everything is okay, then your new account will appear with a green checkmark in the gray bar below.

8. Click on **Create my account** to continue.

9. You will then be prompted to enter a mobile number for validation. You will receive a text message with a verification code. You need to enter it in the next screen and click **Next**. This triggers the process to create your instance:

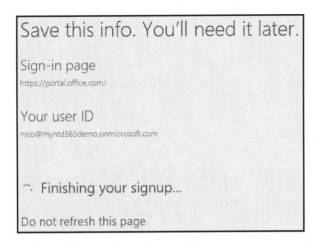

10. When done, click on **Set up** to start configuring your new instance. You need to perform the configuration before anything is accessible:

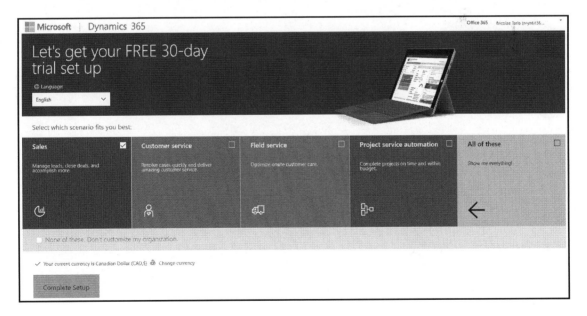

For the purpose of this book, we are only looking to set up Dynamics 365 for Sales right now, so make sure the check box for Sales is selected. Validate the currency based on the country you selected in the setup. You could change the default currency here. Make sure that you select the currency that is the most relevant. While you can use multiple currencies on the platform, you will always have a base currency that cannot be changed once set.

11. Now, click on **Complete Setup** and grab a coffee because this takes a moment. Behind the scenes, a new instance in Dynamics 365 for Sales is created based on the configurations you provided during the setup wizard. This involves, among other things, creating a new *Azure Active Directory* that provides authentication, an Office 365 Admin portal for the configuration of services, and the Dynamics 365 tenant with the Sales application installed.

12. When done, you will be forwarded to the newly created instance. Sample data will already be populated by default, but can easily be removed:

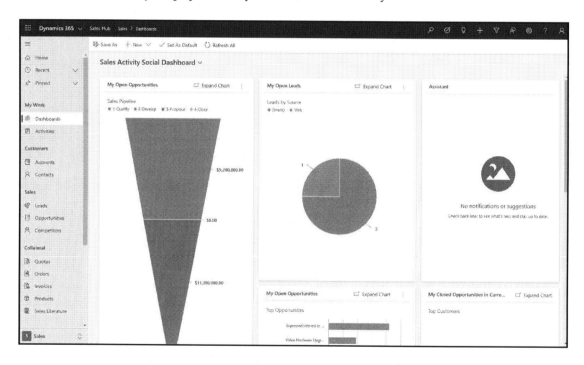

And with this, we now have a functional Dynamics 365 for Sales organization. We will be adding the additional modules as we get to review the functionality for each in the following chapters.

Once we have created the default instance, we can access it directly by the URL, which is going to be in the format `https://[orgName].crm[x].dynamics.com`, with `[orgName]` being the name of the organization you selected and `crm[x]` representing the geolocation of the data center that your instance is served from.

Note that once you have a domain configured, you can reference your current instance by the URL you configure for it, leveraging your domain name.

Now, let's check out the other ways in which can we access this instance.

Tenant access through the Office 365 Admin console

An alternative way to access this instance is by logging in to your Office 365 tenant at `https://portal.office.com/` and following these steps:

1. Log in using the previously created account and password. Once in, assuming that you are an admin and have the necessary permissions, you can navigate to the Microsoft 365 Admin Center, expand **All Admin Centers**, and find the Dynamics 365 Admin Center listed on the left side:

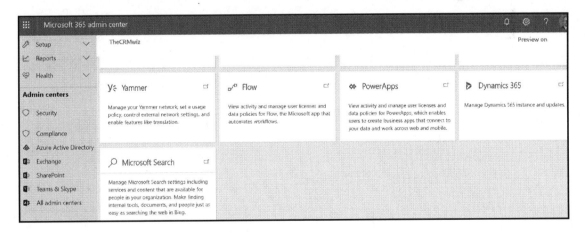

2. This opens the **Administration Center**. Here, you will find your current trial organization. If you are on a paid subscription, you will get the opportunity to manage multiple paid production instances, as well as various nonproduction instances:

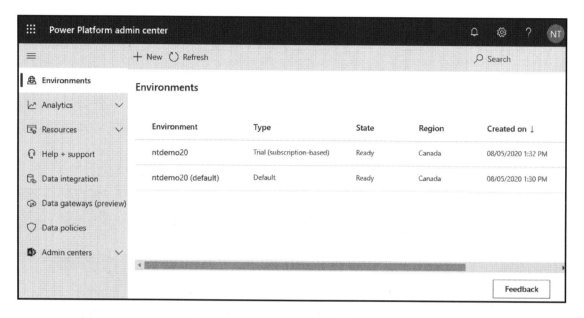

3. You can navigate through the tabs at the top to see the available updates for your instances and the status of the service health and announcements, and manage backups and the various applications installed in your instances.

Back on the instances screen, we have the option to edit our instance properties. Selecting this option takes us to a form that allows us to change the name and URL of our organization, as well as provide a detailed message on the purpose of this organization. We can also copy our current instance to a new sandbox instance. This allows us to create a copy of a production instance for various tests. The notifications option allows us to configure additional users to be notified by email when administrative notices are distributed.

As you can see, besides the **Production** instance, we also get a **Sandbox** instance. In the next section, we will learn what the sandbox environment is.

What is a sandbox instance?

What are the different instance types, you might ask. Well, a **Sandbox instance** is basically a *nonproduction instance*. Depending on your licensing agreement, you could have one or more production instances, as well as several nonproduction sandbox instances. Once in an instance, a sandbox instance is clearly marked by a sandbox overlay over the top header.

From a functionality perspective, no functional changes are made to a sandbox instance. They offer the same functionality as a production instance. One very important aspect of sandbox instances is the fact that, while functionality is maintained on a par with production instances, the database is completely isolated from production. A sandbox instance can contain a full set or a subset of production data, users, and customizations.

As such, sandbox instances can be used for development, **quality assurance (QA)**, and **user acceptance testing (UAT)** environments.

Finally, selecting the **Open** button allows you to open the selected instance and navigate directly to the application. Make sure that you have at least one security role assigned to your user in order to access an instance. Since you created this trial, you should have the Administrator role assigned.

The final chapter of this book deals with administration, and that's where we will come back to the Dynamics 365 Administration Center to visit the remaining tabs and options. Until then, let's focus on our current trial instance.

The trial instance of Dynamics 365 for Sales comes preloaded with some sample data. This makes it easy for a first-time user to see some of the visual representations on the dashboards, and also gives said user the opportunity to track some of the data relationships and see how related data is presented in certain records.

In the next few chapters, we will start investigating all the available features of the Dynamics 365 platform. For now, in the next section, let's learn more about how to configure a domain name for your environment.

Configuring a domain name for your environment

One of the setup steps available with an Office 365 instance is the ability to configure a domain name associated with your instance. While you can continue working with Dynamics 365 for Sales without setting up a domain, it is a good idea to do it now. With the domain setup, you have one less configuration step to take before turning your trial into a production instance. In order to provide a better user experience, you should always configure your domain before going to production.

If you want to proceed with setting up a domain, you can either use an existing domain that you own or, for a few dollars, you can purchase a domain from various registrars. For the purpose of this book, I have purchased a `.info` domain from GoDaddy at `https://godaddy.com/`.

Let's look at the steps to configure a domain, as follows:

1. Access the Office 365 admin center by navigating to `https://portal.office.com/`.

2. You will be prompted to log in. Use the previously created account; this will get you to the main admin center console:

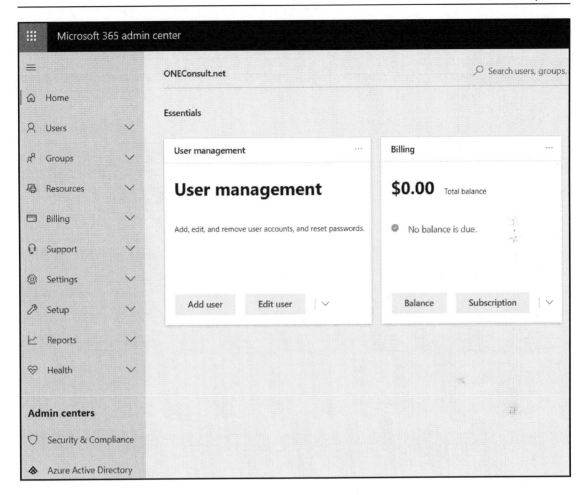

If you do not see the updated interface for the Office 365 Admin Center, look for a **Try the Preview** switch close to the top-right side of the page. Most likely, by the time you read this book, this will be the new interface standard. If you only see a subset of available options on the left navigation, click on the **Show all** option at the bottom. This will expand the listing of configurations.

3. Next, expand **Setup** and select **Domains**. Here, you have the option to purchase a domain (if you haven't already done so) or just add a new domain:

For the purpose of this trial, I am assuming that you have already purchased a domain and you are just configuring it. If you choose not to use a domain, you can skip to the next section while using the default configuration.

4. Go to **Add domain**. This will take you to the first page of the domain configuration wizard. This first page displays a nice process flow at the top, showing the stages that you have to pass through to configure your new domain and collecting the domain details that you intend to use with your instance:

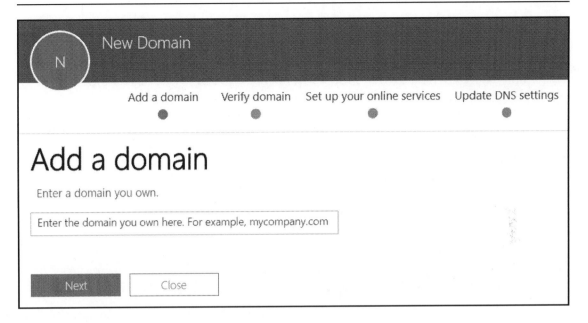

5. Follow the wizard to complete the domain configuration. When it is done, in the administration console you will have the ability to grant your users the ability to use the added domain instead of the default `@[orgName].onmicrosoft.com` account names. Now it all looks much more professional, and you have one less step to configure when you decide to turn this into a production instance.

Let's have a look at the Office 365 services that are available to be configured and integrated with our platform.

Integrating with Office 365 E3 trial services

Office 365 is offered in a variety of flavors, each including a different set of services. One of the common tiers offered as a trial is the **E3**. It includes services such as the Office suite, email, document and file management, conferencing and Skype, team sites, and so on.

 For additional details on what is included in Office 365 E3, refer to `https://products.office.com/en-us/business/office-365-enterprise-e3-business-software`.

From your existing Office 365 instance where you created your Dynamics 365 for Sales trial, you can add this additional trial service by going through the following steps:

1. Start by navigating on the left navigation area to **BILLING** | **Purchase services**.
2. Find the **Office apps and services** section and scroll to find the **Office 365 Enterprise E3** selection. Click on it:

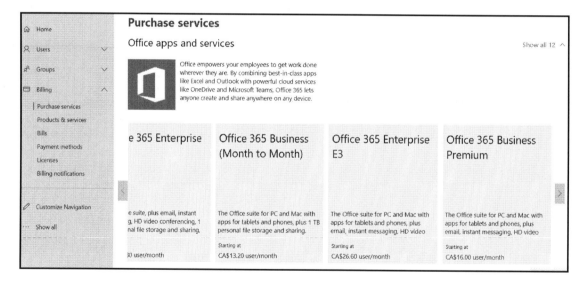

3. On the page that opens, click the **Get free trial** button to add this trial to your existing instance:

Purchase services

Office 365 Enterprise E3

The Office suite for PC and Mac with apps for tablets and phones, plus email, instant messaging, HD video conferencing, 1 TB personal file storage and sharing, and available add-ons like PSTN calling.

Starting at
CA$26.60 user/month

Subscription options
- CA$26.60 user/month
- CA$319.20 user/year

Pick subscription   Get free trial ⓘ

4. You will be asked to provide a valid mobile number for validation. A text message will be sent with a validation code. Once you complete the wizard, you will be asked to confirm your selection. Click the **Try now** button to activate this trial:

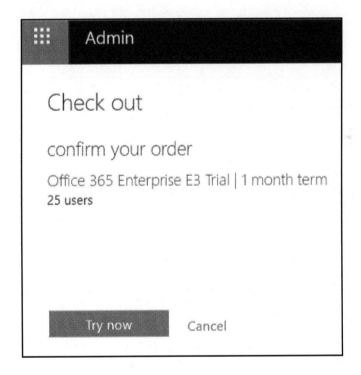

5. And with that, all the additional services associated with the **Office 365 Enterprise E3** services will be enabled and associated with your existing instance. To confirm, look at the expanded **Billing** section in the **Admin** center and select **Products & services**. You should see both trials listed with the available licenses:

Now we can configure all of the default integrations that should be available. We will look at those tasks in some of the future chapters.

Summary

In this chapter, we looked at how to create a new free trial environment for Dynamics 365 for Sales.

We also learned how to add an Office 365 Enterprise E3 trial to our current Dynamics 365 trial in order to leverage the services that are available with the Office 365 service. This allows us to configure additional integration points; we'll be looking at these in future chapters.

We looked at the various geographical locations in which this service is hosted in Microsoft data centers and how it is served to various geographies. We learned that, while you should have your instance created in the closest geographical location for better performance, there are situations where you might want to deploy to a different location, or even to multiple locations for global organizations. That is a much more complex scenario and could involve different deployments and real-time synchronization of data.

The next chapter delves into the platform structure. We will look at the standard modules available with the platform, the elements that are available for customization, and their relationship to each module and each other.

2
Dynamics 365 Platform Structure

The first chapter of this book focused on getting us going on this journey, reviewing the components that make up the Dynamics 365 platform, the various deployment models available, and online deployment locations, as well as walking you through the process to create a trial instance.

At this point, it is assumed that your 30-day trial of Dynamics 365 for Sales is up and running and you can easily follow and execute the concepts described in this book.

In this chapter, we're shifting our focus to the platform structure. There have been some changes with the move to Dynamics 365. Where before, in Dynamics CRM, we used to have one complete monolithic application that included Sales, Service, and Marketing, the updated platform now follows a more modular model.

This chapter focuses on the following topics:

- Experiencing the platform evolution
- Modularity for everyone
- Dynamics 365 application elements
- The extensibility options
- Understanding platform navigation
- Exploring the modular concept

Let's get started with this chapter!

Experiencing the platform evolution

Let's look at how this platform has evolved over the last few years. We've transitioned from what used to be Dynamics CRM to a new unified model under the branding of Dynamics 365. This is the merging of the ERP and CRM platforms under a unified naming convention. As with all major changes, behind the scenes, things took a little longer to take shape.

In order to differentiate between the various platform purposes, we had Dynamics 365 Customer Engagement covering the former Dynamics CRM functionality. The platform evolved behind the scenes, and this allowed the separation of various functionality modules. The current offering includes separate modules for Sales, Service, Marketing, Field Service, and Project Service Automation. In addition, some new modules made their way into the bigger family, including the ERP functional modules, as well as new modules such as Talent.

Microsoft Dynamics 365 Customer Engagement allows a company to manage interactions with current and future potential customers. Usually, a CRM system is part of a bigger picture, involving customer service, customer experience, customer retention, and other aspects. The CRM platform fits in this puzzle as the software platform that provides a company with the tools necessary to perform all the other tasks. With the modularization taking place, your organization can now choose which modules need to be implemented first, in what order, and which ones are actually required.

A robust system allows both **reactive** and **proactive actions** from the various staff using it. While most of the service aspects are primarily reactive, through extensive analysis and solid business processes, proactive actions can be taken to increase customer retention, quality of service, and sales, and create more robust marketing campaigns. Various **Artificial Intelligence (AI)** offerings are now available to help with these proactive actions. AI for Sales, Customer Service, and Market Insights provide added value when it comes to proactively handling situations.

A system based on Dynamics 365 modules provides a 360-degree view of a customer, with all historical interactions, purchase history, contact preferences, and survey responses, along with additional related data as needed. This collected data can be further analyzed to determine the best strategies for increasing customer satisfaction and providing better-quality services. The proactive features allow better customer satisfaction, resulting in increased retention.

In the next section, we will learn about modularity options offered by Dynamics 365.

Modularity for everyone

While Microsoft used to market Dynamics CRM as a rapid development platform under the xRM term and is encouraging partners to extend it to cover various aspects of businesses, by default, the product included three major modules. They were **Sales**, **Service**, and **Marketing**.

At the time of this writing, the platform is sold under the umbrella name of Dynamics 365. It offers various modules that can be purchased separately or packaged under the Customer Engagement Plan license. This plan includes the following functional modules:

- Dynamics 365 for Sales
- Dynamics 365 for Customer Service
- Dynamics 365 for Project Service Automation
- Dynamics 365 for Field Service
- Dynamics 365 for Marketing

The platform has greatly evolved over the years and is currently one of the top players in the market. With this evolution, all the standard modules have been enhanced, and new functionalities have been added. Currently, each one of the modules can function either independently or in conjunction with the others, sharing data and providing full visibility on customers across all modules.

The clear definitions between the data shared between these modules are getting blurrier as the need to transfer data records across practices evolves. Business processes can span across these modules also and gain a more central role in the way the user interacts with the platform, to the point that they often pass across from one module to another.

As the licensing model evolves, and the platform has been revamped to support a modular approach, now individual applications can be purchased for each set of functionality. You can now start with Sales as an example, then later on when you are ready to add new features, you can include Customer Service, and so on. This allows a slower roll-out based on the individual level of comfort or each client organization. All this is possible because of great investment made into the Unified Interface and the ability to segment individual apps.

But let's have a quick look at each of these modules separately and see the functionality covered.

Dynamics 365 for Sales

The Microsoft Dynamics 365 for Sales module facilitates the sales teams in managing leads and opportunities, as well as closing these opportunities in a quicker and more orderly fashion. It helps to increase the opportunity success rate. Building stronger relationships with customers is a differentiator that most companies are striving for. A focus on better, more optimized sales processes can make a huge difference in the success of an enterprise.

Within the Sales module, the sales team can manage their own customers and contacts and get full visibility on customers, current orders and services, existing issues, and resolutions. Nurturing sales from lead to order, as well as capturing collateral information along the way, is at the core of the Sales module. With all this information at your fingertips, a salesperson can walk into any new opportunity fully prepared, avoiding any unexpected surprises. Furthermore, they can show full knowledge of the customer and their current needs, level of satisfaction, and potential issues.

Your typical Sales module navigation is presented in the following screenshot:

Dynamics 365 for Sales presents several user experiences, depending on the way you access the application.

The Classical interface is simply an evolution of the interface we've seen over the last few versions. Certain enhancements have been made for better visibility, better use of real estate space, and overall better user experience. A lot of feedback from the community has played an important role in shaping up this interface. With the platform evolution, this interface is now deprecated in favor of the new Unified Interface.

The new Unified Interface gives a collapsible left navigation bar, structured clearly with categories to give you the ability to easily bubble up recent and pinned records. The remainder of the screen presents the data. The following screenshot shows you the new Unified Interface in the **Sales** module:

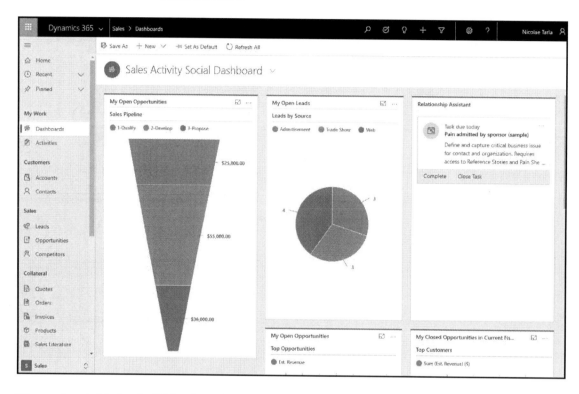

Throughout this book, I'll be focusing mostly on the Unified Interface. This new interface, introduced with Dynamics 365 as of version 9.0, provides an enhanced and responsive user experience. This is a much richer interface, allowing not only responsiveness but also major accessibility improvements.

In addition, this new interface now supports a set of much richer controls, such as timeline control. In time, there is a possibility that developers could start building additional controls to enhance the user experience using supported methods.

For mobile access, the Sales application has been updated to leverage the same Unified Interface. This application can be installed on all mobile devices and has the same familiar look and feel.

Microsoft has introduced the **Home** page, a way to collate all available applications for a specific user. This page not only collects together all applications the logged-in user has access to, but also provides the ability to surface Power Apps and to retrieve additional apps from various third-party **Independent Software Vendors (ISVs)**:

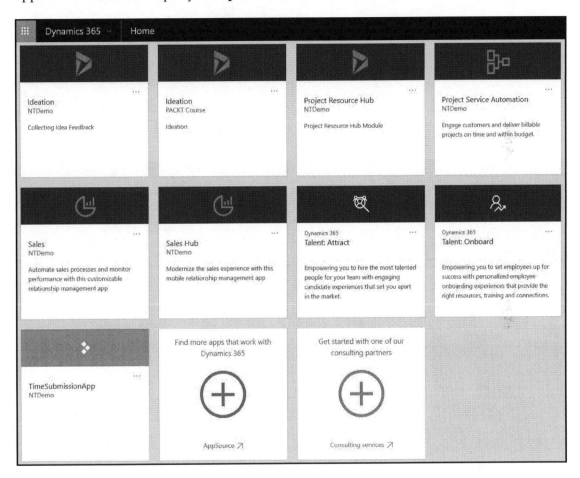

The next module to go over covers the customer service functionality. Let's look at it.

Dynamics 365 for Customer Service

The Customer Service module includes a set of powerful features that allow service users and managers to manage and track customer complaints, service activities, and customer interactions within your organization.

Great customer service can make the difference between a successful or failing organization. Customers nowadays demand better, faster, more personalized support. The new generation is pushing the envelope by expecting support on new channels while leaving behind traditional channels.

The Customer Service module collects features and tools to manage the service and customer experience. Great customer experience can easily transform into new referrals and new business opportunities.

The main features of this module include capabilities to do with the following:

- Capturing customer issues in cases
- Recording and keeping track of all customer interactions in the process to resolve a case
- Providing users with the ability to share product and support documentation to customers demanding assistance
- Creating and managing various **Service Level Agreement (SLA)** tiers
- Reporting on SLA performance through real-time dashboards
- Defining customer categories and entitlements
- Managing cases between various teams through queues, and routing cases to the correct queues based on the defined business rules
- Creating and managing services to customers
- Surfacing real-time details on performance and productivity through reports and dashboards
- GDPR and local regulatory compliance enforcement

Just like we've seen in the Sales module, the Customer Service module also provides access through the Classical interface, which has received a refresh. Your navigation looks as shown in the following screenshot:

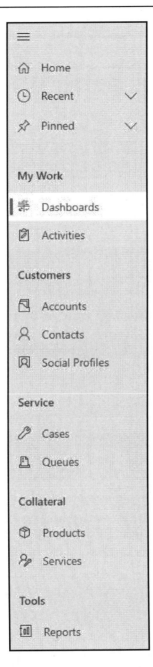

Observe not only the standard categories but also the ability to surface your customizations in the Extensions section.

The Customer Service Hub is the new Unified Interface app made available both on desktop computers and mobile devices. Just like the Sales app, it has a responsive web design and support for accessibility. As these apps evolve, some changes will be obvious in the user interface. At the time of this writing, the Customer Service app provides access to **Cases**, **Queues**, and **Knowledge Articles**, while the **Service Management** area provides access to **Case Settings**, **Service Terms**, **Templates**, and **Knowledge Base Management**:

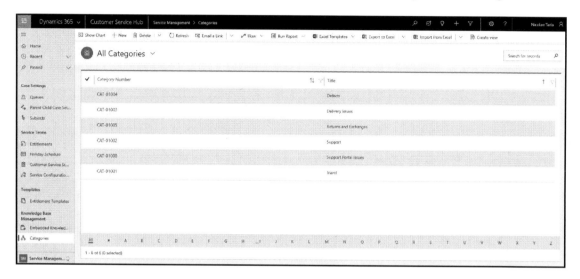

Let's move our attention to Project Service Automation in the next section.

Dynamics 365 for Project Service Automation

The **Project Service Automation (PSA)** module is a relatively new module to the platform. In its current incarnation, at the time of writing, it is at version 3. The default navigation in the Classical interface looks as follows:

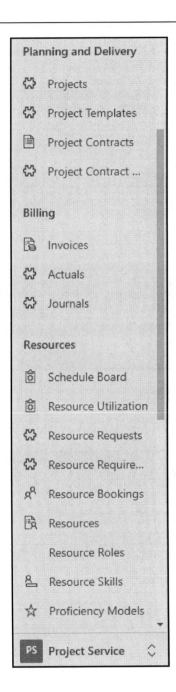

This module provides functionality for managing and delivering project-based services. Some of the main functionality includes the following:

- Planning, estimating, and scheduling projects
- Managing project costs and revenue
- Resource forecasting
- Managing and assigning or re-assigning resources at various project stages
- Tracking and reporting on project progress
- Extensive reporting on various defined **Key Performance Indicators** (**KPIs**)
- Tracking resource time submission

The following screenshot shows the ability to track a user's time reporting across various projects:

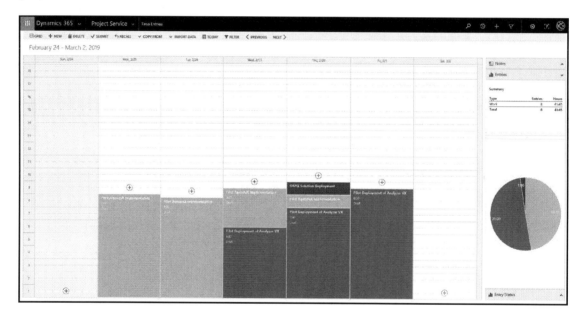

Like the other modules, the Project Resource Hub leverages the Unified Interface and presents another way to look into the application. The following screenshot shows the same time entries from the previous screenshot presented in a standard view:

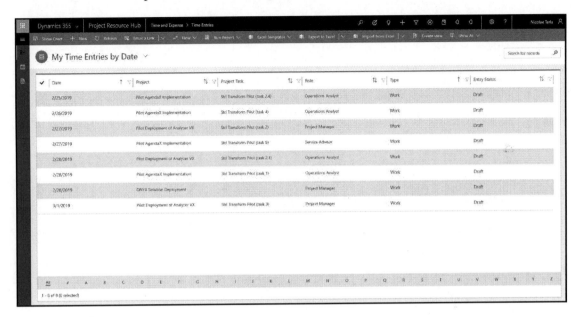

The next module in Dynamics 365 is the Field Service module.

Dynamics 365 for Field Service

The Field Service offering focuses on managing onsite service to customers. It provides a robust scheduling engine, working in conjunction with resource availability, automation, and mobility to deliver a comprehensive solution around managing resources in the field.

The default navigation of this module is presented in the following screenshot:

The core module functionality revolves around the following aspects:

- Optimizing the volume of service response activities
- Improving the rate of fixes on the first attempt
- Reducing costs and efforts associated with travel time by optimizing routes and service schedules

- Providing enhanced customer service around notification of arrival time, status updates, and resolutions, and providing accurate resolution details to customers
- Preventative maintenance and service by analyzing trends
- Providing accurate customer and site history of previous service visits
- Enhancing analytics and reporting around service calls, service success, and equipment maintenance

The following roles are directly involved in leveraging the services provided in this module: **Customer Service Representatives (CSRs)**, dispatchers, and field service technicians. In addition, service managers, asset managers, and inventory managers can take advantage of the reporting facilities to provide enhanced optimization of inventory and service quality.

Just as with the other modules, the Field Resource Hub takes advantage of the new Unified Interface to present data in a mobile-friendly, responsive way to users. The following screenshot depicts the resource booking in the hub, with the left navigation pane allowing easy access to work-specific details, customers, and other features:

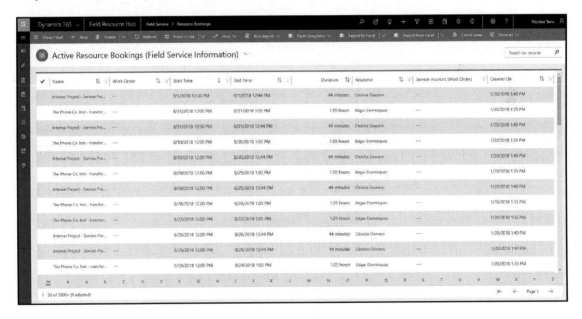

Within the Field Service app, we have the main navigation pane differentiating between the core Field Service functionality areas, including work orders and scheduling, service delivery, and inventory management, as seen in the following screenshot:

In addition, Scheduling handles all the scheduling activities, along with a schedule board and configuration elements:

Next, let's see the last module on the list.

Dynamics 365 for Marketing

While the original platform included some marketing functionality, which is still available if you choose not to customize your installation when creating your tenant, the new Marketing module is a greatly enhanced tool that provides additional functionality and enhancements that customers have been requesting for a long time.

The original Marketing navigation functionality is presented as a part of the Sales module, with the ability to create marketing lists and quick campaigns, as they relate to Sales. This is presented in the following screenshot:

Features around Marketing and collateral elements and tools around reporting and primary alerts are all included.

But this version fell short when it came to modern customer marketing activities. There was no support for testing marketing campaigns, providing modern messaging templates to customers, portal functionality, and so on.

The new Marketing offering, which was launched with Dynamics 365 version 9, includes a much richer set of components, along with a new modern user interface based on the Unified Interface.

The main highlights of the new Marketing offering include the following:

- Graphical editor for rich emails to customers
- Nurture lead processing with an enhanced user experience
- Events management, including organizing and publicizing events through a public portal
- Integration with LinkedIn for business prospects
- Customer surveys through the updated **Voice of the Customer (VoC)**

The new Marketing module was built from the ground up leveraging the new Unified Interface. As such, in the Classical UI, only the former Marketing functionality is available. The following screenshot shows the new experience of Marketing module navigation:

Next, let's look at the main features of this offering.

Dynamics 365 application elements

Dynamics 365 comprises a few standard elements working together to achieve the system's functionality. These include (but are not limited to) the elements we will be covering in the following sections.

Modular design

As seen earlier in this chapter, modules are groups of functionalities that serve a specific business scope. The standard modules in the previous versions provided by Microsoft include Sales, Service, and Marketing. Since then, new modules have been added, as we've seen previously.

This modularity has been driven by the need to provide a unified model for partners and ISVs to further extend the platform with custom functionality. Microsoft took the first step by not only providing modular capabilities to the platform but also redesigning its original application to take advantage of this new model. Hence, now all modules leveraging the Unified Interface are built to leverage the new modular model.

Entities

Entities are containers used to model, store, and manage business data. Through the use of entities, the platform allows us to structure data, create relationships, and manage actions.

Each entity comprises a **varying number of attributes**. These attributes are in fact data items, of a particular type, stored in the database. Each one of these attributes can be displayed on an entity form as a field. For example, an account will have a name attribute, possibly an ID attribute, a description attribute, and many others.

From a tabular point of view, we can think of each entity as a table or an Excel spreadsheet. Each column is an attribute. Each record is a line in this table. Each field is a specific record's attribute and can be defined as one of the available data types.

Within Dynamics 365, entities are classified into three major categories:

- **System entities**: System entities are used internally by the framework. They can handle workflows and asynchronous jobs.

 System entities cannot be deleted and/or customized.

- **Business entities**: Business entities are the standard entities provided by the framework as part of the three available modules. They are present in the default user interface and are available for customization.
- **Custom entities**: Custom entities are entities that are created as part of extending the standard framework with new functionality. They can be made visible through the standard user interface or can be kept hidden and participate in custom processes only.

Business and custom entities can be configured as customizable or non-customizable. A customizable entity can be modified by modifying its attributes, renaming it, or changing processes associated with it.

Processes

Dynamics 365 allows businesses to define and enforce consistent business processes, helping users to focus more on performing their regular work and less on remembering what needs to be done at each step along the way.

The processes defined can be as complex as needed and can be grouped and related to achieving even greater complexity. The processes on the Dynamics 365 platform can be created and managed by non-developers. This brings ease of use and allows managers and power users to manage them and update them as time goes by. For this reason, the system can easily stay up to date with the business as it evolves.

 Giving power users permissions to make modifications to the platform carries an associated risk of certain configurations having a negative impact on the overall health of the platform or data associated.

Within the Dynamics 365 platform, at the time of this writing, there are four categories of processes available—dialogs, workflows, actions, and business process flows. We will look at each one individually, and we will identify when you should use one over another.

Dialogs

Dialogs in Dynamics 365 are used to create a graphical interface to guide a user through a process to be followed when interacting with a customer or performing a set of actions. They are similar to scripts used in call center scenarios. They are meant to be executed in one session from beginning to end.

 At the time of writing, dialogs have been marked as deprecated. This means that at a future date, they will be dropped from the platform. To replace the dialogs functionality, consider embedding a canvas app into your form. More details on canvas apps are to be found in `Chapter 8`, *Dynamics 365 Customer Engagement and the Power Platform*.

Dialogs help users collect data and create new records, and they guide the user through a set of actions to be performed based on various answers from a customer. A running dialog collecting user input looks like this:

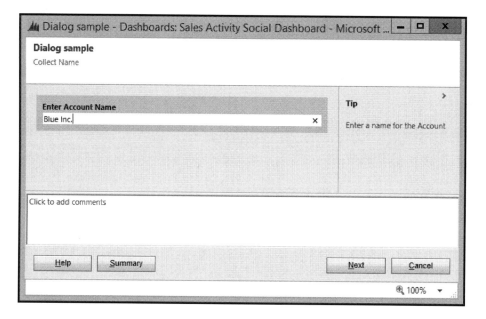

Next, let's look at the next category of processes—workflows.

Workflows

Workflows help to automate actions behind the scenes. They do not present a user interface and are not limited to being completed in a single session. Workflows can run over a period of time to completion.

A workflow is usually initiated by a system action, but they can also be customized to be triggered by a user directly. They can work asynchronously or synchronously. The synchronous workflows are also referred to as real-time workflows, and they were introduced with CRM version 2013. Starting with the same version, we have the ability to convert an asynchronous workflow to a real-time workflow.

Actions

An action in Dynamics 365 is a custom process that allows us to create a custom message. They are used to add new functionality to the application or to combine multiple requests into a single one. They use the underlying web service architecture to group complex or specific actions.

Creating an action is very similar to creating a workflow. They can be created using the wizard-driven interface or custom code. Custom code is only supported for on-premises deployments.

An action is associated with a specific entity or can be defined at a global level. Through actions, we can invoke plugins, which are custom components built by developers.

New actions are exposed through the standard API and can be triggered through custom code and through integration from other applications.

One very important aspect of actions is that they are not supported by offline clients.

Business process flows

Business process flows are visual elements that allow a system user to input required data by grouping the required fields together at the top of the screen. They can be created using the wizard-driven user interface and show the user the progress of a process through a predetermined set of steps to completion.

The opportunity sales process is a very good example of such customization. From a user perspective, they will see the following section on their screen:

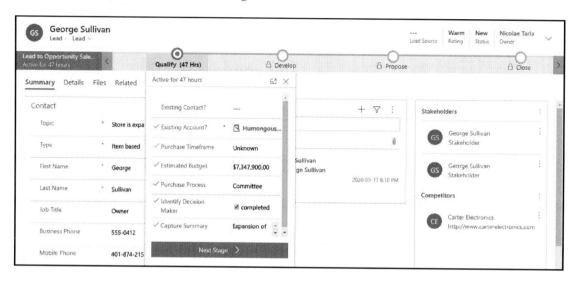

For the system customizers, the interface to generate this is quite simplistic and easy to use, and looks as follows:

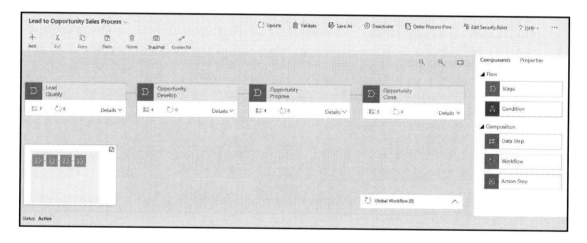

Each stage of the process is defined, and within it, each required field can be added and marked as required or not required. Progressing through stages requires that all fields marked as required are filled in before advancing to the next stage. The control also allows users to navigate back and forward to see what is required at each stage.

With business process flows, we can create conditional branches. This functionality was added with version 2015 to solve the if/else scenario. For example, if the customer's status is "gold," take one path; otherwise, take another path.

Dashboards

Dashboards in Dynamics 365 are visual components that allow users quick access to aggregated data in a system. They are a visualization and analytics tool that enhances the value of your system by allowing users to quickly glance at aggregated data and to dig deeper into underlying data used to generate the visualization.

They act as business intelligence tools, providing snapshots of system data presented in various forms.

Dashboards comprise various elements, including charts, grids, IFRAMES, and web resources. With additional customizations, reports can be incorporated into dashboards also.

Dashboards are in fact containers for these elements and can present up to six visualizations at a time. They comprise tabs, sections, and components, they can be created easily through the wizard-based interface, and they can be targeted to a specific module, user, or team.

From an ownership perspective, dashboards can be organization-owned or user-owned. A user-owned dashboard can be shared with other users.

A typical Sales dashboard looks as follows:

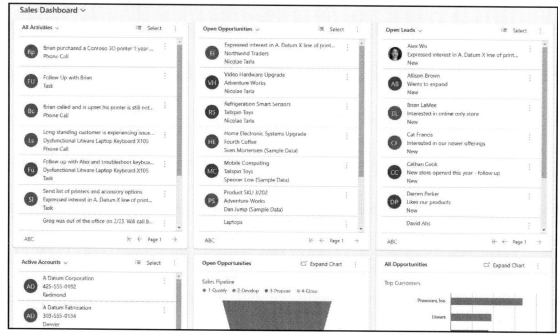

In addition to the standard Dynamics 365 dashboards, the platform supports integrating and surfacing more visually appealing dashboards built leveraging Power BI. Power BI is part of the Power Platform and is a business intelligence tool that allows extensive data analytics and visualization.

Reports

A user can report on system data in various ways: from the simplistic Advanced Find tool, where tabular data can be retrieved and exported to Excel for further analytics, to wizard-driven report generation, and all the way to custom **SQL Server Reporting Services (SSRS)** reports. Data can also be used as a data source in Power BI, and it can be mashed with data from other sources for a more comprehensive view of business performance.

This great degree of flexibility makes reporting easy to do and very powerful.

Each one of these options has its own strong points and weaknesses. For example, custom SSRS reports are the most powerful, not only for the amount of data collected but also for the complexity of data relationships. The downside is that they require a developer with extensive SSRS reporting and Dynamics 365 knowledge to produce. Furthermore, SSRS reports built for the on-premises version access data on the backend differently from reports leveraging the online offering.

> For complex reporting scenarios when leveraging the online offering, you should also consider using a **Data Warehouse** (**DW**) model, where data is extracted from your Dynamics 365 environment in an external source and re-mapped for more efficient reporting needs.

Power users of the system will find it easy to create wizard-driven reports. While limited in complexity and having a standard user interface, the ease of creating them will appeal to users with no development background.

These reports support the use of custom parameters for filtering data and allow us to save for offline use as well as export in some of the most common formats, including Excel, Word, and PDF.

The extensibility options

Dynamics 365 is a very flexible platform with a multitude of extensibility options. The system can be extended through various methods and components. Third-party solutions can be acquired from Dynamics Marketplace, and internal customizations can be performed, packaged, and exported from one environment to another.

Understanding platform navigation

User experience has evolved a lot with each new version of Dynamics CRM. This continues with the release of Dynamics 365 version 9, where the navigation was again redesigned based on user feedback. As part of this process, now navigation is less obtrusive, takes less screen real estate, and is more dynamic. The sub-layers of navigation have been restructured to minimize the amount of scrolling needed. As such, new groups have been created and present options vertically as smaller tiles.

The default navigation is presented in the Classical UI as follows:

The navigation remains highly customizable, and the logical modules are clearly presented. This navigation can easily be changed to add new modules, remove existing ones, and re-arrange items.

With the introduction of the various hubs and the application model, leveraging the Unified Interface, the navigation is now fully configurable to reflect only the necessary elements for a specific application. This navigation has been extracted from the top-most location where we had it in the Classical UI and has been relocated to a side blade, which can be extended when needed:

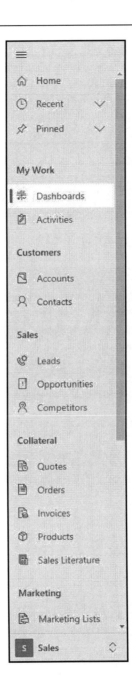

The application ribbons have also been redesigned both in the Classical UI as well as the Unified Interface, with a similar horizontal display at the top of the form. The most common actions are left visible, with additional ribbon elements collected under an ellipsis menu. In addition, tabs on forms have now been added underneath the record name for easy access and navigation:

Let's have a look at **Common Data Model** (**CDM**) and how this design allows modularity.

Exploring the modular concept

In order for Microsoft to be able to deliver on the new modular concept, the platform has been redesigned around a new structural approach. At the core of the platform, we have CDM. CDM is a metadata-driven layer that simplifies data integration and sharing across various apps and platforms by providing a set of common data entities. This allows consistency across all apps and platforms and simplifies integration to other platforms and products.

CDM provides a set of standard core entities, the most common of which are these:

- Account
- Contact
- Activity
- Owner
- Currency
- Task

These entities are leveraged in the various Dynamics 365 modules, as well as the Talent application for HR and other accelerators. Partners and ISVs also use these entities, along with their own custom entities, when building new solutions for their platforms.

CDM's value comes from its ability to provide consistency in both a structural and semantic way for all integrated apps. Furthermore, it simplifies integration efforts by collecting and surfacing data to all apps from a common dataset. Its strength is the ability to extend this model as needed, in order to build new applications and solutions for various specialized purposes.

Overall, representing CDM in a visual way, you can think of it as the following diagram depicts it:

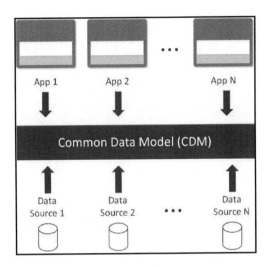

This depicts the modular approach: the ability to source data from various sources, to merge it into a common data store in CDM, and to surface only subsets of functionality in individual applications targeted to specific roles.

Now that we have reached the end of this chapter, let's summarize what we have learned.

Summary

Throughout this chapter, we looked at some of the most important elements comprising the Microsoft Dynamics 365 platform. We have reviewed the standard modules that form the default Dynamics 365 platform: Sales, Customer Service, Project Service Automation, Field Service, and Marketing. We also looked at the major components of the modules and how they relate to a specific module or work across multiple modules. We looked at entities and what an entity is in the context of Dynamics 365, and we reviewed dashboards, reports, and the default navigation throughout the application.

At this point, we should have an understanding of how everything ties together and what to look for when we need to customize a system.

The next chapters will take you into more detail regarding the individual app modules and each module's target audience and functionality.

Section 2 - Default Modules Available with the Platform

2

In this section, we will focus our attention on the various modules offered by Microsoft as solutions for the platform.

This section comprises the following chapters:

3
Dynamics 365 Sales Application

The first two chapters of this book focused on getting us on this journey by introducing us to the overall platform, looking at the deployment models and the various geolocations where the online service is offered, as well as getting us going with a trial environment. We also explored the platform's modularity and the benefits available as part of the restructuring process that took place with the move to Dynamics 365.

At this point, you should be familiar with creating a trial instance, and you should already have a new Sales instance created. We will be using this instance in this chapter to review the Sales application's functionality. If you do not have a trial instance, revise the steps to create one that were presented in Chapter 1, *Getting Started with Dynamics 365*.

In this chapter, we will look at the first and most widely used application that can be built on the platform: the Sales application.

This chapter focuses on the following topics:

- The functionality of the Sales application, including entities that support the Sales application and standard Sales processes
- Standard scenarios supported by the Sales offering
- The Sales Hub and the new **Unified Interface (UI)**

By the end of this chapter, you will have a good understanding of the Sales application's functionality, the standard process for managing sales and related activities, and how to make this functionality available to your organization. You should also be able to clearly identify and work with the new UI features. With the move to the new UI, new capabilities are made available, greatly improving the user experience and the application's overall usability.

Reviewing the Dynamics 365 Sales app

With the move to the new app model, Microsoft has separated the various functional modules into distinct applications, available for purchase in a modular way. At its core, the Sales application focuses on the capabilities of building relationships with prospects and customers:

- The ability to close sales faster
- Track progress and interactions with customers
- Have an overall view of all customer activities
- Interactions within your organization

The Microsoft Dynamics 365 for Sales module facilitates sales teams in managing leads and opportunities, as well as closing these opportunities in a shorter, more orderly fashion. It helps to increase the opportunity success rate.

From the standard application drawer, which presents the various applications available to a user, we will find **Sales Hub**, as shown in the following screenshot:

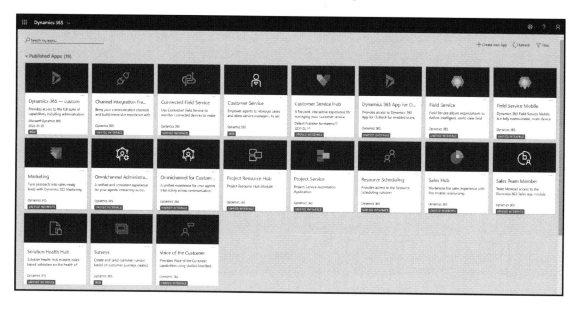

Sales Hub is the core application that handles the Sales functionality and is your starting point when working with the platform in a Sales or Sales Manager role.

Within the Sales module, the sales team can manage their own customers and contacts and get full visibility on potential and existing customers, current orders and services, existing issues, and their resolutions. With all this information at your fingertips, a salesperson can walk into any new opportunity, fully prepared, while avoiding any unexpected surprises. Furthermore, they can show full knowledge of the customer and their current needs, level of satisfaction, and potential issues.

The Sales module is comprised of a set of entities, processes, dashboards, and reports, as well as the ability to see the products and services offered and the associated sales literature. Within this same module, the sales team can see their progress against pre-defined goals. In addition, each sales team member can manage their own customer interactions using some of the basic marketing features built on the platform.

For those of you that have worked with this platform over the years, you will find that the classical navigation is now redesigned in the UI. The following screenshot shows the classical way of navigating to the various elements of the platform:

As a result of the redesign and the transition to the UI, opening **Sales Hub** will now present a new experience for the user, as shown in the following screenshot:

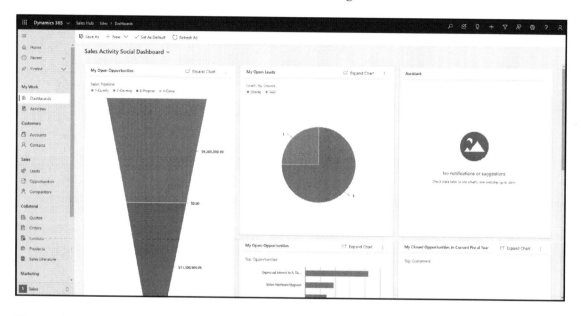

The entire navigation is now shifted to the sidebar, allowing better visibility of the sections and elements available for navigation. You are still taken to the Sales Activity Social Dashboard by default, and small user experience tweaks are apparent throughout the entire application.

 This book will continue to focus on the new UI experience since the classical web interface is slated to be deprecated with the second wave release of 2020.

The entities available are structured by categories, with the **Customers** section focusing on keeping track of and managing **Accounts** and **Contacts**. The **Sales** section allows us to create and nurture sales from leads to orders, while collateral entities allow the user to manage and track related records of information, such as **Quotes**, **Orders**, and **Invoices**, as well as specific products or services and related sales literature. Other sections include items such as goal management, which allows us to set up and track sales goals for each sales representative. Additional tools such as reports and alerts are related to specific sales activities, and there's also a calendar view of activities related to the respective sales representative.

You will observe a **Marketing** section during the navigation. Not to be confused with the newer Marketing application offering, this section allows basic sales-specific marketing operations, such as managing static and dynamic marketing lists, as well as quick campaigns. These quick campaigns are typically email blasts sent by a salesperson to one or more marketing lists that they own.

In order to support the standard flow and actions required to close a sale, business processes are created and include the standard out-of-the-box **Lead** to **Opportunity** process, which guides the staff through the necessary actions and steps to close a sale, as well as the **Opportunity Sales** process. Your custom sales processes will be at the core of your business, whether they are an extension or customization of the existing processes, or entirely new processes mapping your existing business needs.

Leveraging the new app model and the new UI, the sales functionality is brought to life through a revamped model. The following screenshot shows the navigation that's available when leveraging **Sales Hub**:

The Dynamics 365 Sales module includes a set of entities that are shared across modules, as well as entities specific to Sales. We will look at these two generic categories and each of the entities included in them.

Besides these Sales application-specific entities, shared entities are entities that are used across multiple modules. While they are not specific to a certain application, they tend to be tightly integrated with the functionality of each application where they are present. Some of the most obvious ones include the **Account** and **Contact** entities, which span across the whole platform and tightly integrate with all applications.

Now, let's move our attention to Sales-specific entities.

Understanding Sales-specific entities

Sales-specific entities are entities that are used mainly within the Sales module. Some of these include **Leads**, **Opportunities**, and **Competitors**, as well as additional collateral entities such as **Quotes**, **Orders**, **Invoices**, **Products**, and **Sales Literature**. Another set of entities directly related to Sales module includes **Goals** and **Goal Metrics**, which are used to track sales performance.

When customizing the system, the scope of each of the existing entities can be changed simply by modifying the navigation and its associations. For example, a new entity can be made accessible only through a specific application, or an entity from one application can be surfaced in another.

Furthermore, a custom application can be created to either reduce the navigational scope for specific user roles or to surface elements from multiple applications into a single, unified interface.

Now, let's look at some of the entities that support the Sales application.

Leads

The **Leads** entity is a representation of a person or organization interested in the company's products and/or services. The lead entity is meant to track a potential customer that has not been qualified yet. It will track all communication activities through the qualification process. An example of collecting leads is at a trade show, where people drop a business card in a jar. Using a Power App, a user can scan those cards and generate new leads in the system. These leads are then assigned to the sales staff to follow up and identify potential opportunities.

The following screenshot shows a standard new lead form in Dynamics 365 Sales:

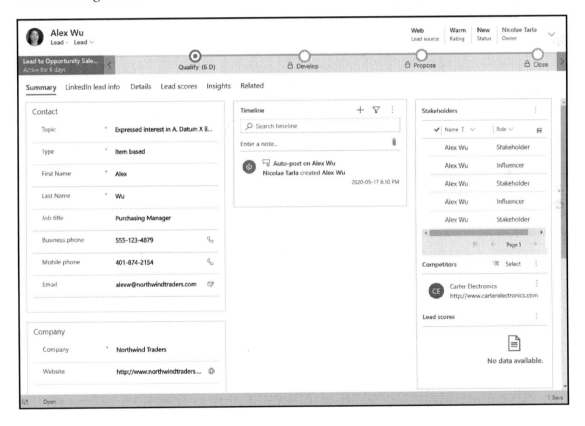

Note that these Leads can also be created manually by a salesperson, as a result of cold calls or any other mechanisms used to identify potential new customers.

The Lead management qualification process is a process for managing a possible opportunity through to qualification. This process is kept separate from the opportunity management process through the use of the Lead entity. The following screenshot shows the standard business process flow for working with a Lead. Observe the **Qualify** stage being opened and providing additional details to be collected at this stage:

A Lead record can be in one of the three default states: **New**, **Qualified**, or **Disqualified**. Once a Lead is qualified, it can be converted into an Opportunity. Upon qualification, from the associated data that's been collected, an **Account** and a **Contact** can be created.

The Lead record can be associated with other system data, including various **Activities**, **Notes**, and **Playbooks**, as well as **Marketing Lists**. Also, documents can be attached to Leads, but we will talk about better ways to handle related documents in later chapters of this book.

The following screenshot shows the **Timeline** control of the Lead, which collates all the activities and actions that took place as they relate to this Lead record:

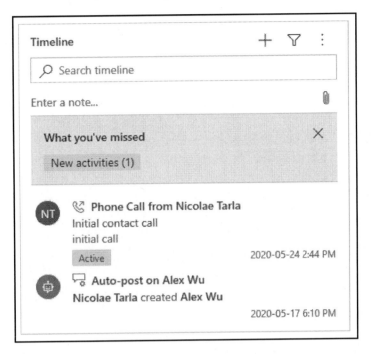

By default, a Lead can also be disqualified. When disqualifying a Lead, the following options are available: **Lost**, **Cannot Contact**, **No Longer Interested**, and **Cancelled**. These values can be customized to represent the business terminology.

Even once you qualify a Lead, this does not necessarily mean an Opportunity is won. You can close a Lead as Lost by selecting the **Close as Lost** option on the Lead screen, as shown in the following screenshot:

The popup allows you to define a **Status Reason**, **Close Date**, **Competitor**, and a detailed **Description**, as shown in the following screenshot:

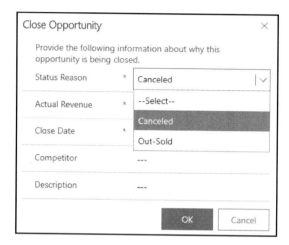

Qualifying a Lead is a more complex process, with a couple of actions taking place in the background. Besides moving the **Business Process Flow** into the **Develop** stage, the current Lead record is closed, and in the background, an Opportunity record is created, with all the data captured on the originating Lead.

 Note that some organizations choose to completely skip the use of leads and directly use opportunities. This is okay, and a decision should be made by the business regarding what model fits your organization better.

Since a lead turns into an opportunity, we'll look at opportunities next.

Opportunities

The Opportunity entity is meant to capture a potential sale for an existing customer. It is used by sales staff to keep track of and forecast sales engagements they are working on. An opportunity can be created directly in the system or generated as a result of qualifying a Lead. As mentioned previously, some organizations prefer to not use Leads, but rather start the sales process directly at the Opportunity.

Based on business opportunities, a company can forecast business demands for products and services, as well as sales revenues.

An opportunity in the system must be related to an **Account** and/or **Contact**. This is one of the differences between Leads and Opportunities, where an **Account** or **Contact** must already be qualified in the system for an opportunity to be able to associate with it.

The same as with leads, a sales representative can track phone calls, emails, and other activities against the Opportunity. This gives the representative complete visibility of all the steps that were performed while working with each Opportunity.

The following screenshot shows a standard listing of all Opportunities:

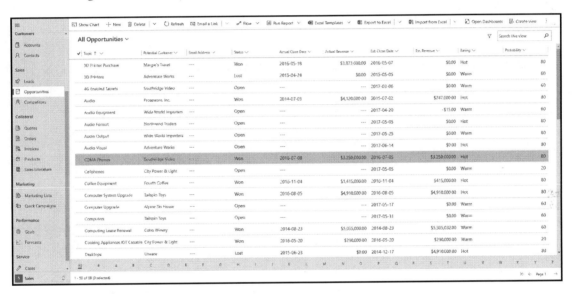

You can configure the view to present other columns, remove some of the existing columns, or add new columns of data as needed.

You can create new Opportunities in various ways. You can either import a set of Opportunities from an external source, most commonly from an Excel spreadsheet; you can have Opportunities generated in another system and integrated with your Sales application so that they are automatically created; or you can create new Opportunities manually. You can do that by navigating to the **Opportunities** view and selecting **New** on the ribbon. The **New Opportunity** screen is shown in the following screenshot:

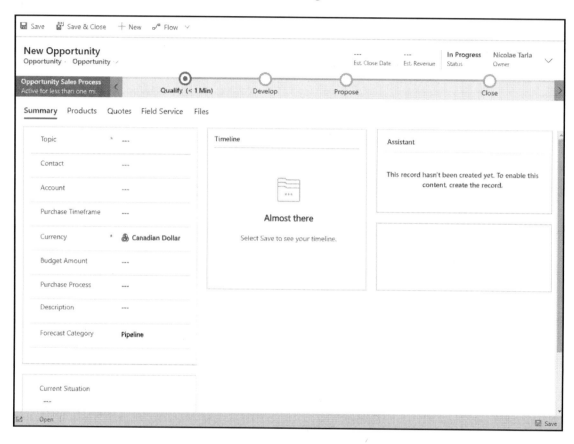

Each Opportunity in the system usually has one or more products/services associated with it. This association is achieved through the use of a relational system entity called **Opportunity Product**. In addition, processes can be put in place to validate that only certain **Products/Services** are available for a specific opportunity, based on either the **Account/Contact** selected or any other set of business rules. Associated Opportunity product lines are presented and can be managed from the **Products** line's **Items** section, as shown in the following screenshot:

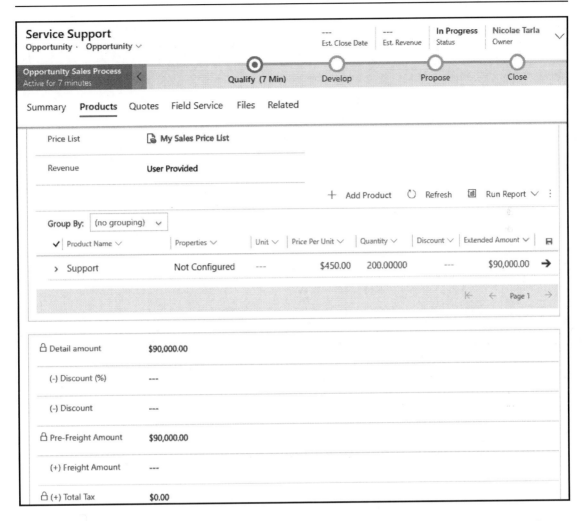

You can add products from an existing **Price List** that has already been configured in the system, or you can add new products by putting in a new write-in product and price. For the most part, you will want to work with an existing price list that includes existing products that have been predefined in the system.

Processing an Opportunity results in its closure. An Opportunity can be closed either as **Won** or **Lost**. Upon closing an opportunity, an **Opportunity close** activity is generated. This activity record stores information about the close reason, date, and revenue. This is also reflected in the **Timeline** for the respective Opportunity, as shown in the following screenshot:

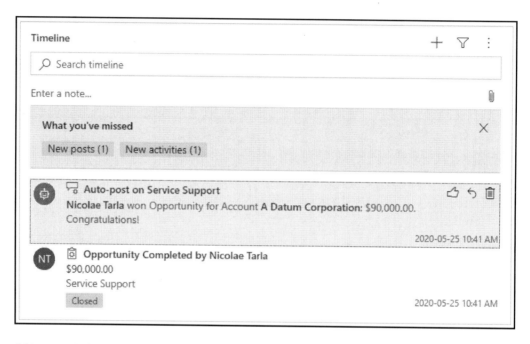

In addition, while working on an Opportunity, it can be associated with **Accounts**, **Contacts**, **Competitors**, **Quotes**, **Orders**, and **Activities**. You can put notes against an open Opportunity, as well as related **Sales Literature**.

 Note that, even if an Opportunity is **Closed**, it can later be reopened for additional corrections or processing.

Next, we'll look at Quotes associated with Opportunities. You would generate a Quote in order to provide a customer with an estimate of the cost associated with the requested products and/or services.

Quotes

The Quote entity is an important part of the sales process defined within the Dynamics 365 Sales platform. It works in conjunction with Products and Orders to complete the sales cycle.

The Quote entity represents an offer of Products and/or Services at a predetermined price. In addition, payment terms are associated with the respective quote.

A Quote in the system can be stored as **Draft**, **Active**, or **Closed**. A Draft quote is a quote that is still being worked on. Once work is completed and it is ready to be sent to the customer, the quote becomes Active. On completion, whether accepted or rejected, the quote becomes Closed. A completed quote that is accepted by the customer can be converted into an Order.

The following screenshot shows a standard new quote form since the quote was generated from the **PRODUCTS** associated with an Opportunity:

When a Quote is created from an Opportunity, the products and services associated with the Opportunity are automatically added to the Quote. When an Order is generated from a Quote, all products and services are also kept, and the Quote can be left open or closed.

You can also generate a Quote as a new record. When generating a new Quote directly, you must provide, at a minimum, an association to a **Potential Customer**, which is an Account in the system. The following screenshot shows a blank new Quote with the required fields marked with a red asterisk:

For such a Quote, you must manually add the necessary products or services to the quote in order for the total to be calculated.

As shown in the center column, below **PRODUCTS**, you can add additional discounts either as a percentage of the total or a fixed amount, as well as freight charges. These fields can be customized, and unnecessary ones can be hidden. For example, if all discounts are applied only as a percentage of the total, you can remove the discount as a fixed amount and only leave the discount as a percentage.

Information stored with the Quote includes various dates as they relate to processing the Quote. These include effective from and to dates, as seen on the header of the form:

This information is very important as a certain price or discount might only be available for a limited time.

The Quote also stores **Bill To Address** and **Ship To Address**. Ship to Address can also be defined by product or service.

Other entities that can be associated with a Quote include the Customer, as an Account and/or Contact, which is a required field, along with Competitors, Products and/or Services, Opportunities, as well as customer Addresses. Within a Quote, we can track **Notes**, which store various details for the resources working with the Quote record.

Orders

The Order entity is, in fact, a Quote that has been accepted by a customer. They can be created from a Quote, or directly as a new Order. You generate an Order from an active Quote by selecting the **Create Order** option on the ribbon. This brings up a popup that allows you to define the parameters for closing the existing Quote as **Won**, as well as whether to close the Opportunity and calculate the revenue based on the values in the Quote. The following screenshot shows this screen:

The following screenshot presents the standard Order form, as created from our previous Quote:

The Order form is quite similar to the Quote form in terms of layout and allows us to track similar information. It also allows us to associate the same related entities.

Invoice

An Invoice represents the next step in the process. You can generate an Invoice from an existing Order by selecting the **Create Invoice** option on the ribbon. Following our previous example, the following screenshot shows our Order converted into an Invoice:

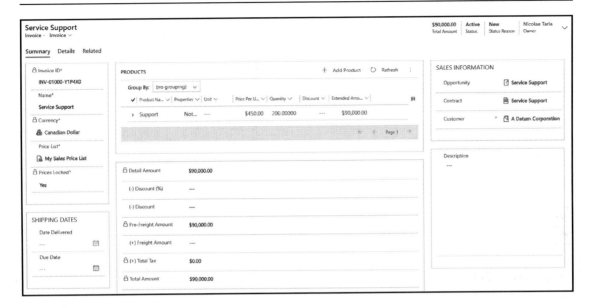

You can also generate an Invoice as a new record. This is valuable in situations where a sale is made directly. The following screenshot shows this **New Invoice** form prior to being saved:

Just like the Order, you must relate this Invoice to a Customer, which is an Account in the system.

Just like Orders and Quotes, the user interface presents similar information and the ability to associate Products and/or Services. When an Invoice is generated from an Order, all the Order details are pre-populated on the Invoice. They can be adjusted later, before the Invoice is marked as **Paid**.

Once you've finished working on an invoice, typically, control is transferred to your ERP system for financial processing through integration, as described later on, in Chapter 12, *Custom Integration Capabilities*.

Competitor

The **Competitor** entity stores details about another organization offering similar Products and/or Services. This allows us to associate a Competitor record throughout the sales cycle. In addition, we can store details about the competitor, including a list of their products competing directly with ours, sales literature, and any other sales materials. This allows better insights into the challenges we are facing in the marketplace, as well as how our main competitors influence our revenue.

 Note that a Competitor can be a **Partner** and a **Customer** at the same time, depending on the business model.

The following screenshot depicts the standard **Competitor** form:

Competitors can be categorized, and details can be recorded about each competitor's strengths and weaknesses, along with their profile. All this data that's collected allows sales representatives to make more informed decisions about each Opportunity, in order to increase its potential. The following screenshot shows the **Analysis** tab of a Competitor record, which is where we capture all these details:

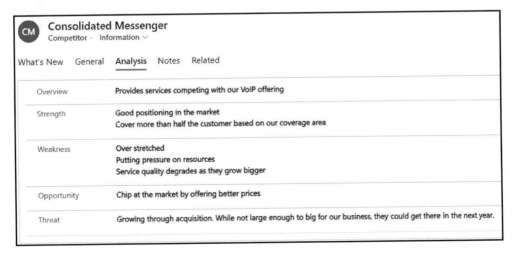

One or many Competitor records can be associated with every Opportunity.

In a way, even though it is being captured differently, a Competitor can be viewed as another Account. In fact, an organization can be both a Competitor and an Account (customer). The reason such an Account is captured instead as a Competitor is to allow us to track various other information that's specific to the role of Competitor. This includes strengths and weaknesses, as well as related Opportunities where this Competitor is involved in the sales process. Further analysis can be performed to determine the Opportunities where we encounter the same Competitor or the Competitors we struggle against the most.

Products

Part of the **Product Catalog** entity, the Product is a record that represents an individual Product or Service offered to customers. Products can be associated with Opportunities, Quotes, Orders, and Service Cases.

A Product can contain associated sales materials, as well as details about competitor offerings.

The following screenshot shows the standard **Product** form with an already defined product:

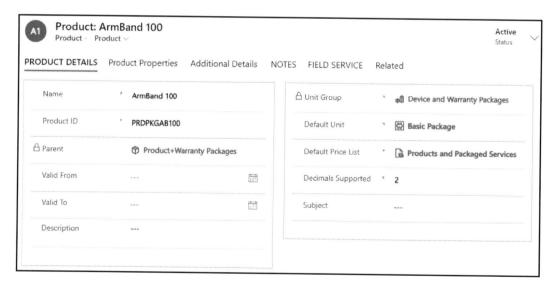

As part of the Product Catalog, a Product can have one or more pricing models and discount lists associated with it.

Based on user permissions, Products can be created, updated, disabled, or deleted. It is not recommended to delete any product records since they are already associated with older Opportunities, Quotes, Orders, and Invoices, and removing them would break the integrity of the data.

Always disable products rather than deleting them.

In order to see which Price Lists a Product is a part of, you can navigate to the **Additional Details** tab and find the **Price List Items** section, as shown in the following screenshot:

Products can be configured in a hierarchical relationship. This hierarchy can be visualized like so:

In addition to hierarchical relationships, products can also be grouped into bundles. A bundle is a grouping of products sold together, usually at a discounted price compared to the total cost of each individual product:

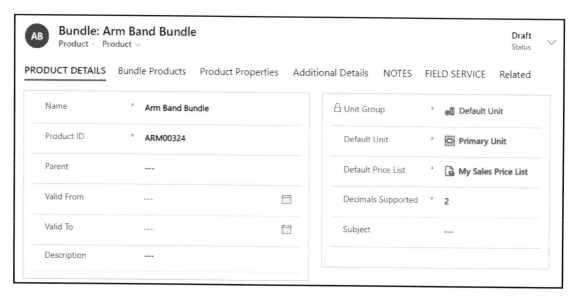

To see the Products that make up the current product bundle, you can navigate to the **Bundle Products** tab, as shown here:

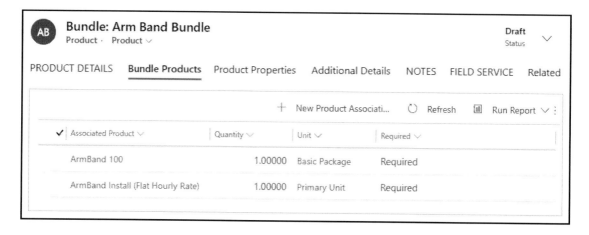

When looking at the generic view for **All Products, Families & Bundles**, each hierarchy is clearly represented by the icons preceding **Name**:

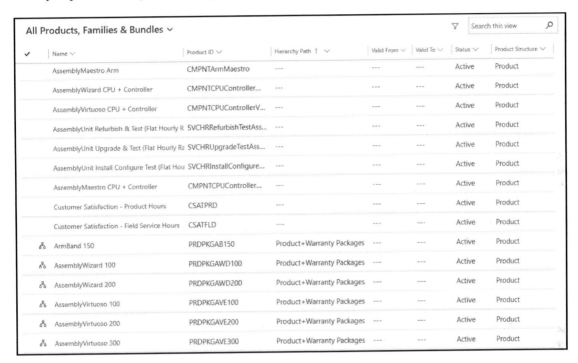

For bundles, we now have a separate view. You can select the **Active Product Bundles** view from the dropdown, as shown here:

Note that while the new UI in the Sales Hub strives for parity, some of the features we might be used to using are missing or have been relocated. For example, the **All Products, Families & Bundles** view used to have a visual representation in the classical web interface for both hierarchies and bundles. In the current incarnation of the UI, at the time of writing, only the hierarchies icons are presented, while a separate view has been provided for bundles.

New updates are being pushed at a fast rate, and the UI is being updated to bring all functionality over. It is quite possible that, by the time you read this, some features will have been updated and reflected slightly differently compared to what you have seen throughout the screenshots in this book.

Sales Goals

The **Goals** configuration and tracking process allows managers to monitor progress against targets. Taking advantage of the goal management processes across Sales and other business aspects allows better planning and growth for the business.

Goals in Dynamics 365 Sales can be created in a hierarchical structure and can be rolled up from the individual users to the team and department level. This allows greater visibility into the success of certain new initiatives and regular processes, or regions.

A Goal entity interacts directly with two types of user records: the goal manager as the record owner, with rights to update and modify the goal properties, and the goal owner as the user, who has to meet the goal targets. In addition, the goal is set for a certain period of time, either mapped to a fiscal period or a custom arbitrary period.

The following screenshot shows the standard **New Goal** form in Dynamics 365:

The **Time Period** tab allows you to define the duration of a Goal. You can choose between **Fiscal Period** or **Custom Period**. The following screenshot shows these settings for a **Fiscal Period**:

On the **Targets** tab, you can define the actual target to be reached for the goal to be achieved. When defining **Goal Metric** as **Revenue**, your target will be a specific amount you define here, as shown here:

Other options for goal metrics include the number of units sold, or for case management, the number of cases resolved.

When working with goals, as mentioned previously, these could be defined as **Rollup Goals**. You can configure this by going to the **Child Goals** tab and defining a set of child goals that roll up to the parent goal.

Finally, you can track progress against your goal by looking at the **Actuals** tab, which presents the actuals calculated values and the **Percentage Achieved** for your goal. You can also view the in-progress data here, as well as the actual values.

Now, let's have a look at the actual process a Salesperson follows to capture a Lead, work on an Opportunity, and make a Sale. These processes are standard and defined out of the box but can be configured to fit your organization's needs.

Standard Sales processes

The **Business Process Flow** (**BPF**) is a feature that was introduced back in Dynamics CRM 2013 and was greatly enhanced in later versions. It allows the system user to follow a predefined business process path to completion, and to track progress in a visual way. On an entity form, these are presented through a visual representation at the top of the form. We have already seen these on the Lead and Opportunity entities.

The following screenshot shows the standard BPF graphical representation, as shown on the default new lead form:

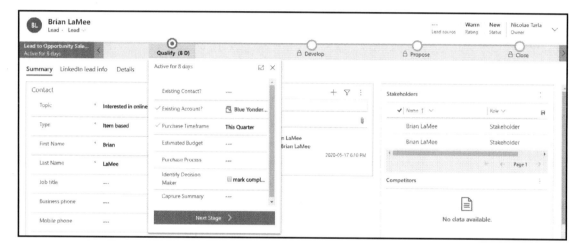

Each step of the process can be expanded so that we can view the specific actions and fields to be collected at that stage. You can also expand steps that have been completed or steps to be completed.

On a default base installation of Dynamics 365 Sales, two sales processes are included as part of the Sales module. These processes are provided as an example, but for some organizations, they might be just enough. Alternatively, you can configure them in order to add or remove steps, rename existing steps, or define new fields of data to be captured and processed at each step. These two processes are as follows:

- Lead to Opportunity Sales Process
- Opportunity Sales Process

We'll explore these processes in the subsequent sections.

Lead to Opportunity Sales Process

This BPF guides the user through the qualification process of a new **Lead to an Opportunity** record.

The following screenshot shows the **Lead to Opportunity Sales Process** customization form:

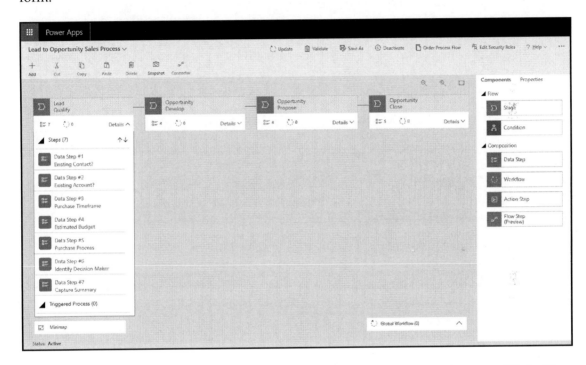

This process defines the data that needs to be captured on a Lead in order to qualify it. The preceding screenshot lists the data steps needed.

A process will typically span across several entities in the system. This process starts at the Lead entity and works through to the Opportunity. Others will include more entities, as we will see in the next process. The entity name is clearly displayed at the top of each stage, and each stage will be associated with only one entity. You can have a process that hops back and forth between entities as needed.

In this process, the user walks through the following steps:

1. We start at the Lead record by creating a new Lead. We work with the Lead and when we are ready, we qualify it and convert it into an Opportunity.
2. The **Develop** stage in the process is already using the Opportunity record, as generated from the original Lead. Additional information is collected and recorded on the Opportunity.
3. The **Proposed** stage further expands the work on the Opportunity by tracking the creation and presentation of a proposal to a Customer.
4. Finally, the **Close** stage handles the final Proposal presentation to a customer, capturing the win and final communication to the client, as part of the Sales process. At this point, we are ready to hand the sale to fulfillment.

We'll look at the second process next.

Opportunity Sales Process

This business process defines the stages that are followed to qualify an Opportunity. Just like the previous business process, the fields that are required at each stage are highlighted.

The following screenshot shows the **Opportunity Sales Process** customization form:

As you can see, these standard stages map to various steps for progressing an opportunity through the typical sales pipeline. This not only guides the salesperson through a process but allows bubbling up information to a sales manager, who can then make informed decisions based on information that has been collected from an entire sales group.

A BPF stage can not only collect data points but also trigger other actions. As shown on the sidebar on the right-hand side of the screen, you can use the standard data steps to collect information, but you can also trigger **Workflows**, **Action Steps**, or **Flows** designed with Microsoft Flow. This allows more complex actions to be configured and triggered when moving between process stages.

So far, we've looked at two sales processes. Now, it's time to understand the Sales Literature.

Sales Literature

In Dynamics 365 Sales, the **Sales Literature** is a collection of records pertaining to various product documentation that's stored in various file type formats. This is information that is referenced or attached from external sources. Each Sales Literature record can include one or more individual sales attachments. Each attachment has a defined set of keywords, an author, and a title. It also includes an abstract.

A Sales Literature record is presented in the following screenshot:

The **SALES ATTACHMENTS** record captures metadata about the document attached to a **Sales Literature** record, as well as the document itself. This information makes it easy for the document to be retrieved later when it's needed, either to support a customer or for any other purpose. The **New Sales Attachment** record in the Sales Hub looks as follows:

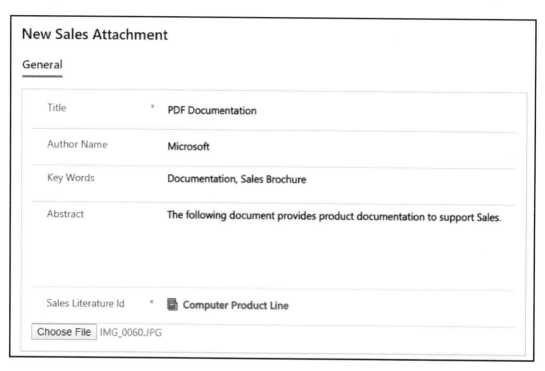

Since Sales documentation is added to a Sales Literature record, this is displayed in the **SALES ATTACHMENTS** section, as shown here:

The Sales Literature is a repository driven by metadata. The **Subject** field allows you to associate each document with a specific topic defined in a taxonomy. Defining a clear, concise, and correct taxonomy from the get-go will help a lot when it comes to building a well-structured library and providing increased value to your staff.

Each item in the Sales Literature repository can be associated with one or more Products and Competitors. They can then be retrieved and forwarded to Customers.

When creating Sales Literature, on the header line, an **Expiration Dat**e can be defined on each record so that the information that's been captured becomes obsolete and unavailable to be referenced after a specified date. In addition, an owner responsible for maintaining this record is defined in the **Employee Contact** field.

In the next section, we'll look at visualizing data through dashboards.

Reviewing Sales dashboards

A part of Dynamics 365 Sales, Microsoft provides a set of default dashboards specific to Sales staff. They are as follows:

- Sales Activity Dashboard
- Sales Activity Social Dashboard
- Sales Dashboard

Let's have a look at each dashboard and their differences. We're only going to be looking at the presentation provided through the Sales Hub, with the understanding that their layout and content will be similar in the classical web interface.

Sales Activity Dashboard

The **Sales Activity Dashboard** consolidates the day-to-day data required by a sales representative to complete their tasks. It includes charts that represent the sales pipeline, a view into open and won opportunities, a listing of **Open Leads** and **Open Opportunities**, as well as the personal activities for the currently logged-in user. The following screenshot shows the top section of this dashboard:

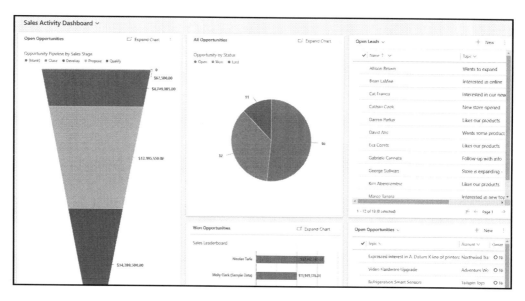

All the data represented on this dashboard is data that's relevant to the sales representative that's currently logged in. This is also called security trimming, and only presents dashboard information that the currently logged-in user has permission to see. We will review security and ways to restrict access to only specific data in `Chapter 13`, *Core Administration Concepts*.

This dashboard is also a good starting point for a sales representative logging into the system. Besides having visibility into a graphical representation of various **Key Performance Indicators** (**KPIs**), the bottom of the dashboard also presents a list of activities that require the user's attention. These include tasks, email, appointments, phone calls, letters, and faxes, as well as custom activities that might be defined as part of customization. The sales representative can now start working and closing these activities. They can tackle these by applying filters based on **Priority**, **Due Date**, **Activity Type**, or any other configured filtering option made available through column headers in the view. A user can also use the search provided at the top-left-hand side of the view to retrieve a specific record to be worked on:

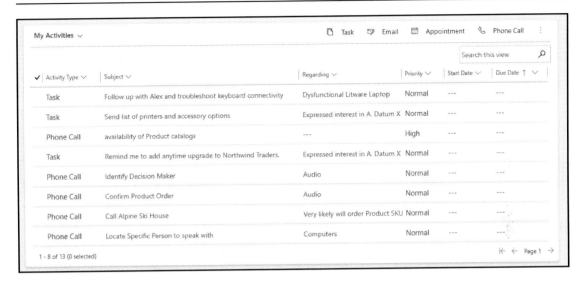

While the default view only shows records owned by the current user, this view can be extended to all records on the platform or select views into remaining open or closed activity records. However, note that, even on these views, security trimming is applied, which means the user can only see the records they have permission to view:

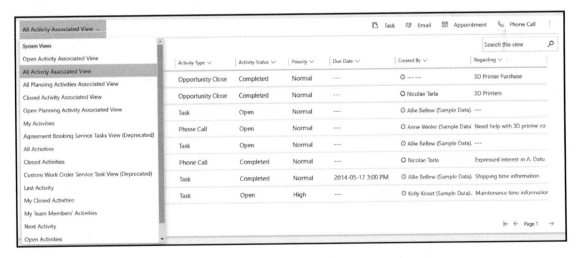

Sales Activity Social Dashboard

The Sales Activity Social Dashboard takes most of its data representations from the regular Sales Activity Dashboard, but it adds the **Assistant** section. This is a piece of AI that was added to enhance functionality across Sales:

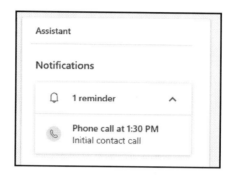

This section surfaces various pertinent activities based on internal matching. The cards presented are contextual recommendations. You can also configure it to surface email alerts. This feature must be enabled separately as it requires access to the user's email inbox for indexing and analysis.

Sales Dashboard

The standard **Sales Dashboard** is less focused on charts and visual elements. Instead, it digs right into the data and presents lists of **All Activities**, **Open Opportunities**, **Open Leads**, and **Active Accounts**. We also get to look at the sales pipeline, as well as a graphical representation of **All Opportunities**. The following screenshot shows the top portion of this dashboard:

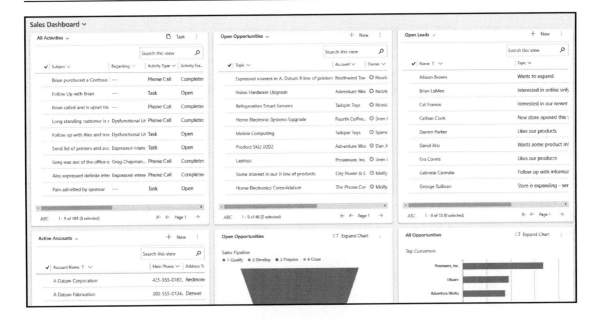

New Dashboards can be created to serve various purposes. You can create your own personal dashboards, or the organization can provide a set of custom dashboards as needed. When creating custom dashboards, you can share them with your team for better visibility. Note that data will always be security trimmed, meaning that even when sharing a Dashboard, the layout and queries are shared, but the data content is presented only based on what the user has permission to see.

In the next section, we'll tackle another way of visualizing data: reports.

Leveraging Sales reports

A default installation of Dynamics 365 Sales will include a set of reports to get you started. There are reports for each application, as well as general reports that span across data from multiple applications.

When working with reports, in most cases, you will end up customizing your own reports. The default ones that are provided are presented as guidance, but they can, on certain occasions, be useful with no customization.

The standard reports revolve around **Accounts** and **Contacts**, as well as **Activities**, **Leads**, **Sales History**, and **Sales Pipelines**.

The Dynamics 365 platform allows us to report on data in various ways. Starting from aggregated and filtered data presented in views, and continuing with charts, dashboards, and wizard-driven reports, the platform capabilities are quite extensive. Add to that the ability to export to Excel and perform further analysis or use Dynamics 365 Sales data as a data source for Power BI, and suddenly you can start creating some very complex visualizations.

For special circumstances where none of these options are enough, we still retain the ability to build specific **SQL Server Reporting Services (SSRS)** reports. This method varies between Dynamics 365 Online versus on-premise, but at this point, a developer should be involved in the process. This approach is quite different when building for Online as certain constraints are in place to protect the cloud environment from unexpected load or other issues that would cripple the service.

Marketing features

While the Sales module is logically separate from the Marketing one, certain features from Marketing are exposed here. As such, a sales representative has the ability to create their own marketing lists and generate quick campaigns. This is meant to allow sales staff to contact a group of customers and track this interaction within the system. This functionality is built on top of the regular direct customer interaction and is tracked in the same way as any other customer contact.

You can find the limited Marketing features in the **Marketing** section in the **Sales** navigation menu, as shown in the following screenshot:

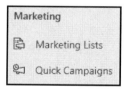

Let's learn how to use this functionality:

1. From **Marketing Lists**, we create a new list that we want to target with a promotional discount. Click on **New Marketing list** on the ribbon to create your first list. You will be taken to the following screen:

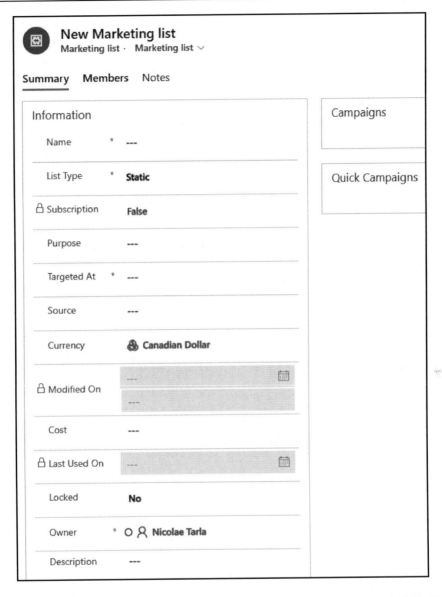

2. You can choose to define a **Static** or **Dynamic List Type**. A **Static List Type** will always have the same contacts defined, while a **Dynamic List Type** will run a query based on specified parameters and rebuild the list every time.

3. When defining the **Marketing list**, you must select the target as either **Contact**, or **Accounts**, or **Leads**.

4. Navigate to the **Members** tab and start adding the members to this list. You can do this by selecting **Add** from the ribbon and selecting the contact to be added. Your complete list will look as follows:

5. And with that, you now have a static marketing list that you can use for quick campaigns.

To create a Quick Campaign from this current list, follow these steps:

1. From the main **Summary** tab on a **Marketing** list, locate the **Quick Campaigns** section and select the **New Quick Campaign** option on the ribbon, as shown here:

2. A wizard will start, allowing you to configure the **Quick Campaigns** properties. Follow the prompts to define the **Name**, the **Activity Type**, the **Assignment**, as well as the **Content**. The following screenshot shows one of the wizard steps where we define the Content:

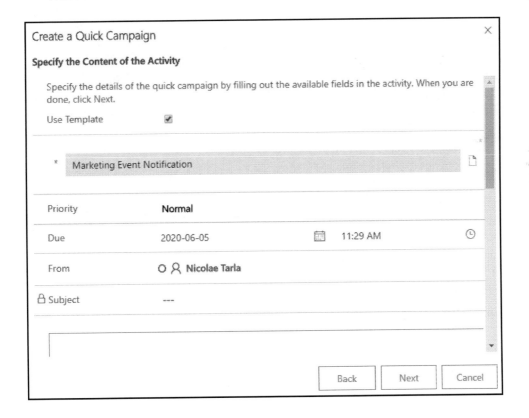

3. Finally, click **Create** to complete the wizard. Your new **Quick Campaign** will now be displayed in the list of **Quick Campaigns** on the **Marketing list** view. You can also find this newly created quick campaign by navigating to **Quick Campaigns** from the sidebar, as shown in the following screenshot:

My Quick Campaigns ∨								
✓ Subject ∨	Activity Type ∨	Total Members ∨	No. of Successes ∨	No. of Failures ∨	Status Reason ∨	Created On ↓ ∨	Owner ∨	
January 2020 Quick Campaign	Email	7	0	0	Pending	2020-05-26 11:34 ...	O Nicolae Tarla	

Like marketing lists, you can define a subscription list. This follows the same approach. The difference is primarily in scope. A Marketing List can come from Marketing, be shared with the Sales team, and be used as defined.

Summary

Throughout this chapter, we looked at some of the most important elements that comprise the Microsoft Dynamics 365 for Sales application. We reviewed the entities that make up the functionality of the Sales app; the out-of-the-box defined sales processes and their scope, as well as their intended usage and the capabilities to extend them; and finally, dashboards and their reporting capabilities.

Finally, we looked at some of the light marketing features available for Sales. Keep in mind that salespeople are primarily focused on closing sales, so they will not perform the more extensive marketing functions available in the Marketing app, as described in Chapter 7, *Dynamics 365 Marketing*.

At this point, you should have a good understanding of the features available in this module and the capabilities that support salespeople and their managers.

The next chapter will take you through a similar journey across the Customer Service application and the functionality that's available.

Dynamics 365 Customer Service

4

In the previous chapter, we focused our attention on the Sales functionality available within Microsoft Dynamics 365. In this chapter, we will start looking at the Customer Service functionality.

At this point, you should be familiar with creating a trial instance, and you should already have a new Sales instance created. This brings a set of core functional entities and components with it. We need to add the Customer Service functionality and see what it is all about.

In this chapter, we will cover the following topics since they relate to the Customer Service functionality:

- The functionality of the Customer Service application
- The Customer Service Hub
- The specific entities and processes that support the Customer Service application

By the end of this chapter, you will be familiar with the Customer Service application's functionality, as well as how to deal with customer issues, track communications, how to assign various activities to other teams in support of resolving cases, as well as how to manage and deal with supporting documentation for repeating processes. You should also be able to clearly distinguish between the **Service**, **Service Management**, and **Scheduling** sections of the Customer Service application.

Let's get started by looking at the Customer Service application and its components.

Exploring the Dynamics 365 for Customer Service app

With the move to the new app model, we have several separate applications we can purchase and deploy independently of others. We looked at the Sales application in the previous chapter, so now, we'll focus our attention on the Customer Service application.

As an organization, once you have made a sale, you aren't done – you're nowhere close. Now that you've built a customer base through selling products and services directly to people or other businesses, the challenge becomes how you help those customers with various issues and how you keep them happy. This translates to repeated business sales, and free advertising through word of mouth and recommendations.

Dynamics 365 Customer Service

The Microsoft Dynamics 365 for Customer Service module facilitates your support team when dealing with issues that arise from your customer's challenges. These can be in various forms, including product or service issues, a lack of understanding, requests for help in using the products that have been purchased, various inquiries, or simply calls to congratulate you on a fabulous product or service provided. Yes – sometimes, we get those too!

Within the Customer Service module, the support team can manage all these customer touchpoints, track and reference back to various interactions with the clients, as well as reporting on the success rates and times to resolution.

There is an obvious overlap in entities within the Sales module, as we saw in Chapter 3, *Dynamics 365 Sales Application*. Entities such as Accounts, Contacts, and Activities perform the same and are shared across multiple applications. This allows a single data point, and no need to keep data synchronized across multiple application profiles.

Also, having visibility across the various touchpoints we've had with a customer paints a good picture of how satisfied our customer is, things we can do better, as well as things that are still outstanding and could create problems down the road.

To get started with the Customer Service application, we will be using the **Customer Service Hub**. This is our Service application, and our entry point into the functionality provided.

The Customer Service Hub can be accessed from the main apps page on any Dynamics 365 instance. The tile is called **Customer Service Hub** and is marked with the **Unified Interface (UI)** tag. The following screenshot shows the tile for **Customer Service Hub** alongside other applications we have access to:

Having the app drawer present and showing all the applications a user can access makes for a great experience where you do not need to scout around for the right application at the right time. Furthermore, you can now access separate applications with trimmed down navigation that's relevant only to the application you're using at that time.

The Customer Service Hub includes a set of powerful features in Microsoft Dynamics 365, allowing service users and their managers to manage and track customer complaints and service activities, as well as customer interactions within your organization.

The Customer Service application can be looked at from the point of view of service management and **Service Scheduling**. The management aspect deals primarily with managing service tickets. They are called **Cases** within the context of Dynamics 365, but are sometimes also referred to as **Incidents** by their internal record name. The other aspect, **Scheduling**, allows us to schedule resources for customer-centric activities.

The introduction of the Customer Service Hub marks the move to the UI, which allows for a similar experience across multiple devices. Now, we can immediately recognize the familiar interface across both desktops and mobile devices.

The Customer Service Hub is comprised of a set of entities, processes, dashboards, and reports, and also allows us to view the products and services being offered. Within this module, the customer support team can see their progress against predefined goals for each customer type or incident type, as well as analyzing various trends.

Within this module, the entities are structured by categories. Starting with the **Customers** section, here, we can find core records that are shared across multiple modules. These include **Accounts** and **Contacts**. Social profiles also captures channel and profile names associated with existing customers in your Customer Service module. In addition to this, here, we capture an influence score.

The next section is the meat of this module, with entities for **Cases** and **Queues**. This is where the bulk of support takes place. We track customer issues using Cases, and we can have various activities related to these cases until resolution. Queues allow us to group cases by specific criteria and assign specialized teams to them. This way, we can make sure the right staff is working on the correct Case.

Next, the **Knowledge** section includes **Knowledge Articles**, which are supporting materials we can use to guide the representative through steps to resolve a Case for a customer. We can forward these materials to customers for self-help. We will look at this in more detail later in this chapter. Also in this section is **Knowledge Search**, which allows us to retrieve the relevant articles as needed.

Finally, for automated monitoring using IoT devices, the **Devices** section allows us to track devices and alerts that have been raised by these devices. This area focuses on fully automated monitoring and Case creation via various integrated monitoring devices.

The following screenshot shows the new navigation for the **Service** area of the Customer Service Hub:

Aside from the **Service** area, within the Customer Service Hub, we also have the **Service Management** section. Here, we can track various settings we can use to configure our Customer Service Hub. Here, we have **Case Settings**, **Service Terms**, **Templates**, **Knowledge Base Management**, and settings for record similarity suggestions, as well as configuration for IoT integration.

The following screenshot shows this navigational menu:

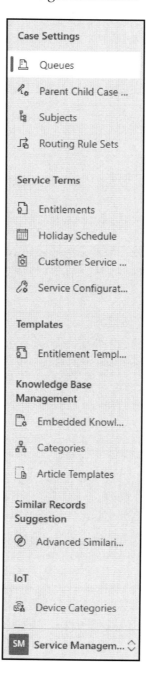

Finally, also part of the Customer Service Hub, we have the **Scheduling** functionality. This area includes **Scheduling** capabilities for resources, facilities, and equipment, as well as additional configurations. The **Tools** area includes a scheduling calendar, which allows us to create blocks of allocation for specific resources needed to service a Case.

The **Settings** area deals with generic system configurations for **Business Closures**, which take part in resource allocation, as well as **Organizational Units**. The following screenshot shows this area's navigation:

Note that these options are always security trimmed. So, if the user does not have permissions to a certain area or entity, that area or entity will not be displayed. Furthermore, the data is security trimmed so that a user will only see records they have permissions to view.

You can switch between these three areas from the option selector at the bottom of the navigation area, as shown here:

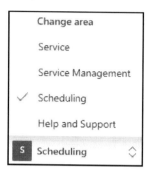

Now, let's move our attention to the Customer Service Hub's functionality, starting with the Service area.

Customer Service Hub – Service area

The Customer Service Hub is the result of a modular approach to consuming the platform's functionality. The **Service** area includes all functionality needed for a customer service representative or their managers to handle customer issues. The main interface starts at **Dashboards**, with **Tier 1**- and **Tier 2**-specific dashboards available, as well as a set of additional system dashboards, as shown in the following screenshot:

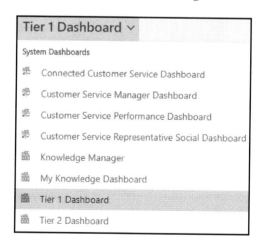

We will review these dashboards later in this chapter, in the *Understanding the Customer Service dashboards* section.

One important aspect to note here that's available throughout all applications is the minimized navigation on the left-hand side, which allows a user to maximize the entire screen space. Using this, we can choose to keep the navigation open or collapse it and take advantage of more screen real estate, as shown in the following screenshot, which shows the navigation collapsed:

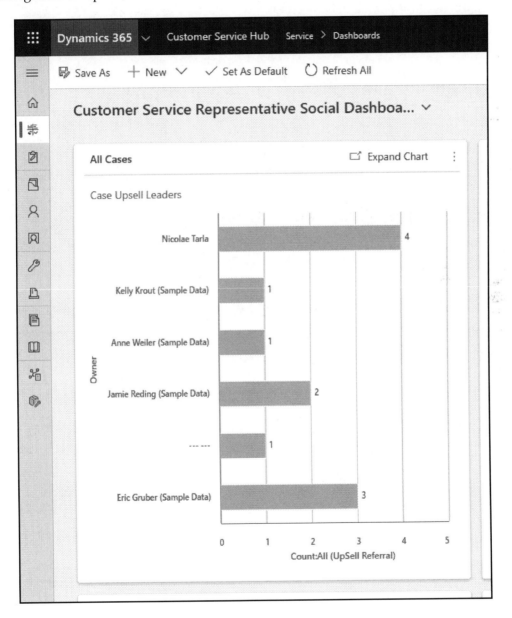

From a functional perspective, the **Customer Service Hub | Service** area provides access to the core customer service elements but leaves some of the elements for the other areas. Separating these areas is essential as a service representative has all that they need to perform their day-to-day duties, without being bogged down by extra fluff. Power users and managers can switch between the areas in the Customer Service Hub to do the additional setup for their teams as needed.

Next, we will look at the **Scheduling** area of the Customer Service Hub.

Customer Service Hub – Scheduling area

This area of the Customer Service Hub focuses on the allocation of resources, facilities, and equipment in order to resolve specific incidents. Besides the ability to configure and manage resources, the bulk of the work in this area will be done in the **Scheduling** calendar. The following screenshot shows a view of the calendar with some allocations in place:

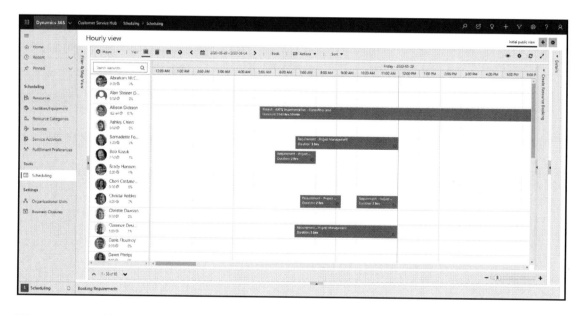

The resource allocation calendar is surfacing in the Field Service schedule board, as we will see in Chapter 5, *Dynamics 365 Field Service*.

Customer Service Hub – Service Management area

This area primarily revolves around the configurations needed for the proper and efficient functionality of the **Service** area. Some of the important aspects include the configuration of queues to store new cases and subjects for case categorization, as well as routing rules for automatically dropping new cases into the correct queue.

Configuring a proper subject taxonomy is essential for the classification of Cases. You can do this through the interface available under **Subjects**, as shown in the following screenshot:

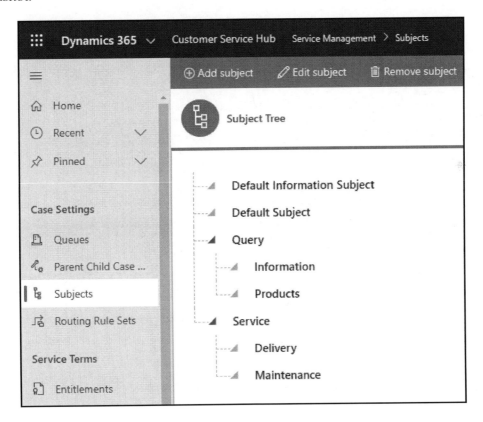

The **Service Terms** section is comprised of configurations for holiday schedules, which define the days when the service is not available, as well as **Entitlements** for existing customers. One example of the entitlement screen is presented here:

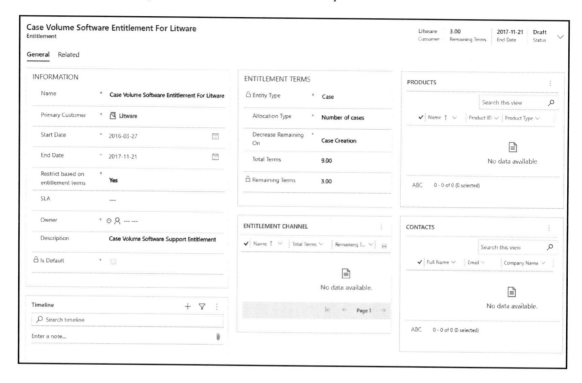

In regard to **Entitlements**, it is important to capture the type of support to be provided for a Customer, as well as the limitations imposed. Some of these limitations could be the maximum number of Cases available for a specific duration or the number of hours available for support.

Now, let's shift our focus to the specific entities that support the Customer Service functionality.

Understanding the Customer Service entities

Just like with the Sales Hub app, the Customer Service Hub app contains specific Service entities, as well as shared entities. These Service-specific entities are as follows:

- **Cases**
- **Queues**
- **Services**
- **Scheduling**
- **Knowledge Articles**

We'll look at these entities in detail in the subsequent sections.

Cases

The Case entity represents an incident or a ticket that's been logged in the system as it relates to a customer. The system users create Cases to track a request, problem, or question from an existing customer. This entity is also the central point for tracking all future communications and actions that are performed while handling the request until completion.

Cases can also be automatically created from communication coming over email, or through integration with other systems.

The Cases that are tracked in the system can be in one of the following states:

- **In Progress**
- **Resolved**
- **Canceled**

The following screenshot shows a new **Case** form, as presented in the Customer Service Hub:

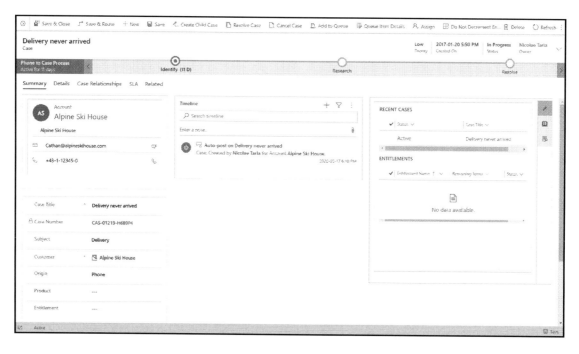

Just as we saw for Leads and Opportunities, a Case has a **business process flow (BPF)**, which helps guide users through the necessary steps to resolve it.

Starting with Dynamics CRM 2013 Service Pack 1, we can relate Cases hierarchically. This allows better organization of the data and easier management of Cases by users.

Only one level of the hierarchy is supported. A case cannot be associated with another case if it is associated with another one. For child cases, a view into their own child cases is not available.

You can associate up to 100 child cases to a parent case.

We can observe related **Child Cases**, as well as **Merged Cases**, by navigating to the **Case Relationships** tab, as shown in the following screenshot:

When multiple cases are logged in the system, either as a result of various channels they arrived through, such as email and phone calls, or a result of another customer service representative raising a case by mistake instead of working on an already existing Case, these Cases can be merged into a single Case to be resolved. These merged Cases are presented on the current Case, as shown in the preceding screenshot.

When closing a case, a case resolution activity is created, which stores details about the resolution, the time spent on resolving the case, and other remarks, as shown in the following screenshot:

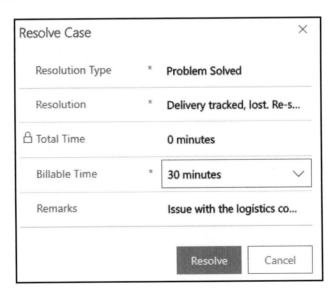

Now, let's look at how to group cases using queues.

Queues

Queues are used within Dynamics 365 Customer Service to organize, prioritize, and monitor a user or team's work. In conjunction with routing workflows, queues play an important part in automating standard business processes and improving efficiency.

From an underlying point of view, queues are comprised of queue items. Each queue item is a record that points to an existing system entity. For example, you can have a queue that holds various cases. Each queue item would point back to an existing case. A queue item can point to a task, email, or case. In addition, new custom entities can be enabled for queues.

 A queue can hold more than one entity type. Thus, a queue can hold tasks and cases at the same time.

Each system user gets a personal queue associated with the respective user profile. In addition, new queues can be created, and they can be either private or public. A queue definition looks as follows:

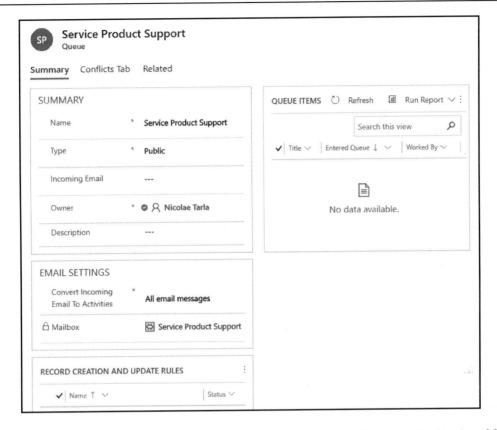

A private queue limits the number of users who have access to the queue items. A public queue, on the other hand, allows everyone in the organization to view the queue and its associated items. We'll look at the Services entity next.

Services

The Service entity is another configurable entity that represents work to be performed for a customer. It is defined by the date and time, duration, name, resource(s) assigned, and other fields as needed.

The following screenshot shows a **Service** that's been defined, along with its related **Resource Requirements**:

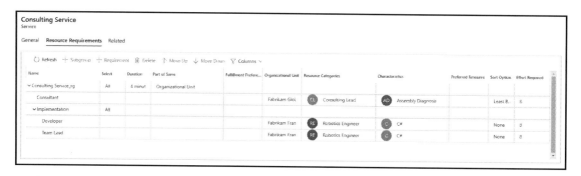

Service Activity works in conjunction with the **Service** declaration by referencing a specific **Service** on the **Activity** record, as shown in the following screenshot:

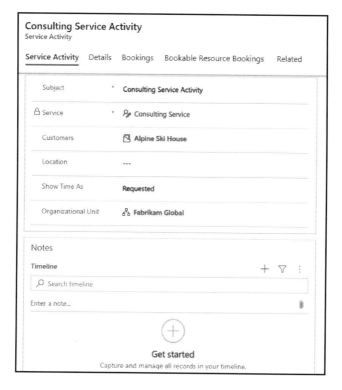

More details on booking and **Scheduling** will be covered later in this book.

Scheduling

The service calendar represents all the service records that have been created based on resources and equipment availability, as well as the duration of service activity. The Calendar entity aggregates the Service data through holiday schedules and business closures and allows us to schedule new service activities.

Calendars are related to Calendar Rules, which define the calendar's duration and availability, recurrence, and start/end times. These rules can be ordered and ranked to determine precedence. Rules can overlap.

A **Scheduling** calendar is shown in the following screenshot:

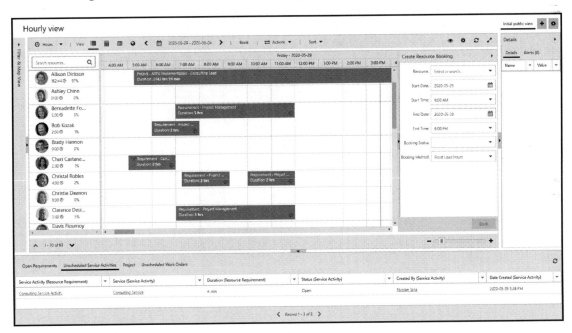

Of course, in a real-life scenario, this calendar view could become quite busy. The visual aspect of the calendar creates a familiar experience, similar to the Outlook client.

What if the customers need repetitive support information for specific products or services? We'll look at this in the next section.

Knowledge Articles

Knowledge Articles are the central elements for providing customers with repetitive support information for specific products or services that are sold. Typically, these articles are the domain of a specific group within the organization that creates these materials, reviews them, and proves them for publishing.

Once published, these articles can either be surfaced on a self-service portal for customers to access, sent via email, or referenced by support technicians to help customers.

A typical new **Knowledge Article** screen is presented in the following screenshot:

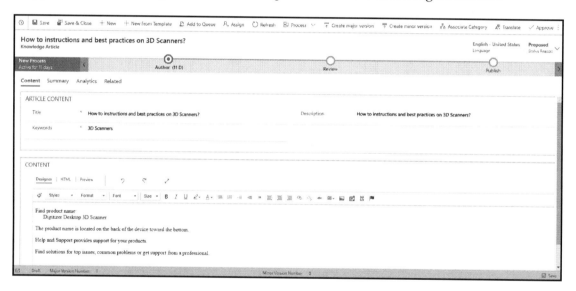

A couple of things are very important to observe here. Like Leads and Opportunities, as well as Cases, we have a BPF that guides the user through managing knowledgebase articles. The scope is somewhat different, though. In this case, we're looking at a normal flow that's used to create, manage, and publish articles to make them available to their intended audience.

The standard BPF in this scenario handles authorizing, reviewing, and publishing the article. At each step, other players are typically involved. The **Authors** group, as mentioned previously, is typically a different group in the organization that manages the creation of documentation. The reviewers are tasked with approving the created content for publishing. Once a Knowledge Article has been published, it becomes available for use by a larger audience.

During the creation and approval process, a Knowledge Article will switch between several status reasons, as shown in the following screenshot:

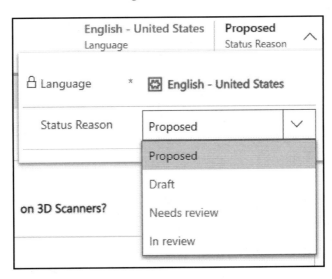

From a content perspective, we can create and manage rich content. The new editor allows style definitions and formatting to be created, as well as HTML design to be created and embedded. The **Preview** feature allows us to verify the format, look, and feel across various devices, as shown in the following screenshot:

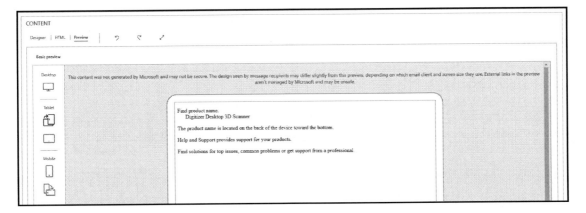

Versioning is also very important when working with a library of articles. You can define and manage versions by navigating to the **Summary** tab of an article and looking at the **BASIC SETTINGS** area, as shown here:

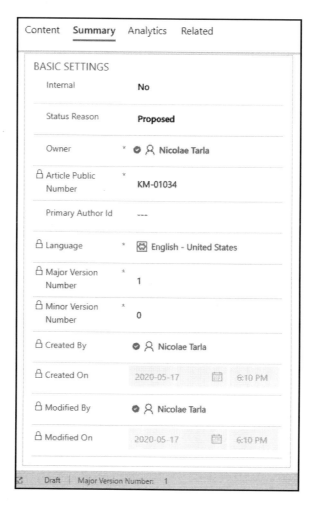

Since the version is very important, it is also displayed on the bottom status bar.

On that same tab, we have access to additional details in the **RELATED INFORMATION** area. We can easily track related versions of the same article, as well as related translations, categories, articles, and products. The following screenshot shows this section reflecting the related article version:

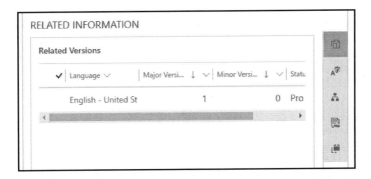

As you can probably guess, this allows a multi-faceted structure of articles to be built and managed, allowing large organizations with complex requirements to leverage the system, while smaller organizations can only use a subset as needed.

The **Analytics** tab allows information and feedback to be collected and analyzed. This becomes even more relevant when these articles are surfaced on a self-service portal and users provide feedback. The following screenshot shows a typical **Analytics** tab for an article:

With this information, in order to create and make a new article available to readers, we go through the following steps:

1. Create the content in a new knowledge article.
2. Review how the content will be presented in various screen formats and sizes.
3. Mark the article Complete and ready for Review.
4. Submit the Article for Review.
5. A reviewer receives the article and analyzes the content. At this point, the reviewer can either reject the article, thus returning it to the author with comments and feedback for additional improvements, or approve it if everything looks good.

6. Once an article has been Approved, it is ready to be Published.

7. Finally, the Knowledge Article is Published and an Expiration Date and Time is provided (if needed). The article will remain published and available to users until the Expiration Date and Time are reached, or another user Un-publishes it.

In the next section, we'll look at Service Processes, which are the glue that tie the separate pieces together and guides the user through a logical approach to solving a business need.

Understanding Service Processes

With a default Dynamics 365 for Customer Service deployment, for the Service app, we only get one predefined business process flow. This is known as **Phone to Case Process**.

The business process flow for **Phone to Case Process** looks as follows:

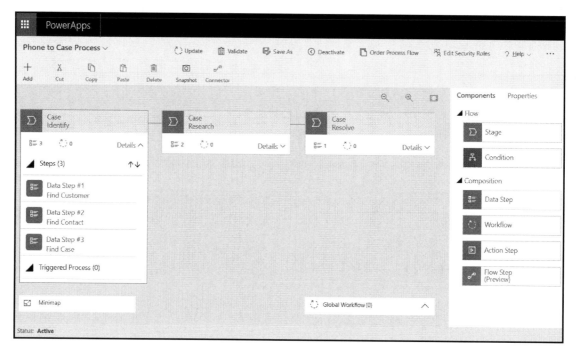

For those familiar with the previous versions of the business process flow editor, observe the updated and more streamlined card-like approach to the design. This is a much more visual and intuitive way to design complex business process flows.

This process lives on the Case entity and handles the standard approach to solving Cases through three predefined stages.

This business process flow, which was created in the preceding wizard, will display on a new case form like so:

To maximize the screen real estate, the entire business process flow is collapsed, and each stage opens its details in a hovering window. This makes it much more clear from a usability standpoint.

In addition, you can expand each BPF stage as a blade that appears on the right-hand side of the screen, as shown in the following screenshot:

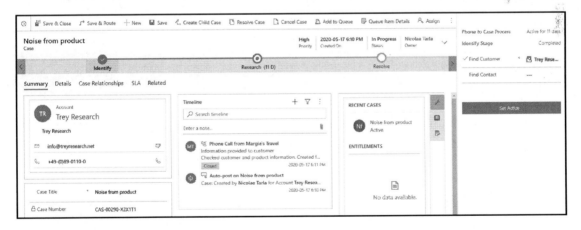

Putting all this functionality aside, most of the time, you simply need to make sense of the data. You can easily do that on this platform through the use of dashboards, as described in the following section.

Understanding the Customer Service dashboards

Just like all the other available applications with Dynamics 365, the Customer Service Hub provides a set of default dashboards built to leverage the standard configuration. Of course, the moment you start building up and expanding the core platform functionality, you must consider updating these dashboards or creating new ones to include the newly configured elements.

The Customer Service Hub adds on top of the standard dashboards; that is, the **Tier 1 Dashboard** and the **Tier 2 Dashboard**. These two dashboards are, in a way, different from the regular dashboards as they provide a richer experience. You can change the view from the standard **Stream View** to a **Tiled View**. The **Tiled View** shows aggregated totals in card format, as shown here:

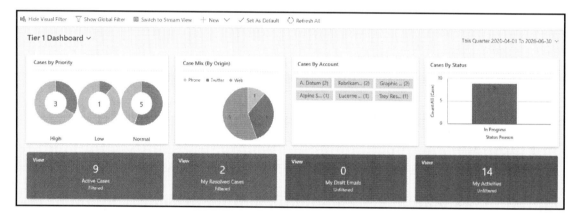

Furthermore, filters can be applied so that we can only view a subset of the data presented in these dashboards. This way, if you are assigned only a specific type of Case to work on, you can directly filter these by expanding **Global Filter** and applying the necessary condition. The following screenshot shows a filter that's been applied to only show Case records of the **Problem** type:

This provides great flexibility when you're starting your workday from a dashboard.

The **Tier 2 Dashboard** is designed to give a user a more comprehensive overview across not only their activities and cases that need attention but also more aggregated details about the system's overall performance. This dashboard mixes the **Tiled View** and **Stream View** together, for a very visual experience:

Of course, just like the **Tier 1 Dashboard**, you can apply **Global Filters** to narrow down the data to only the relevant types of Cases.

While these dashboards are great for presenting visual representations of data, we can also interact with various elements. We'll look at this in the next section.

Interacting with Streams and Tiles

On the new UI dashboards, the concept of Streams and Tiles has been added. This gives a more visual appeal to the data and allows us to interact with the individual elements.

First off, we can apply date period filters to all the data elements presented on the dashboard. This is a generic setting for the entire dashboard, and it is present at the top-right corner of the dashboard:

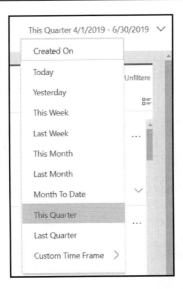

You can choose from predefined time periods or define your own custom period for filtering the results.

The Streams display shows a list of elements in card format. At each stream level, you have the option to apply additional sorting and filtering. On each record, you can expand the card to display more details by selecting the down arrow in the bottom-right corner of the card. The following screenshot shows two cards; the first is expanded, while the second is collapsed:

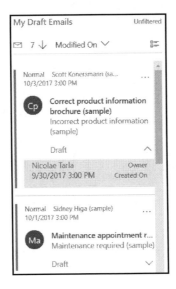

The Tiles display shows aggregated totals for specific groups of records. For example, you have totals for Activities, Cases, and so on, as shown in the following screenshot:

Clicking each of these tiles brings up a popup showing the individual records that make up these totals. It allows the user to directly navigate to any of those records.

Standard dashboards

For the Customer Service aspect of the business, just like for Sales, dashboards are an invaluable resource used to present data to the system users in a variety of ways. By default, the Customer Service app comes with five standard dashboards that serve various roles.

These remaining dashboards are available in the Classical Interface and UI. They include the following:

- **Customer Service Representative Social Dashboard**
- **Customer Service Performance Dashboard**
- **Customer Service Manager Dashboard**
- **My Knowledge Dashboard**
- **Knowledge Manager**
- **Connected Customer Service Dashboard**

Let's look at each of these and see what the major highlights and differences are.

Customer Service Representative Social Dashboard

As an aggregation of various Case details, along with providing a list of activities relevant to the currently logged-in user, the **Customer Service Representative Social Dashboard** is the default dashboard for the Service Module. The following screenshot shows the components that make up this area:

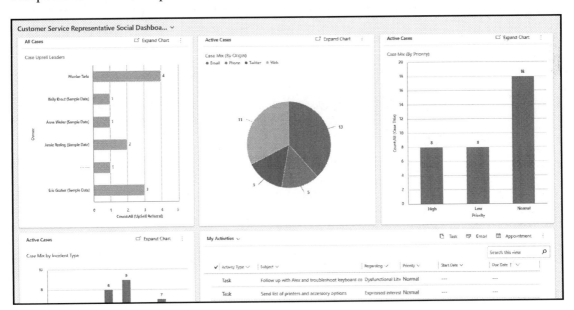

With a somewhat similar flavor, the next dashboard slightly changes the focus to performance.

Customer Service Performance Dashboard

The **Customer Service Performance Dashboard** focuses primarily on the service representative's overall performance and looks at Case mixes and trends. It is a charting dashboard that provides a quick overview of the status. The following screenshot shows an example dashboard prepopulated with sample data:

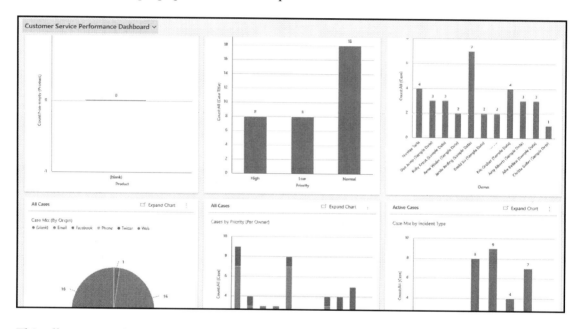

This allows a service representative to have direct access to cases by categories, in a visually simple format. With a quick glance, you can determine who is your busiest agent, or which case priority is the most popular.

Customer Service Manager Dashboard

The **Customer Service Manager Dashboard** combines relevant information across the whole team. The various sections of this dashboard present views into Cases by agents or team, queues, and entitlement, as well as Cases by priority. The following screenshot shows this dashboard, with a focus on cases by other filtering criteria:

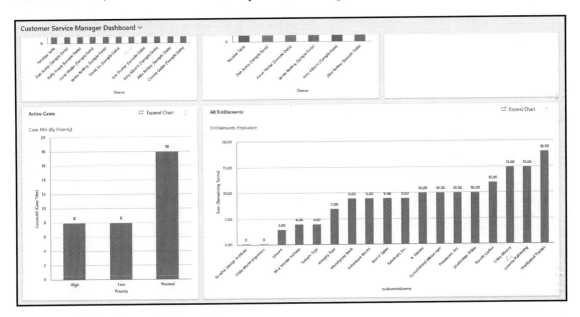

Having the ability to get to cases by a specific agent or those that have been filtered by various entitlements is important in optimizing the process flow and allowing the service representative to focus on what is important at that time.

My Knowledge Dashboard

The **My Knowledge Dashboard** is entirely focused on a user that creates and manages content for Knowledge Articles. It presents a Stream of last modified articles by date, along with cloud tags for subject and owners. In addition, we have information aggregated by status and subject, as well as tiles with totals.

The following screenshot shows this dashboard with some sample data in the system:

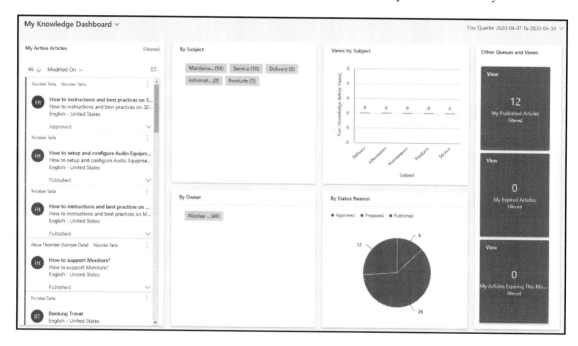

You can drill down into any of the tiles to see the content that makes up the visualization, as shown here:

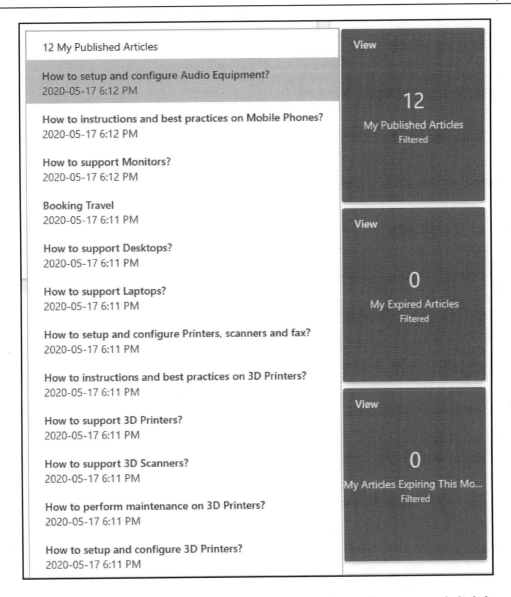

From a manager perspective, sometimes, the information has to be structured slightly differently. We'll look at this in the next section.

Knowledge Manager

This dashboard is somewhat less visual. It presents several streams with relevant information for a Manager role. It captures details on proposed, draft, and expired articles, as well as the most popular and highest-rated articles. The default **Stream View** of this dashboard is shown in the following screenshot:

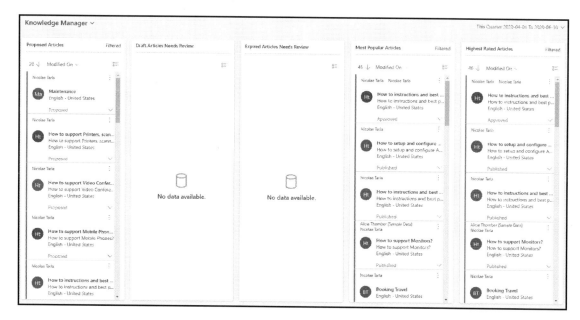

This view can also be switched to a **Tile View**, as shown in the following screenshot:

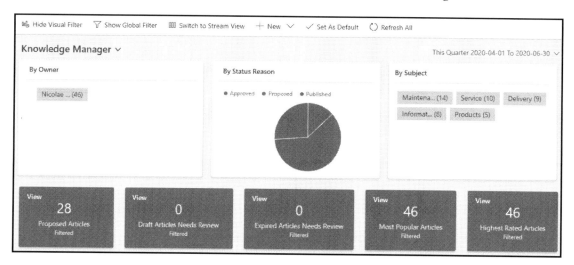

But there's more. The next dashboard has a totally different look and feel.

Connected Customer Service Dashboard

Finally, the last available dashboard relies heavily on integrating with IoT. When your platform is integrated either with an existing IoT hub or Azure IoT, streamed data from various devices can create various alerts and generate Cases on the platform.

The default look of this dashboard is shown in the following screenshot, with no data being populated:

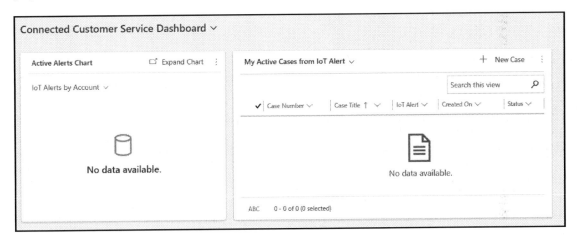

In order to see data in a more printable/formatted way, we can create reports. These reports enhance the dashboard's functionality by giving us another way to aggregate and present the data. We will look at reporting in the next section.

Service Reports

Just like the other modules, the Service module presents us with a set of standard reports. These include, but are not limited to, reports around Activities, Case Summaries, and Service Activity Volumes.

A large variety of additional reports can be customized in various ways.

With the added support for Power BI, this is quickly becoming the go-to tool for dynamic and highly visual reports that allow us to drill down into complex data. It is seldom that a classical SSRS report is built, and when that's the case, due to the cloud model's limitations, FetchXML must be used, which comes with its own set of limitations from a performance standpoint. It also shows the maximum number of records that have been returned from a query.

You will typically want a new set of reports to be created once you've started to configure and extend the platform. While it is not uncommon to leave the default reports available to users, to get the most out of this module, it is recommended to create custom specific reports to present data to system users.

Summary

Throughout this chapter, we looked at some of the most important elements that comprise the Microsoft Dynamics 365 Customer Service offering. We reviewed the Customer Service Hub options, areas, and its functionality. We also looked at the main entities that make up this application, as well as the other components that glue together the separate parts to create a comprehensive, functional solution.

We finished this chapter by learning how to visualize data through Streams and Tiles, as well as dashboards and reports. We also looked at the application hub and how it brings all the required information together through a friendly user experience.

The next chapter will expand on the standard Customer Service by looking at the Field Service offering. The Dynamics 365 Field Service application presents some similarities to the Customer Service offering we have seen so far, but also provides more robust functionality in order to support organizations that manage field technicians.

Dynamics 365 Field Service

5

In the previous chapter, we focused our attention on the customer service functionality available with Microsoft Dynamics 365 Customer Engagement. This time, we will move on to the Field Service offering.

We've so far seen the Sales app, where we enroll customers by selling them existing products and services, as well as the Customer Service app, where we provide the necessary support to our existing customers over the phone or in the form of knowledge base articles. This is a remote type of support, based primarily on the customer participating actively in fixing existing issues with a product or a service offered.

The Dynamics 365 for Field Service app shifts focus to delivering on-site customer support. This serves situations where, for example, for an internet provider, a technician needs to be sent to a customer to install a modem or fix connectivity issues that the customer cannot debug using standard customer support practices.

In this chapter, we are looking at the following aspects, as they relate to the Field Service functionality:

- The core functionality of the Field Service application
- The personas leveraging this application
- Common scenarios for Field Service, including working with work orders and the resource scheduling board
- The various apps available to access this service

By the end of this chapter, you will be familiar with the Field Service functionality, the typical roles interacting with this set of functionalities, as well as the various applications supporting this module. You should also be able to understand the difference between the different applications leveraging the Unified Interface as well as the mobile offering.

Solution features of Dynamics 365 for Field Service

As mentioned, the Field Service app functionality shifts the focus from standard customer service, as described in `Chapter 4`, *Dynamics 365 Customer Service*, and takes support out into the field. The solution handles scenarios where delivering service to customers at the customer location is essential. This solution handles the dispatching of necessary resources at various client locations when needed, and with the necessary skills and resources to handle a situation in a single visit, with no repeat visits.

How many times have you had a technician come over to inspect an issue, followed by another visit from the same or another technician to try to fix the issue, just to find out they require another part they do not have with them? With Field Service, you can easily track what an issue is, schedule a visit for a repair, and make sure that the dispatched resource has the skills and parts needed to complete the repair in a single visit. This basically means aiming for a first-time fix. There are obvious advantages to achieving this, including increased customer satisfaction, as well as savings for an organization. Scheduling resources intelligently is essential to achieving this.

Furthermore, in conjunction with standard customer service functionality and the proactive monitoring of appliances and devices, as well as specific hardware devices and components reaching their end of life, a proactive approach to service delivery can be achieved.

With Dynamics 365 for Field Service, three very common scenarios are served:

- Installation
- Regular maintenance
- Break-fix scenarios

Let's understand each one of these scenarios in detail.

Installation

Typically, if we think of an example that we have mentioned earlier, where an internet service provider deploys new modems, once we have sold the service to a customer, we need to get that customer online. For those more technically inclined, this could be as simple as sending the hardware via mail and relying on the customer to perform the installation. Customer service might be engaged to assist by either providing phone support or by providing links to installation instructions.

For everyone else, a technician needs to be dispatched to the customer to perform the installation. This could be either for setup outside the house, like the actual physical connection of cables, which, in most cases, is transparent to the user, or for setup required inside the residence, like the actual modem installation.

Regular maintenance

In a regular maintenance scenario, once a piece of equipment has been sold and installed at a customer site, regular preventative maintenance might be required. If you think of an example where a firm sells large printers and laminating machines, regularly scheduled maintenance is required at timed intervals. This is preventative maintenance to keep the equipment running at optimal performance. Depending on the usage and volumes of print or laminating, this could be monthly, quarterly, semi-annually, or any other schedule deemed necessary by the manufacturer.

Regular maintenance could also include scenarios where machinery requires servicing and parts to be replaced proactively. Rather than waiting for a customer to call in with broken machinery, a firm leasing laminating equipment might proactively send service technicians to replace drums on the laminating machine prior to a break-fix scenario occurring.

Break-fix scenarios

This is the scenario where, outside of regular preventative maintenance, additional servicing is needed when something stops working correctly. This could include situations where equipment fails completely, or as regards the previous scenario, the quality of prints or laminate degrades substantially, thus impacting the quality of the final product and, implicitly, the client firm's reputation for delivering excellent services and products. In these scenarios, a technician is dispatched on request from the customer. Prior knowledge of the machinery model and service schedule, as well as notes from previous visits, can paint a clear picture of what skills are required from the technician to service this machinery, as well as the parts needed to complete a first-time fix, with no need for additional site visits.

In the next two sections, we will be looking at the classical web UI as well as the Unified Interface app for Dynamics 365 Field Service. This will help you understand, compare, and differentiate between these two interfaces.

Dynamics 365 for Field Service – the classical web UI

The classical web UI will be deprecated, but at this time, it is still available from the application drawer. Customers are encouraged to move to the new Unified Interface before support is dropped for the classical web UI. The classical interface is marked clearly with the WEB label on the app launcher and is called **Field Service**. Let's first have a quick look at it before we can dedicate our attention to the new app.

 If you are implementing Dynamics 365 for Field Service at this time, you should not even consider the classical web UI, but rather you should be implementing the new Unified Interface from the get-go.

This section provides a quick overview of the classical web UI for those organizations that are still yet to transition. It is meant more as a comparison of what was there, versus what is coming.

In the classical interface, the entire navigation is structured around two main areas. The **Field Service** area caters to everyday operations and configurations. The following screenshot shows the **Field Service** area and its sub-components:

Here, we have a section dedicated to **Work Orders and Scheduling**. This covers the core entities for this app, which include the **Work Orders**, along with the **Schedule Board** for assigning work to field resources, and **Resource Bookings**, which presents a listing of scheduled appointments.

As we have seen in the other apps, there is always overlap with core entities from other modules. The **Sales** section includes the core sales entities that are relevant for Field Service.

Next, the **Service Delivery** section includes some other core entities, such as **Orders** and **Invoices**, as well as specific configurations for **Agreements**, **Customer Assets**, and **Time Off Requests**. These work in conjunction with the other core Field Service entities to assist in configuring the type of service available to customers, as well as the resources available to service a specific type of request.

Finally, the **Inventory & Purchasing** area collects the necessary entities required for handling inventory, inventory location, and customer purchased products and services, as well as return requests.

In addition to the core **Field Service** area, we also have the **Resource Scheduling** area:

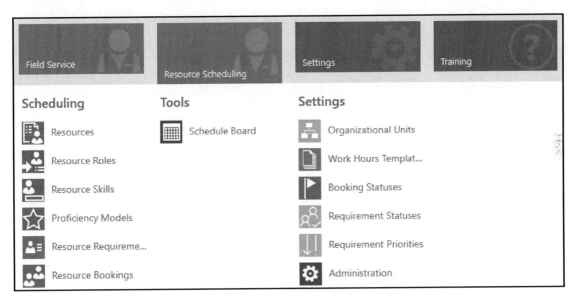

This area includes all the necessary tools for scheduling the right resource for the right service request, taking into consideration resource availability and other constraints.

Schedule Board, being the central point of this functional module, is accessible from the **Tools** area.

Finally, the **Settings** area, where permissions allow a user to access it, allows for specific configurations for best operation. Typically, these options will be filtered by user role, and will only provide access to features a user is authorized to edit or view.

At this time, since the classical web UI is being deprecated, let's shift our attention to the new experience provided by the Unified Interface app for Field Service. Most of the functionality remains the same, or new features are being added and enhanced. The user experience receives an overhaul, making things more friendly in presentation, and simplifying the effort needed for a platform user to interact with the application. The new Unified Interface presents a modern experience, with a responsive design and clear screen layouts that improve the overall user experience. This new interface supports richer controls, better dashboards and charts, as well as the ability to create custom controls that provide better visibility into the data, new ways to present this data, and overall better performance.

Dynamics 365 for Field Service – the Unified Interface app

With the move to the new app model, we now find the Field Service applications in the App drawer. These are new apps built on the Unified Interface. The following screenshot shows the App drawer with several applications you have access to, depending on user roles and permissions. You might see more or other applications than what is presented in the following screenshot. In this list, we find the **Field Service** and the **Resource Scheduling** application. These are two separate scenarios we will look at during this chapter.

Note that, at the bottom of each tile, you have an indication of the interface being used. The tiles marked with **UNIFIED INTERFACE** are the new modern applications, as seen here:

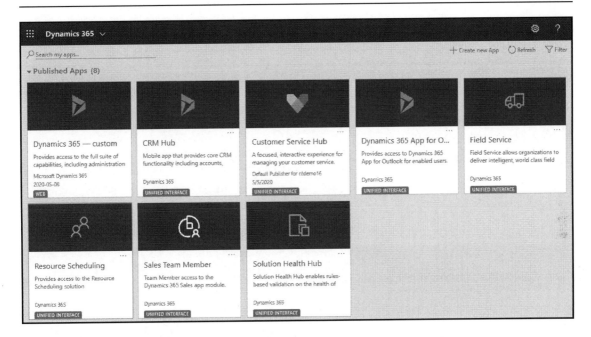

Navigate from the app drawer to the **Field Service** app.

The core entity around this module is **Bookings**. Hence, once you open this app, you can navigate to the **Scheduling** section and find the **Bookings** option. Once you select it, you will see a view of active bookings, as seen in the following screenshot:

As opposed to other apps in the family, the Field Service app is focused entirely on booking resources to complete on-site work. The app does not present us with a dashboard, but rather takes us directly to the necessary work orders that require our attention.

The work revolves around two main items, **Bookings** and **Work Orders**. **Work Orders** is what dictates what needs to be done and where, while **Bookings** deals with assigning the right resource for a specific work order. This assignment happens based on various criteria, including availability, skillset, and so on.

From a user's persona perspective, there are two typical user categories leveraging the functionality available with Field Service. These include the **service technicians**, who perform the assigned work on-site at the customer's premises, and the **service scheduling agents**, who monitor the schedule and assign the best resources for each work order type.

From a usability perspective, it is expected that the scheduling agents will always use the app from a back-office machine.

On the opposite side, the field technicians could leverage, depending on the mobile setup they have, either the desktop app or a mobile app when out in the field.

Let's now focus our attention on the core entities in Field Service in the next section.

Understanding core entities in Field Service

The Field Service app leverages some core common entities with the rest of the apps in the family. These are a set of defined entities that form the initial model for **Common Data Service** (**CDS**) and include elements such as accounts and contacts. This **Common Data Mode** (**CDM**) has been agreed upon in collaboration with multiple partners, in the hope of standardizing and unifying various applications. In addition, entities such as the work order, which is at the core of this module, are specific to Field Service.

Let's look at these in more detail.

Accounts and contacts

As mentioned, accounts and contacts are shared across the entire family of Dynamics 365 products. Accounts are the main customer organization. This represents a company we do business with. Contacts, on the other hand, are people. These are individuals we communicate with directly. They are associated with an account as the organization they work for.

Work orders

An important aspect of work orders is how they relate to the core shared entities. A work order is always associated with an account. There will be one or more contact records associated with the account, but the work order is always related to an account.

The work order, by definition, represents a request for service.

We will delve deeper into work orders in the *Creating and capturing work orders* scenario later in this chapter.

Incident types

An important concept when working with the Field Service offering is the **incident type**. This is available as a selection from the work order screen, in the **Primary Incident** section.

As we will see in the work order screenshot later on, there is quite a bit of information required to manually populate when creating a new work order from scratch. This can be tedious and error-prone.

The platform supports a set of defined and configurable incident types. These act as a template for work orders, allowing us to quickly create new work orders with a set of pre-populated values as needed. These are usually configured as part of the deployment and maintained by a super user or administrator to reflect field agents' feedback or the addition of new services. It is important to have these incident types configured and regularly maintained in order to simplify the frontline agents' work when creating and imputing data into new work orders.

An incident type includes items such as service tasks, products associated with the service call, the skills required for the technician to be dispatched to the customer's site, and an estimated duration for the fix. This comes into play when scheduling technicians to optimize the schedule and make sure that the on-site booking is as accurate as it can be.

Incident types are typically associated with a specific product to be serviced. They can also be configured at a more granular level or can include a set of service tasks adding up to the total amount of time required to complete the service request. The following screenshot depicts the general information captured in relation to a new incident type:

In addition to defining the standard incident type properties, the tabs at the top allow us to see the other characteristics. The **Details** tab presents the estimated time to complete this service, as well as the work order this incident type is associated with:

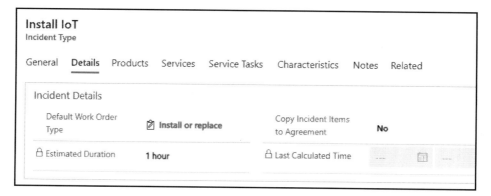

The **Service Tasks** tab presents a listing of all the necessary tasks to be completed as part of this service visit, along with the estimated duration of each task. This acts as a checklist for the technician on site. Of course, the more senior the technician, or the more common the issue, the smaller the value of this checklist:

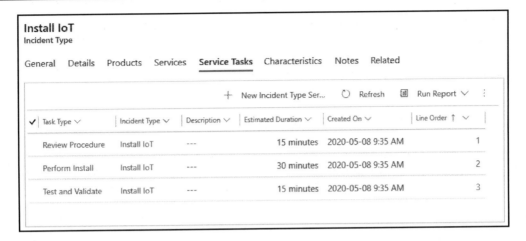

The **Line Order** is typically the order in which these tasks need to be performed.

The two tabs after **Details** in the preceding screenshots include **Products**, which presents a listing of necessary parts required to complete the service request, and **Services,** which shows a list of standard services with their associated duration. This is what gets billed to the customer. Finally, the **Notes** tab allows the service technician to include specific notes detailing the type of work done, or other items related to this client visit, as well as **Related** items, including details and common properties:

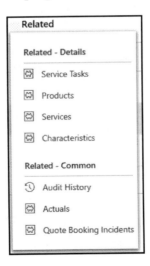

You use the incident type on a work order by selecting one of the predefined **Incident Types** in the **Primary Incident Type** field under **Work Order** in the **Primary Incident** section.

Let's take a look at a number of scenarios specific for Field Service in the next section.

Handling scenarios in Field Service

Typically, working with the Field Service functionality involves several users, and a standard multi-step process. The main categories are as follows:

1. **Capturing a work order**: We begin our work with the first scenario, which includes the creation of a new work order. This can be created either manually, basically starting from scratch, or automated based on real-time data supplied from IoT devices. Alternatively, a case in customer service can result in the creation of a work order. This process can be automated, resulting in less manual input. This is typically done by a customer service representative role user.

2. **Scheduling resources**: Once a work order is created, we move on to the second scenario, which is scheduling. Now that we know what the issue is, and the expected resolution, we need to look for the best available resource to complete this work, at the earliest available date and time. This is done typically by a resource scheduler role user. Once the work is assigned, the service technician is notified. He or she can decide to accept the allocation or reject it.

3. **Fulfilling the work order**: Finally, once a work order is accepted, the technician can then proceed to the customer's site to complete the work. Various statuses allow the technician to flag back to the system when they are in transit, when the work starts on site, as well as when it is completed. Once completed, the technician can then mark the work as complete on their mobile device through the mobile app and capture a customer signature to certify completion.

Other post-execution steps could include the following:

1. **Monitoring by a supervisor**: When the work is marked as complete by a technician, typically, a supervisor will monitor and make sure that the work is indeed complete, that the customer is satisfied, that the expected outcome has been achieved, and then approve completion. This final approval is not mandatory, but it is a common step in the process.

2. **Generating the invoice**: With final approval in place, an invoice is generated, and if any supporting parts were used to complete the fix, the inventory can be automatically or manually updated. Typically, an invoice is only generated in Dynamics 365 for Field Service and processed to the customer through integration with the ERP solution in place.

This describes a typical process at a high level. Steps can be configured and automated as needed. Let's now have a look at each of these three steps in detail, in the subsequent sections.

Creating and capturing work orders

This is the starting point in the process flow. In our first scenario, a customer requests a service, resulting in a work order being created in the system. Alternatively, this work order can be automatically generated through integration with smart devices (IoT) that send a direct stream of data about a device or machine's performance. When a certain threshold is reached continuously over a defined period, this could be an indication of a malfunction, resulting in a work order being generated proactively.

In the context of Field Service, the service requested is delivered on-site to the customer. There are some similarities here with the case in the customer service module we have reviewed in the previous chapter. The main difference, rather than helping over the phone, email, or through a knowledge base article, is the fact that support is provided in person, at the client's site.

A typical work order in the app looks like the following screenshot:

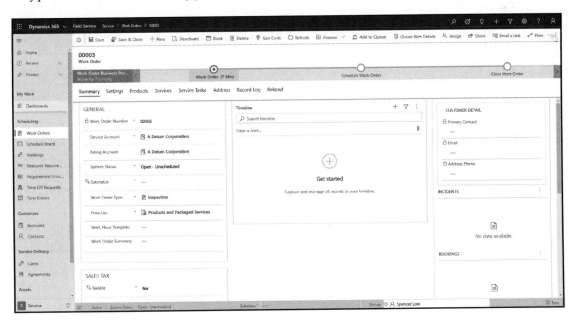

As you can see, the work order is a collection of related information. This information includes items such as a description of the work to be done, the customer window of availability for on-site service, as well as the **Work Order Type**. You can use types to define the most common support scenarios and have attached the defined details on price lists and products, the time required, and service tasks to be performed.

Scheduling resources

We have seen in the first scenario how a support user creates a new work order. With an existing work order in place, the next scenario is to look at scheduling the necessary work. This is done by a user managing resource allocation. This role could be part of the responsibilities assigned to the same support user, or a totally different group of users in the organization.

We can now shift our attention from the Field Service app to the Resource Scheduling app. Opening this app takes you directly to the **Active Resource Requirements** screen, where you can see a listing of work orders to be processed, as seen in this screenshot:

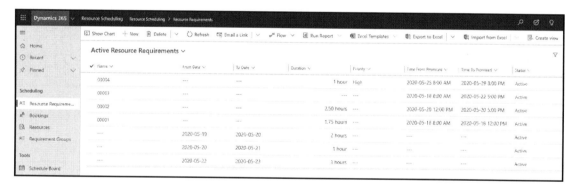

When it comes to scheduling, some important aspects need to be considered. These include the following:

- **Technician availability**: The ability to schedule a service hinges on the availability of resources to perform the work. This can include field service technicians as the obvious requirement, but also takes into consideration the available skill set for a specific job type. In addition, we can schedule equipment, or custom entities enabled for scheduling.
- **Time frame**: This takes into consideration the availability windows along with coordinated appointments with the customers.

- **Location**: The location of the customer site as well as the location of the technician play an important role in scheduling. It would be quite pointless to schedule a technician on the West Coast for a job to be performed on the East Coast in a short time frame.

An important aspect of scheduling resources is the resource requirement. On the **Scheduling** tab, we find that the location where the work is to be performed, as well as the promised service window, are captured, as agreed with the customer when the work order was created. You can see the details in the following screenshot:

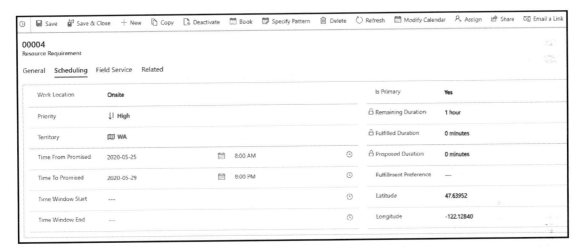

The other components taking part in processing a work order is scheduling the actual resource available to be booked. As mentioned before, this can be your field service technician, but it can also include a resource from the client, equipment, or other values. The following screenshot shows some of the available resources to be booked:

When defining a resource to be available for booking, we need to configure that specific resource with some important information. This is typically done when onboarding resources and the information can be updated once existing resources re-specialize or obtain new skills. It is essential to keep this information updated, as it relates to the availability of that resource for specific work to be performed. This includes **Hourly Rate** and the available skills, among other things. In addition, if configuring a field service technician, you will want to configure whether they have access to the mobile application.

These are all shown in the following screenshot:

From a scheduling perspective, a resource can be enabled for an availability search and can be configured to show on the schedule board:

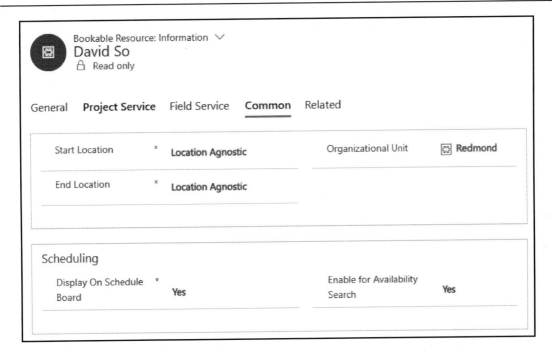

The work order is typically scheduled by a user with a scheduler role in the organization. These are office support personnel who manage bookings and work directly with the schedule board. Let's have a look at the default schedule board:

The board is structured in several areas. On the left-most side, we have the filtering capabilities. Here, we can define parameters to restrict the list of resources to only the specific resources available for a certain area. We can also look at this in a map view if this functionality is enabled.

Next, in the central area, we have the resources and the time slots available. Clicking on a resource name brings up a hover window with additional resource details, while also allowing us to see specific resource information in the **Detail** slides from the right-hand side. From the resource card, we can interact directly with that resource either through messages, by phone, if telephony integration is configured, or by email. We can see here the resource roles, skills, and their time zone, as well as their picture if set up, as demonstrated in the following screenshot:

Also at the bottom of the schedule board screen, we have a view of booking requirements. We can change the view here to see the unscheduled work orders. We can drag any one of those on the board to associate with a user and an available time slot. In the following example, I have booked three appointments for David:

Another way to book a resource is from the work order by looking at **Resource Bookings** and adding a **New Bookable Resource**, as seen in the following screenshot:

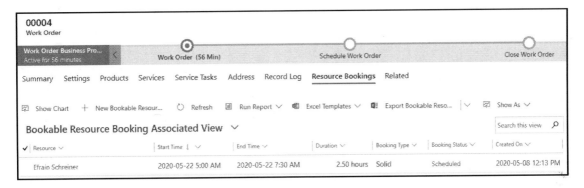

The system is flexible enough to allow a user to work from the location they are most comfortable to start from, based on current business requirements.

Fulfilling/completing the work order

As discussed throughout the chapter, a field service technician is always traveling to client sites to help resolve customer product issues.

It is expected, through the nature of the job, that a mobile application is the best way for these technicians to access the application.

In the first scenario, we saw how a customer service representative captures a new work order. The second scenario has presented a resource in the role of scheduler, handling the assignment of a resource to a work order and creating a booking. Finally, this third scenario looks at a field service technician taking over the work order and executing the job.

We have an available mobile app supporting the major mobile platforms. This allows the field technician to perform the necessary tasks, such as marking a job as complete and updating its status as necessary.

The following screenshot shows the mobile application. Note that this application has gone through several revisions:

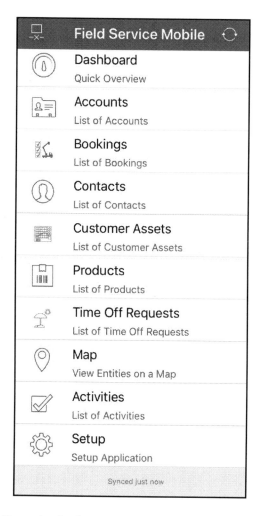

The mobile application allows for both connected and disconnected modes. This allows a technician to update information while offline, and have that information synchronized back to the platform when connectivity is restored.

The **Bookings** link is the starting point for a field service technician. This is where all the scheduled activities are collected and presented.

A field service technician can pick a booking, mark the status as *traveling* once they proceed toward the customer location, and update the status to *in progress* as they commence working on the issue at the customer's premises. Once the job is complete, the technician can mark the work *complete*, and capture a customer signature on completion. The status is updated to the home office and, if needed, a supervisor or an automated process can follow up with a customer satisfaction survey or phone call.

The mobile application is tightly integrated with mobile devices, allowing for integration with the default navigation applications. This is a very handy feature for a technician on the road, allowing for route planning as well as navigation instruction with a single tap on the customer address.

While performing work for customers is at the heart of any business, it is important to monetize that work. Customers expect your organization to be able to enter into service agreements, and be able to track work against a promise agreed upon through an agreement. Let's look at precisely that in the next section.

Working with agreements

An agreement is a mechanism to automatically create work orders on a timed schedule. This allows us to define recurring appointments for regularly scheduled maintenance. We will not be using agreements for standard break-fix issues.

You configure **Agreements** from the **Field Service** app in the **Service Delivery** area. Here, you have access to cases, which could generate work orders or agreements.

A typical **Agreement** configuration screen is presented as follows:

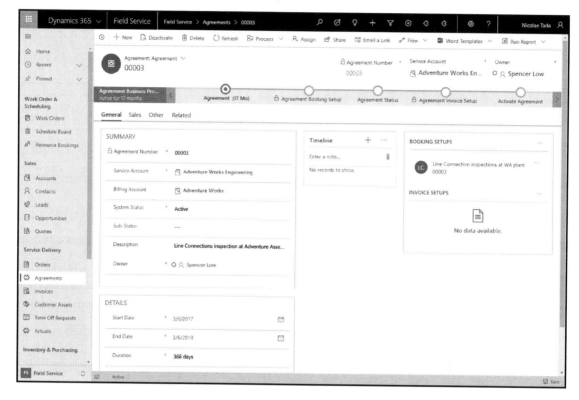

An agreement will have a duration calculated based on a **Start Date** and **End Date**.

Getting into the **Booking Setup** for the specific agreement, we have the capability to configure both the autogeneration of work orders and the ability to generate these work orders a set number of days in advance, in order to allow for client confirmation and other processes to execute. The following screenshot shows the **Agreement Booking Setup** screen:

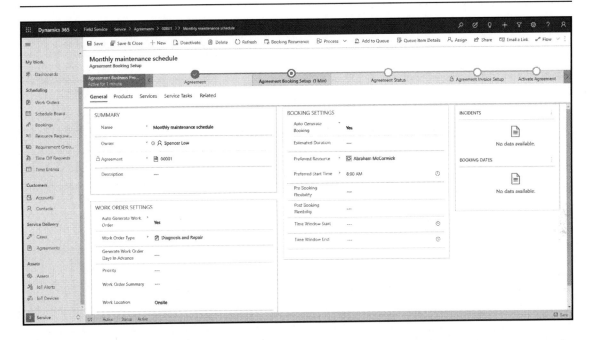

Next, we move on to setting the status of an agreement. For an agreement to generate work orders, it must be set to an **Active** state. Other options include **Estimate**, **Expired**, and **Canceled**:

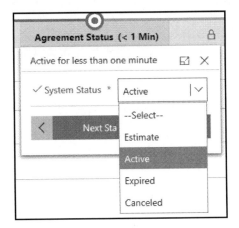

Finally, we can set the system up to generate invoices for work orders automatically.

As we have seen so far, agreements do play an important role in servicing our customers.

The next section will look at some of the additional entities that glue the existing pieces of data together with processes, making this a robust solution.

Supporting entities in Field Service

To capture the bigger picture, some additional entities are necessary. These include customer assets, and inventory and purchasing, as described in the following sub-sections. These additional entities store information relevant to the functionality of the Field Service, and help glue the data together with processes, providing a clear picture of what is being used, when is it used, what is available to provide the best service, and so on.

Let's look at these in more detail in the forthcoming sections.

Customer assets

Customer assets are the serviceable elements located at a client's premises. These can include products our organization has sold and deployed to a customer, or products the customer has engaged us to maintain. The following screenshot shows the listing of assets, as found in the Field Service app, under the **Assets** category:

Tracking customer assets is a very important aspect of providing the best service to our customers. We need to be able to know the product, the exact model, and details to be able to provide the best service.

A customer asset relates a customer to a specific product from our inventory.

The customer asset definition allows us to group assets together, for example, when servicing a computer and its related software. We can define both child assets and related assets. The following screenshot shows a defined asset, along with related sub-assets as presented on the right side of the same screen for ease of use:

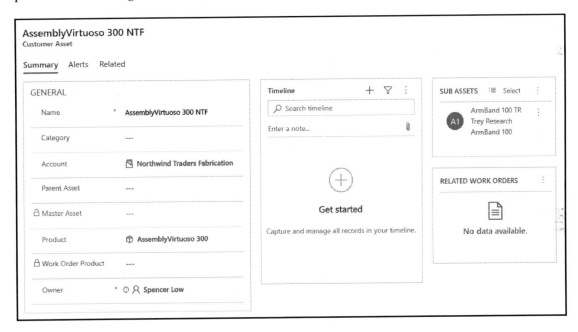

We have the capability to create customer assets automatically every time a product is sold to a customer. This allows us to not only track the products sold, but also reduces the manual work required to create and track the products in relation to customers.

Let's look at the next supporting entity.

Inventory and purchasing

The **Inventory** area includes several standard entities, as shown in the following screenshot:

The functionality regarding inventory management allows the application to track and manage products and required parts related to work orders.

This is where we keep track of all available spare parts required to service a customer product. We can track and replenish inventory as needed to avoid interruptions due to a lack of required parts for work orders.

In addition to typical inventory replenishing through the ordering of new parts, the availability and the need for new parts work in conjunction with the ability to relocate products across various service locations and warehouses, as well as tracking parts returned by customers. This functionality is handled through inventory transfers and inventory adjustments.

A typical inventory transfer screen is presented here:

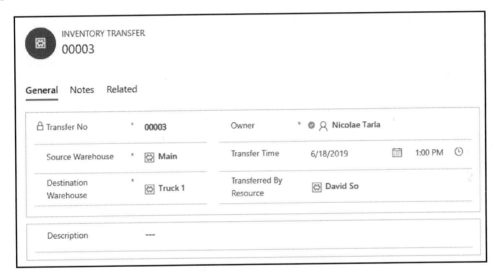

We can see a listing of all products and parts available in a specific warehouse by navigating to **WAREHOUSE** and selecting the **Product Inventory** view. This shows products with available and on-hand quantities, as well as quantities on back order. If a re-order point is configured, it is also displayed here. This represents the minimum inventory quantity on hand when we need to re-order the specific product. We see in the following screenshot that the **AssemblyMaestro CPU + Controller** product needs to be reordered when the **Quantity On-Hand** drops below eight units:

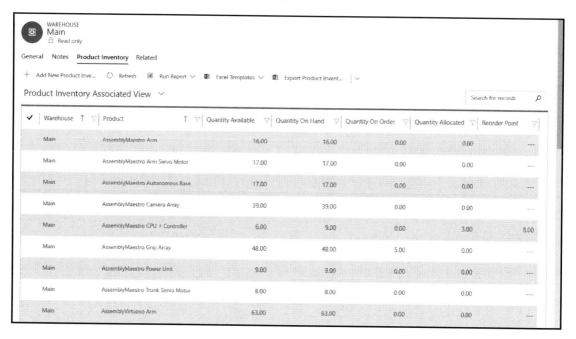

The purchasing part allows us to create purchase orders to maintain stock availability across our warehouses. This allows tacking against various vendors depending on the products required.

The process for managing stock replenishing includes default steps, as seen in the following screenshot:

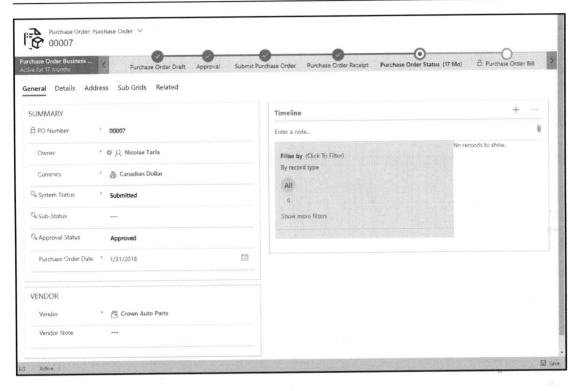

This process allows for the necessary checks and bounds in place, where approval is required before submitting an order. In addition, we track the submission and the receipt of the Order.

Selecting the **Products** tab from the **Related** dropdown displays the products and quantities on each purchase order.

As we have seen so far, managing the products and services offered to our customers is essential in providing accurate estimates and being able to close deals. While this platform is not always the best solution for inventory management, the core functionality provided is enough for many scenarios, and it can be integrated with other more robust inventory management systems for a more comprehensive set of features.

Other supporting integration scenarios

To create a comprehensive ecosystem, Microsoft has provided extensions to enhance the functionality of the Field Service offering.

We can now integrate with IoT through Connected Field Service to receive real-time live data from monitored devices, in order to automatically generate work orders. This scenario has multiple applications, including facilities monitoring, or providing support to a fleet of machinery and devices deployed to multiple customers.

In addition, in order to enhance the ability of a field technician to provide a first-time fix, we can now leverage solutions such as Dynamics 365 Remote Assist to allow real-time interaction with back-office technicians who can assist in resolving an issue, or leverage the Dynamics 365 Guides solution to provide an overlay of documentation and instructions for resolving issues with specific devices being services.

Furthermore, you can extend the reporting capabilities by overlaying business intelligence using Power BI. You can also leverage Power Apps to tap into the platform data and create mobile solutions targeted at specific scenarios.

Summary

Throughout this chapter, we saw several aspects as they relate to the Dynamics 365 for Field Service offering.

We started with a look at the classical web interface, which will be deprecated soon, before moving on to the new Unified Interface applications. We saw the two distinct applications available, the Field Service app and the Resource Scheduling app, both accessible from the app drawer.

We looked at three distinct scenarios: the creation of a work order, the scheduling of a work order, and the handling of a work order by a field technician on a mobile device

Finally, we looked at how inventory and purchases are tracked, as part of maintaining the necessary stock of parts for performing service at the customer sites.

The next chapter moves on and looks at the next app available. This is the Dynamics 365 for Project Service.

6
Dynamics 365 Project Service Automation

In the previous chapter, we focused our attention on the Field Service solution functionality available within Microsoft Dynamics 365. In this chapter, we will look at the Project Service Automation solution.

The **Project Service Automation (PSA)** functionality is targeted at *consulting and service organizations*. The solution brings the Sales process and the Delivery process into one cohesive offering. It allows a complete end-to-end view across the sales process, resulting in an opportunity, along with the implementation of the respective deliverable. The focus is to be able to track and deliver solutions on time and on budget.

The solution covers estimating, quoting, and contracting on the sales side, as well as planning and management, collaboration, tracking time, expenses, and resource allocation, real-time progress, and invoicing on the delivery side.

In this chapter, we will look at the following aspects of the PSA solution:

- The core functionality of PSA
- Common scenarios for PSA, including creating and managing projects, managing schedules, estimation process, and resource scheduling
- Managing an end-to-end project to its successful delivery via the available project progress tracking capabilities

By the end of this chapter, you will be familiar with the PSA functionality, the personas that leverage this tool, and the core entities and processes that make up this solution.

Overview of Dynamics 365 Project Service Automation

As the name implies, the PSA functionality manages projects for consulting and service organizations. There are several core business processes that are handled by the application:

- Creating and managing projects
- Creating and managing project schedules
- Project estimation
- Scheduling resources for projects
- Tracking project progress

We will cover these aspects throughout this chapter. At the time of writing, the PSA functionality is already at version 3. This version brings some incremental updates to the solution and clears some of the quirks of the previous versions. Also, this version is entirely built to leverage the Unified Interface, making it ready for multiple form factors through responsive design and providing full support for accessibility.

PSA users/personas

PSA enhances the standard functionality of the Dynamics 365 Customer Engagement functionality. It tightly integrates with the Sales module for collaboration all the way from inception, through the sales process, through to project completion. This module brings together sales, resourcing, delivery, and billing.

As such, some of the most common user roles that leverage this solution are as follows:

- Sales and Account Managers
- Project Managers
- Resource Managers
- Team Members/Project Resource

Let's start by looking at PSA applications.

PSA applications

We can find PSA applications by going to the app drawer and looking at the applications that we have installed. The user must have access to the instance, have a license for PSA, and have permission to access these applications. The applications will be displayed as follows:

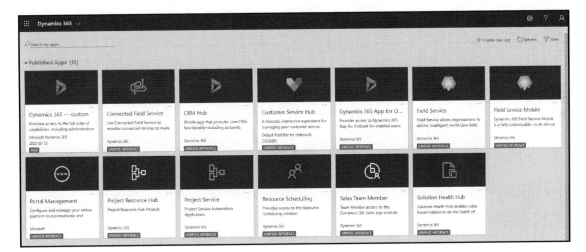

The following are the two applications for PSA:

- **Project Resource Hub**
- **Project Service**

We'll look at these in the following subsections.

Project Resource Hub

The **Project Resource Hub** is an app targeted specifically at resources that have to interact with the platform to submit time entries and expenses. These project resources are presented with an application with reduced functionality in order to simplify tasks and reduce clutter. No project-specific details and actions are available, thus allowing them to focus on efficiency.

The following screenshot shows a default view opening on the **Time Entries** grid:

Entering a new time entry is as simple as selecting **New** on the ribbon and filling in the task's details and time, as shown in the following screenshot:

It is just as easy to submit not only project billable time, but also other types of absence or vacation time, by simply selecting what you want from the **Type** drop-down menu, as shown here:

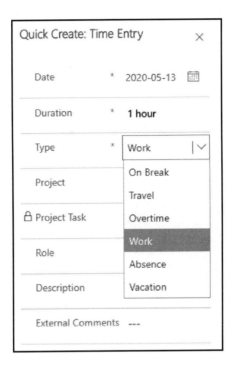

All these options are configurable and can be augmented with other types of time entries as needed.

In a similar manner, submitting expenses is done by navigating from **Time Entries** to **Expenses** and then from the **My Expenses** view, selecting **New** from the top ribbon. This brings up the **Quick Create: Expense** submission form, as shown in the following screenshot:

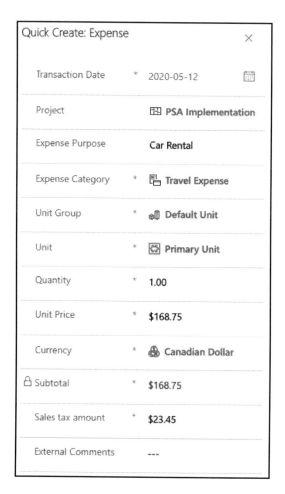

When capturing expenses, the user experience is just as simple, with the ability to capture not only amounts and taxes, but also the relationship to a specific project, expense category, and purpose. Once an expense has been submitted, the totals are rolled up into the overall project budget and reflected across the various reports.

Along with standard expenses, receipts can be captured and tracked for each expense, making life a lot easier.

Note that both Time Entries and Expenses are kept in Draft mode until they're submitted. You must submit your entries so that they can be picked up and processed by the designated approvers. You can do this for Time Entries by selecting either the specific entry or the entire task and selecting the **Submit** button on the ribbon, as shown in the following screenshot:

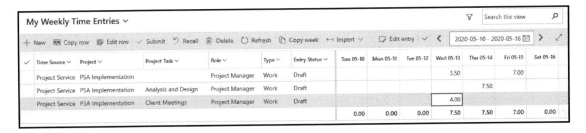

Once submitted, **Entry Status** changes to **Submitted**.

Using a separate app for this functionality makes a lot of sense. Typically, project resources will want to interact with this platform as little as possible while focusing on the task at hand. Furthermore, for resources that track activities into an external platform such as Azure DevOps, having integration in place could allow for timely submission to be inferred from that other platform and simplify things even more.

Now, let's focus our attention on the bulk of the application by closing the Project Resource Hub and navigating to the Project Service app.

Project Service app

The **Project Service** app opens to the Practice Management Dashboard by default. This presents statistics on project success, costs, hours, margins, and utilization. From a management perspective, these are some of the important aspects you want to monitor across your practice.

Along with this dashboard, several additional dashboards are provided out of the box, as shown in the following screenshot:

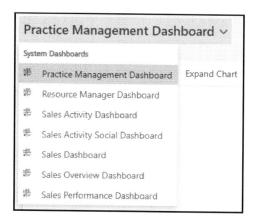

You can configure additional dashboards as needed.

The Project Service app splits functionality into two main categories:

- **Projects**: Looking at the information from a project structure perspective
- **Resources**: Structuring the information around resources and their availability

Only these two are specific to this app. The rest point to existing items, as we've seen in other Dynamics 365 apps so far and throughout this book. You can easily access each category by changing the selection at the bottom of the side navigation, as shown here:

Each of these two categories will present different entities and options on the left navigation, depending on the functionality expected. For example, the **Projects** area shows the following side menu:

Similarly, the **Resources** area shows a menu focused on resource planning, as shown here:

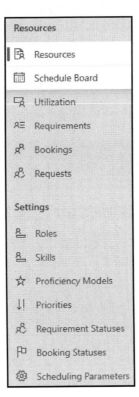

As you can see, different entities take part in this solution at various stages. Now, let's look at some of these entities and identify how they play a role within the PSAs Solution, as well as in the bigger family of Dynamics 365 solutions.

Understanding the PSA core entities

As we have seen with the other modules, certain entities are shared across functional applications. PSA is no exception, and it is tightly integrated with the Sales module. As such, the core Account and Contact entities are common, as well as the core Leads, Opportunities, and Quotes entities. We'll look at these entities in detail in the subsequent sections.

Accounts and Contacts

Accounts and Contacts are leveraged across the entire Dynamics family of products. In this application, the Accounts are renamed to Customers to make it more specific to how this entity is related to the functionality.

When using the PSA application in conjunction with the other applications in the family, the specific records are shared across all applications. As such, Accounts that are created in the Sales application are reflected in the Customer records in PSA.

Navigating to an Account (Customer) with existing ongoing projects allows you to see the projects associated with that respective Customer. You just need to navigate to the **Projects** tab, as shown in the following screenshot:

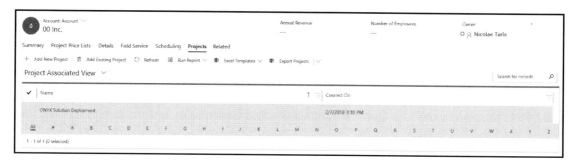

The preceding screenshot shows an associated project on the **Projects** tab.

Now, let's look at some other entities that support this module.

Leads, Opportunities, and Quotes

Because the PSA application allows you to track projects from an early stage, elements from the Sales application such as Leads, Opportunities, and Quotes are leveraged. The individual entity forms and customizations are reflected in PSA.

However, to leverage these Sales artifacts in PSA, certain conditions must be met. For example, for a Lead to be qualified as a Project Opportunity, the Lead Type must be set to **Work-Based**. This tells the system that this will be a PSA qualified Lead that will result in an Opportunity:

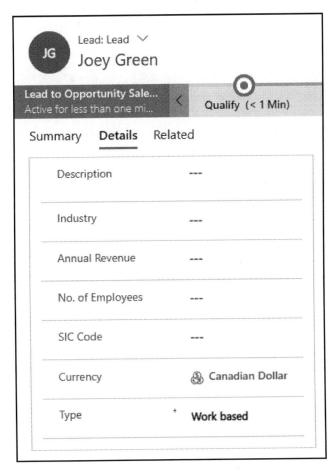

Once you have a Lead qualified as a Project Opportunity, you have a specific PSA form for the Opportunity. If this is not the default form that's loaded, you can change forms from the form drop-down at the top of the record, above the record name. You should be on the **Project Information** form automatically, as long as your Order **Type** field on the Opportunity is defined as **Work based**:

Some of the significant changes that can be made to a project-based Opportunity include the Contracting Unit, as well as a reference to a Services Price List. The **Contracting Unit** is the Organizational Unit in a Professional Services Organization that represents the group or division responsible for the sales and delivery of a project to a customer. This unit employs billable resources that have associated cost rates. The **Service Price List** is like a Products Price List, except that it includes services and rates instead of products.

On the project opportunity, the next logical step is to start tracking related Project Opportunity Lines. These are used to generate a Project Quote. Alternatively, you can generate a Project Quote and fill in the separate lines manually afterward.

As part of the sales process, you can track the Opportunity's associated Quotes by navigating to the **Quotes** tab on the Opportunity form:

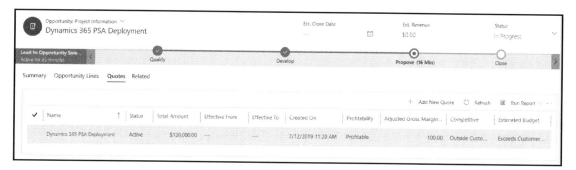

Project Quotes are somewhat like Sales Quotes, except for some differences, as follows:

- Project Quotes line items can be tracked for both projects and products.
- A Project Quote does not support activation and revisions.
- Only one Project Contract can be related to a Project Quote.
- The Project Quote includes some additional fields specific to projects.
- The Type value on the Quote differs between Sales Quotes and Project Quotes.

Quotes support an association with a project. This is typically done toward the tail end of the project sales process when a project is ready to be generated.

Your typical Project Quote screen will look as follows:

When closing a Project Quote, you generate Project Contracts. These are based on the details that have been carried over from the Project Quote.

Now that we have an understanding of entities, which are the smallest units that make up PSA, let's delve into some of the scenarios covered by the solution and understand how these entities are related and can form a functional unit.

Understanding Project Service Automation scenarios

To support the entire PSA functionality, some additional entities and processes are available with this solution. They are divided into the following major scenarios:

- **Planning and Delivering Projects**: Includes functionality for project management to create a project structure and a schedule
- **Billing**: Includes functionality for estimating and tracking project costs and invoicing
- **Resources**: Includes functionality for resource management and scheduling

Let's have a look at these scenarios individually to understand the functionality that's provided for the various aspects of project management.

Creating and managing projects

Once a sale has been successful, we have a project on our hands, and we are ready to start working on it. A standard project screen looks like this:

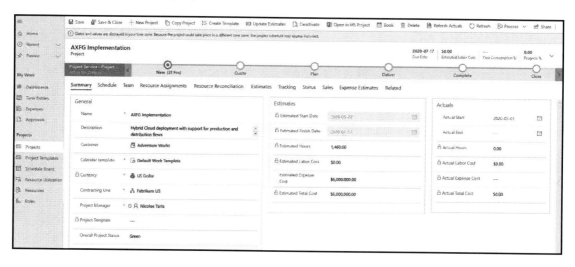

The PSA solution allows you to create Projects in two ways:

- You can create a brand-new project from scratch.
- You can create a project based on a project template. This is applicable when certain services can be repeated.

First, let's have a look at **Project Templates** to understand what is available. Navigating to **Project Templates** and selecting **Project Templates view**, you can view the default templates, along with any custom ones your organization has included. The following screenshot shows a list of available **Project Templates**:

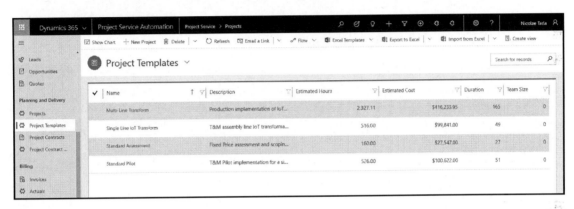

Project Templates help in quickly creating projects for similar engagements. They include items such as schedules, estimates, and team members. They are also based on preconfigured project calendars, roles, and price lists.

Alternatively, you can create a new project without using a template. You can do that when a new engagement type has been identified. When this becomes a repeat engagement type, you can create a new Project Template based on this project.

Now that we've learned how to create and manage projects, let's learn about scheduling them.

Creating and managing project schedules

Project schedules have the same set of elements that a project and a Project Template have. The schedule includes tasks related in a hierarchy, roles associated with each task, as well as dependencies. The project schedule also observes the configured project calendar.

The project schedule is built to reflect the tasks that need to be performed as part of the projects, as well as the estimated time frame for each task to be executed.

The **task** is at the core of the Project Schedule since it's the building block of any schedule. You break down the overall work into specific tasks. These are smaller units of work that revolve around specific sets of functionalities that are easier to estimate.

PSA supports three generic types of tasks:

- **Project root node**: The top-most summary task for the project.
- **Summary tasks**: Rollup tasks for all the leaf node tasks underneath.
- **Leaf node tasks**: These perform the most granular work. They contain an estimate of effort, resources, start and end dates, and duration.

You can add project tasks by navigating to the **Schedule** tab:

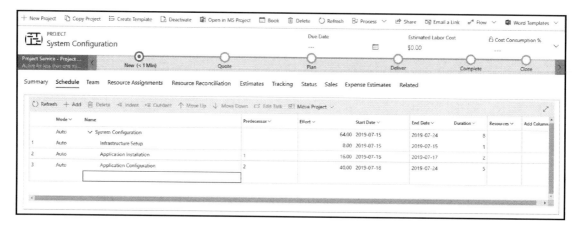

When setting up the tasks, you can define the total effort, the dependencies on previous tasks by defining a predecessor task, and modify the Start Date. The End Date is calculated based on the Start Date and Duration.

Tasks can then be indented so that they're grouped under a **Summary Task**, which groups functional tasks. This is done to make navigating the project plan easier. You can collapse or expand these summary tasks as needed. This can be observed in the following screenshot:

4	Auto	> Task 4	16.00	2019-07-15	2019-07-15	1	
5	Auto	∨ Summary Task	24.00	2019-07-15	2019-07-15	1	
5.1	Auto	Task 5.1	8.00	2019-07-15	2019-07-15	1	
5.2	Auto	Task 5.2	8.00	2019-07-15	2019-07-15	1	
5.3	Auto	Task 5.3	8.00	2019-07-15	2019-07-15	1	
6	Auto	Task 6	8.00	2019-07-15	2019-07-15	1	

For easier management, for the Project Manager roles, you have the ability to integrate with **Microsoft Project (MS Project)**. You will find the **Open in MS Project** button on the ribbon:

This allows you to take a project plan and create it in the familiar MS Project application, read a project from PSA, and publish a project plan back to PSA when it's complete. You can also start by creating the project plan directly in MS Project, and later publish it to PSA. This feature gives great flexibility to project managers, allowing them to use familiar tools and increase productivity.

Also, note that, on the ribbon, you have the ability to either copy an existing project to a new one through **Copy Project** or create a project template by selecting **Create Template**.

Project estimation

As a direct result of building a detailed project plan, you have a much clearer picture of the total duration and value of the project. From the Schedule, you can determine the Effort required to complete this project, as well as the overall duration based on the **Start Date** and **End Date** field values.

If planning needs to be adjusted, you can move the entire project forward by selecting the **Move Project** option on the **Schedule** ribbon:

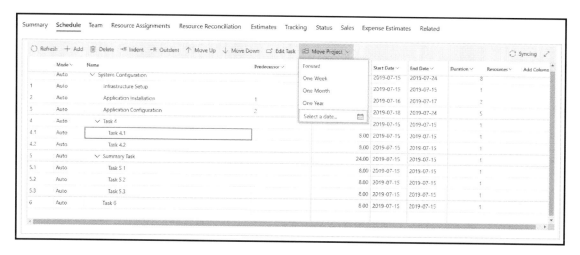

This feature allows you to shift an entire project forward. For situations where only specific tasks need to be adjusted, this is achieved within the project schedule by selecting a task and selecting the **Edit Task** button from the same ribbon.

Leveraging the associated Project Price List, financial estimates can be calculated by using sales prices and cost for tasks, as defined in the Price List.

As a final step, once you have a project schedule and your project estimates complete, you can include this in a Quote Line.

Scheduling resources for projects

With a project schedule in place, it's time to determine the actual resources that take part in the project. First off, we will build our Project Team:

1. Navigate to the **Team** tab on your project. Here, you will find all the resources that have been allocated. When in doubt, or when a resource is not clearly defined, you can use a **Generic Resource**. This is a resource placeholder with a defined role that allows you to plan your work accordingly:

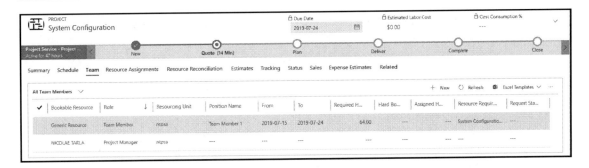

2. With a Team in place, you can now go back to the schedule and start assigning resources to the defined tasks. You can do this by selecting the **Resources** column. Then, for each task, choose to assign one or more of the Project Team resources:

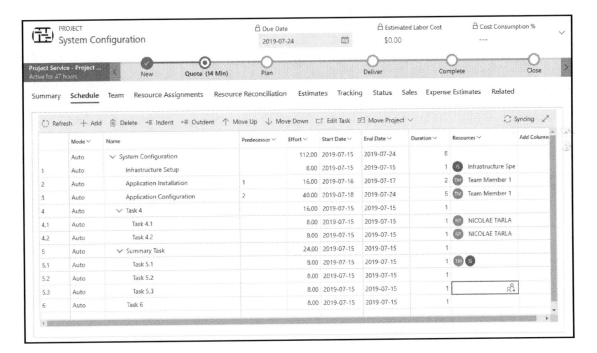

The **Resource Assignment** tab shows the configured project properties in various views. You can select **Group By** on the Ribbon to see various dimensions of the current project. You can group tasks by the following:

- Category
- Role
- Resource

The following is a view that's been done **Resource**, which shows the resource allocation by **Week**:

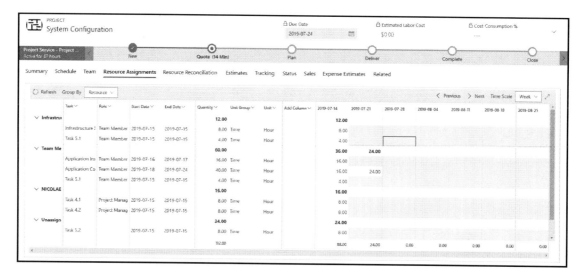

You can also change the time dimension by selecting one of the following options from **Time Scale** on the ribbon:

- Day
- Week
- Month
- Year

3. Finally, the **Resource Reconciliation** tab allows you to view the assignment and resource usage for a named resource in the project. You can easily spot the differences between bookings and assignments in order to make the project efficient. This is where you reconcile the differences between bookings and resource assignments:

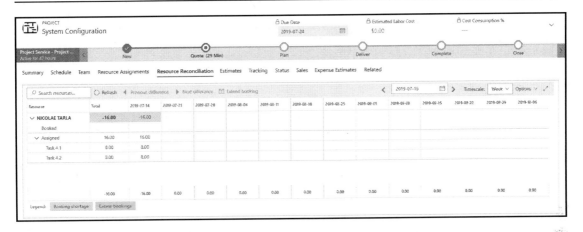

When you are ready to fill in the Generic Resources you have assigned to your project, you can put in a request for a resource. Let's take a look at how to do this:

1. Navigate back to the **Team** tab on your project, select a **Generic Resource**, and find the ellipsis on the top-right of the ribbon. Click the ellipses to expand and find the **Submit Request** option to create a new **Resource Request**:

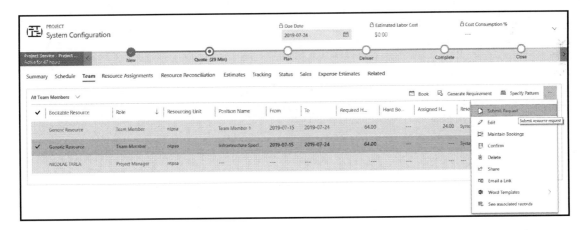

2. Once a Request has been created and submitted, the **Request Status** field is updated to **Submitted**, and a request is sent to the Resource Manager:

3. Finally, to complete the process, once a Resource Manager approves and fulfills the request, the Generic Resource is replaced with a Named Resource in your project Plan. When a Resource Manager does not fulfill the request, the **Request Status** field will be updated to show **Need Review** on the respective Generic Resource record.

Once a project is ongoing, assigned resources can start tracking their time against the various tasks that have been assigned to them. We'll learn how to track an ongoing project's progress next.

Tracking project progress

From a Project Manager's perspective, tracking the progress of the project can easily be done by navigating to the **Tracking** tab of the respective project. Here, you have the ability to track either **Effort** or **Cost**. When tracking by **Cost**, you can choose to track either by the **Cost Rate** or the **Bill Rate**, which give you different aspects of the project's performance.

When looking at Progress by **Effort**, we can determine the completed tasks, the partially completed tasks, and the tasks that haven't been started. The **Progress %** column shows how much of each task or **Summary Task** has been completed.

The following screenshot shows the start of a project, where no time has been tracked against any of the defined tasks or summary tasks:

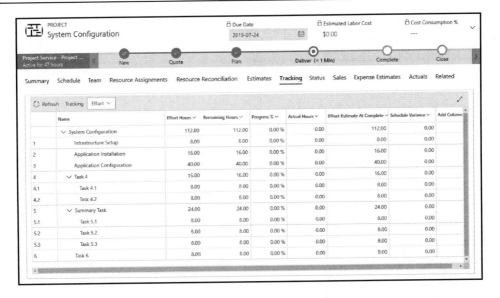

With a plan in place, a Project Manager can start monitoring the time submitted on tasks, progress on tasks, and check the overall project progress toward a complete delivery on time and on budget. This information also supports various billing scenarios, as per the specific project agreement.

As we have seen so far, working with projects and resources, as well as managing the project's completion and success, are done in a manner that helps not only the project manager, but also all team members, understand where we are, what we need to do, when we will be ready, and, most importantly, whether this will be a successful project.

Summary

This chapter has covered the most important features of the Dynamics 365 for Project Service Automation application. We have reviewed functionality around creating and managing projects, project schedules, estimation, resource allocation to a project, as well as the ability to track a project's progress. We have also learned how a Project Manager can have full visibility into the project's progress while various project resources input status data and other relevant project details are fed into the bigger picture.

Armed with this knowledge, you can now create and track your own projects by utilizing the Project Service Automation feature of Dynamics 365 as per your needs.

In the next chapter, we will look at the Dynamics 365 for Marketing solution.

Dynamics 365 Marketing

7

To progress through the various solutions available through Dynamics 365 Customer Engagement, in this chapter, we'll provide an overview of the Marketing application. This is one of the newer additions to the family, with a totally redesigned interface that leverages the Unified Interface concepts, as well as a new set of functionalities.

The standard marketing functionality available with previous versions remains available, but the Marketing application brings troves of value-added functionality, putting it in line with more modern and robust marketing offerings in the marketplace. Integration with LinkedIn, as well as AI-driven insights features, make this a modern and robust offering.

The following are the main elements we'll be looking at in this chapter:

- The core functionalities of the Marketing application
- Core entities and common scenarios for Marketing
- Leveraging the portal in Marketing

By the end of this chapter, you will understand the purpose of the new Marketing application, the main scenarios for using it, and the most important features available.

Dynamics 365 for Marketing

As per the name, the Marketing application handles generating and looking after leads. Through its direct connection to the Sales application, leads are captured, nurtured, and converted into sales. Process automation, as well as AI-driven intelligence and insights, allow for better and faster decisions.

There are several core business processes handled by the application:

- Modern and robust email marketing with support for graphical email templates
- Personalized interactive customer journeys
- Organizing and marketing events
- Leveraging LinkedIn for business prospects
- Core marketing functionality

We'll tackle each of these aspects throughout this chapter.

At the time of this writing, the Marketing application is at version 1. This version has received multiple incremental updates, making it a robust and feature-rich solution. Being built from scratch on the new Unified Interface, the user experience is greatly enhanced, taking advantage of all the visual configurations available for processes, automation, and campaign creation and reporting. You can typically either include the Marketing application with the initial deployment or add it later to an existing environment from the environment's Administration console.

Marketing users/personas

The Marketing application is targeted primarily at the marketing staff. That being said, other roles can take advantage of the Marketing application's features to enhance their experience and serve customers in a better way. These roles include the following:

- Marketing Specialists and Managers
- Marketing Lead Score Specialists and Managers
- Sales and Account Managers
- Event Planners and Event Administrators
- LinkedIn Marketers and Managers
- Survey Designers and Administrators for the Survey package

 As of July 2020 Surveys have been deprecated in favor of Microsoft Forms. For more details, refer to the official documentation at `https://docs.` `microsoft.com/en-us/dynamics365/marketing/surveys`.

Next, let's learn about the Dynamics 365 application for marketing.

The Marketing application

The Marketing application is built from the ground up using the new Unified Interface. This presents a modern interface to users that contains advanced capabilities for them to interact with the platform in a much more visual way. From managing processes and journeys in a visual drag-and-drop manner to creating marketing email templates using modern templates with a high visual impact, the application is a big step forward from the previous incarnation of the marketing functionality available with the platform.

The application starts right off the bat with a **Get started with Dynamics 365 Marketing** dashboard presenting the basic workloads, things to try, an information box, and details of the instance:

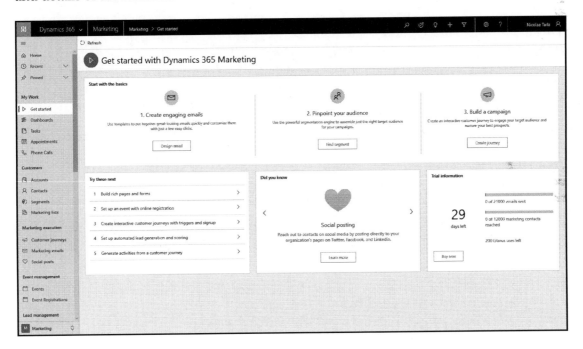

In this chapter, we're going to focus on several common workloads, including the ability to manage customer segments, creating marketing communications, and managing customer journeys, followed by a look at the portal capabilities, including the creation of landing pages. We'll continue with a review of event management capabilities, how to manage surveys, and the ways we can leverage social media. So, let's get started!

Understanding the core marketing entities

Just like we've seen in the previous applications discussed so far in this book, the Marketing application revolves around some shared entities, along with some specific entities that serve the marketing functionality.

We see Contacts and Accounts being shared pretty much across all applications. We also find Leads being shared with the Sales module, but they are enhanced with Lead Scoring capabilities. In addition, common areas are available in this application, just like in the other Dynamics 365 apps we've looked at in this book, including access to **Accounts**, **Contacts**, and **Leads**.

Part of the Marketing menu is presented in the following screenshot. It includes relevant **Customers** links, along with marketing-specific functionality:

The specifics for this application include entities such as the **Customer journeys**; **Segments**; **Marketing lists**, which are extended from the old marketing lists but with added features; **Marketing emails**; portal-specific entities such as **Marketing pages**, **Marketing forms**; **Marketing websites**; and specific marketing content entities and templates.

Throughout this chapter, we will look at the most important features under each of the main categories shown in the preceding screenshot, starting with the **Customers** category.

Understanding customers

Selecting the audience for your marketing campaign is one of the first decisions you must make when creating a new campaign. The ability to filter and select a subset of customers to contact is essential for your marketing endeavors. Creating targeted messages that increase the success rate of your campaign relies heavily on filtering the target audience. This is done through segmentation. Let's see how.

Managing customer segments

Imagine running an Advanced Find on your Contacts and deciding on a filter for all customers residing in Toronto. Your **ADVANCED FIND** query would look something like what's shown in the following screenshot:

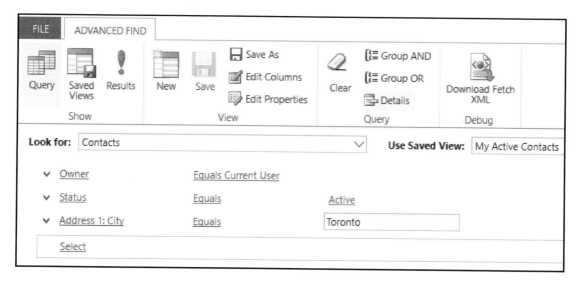

The idea of segmentation is similar in many ways. Your end result is a subset of Contacts to be targeted by your campaign.

If you navigate to **Marketing**, then **Customers** and **Segments**, you will find a listing of already predefined segments. If this is the first time you're running through a trial or a new instance, this list will most likely be empty. Perform the following steps to create and configure a new segment:

1. On the ribbon, find the **New** option to create your first segment. The screen that opens up presents you with a **DESIGNER** view, where you can start creating the filtering conditions in a very similar manner to the **ADVANCED FIND** option we saw in the preceding screenshot:

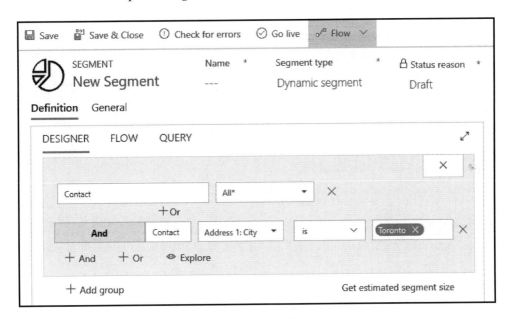

Clicking the **Get estimated segment size** option calculates the total number of Contacts selected by your defined query and filters on the fly.

If you are more code-inclined, you can select the **QUERY** tab and see the format of the query you just created:

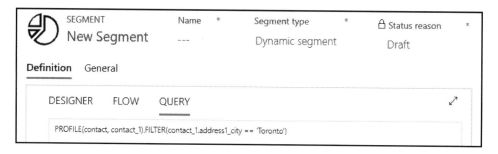

2. Once you are satisfied with the query you've created and the total number of records selected, choose the **General** tab to define the **Name** property of the newly created Segment.

Regarding **Segment type**, you have a choice between **Dynamic segment**, which is a segment created based on a Query that's recalculated at runtime; **Static segment**, which is a segment defined manually that remains fixed; or **Compound segment**, which is a new option that defines logic used to combine existing segments into a new segment. For the purpose of this scenario, we'll leave the **Dynamic segment** option selected:

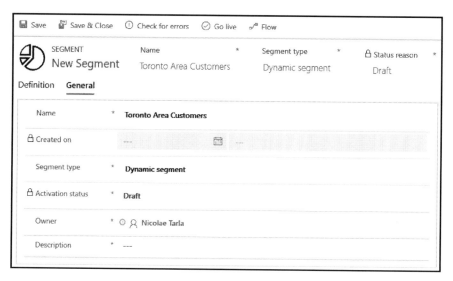

3. When you are ready, on the ribbon, select the **Check for errors** option to validate the segment's definition. If all is good, go ahead and **Save** your new segment definition. Observe that **Activation status** remains as **Draft** until you choose the **Go live** option on the ribbon. Going live performs an error check and updates **Activation status** to **Live**. Now, your newly created segment is ready to be used.

Once a segment has been created, additional details become available. Most importantly, you will see the **Members** tab appear. Here, you will find the result of your segment query in the form of a list of contacts:

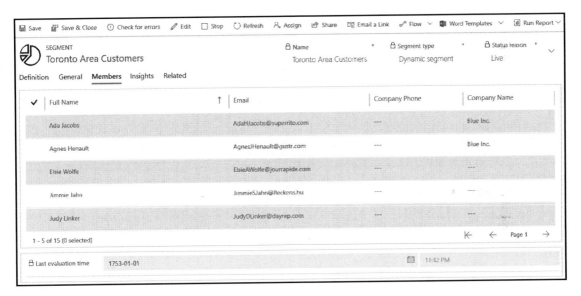

Finally, the **Insights** tab presents a visual rendering of how your selected segment evolved over time. As new Contacts are added to the system and they match the query parameters, the number of selected Contacts will increase:

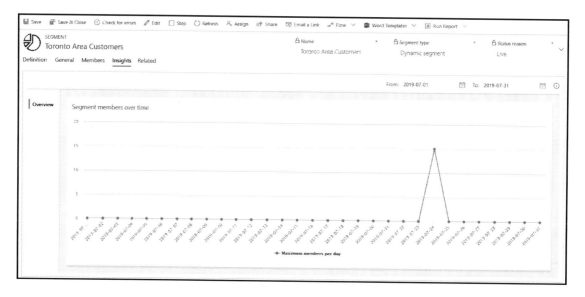

The opposite is also true, where if Contacts are removed from the system or they relocate to another city, they are removed from the segment in a dynamic manner.

The next category available in the Marketing menu is **Marketing execution**. We'll look at it next!

Marketing execution

At the top of the list for marketing channels, email marketing remains king. For this reason, Dynamics 365 for Marketing includes a new robust set of features. For those familiar with the marketing features in previous versions, you might remember the clunky interface and the limited capabilities around creating dynamic emails. Yes, you had the ability to populate dynamic values in your emails, but that's where the flexibility stopped. These emails were bland and non-formatted – enough for internal notifications but not much more.

Welcome to the new generation of email marketing. Dynamics 365 for Marketing now allows not only dynamic content but also allows us to format email messages with rich, graphical presentations. In addition, now, we have support for an increased volume of email communications, capabilities to monitor the user's interaction with these emails, and can also map customer journeys based on these interactions. Advanced analytics now allows us to determine the success and best approaches to marketing.

The next section will focus on creating marketing-specific communications.

Creating marketing communications

To create your first marketing email, navigate in the Marketing application to the **Marketing execution** section and select the **Marketing emails** option. You will be presented with a list of all **Active marketing emails**:

These are existing templates for marketing emails. Select one of them to see the content as an example. Close it after you see the designer interface. Let's get started:

1. In order to create a new template, find the **New** option on the ribbon. When you select **New**, you will be presented with a list of standard email templates. These are modern and graphically appealing templates. You can add your own to this library or use an existing one already provided by the solution. Let's select **ercolano**, for example. Your screen should look as follows:

   If you choose the **blank** option, you can go ahead and create your own templates from scratch. Sometimes, this option makes total sense, but for the most part, it's enough to start with an existing template and modify it as needed.

2. When you're satisfied with the selected template, choose the **Select** option to load the template into your designer window. This is where the fun starts. You are now on the **Design** tab, in the **Designer** window. You have the choice to change the view to HTML or see a preview as it will appear on either a desktop, tablet, or mobile device. The true nature of responsive design kicks in and allows for dynamic formatting, depending on various screen sizes.

3. When on the **Designer** tab, look to the right of the work area. You'll see a section with the default **Toolbox** presented. Here, you can choose to add various elements in a drag-and-drop fashion. You can easily add text areas, images, buttons, and other elements as needed:

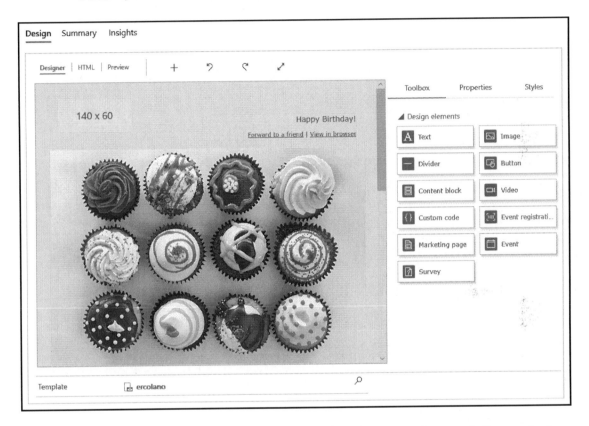

The **Properties** tab allows you to modify the parameters for an existing content block, while the **Styles** tab allows you to change the style of the selected area.

As you can see, the interface is a lot more user-friendly. This allows any user with permissions to easily design email templates with an increased graphical impact. Note that, while designing email templates, you should still rely on a designer or a resource with visual skills for a better impact.

4. When you are satisfied with the template, move on to the **Summary** tab and make sure you have filled in all the necessary fields properly. Here, you can define generic information about this new template, along with sender and receiver information, as depicted in the following screenshot:

5. Finally, when satisfied, select the **Save** option on the ribbon. Observe how the plain text version is generated automatically based on the template we defined earlier.

If you are ready to release this template for use, select the **Go live** option on the ribbon. This triggers a **Check for errors** call. When this has completed, the email template will be ready. Now, if you navigate to the **Insights** tab, you will find a set of cards with details about the performance of this template. The **Overview** tab shows all this information collected in one place, making it easy to view. The other tabs provide additional details based on various scenarios:

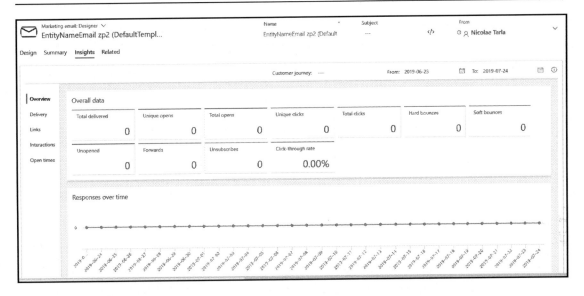

6. Finally, the last step in leveraging the newly designed template is to run a test to make sure the outcome is as expected. You do this by sending the message to yourself. On the ribbon, find and select the option to **Test and Send**. A side blade will open that contains the required information for the test to be run. Fill in all three required fields and click **Save and Close**:

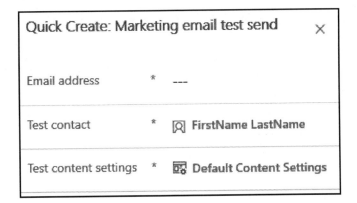

And this concludes creating a simple email template. The functionality is robust, thus inspiring users to be more productive and engage better with existing clients and stakeholders. In the next section, we'll look at customer journeys. We'll find out what a customer journey is, how to map one, and how to manage it.

Creating and managing customer journeys

The customer journey is the process a typical customer goes through to complete a purchase. This typically starts with product or service discovery, then evaluation, research, and finally then purchasing the product/service. Defining various journeys allows us to determine how we will guide our customers through the various steps, provide the most relevant information each step of the way, and successfully close a sale. We can introduce automation to speed things up, as well as provide an interactive way to assist in the decision-making process.

In order to create new customer journeys, we need to define a segment of customers we are targeting, based on specific filtering criteria, as well as a marketing email.

Creating a new customer journey is done from the Marketing application, by navigating to the **Marketing execution** section and selecting the **Customer Journeys** option. This provides us with a view of all the existing journeys defined in the system. The sample data includes several such examples:

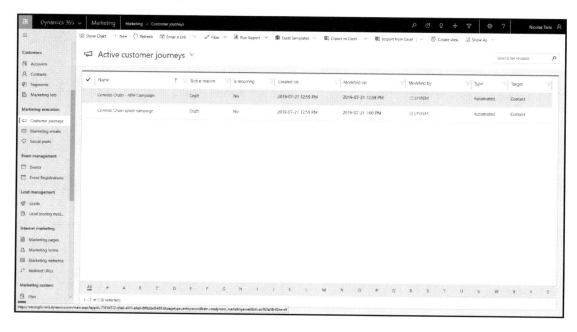

Opening one of the sample records, we can see how the same visual interface allows us to define the steps in each journey and the decision points along the way. This is, again, a simple and easy drag-and-drop interface, similar to what we saw previously in `Chapter 4`, *Dynamics 365 Customer Service*, when looking at Service Processes:

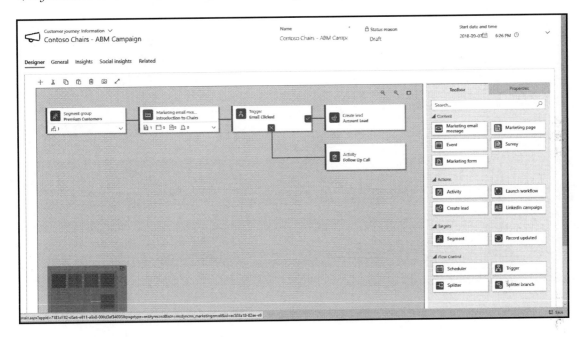

You can include specific content, actions, targets, and flow control elements to create a robust set of steps in the journey.

From a visual perspective, creating a new customer journey is done similarly to creating a simple process. From the listing view, select the **New** option on the ribbon. You will be presented with a list of available customer journeys templates to select from. You can start from an existing, predefined template or select to start from a **Blank Template**.

Select the **Blank Template** option and make sure the required fields are pre-populated:

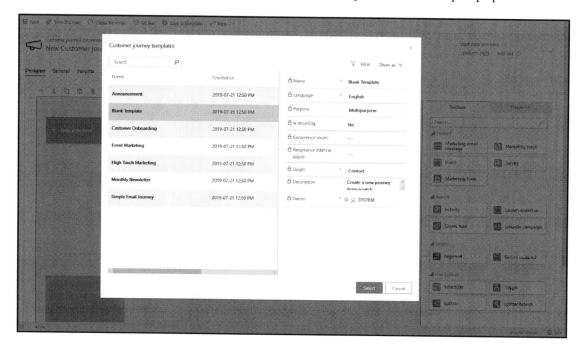

When satisfied, click the **Select** button to start configuring the newly created customer journey. You will be taken to the **Designer** area, where you can start dragging the various elements from the **Toolbox** tab from the right-hand side of the screen:

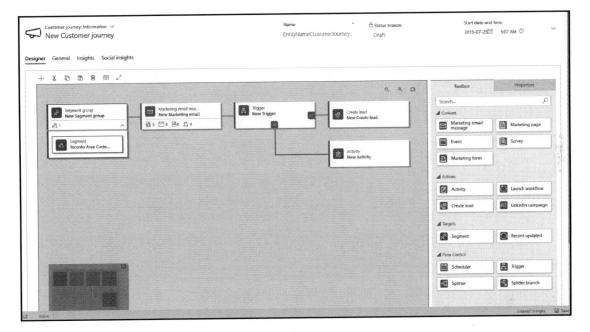

Make sure that each step along the way is configured by selecting it and checking the **Properties** tab on the right-hand side. Fill in the necessary details as needed:

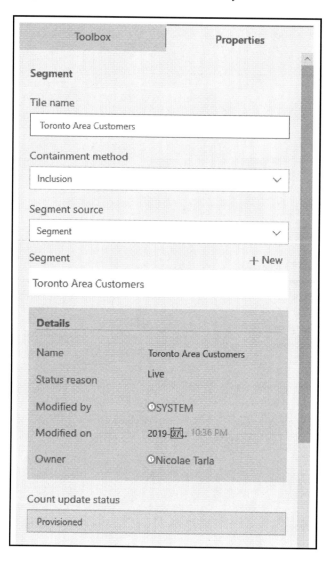

When complete, give your customer journey a **Name** and select the **Save** option on the ribbon. Check the **General** tab for additional details on the newly defined **Journey** record, as depicted in the following screenshot:

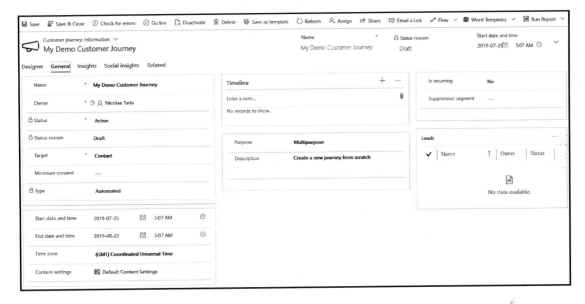

The additional **Insights** tab provides analytics around the success of a specific customer journey.

When connected to the Microsoft Social Engagement offering, Social Insights can augment the data through additional analytics.

Finally, just like we did for marketing emails, you need to select the **Go Live** option on the ribbon to activate your newly created customer journey record. This completes the necessary validations and notifies us if anything unexpected is found in the customer journey definition.

You can take the same approach to generate more complex journeys, including triggering specific actions on the platform or creating a journey that interacts with the customer in a more dynamic way, through additional emails, marketing pages (also known as landing pages), surveys, or other means.

In the next section, we'll focus on how to track and manage social media posts.

Managing social media posts

The Marketing application extends beyond the normal borders of email marketing and event management, and into social media networks. The platform allows you to schedule and publish events on social media through your corporate accounts.

We can find this functionality on the navigation bar, under the **Marketing execution** section. The option is called **Social posts**. Selecting this presents you with a calendar view displaying all future scheduled posts, as well as previously posted messages:

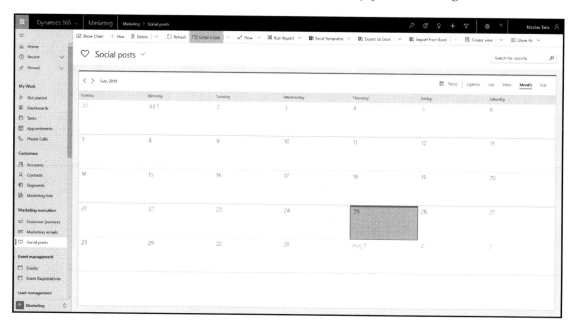

You can add a new post by selecting a date and then clicking one more time to open the fly-out menu for **New item**:

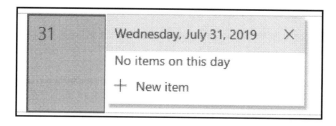

This takes you to the **Post creation** page. Here, you define the post's **Name** and the social account you want to post to. In this example, we're posting to a Facebook page. Make sure you have created your social profiles prior to attempting to create Social Posts; otherwise, you will not be able to select the mandatory channel field:

You can add images related to your post and edit the post content in the **Add post** multi-line text field. The schedule is based on the scheduled date you began the process from.

When you're ready to post, you can choose to post at a scheduled date and time or post immediately. If you choose to post at a future date, the post will be presented on the calendar at the selected date. As time progresses, older posts will stay represented on the calendar. The following screenshot presents a view of the **Social posts** calendar with a few Facebook posts added:

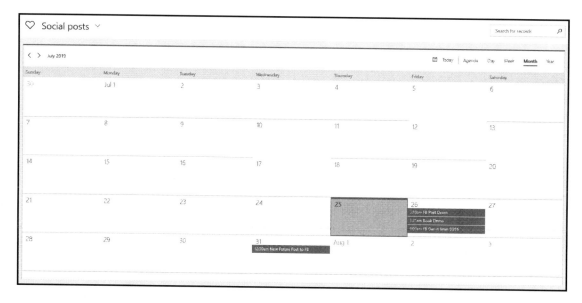

At the other end, when checking the Facebook page we selected to post to, we can see the posts already populating the feed:

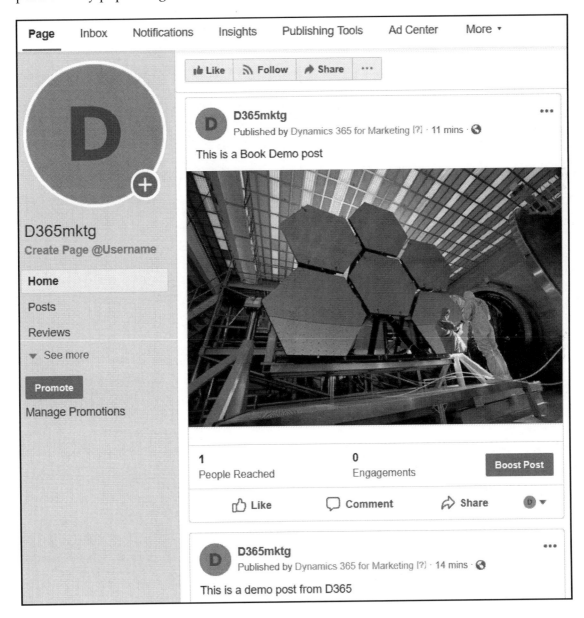

You can easily do the same with Twitter and LinkedIn posts.

In order to configure social profiles, you need to have your corporate credentials for these social networks ready. You simply navigate to **Settings** from the bottom section and find the **Social Configuration** option under **Marketing Settings**:

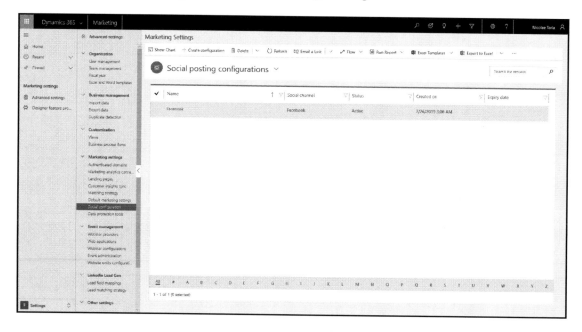

Then, select the **Create configuration** option from the ribbon to start creating a new Social Profile. A fly-out will open on the right-hand side that allows you to select a channel and give the configuration a name. When selecting a channel, additional details are populated, including the privacy and terms of service, as well as the terms and conditions. You must check the checkbox to agree and then select **Create**:

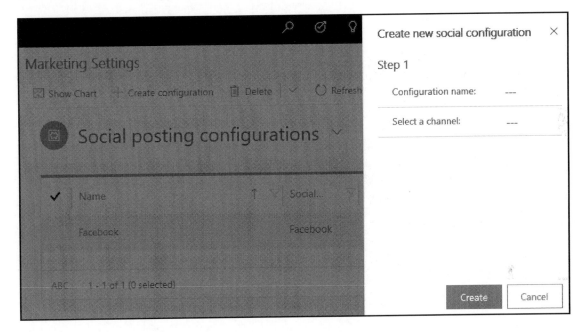

If you have interrupted the setup process, or you have updated the social account password, you can come back and select the **Reauthorize** button from the ribbon. This will cause your social network of choice to be reauthenticated:

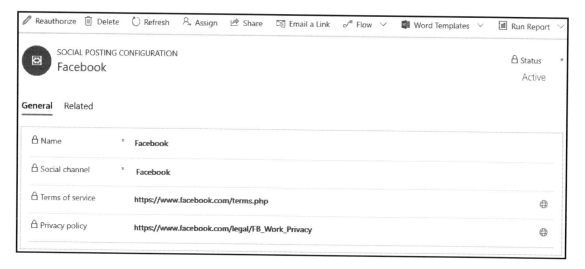

Make sure the status is set to **Active** as this denotes the record has been configured correctly and is functional.

The next category available in the Marketing application is event management. We'll look at this in the next section.

Event management

Another way of targeting a customer is through coordinating public events. Whether these are simple seminars or full conferences, Dynamics 365 for Marketing allows us to plan, budget, promote, and analyze attendance. Furthermore, you can evaluate the success of specific events and compare them to determine the most successful avenues you can use to reach your prospects.

The Event Management area is located on the main navigation bar, under **Events**:

Options for event management include managing events, participants, venues, logistics, and sponsorship. This provides a robust tool we can use to manage the entire event's life cycle. Post-event capabilities allow us to track leads generated by the event and move those into the standard Sales pipeline.

Next, we'll learn how to create and manage various events on the platform.

Creating and managing events

As soon as you navigate to **Events**, you will be presented with a list of existing events in the system. If you have sample data loaded or this is a currently active environment, you will already see the listing pre-populated with a set of records.

On the top ribbon, you will be presented with the option to create an event template, create an event from a template, or create a new, blank event.

Creating a new event from scratch allows for a full gamut of configurations. Once you select **New** on the ribbon, you will be presented with the General Event configuration form. Observe the process flow at the top, which guides you through the necessary steps to configure, track, launch, and analyze the event successfully:

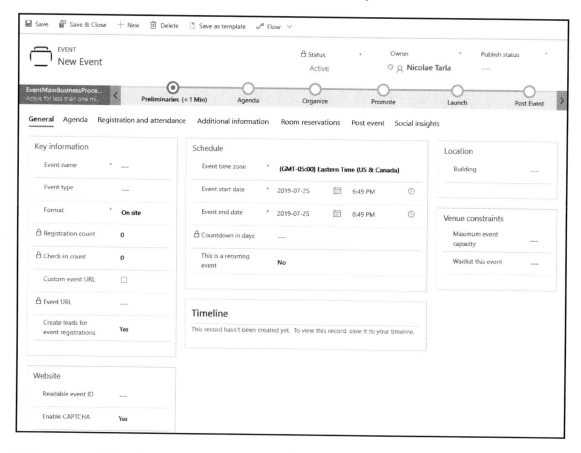

Make sure to fill in the required fields, then click on **Save**. Observe that you can define this as a recurring event or an event spanning multiple days, as well as additional properties such as the event URL and an event image.

The record we just created is called a **Root event record**. From this point on, we can add event configuration options as needed. At this point, you can think of the newly created event as a *container* for further configuration. Note that an event does not show on the events portal until it is finalized and published.

The following tabs display the schedule for the event:

- Registrants on the **Agenda** tab
- Attendance and cancellations on the **Registration** tab
- Additional details on the **Additional information** tab

Once you have created the event record, the next step is to set up the team that will participate in this event. Do that by navigating to **Event team members**. Here, you can define team members based on existing Contacts in the system:

On the Team Member record, you can associate the respective events with the person who fills in the defined roles. You can view the same information using the event by navigating to the **Additional information** tab on the event record and scrolling down to find the **Event team members** grid. You can also add additional event team members from here as needed:

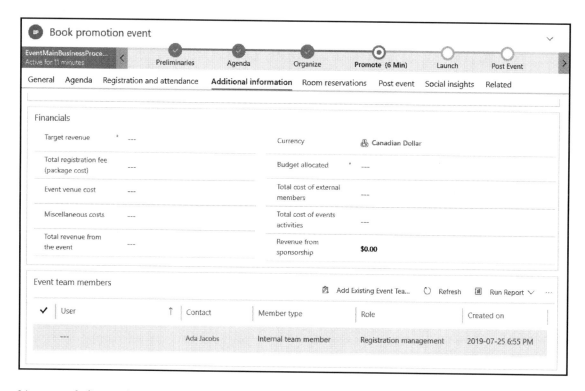

You can define either internal or external team members to participate in the event. This allows you to configure large events where not all your staff are on the payroll.

With a support team created, the next step is to capture and organize the sessions and presenters. Do that by navigating to the **Participants** section and finding the **Speakers** option. This presents you with a view of all existing recorded speakers:

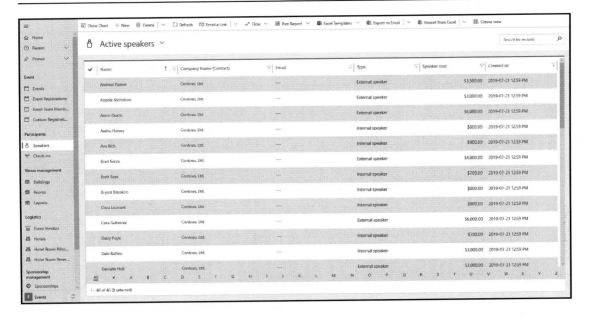

When you have a repeat speaker, you will find the existing record already on file. This saves creating a new record each time that the speaker presents at one of your events. With the speaker created along with the event and Sessions, the next step is to create a Speaker Engagement record, which ties a selected Speaker to a particular event Session:

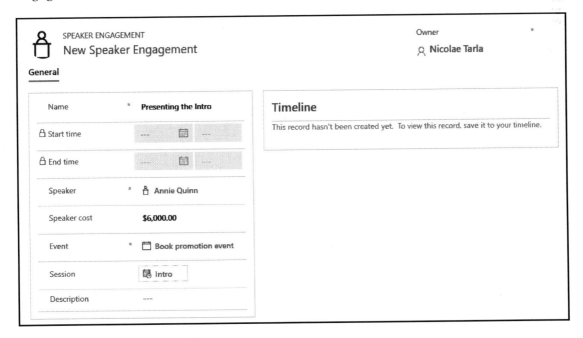

Looking at the Session from the event side, we can see the Speaker we selected on the **Agenda** tab. From here, you can add the additional **Speaker engagements** for when you have multiple speakers co-presenting:

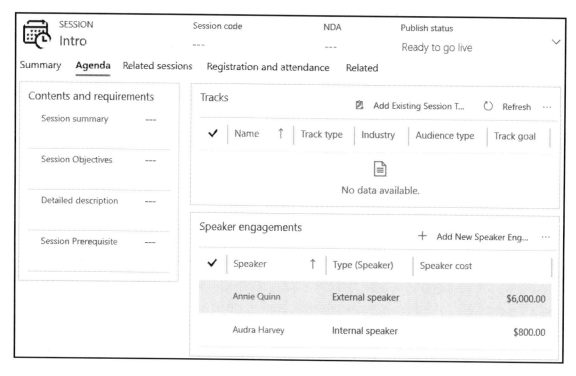

Events that do not contain multiple sessions act as sessions themselves.

Now that we've defined our Speakers, let's configure the Venue for the event. This can be done right after the event record has been created, or at any time after. Do this by navigating to the **Venue management** section on the navigation bar. Here, you can start setting up the **Buildings** and **Rooms** available for your event, as well as a **Layout**. You use a **Layout** when the same room is shared between different types of sessions. You could have one layout for an earlier presentation session, followed by a different layout for a section that requires more interaction between session participants.

You can find the **Venue management** section on the navigation menu as per the following screenshot:

Now, there's one more thing left to capture: handling event registration and providing some passes to the event.

Handling event registration

Event passes can be either sold or given away for free, depending on the setup. It is totally optional to use passes. Passes can be issued for different categories, including regular attendees, speakers, sponsors, media, and so on.

You can add passes for an event by navigating to the **Registration and attendance** tab in the event record. Here, under the **Passes** section, you can start adding new passes:

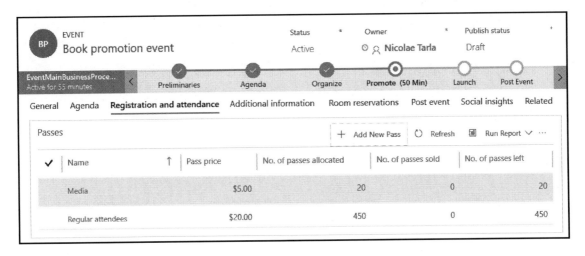

When defining passes, you name the category they apply to, the allocated number, and the cost.

You can also further restrict the use of passes by only making them available for specific sessions in an Event. You can do that from the pass record by navigating to the **Eligible sessions** tab and adding the sessions you want the pass to be valid for:

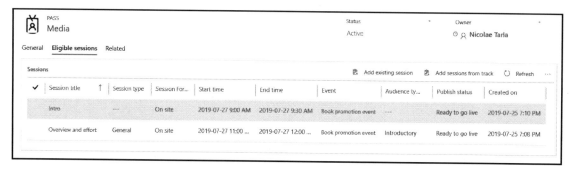

Additional sessions and event features allow us to limit the number of attendees. You can only allow a maximum number of registrations for an event or a session, with a waitlist to capture additional registrations over the maximum capacity.

And with the configuration in place, you are ready to open the event for registration. Good luck!

For the manager role, when you need to monitor the status of all the events that have been organized, the **Event management dashboard** is the place to go. You can find it under the **Dashboards** menu:

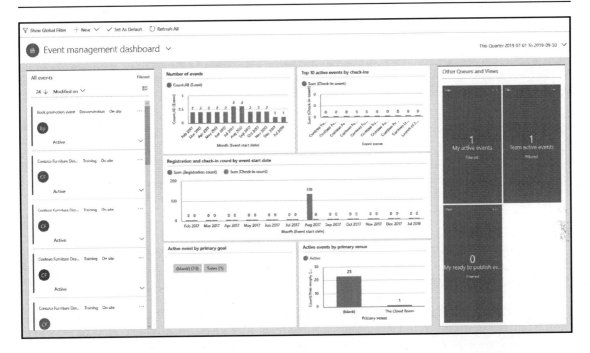

This dashboard allows us to query over a specific time period, with additional filters defined. By default, you get a list of all events and their statuses, along with the topmost active events, registrations, and actual check-ins, events by venue, and events by pre-configured goals to be achieved through a specific marketing activity or campaign.

And that covers our overview of the **Event management** functionality. For additional information, please refer to the Microsoft documentation available at `http://docs.microsoft.com`. Now, let's look at the next category available in the Marketing application menu: internet marketing.

Internet marketing

The Microsoft Dynamics for Marketing application comes with support for Marketing portals. This is a portal solution based on Dynamics Portals, but specific to Marketing functionality. You will want to extend a current portal with the Marketing functionality or create a new portal for marketing in order to leverage marketing specific features, such as the event management website. Leveraging a portal allows for specific Marketing functionality, including the ability to create and use the following elements:

- **Landing pages**: Provides data collection forms, such as a Contact Us page.
- **Subscription Centers**: Provides functionality necessary for a site user or customer to manage their mailing list subscriptions.
- **Forwarding Pages**: Allows email forwarding with full tracking capabilities.
- **Event Websites**: Enables functionality for event registration and promotion.

You can provide this Marketing functionality by leveraging either the Power Apps portals functionality for a custom website or use a **Content Management System (CMS)** of your choice. You can also choose to use both options together since, technically, this is possible and supported.

Let's start by looking at the process of deploying Marketing functionality using the Marketing portal.

Deploying the Marketing portal

Note that, during the portal's deployment, you have a choice between using the Dynamics Portal solution or your own custom Marketing portal. If you choose to use the Dynamics Portal solution, make sure your license allows you to create yet another portal side-by-side with any possible Dynamics Portal you already use with Sales or Service.

In order to deploy the Marketing portal, you need to go through **Administration Center**, on the **Application** tab, and choose to configure the Dynamics 365 Marketing application. This starts the configuration wizard, as shown in the following screenshot. Here, you can choose between using your own portal or configuring the Dynamics 365 portal for Marketing:

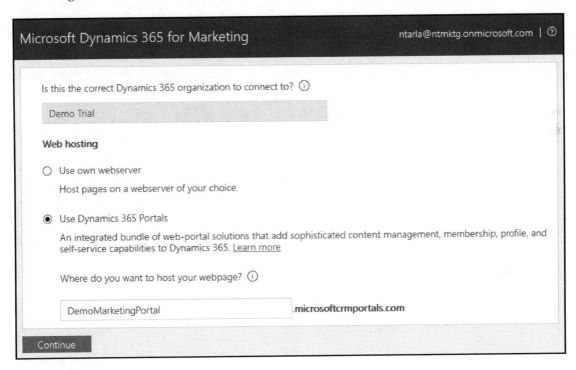

The setup takes several minutes to provision the necessary resources, after which you are ready to start using the portal.

Next, let's learn how to create a landing page for users to reach on the portal.

Creating a landing page

A landing page is typically a page in the portal that hosts marketing form. The data captured in this form flows back into your Dynamics 365 for Marketing instance.

To create new marketing pages on the portal, find the **Internet marketing** area on the navigation bar, below the **Marketing pages** option. This presents a listing of existing marketing pages, along with the option to create a brand-new page. Triggering the creation of a new page starts the wizard, which allows you to select one of the pre-existing templates for pages. This user interface experience is very similar to creating a marketing email, but the templates are specific to web pages now:

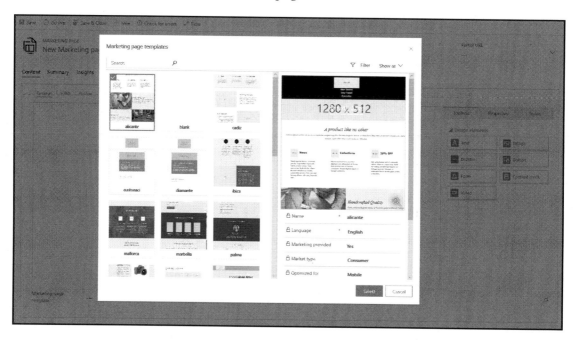

Selecting a template puts you in edit mode on the page designer. Here, similar to creating email content, you have the graphical designer, the HTML view, and the **Preview** option. With this option, you can preview how the template will be presented on various devices. The **Toolbox** tab on the right-hand side gives you the tools you'll need to create page templates. The **Properties** tab provides features you can use to define granular properties for each added page element. Finally, the **Styles configuration** tab allows you to format selected page elements. The following screenshot shows the entire designer screen and the aforementioned features:

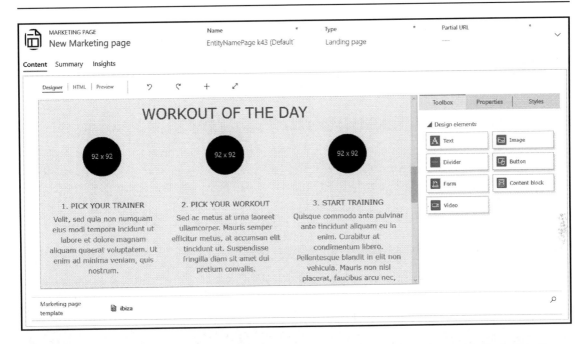

The additional **Summary** tab allows you to update the **Name** you've provided, define the partial URL, and modify other properties. When done, save the page by selecting the **Save** option on the top ribbon. Then, select **Go live** to publish this new page.

The **Insights** tab will present a graphical analysis of the page's usage once it's live. When this page captures a form, you get additional details on page visits and submissions. This is essential information you can use to track the success of a specific marketing initiative.

Marketing pages come in different flavors. These include the following:

- **Landing pages:** Pages with input to capture customer data. These are typically used for sign-up forms in order to capture potential customer details.
- **Subscription centers**: This allows a user to select the subscriptions needed, or to unsubscribe from existing mailing lists.
- **Forward pages**: These are pages that are designed to allow us to forward marketing messages to another user. The platform has the ability to track forwarded messages using forward pages but will not track emails forwarded directly.

You can easily integrate these types of pages in customer journeys, as we've seen in the previous sections.

So far, we have looked at the major categories available in the Marketing application. In the next section, we'll learn more about Surveys as an important functionality of the application.

Creating and managing Surveys

As part of the Marketing application, we have the ability to work with Surveys. We use Surveys and the Survey app to design and publish online surveys. You can integrate these Surveys with events, marketing emails, and defined customer journeys. It is yet another way to reach out and collect feedback from your customers, as opposed to the portal functionality. This functionality is provided as a separate app but leverages the same backend as the Marketing application. This means that it has access to the same data records, such as Accounts and Contacts.

You can find the Surveys app by going to the **My apps** menu and selecting **Surveys** from the drop-down options:

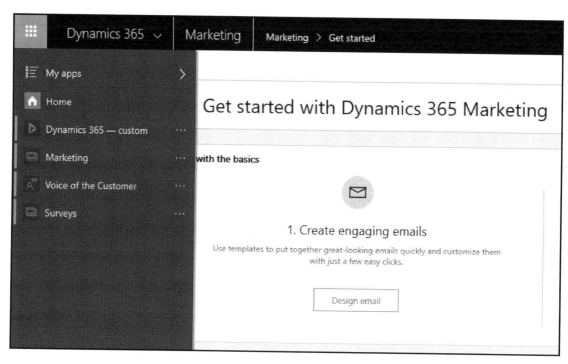

This app leverages the **Voice of the Customer** functionality that we've seen in previous versions. There is limited functionality, however: you can only create anonymous surveys and attach them to emails, but this functionality can't trigger any actions on customer journeys.

From a functionality standpoint, you have the ability to create Surveys, as well as track responses and see outcomes. You can define themes and images to be associated with surveys.

You can create a new Survey by navigating to the **Voice of the Customer** section from the menu and finding the **Surveys** option. This opens up a view of active Surveys. Create a new Survey from the ribbon's **New** option:

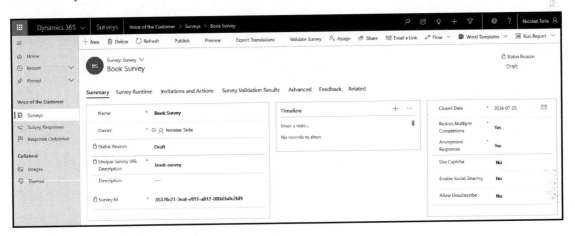

Then, on the **Survey Runtime** tab, you can define the logo, header, footer, and other options.

In order to generate the Survey questions, change the record view from **Survey** to **Designer**:

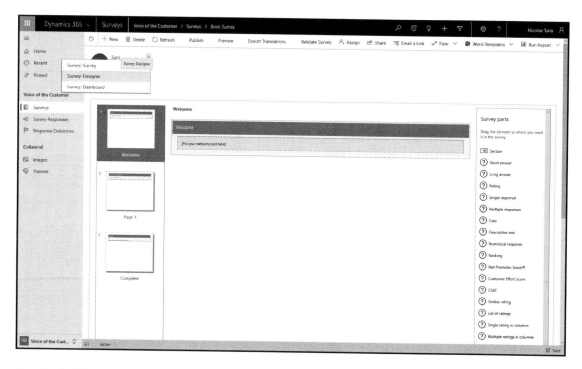

On the left-hand side, you define the pages that make up your survey, while on the right-hand side, you define the controls to add to each page. This is as simple as dragging controls onto the pages and defining properties such as questions, available answers, and other text.

When you are satisfied with your survey, save it and select **Preview** on the ribbon to see how it will look:

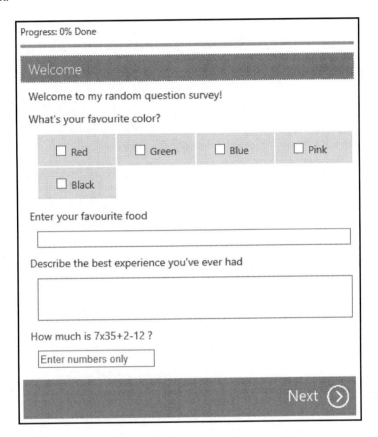

When satisfied, select the **Publish** option on the ribbon to make the survey available. On the **Invitations and Actions** tab of the Survey, you will find the **Anonymous Link** option. You can use that to publish your Survey to users and start collecting answers.

Once you have published the survey, you can view the answers trickling in by navigating to **Survey Responses**:

Some basic reports are pre-built and leverage the standard wizard-driven reporting capabilities. An example is the Summary report presented here:

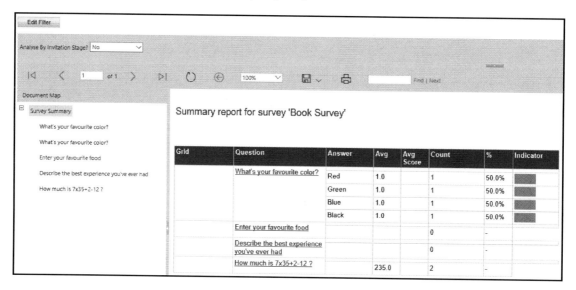

For a better experience reporting on Survey outcomes, you should consider leveraging a BI tool such as Power BI. With this, we have come to the end of this chapter. Let's summarize what we have learned!

Summary

This chapter has covered the core features of the Dynamics 365 Marketing application. We looked at the functionality around managing and segmenting customers for marketing activities, creating modern and responsive email templates, managing customer journeys, capabilities around leveraging social media, event creation and management, portal capabilities, and the ability to create surveys.

With this knowledge, you can now create and run marketing campaigns and manage modern email templates for various communication needs, as well as entire customer journeys.

In addition, we learned how to leverage Dynamics 365 Marketing to collect customer information through surveys, as well as present and manage events through the use of a public portal. With this knowledge, you are now ready to target your customers in various ways and enhance their experience at each interaction point.

In the next chapter, we'll look at the Power Platform and its overlapping capabilities.

Section 3 - Customization, Configuration, and Extensibility

3

In this section, we will focus on configurations and customizations that extend the basic functionality of the platform. We'll also be looking at the Power Platform not as a common set of functionalities, but rather at its ability to extend the platform and provide added value to users.

This section comprises of the following chapters:

- Chapter 8, *Dynamics 365 Customer Engagement and Power Platform*
- Chapter 9, *Customizing Dynamics 365*
- Chapter 10, *Building Better Business Functionality*

8
Dynamics 365 Customer Engagement and Power Platform

In the previous chapters, we looked at the various applications available for Dynamics 365 Customer Engagement. These include **Sales**, **Customer Service**, **Field Service**, **Project Service Automation (PSA)**, and the new **Marketing** applications. Often enough, though, we tackle a new project that falls outside of these applications. Yes, it might integrate with one or more of these applications, leveraging some or all of the functionality, but the scope is so different that it does not fall within any of these functional offerings. Back in the day, we used to call this xRM, where x stands for *anything* – for example, **Member Relationship Management (MRM)** solutions, or other very specialized solutions.

With the evolution of the cloud and the total revamp of the Dynamics platform, we now have what's called the **Power Platform**. This is a combination of the following solutions:

- Power BI
- Power Apps
- Power Automate
- Power Virtual Agents

When it comes to Power BI, this is a topic better handled on its own, and there are many books out there covering this topic in detail. Suffice to say, it is a powerful **Business Intelligence (BI)** tool that allows you to create data-driven visualizations for better analysis and decision making.

In this chapter, we're focusing primarily on Power Apps and how to leverage **Microsoft Flow** (currently known as **Power Automate**) for task automation. Through the separation of **Common Data Service (CDS)**, we now can build custom applications leveraging the same backend but build our own custom apps.

We will be covering the following topics:

- What is in Power Apps?
- Common roles and scenarios for Power Apps
- Tying it all together with Microsoft Flow

By the end of the chapter, you should be able to quickly build applications with no/low code. As you will see in the examples provided, low code refers to the ability to create Excel-like formulas and no actual custom code.

Understanding the Power Apps way

Power Apps is a collection of applications, services, connectors, and backend data platforms that allows makers or creators to develop applications at a rapid pace, with no or minimal code. It provides a set of tools allowing the creation of custom business applications. The idea is to put the power in the hands of the business users and provide them with the ability to create the necessary tools to be leveraged by the business.

The underlying data platform, called CDS, allows storing business data in a structured manner but is not the only backend available. Power Apps can leverage structured data stores, either through CDS or other structured databases supported by a large number of available connectors or through loosely structured data stores such as SharePoint. We can leverage either online or on-premises data sources. The most common ones include, but are not limited to, the following:

- Office 365
- Excel
- Dynamics 365
- SharePoint
- SQL Server

A Power Apps application, depending on how it's built, can leverage the business logic and workflow capabilities we've become familiar with Dynamics over the years. This provides extensive capabilities to automate former manual processes, and digitally transform your business from the ground up.

In addition, and by design, Power Apps apps are built respecting all responsive design restrictions, allowing these apps to run on any device. We can have the same app displaying one way on a smaller phone screen while leveraging the additional screen real estate on a larger tablet or on the desktop.

This is a true *build once, use anywhere* transformation.

In addition, possibly the most powerful feature is the ability to build a new app with no code. The low-code/no-code approach is gaining ever more popularity, and Microsoft is yet again at the forefront of the pack, being recognized by Gartner as a leader in the no-code/low-code application development world.

The platform is not limited only to makers and creators though. It has all the necessary plumbing in place to allow developers to programmatically interact with the platform components. They have the ability to build custom extensions, interact with data, create new business logic and custom connectors, as well as tap into external data sources.

With such great features, it is not hard to see why this platform is so powerful, and it's getting more and more traction every day. The fact that Microsoft is recognized as a leader for the effort in this space stands only to validate the fact that this is a step in the right direction. Putting the power in the hands of all users, whether developers or business users, opens the potential for new, creative ways to build fabulous functionality – the likes of which we haven't seen so far.

Users/personas leveraging Power Apps

As we've just seen, Power Apps apps can be created by business users, with a no-code/low-code approach, or by hardcore developers. This speaks to the platform's ability to grow and change in order to create new and revolutionary solutions.

We often encounter the following categories of users interacting with this platform:

- Makers/creators
- Standard users
- Administrators
- Developers

Let's take each separately and see how they leverage Power Apps.

Power Apps for makers/creators

With Power Apps, you can create the following types of applications:

- Canvas apps
- Model-driven apps
- Portal apps

Typically, an app maker will start from `http://web.powerapps.com`.

This is the starting page, allowing you direct access to the various components of the platform:

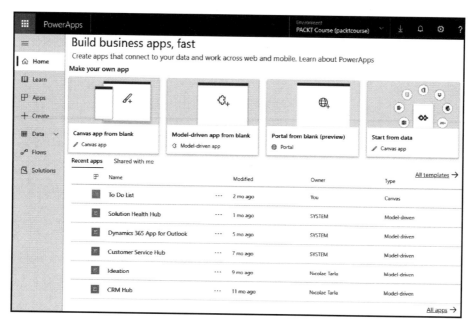

The **Home** page presents the user with navigation on the left side of the screen, allowing you easy access to **Apps**, **Data**, **Flows**, and **Solutions**.

On the main screen, you are presented with a list of options to start creating your new app. You can either choose one of the three app types or select to start from an existing template. Selecting the **All Templates** link presents you with a listing of predefined sample applications. Some of them, while primarily created as a demo of what can be done, can be used as is. Solutions such as **To Do List**, **Book A Room**, or **Asset Checkout** are simple examples to start from. Open some of these and observe how they are built. This will help you understand the capabilities and options to expand in detail.

Looking at an app card, you will observe the app type in the bottom corner of the card, as in the following screenshot:

Switching the filter from **All** to **Office** presents a listing of templates related to Office 365 functionality. These are apps leveraging the Office 365 services either through integration or by using the Office 365 backend. The next screenshot shows the filter with the Office apps selected:

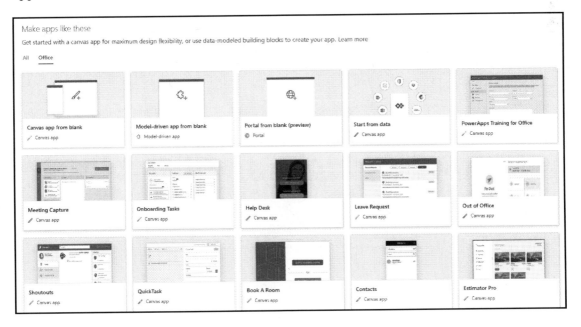

Typically, you would use the following tools, depending on the app type you are creating:

- Power Apps Studio is the designer used for creating canvas apps. We will see what those are later in this chapter in the *Comparing canvas versus model-driven apps* section. Simply put, at this time, the designer allows the creation of apps in a manner very similar to creating a PowerPoint slide.
- The app designer is used for building model-driven apps. These are apps built based on a pre-existing data model. The designer allows the creation of the components based on existing data structures, and wraps them all in a site map, thereby creating an application with custom navigation.

Power Apps for application users

Another category of personas is the application users. These are the application consumers. They can leverage the pre-built apps either through a computer, tablet, or mobile device.

These users will have access to corporate applications based on permissions and the applications shared with them. They are not the ones creating apps.

Typically, on a mobile device, opening the Power Apps application presents you with a listing of various corporate apps you have access to, as in the following screenshot:

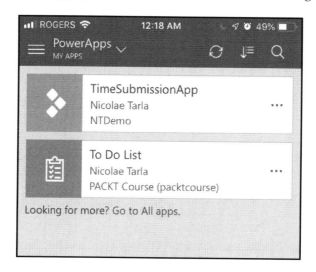

Selecting one of the apps launches the application and puts the user directly into the application interface. The following screenshot shows the main screen for **TimeSubmissionApp**:

Let's move on to the next category of users of Power Apps.

Power Apps for administrators

Administrators are typically people that manage applications and access. They do not always create new applications for the enterprise but are involved in proper application management, including access security and various policies.

Administrators have access to two distinct administration centers. They are as follows:

- The Power Apps admin center is available at `https://admin.powerapps.com`.
- The Power Platform admin center available at `https://admin.powerplatform.microsoft.com`.

The subsequent sections will explain these data centers in detail.

The Power Apps admin center

The Power Apps admin center has a layout somewhat similar to the App Maker interface. We find on the left side the navigation options, including the management of various environments and data policies, the definitions of the various integrations configured, and the general tenant details.

The main page shows the details of each navigation option selected. The following screenshot shows the Power Apps admin center with the **Data policies** navigation selected:

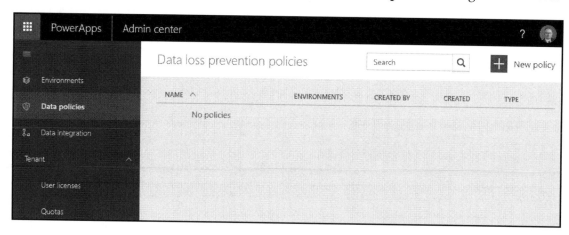

Selecting the **New policy** option at the top right of the screen allows an admin to create a new policy.

The Power Platform admin center

The Power Platform admin center, on the other hand, while presenting a similar interface with navigation to the left and content on the main page, includes several other options. Besides environment management, which is common across both admin centers, as well as data integration and data policies, we have some additional options. Here, we have access to create and review various support cases opened with Microsoft, as well as to the option to configure data gateways. Data gateways are used to configure connections from the app to an on-premises data source.

The following screenshot shows the **Power Platform admin center** screen with the **Help + support** navigation option selected:

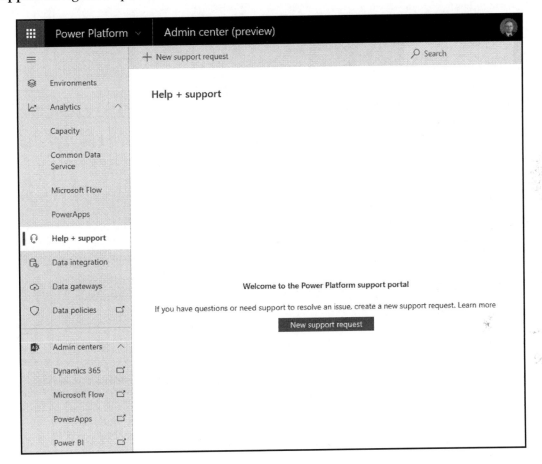

As you can see, in addition to the standard options, we can see analytics on the various components of the Power Platform service, including details on the following:

- Capacity
- CDS
- Microsoft Flow
- Power Apps

We also have access here to other admin centers within the same tenant. These include the standard Power BI, Power Apps, and Microsoft Flow, as well as Dynamics 365 if it's part of the same tenant.

Power Apps for developers

Finally, developers are application creators that can do a little bit more than app makers. They typically get involved in app creation when custom code is used to extend the available functionality. They can create Azure functions, plugins, and custom workflow extensions, as well as customize client-side functionality leveraging JavaScript. Typically, when using a model-driven app, a Dynamics 365 developer's skillset applies.

The Microsoft docs provide extensive developer documentation and code samples, including extending canvas and model-driven apps, working with CDS, creating custom business logic, creating integrations and packaging, and distributing these applications. This is a really good source of information and it should be bookmarked so that it is one click away.

Let's look next at the process to create Power Apps.

Creating Power Apps

Power Apps provides more than just the capability to create no-/low-code apps. The entire suite of business apps is comprised of four main components.

CDS is the data platform. It serves as the backend data store for multiple applications, including Dynamics 365. It includes several predefined entities representing tables in the database. As time progresses, more and more applications start to leverage the same common data store, resulting in fewer synchronizations between applications, less integration work, and no need to define a specific source of truth.

Portals is the newest feature added, where we now can create public websites, with support for various authentication mechanisms, as well as present CDS data. We will be looking at Portals in detail in a later part of this chapter.

Canvas apps are custom applications created based on a specific user experience. They are typically very visual, with excellent support for various mobile platforms. These applications are typically responsive and can scale on various screen sizes and resolutions, making them a great choice for simple business process execution apps. In addition, the platform supports a large number of connectors to other applications and platforms. This makes a canvas application ideal for when you want to use a backend other than CDS.

Model-driven apps are applications built based on an existing data model. These are based on a schema defined in CDS. Model-driven apps generate a user interface along the lines of the core functional modules in Dynamics 365, which should be familiar to all CRM users.

Let's look at these application types in the next section.

Comparing canvas versus model-driven apps

As mentioned, from a user experience perspective, the two main categories of apps that can be created by leveraging Power Apps are canvas apps and model-driven apps. Fundamentally, these application models are quite different from each other, and they apply to different scenarios. It is also possible to mix canvas and model-driven apps and incorporate a canvas app into a model-driven app, for example.

While a model-driven app is focused primarily on the data, while keeping a somewhat standard visualization, a canvas app allows creativity to take over to create visually appealing user experiences.

In the subsequent section, we will see how to create canvas apps and model-driven apps.

Creating a canvas app

Canvas apps are applications built in a very visual manner, like designing a PowerPoint presentation deck. Each app page is a slide in your deck, and you can skip between various pages based on links or rules on each page or controls.

Canvas apps are created through a simplistic drag-and-drop interface, by positioning predefined controls on a canvas, then defining properties and actions for each of these controls.

Connectors for various data sources are at the core of this app type functionality. Microsoft has built many connectors already, and that number is increasing with every new release. Developers have also the ability to extend and create new connectors.

We can create a simple canvas app by navigating to the maker environment, available at `https://make.powerapps.com`.

Make sure you select the correct environment where you want your application created from the top-right side of the screen. You can see the **PACKT Course (packtcourse)** environment selected in the following screenshot:

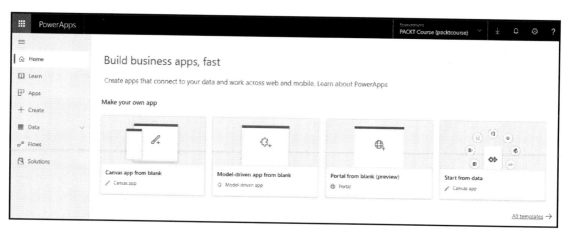

If you choose to start a new application from scratch, you can select, from the **Make your own app** area, the section for **Canvas app from blank**, as you can see in the preceding screenshot.

This launches a wizard where you get to define the app properties and target. The following screenshot shows the first step in the wizard to create a new app called **PACKT Canvas App**.

We'll target the mobile format:

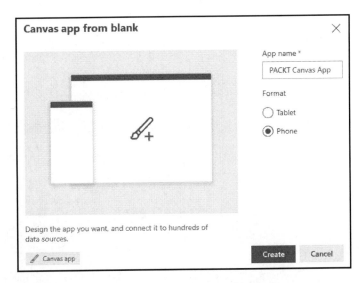

Selecting **Create** opens the Power Apps Studio application in a new browser tab, where we can start composing our new app. Observe that, from the start, the format is configured for mobile:

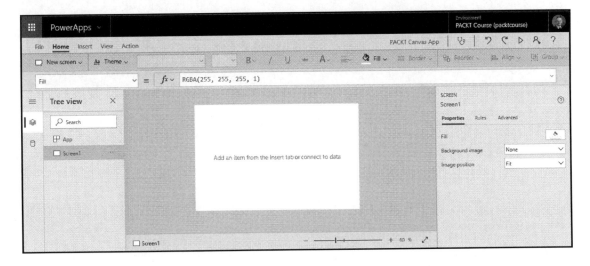

 Note that Power Apps Studio is available both as a web application accessible through the browser and as a client application that you can install on Windows from Microsoft Store.

Opening Microsoft Store and looking for Power Apps Studio will take you to the app installation page:

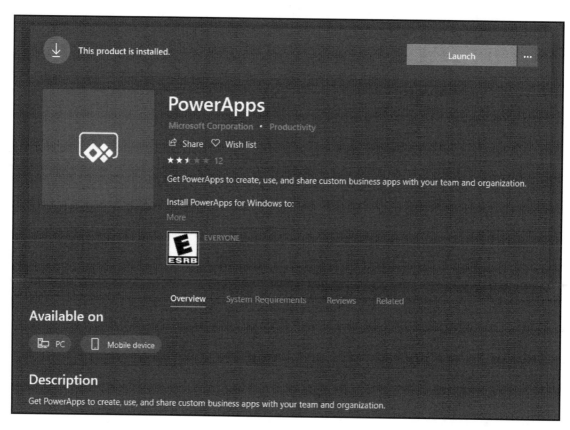

In Power Apps Studio, expanding the hamburger icon on the left side opens the slider containing the selection between a tree view of application elements or data sources. The following screenshot shows the expanded menu:

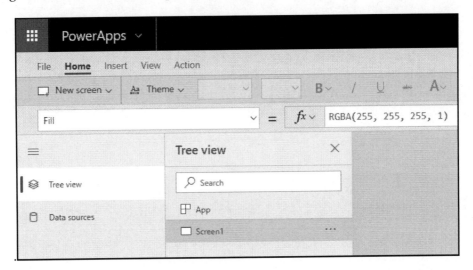

We want to use an Excel file stored on our personal OneDrive as a data source for this application. For this reason, we first need to do a little legwork to set everything up. Navigate to your OneDrive, create a folder called `PowerApps`, and create a new Excel file. We'll call this file `Customers.xlsx`.

Open the Excel file, and on the only sheet, create the following headers:

- `FirstName`
- `LastName`
- `PhoneNo`
- `EmailAddress`

Select the four columns, and from the ribbon, select **Format as Table**. You need to have a formatted table in Excel in order to use the data in Power Apps.

Select a layout and your screen should look as in the following screenshot:

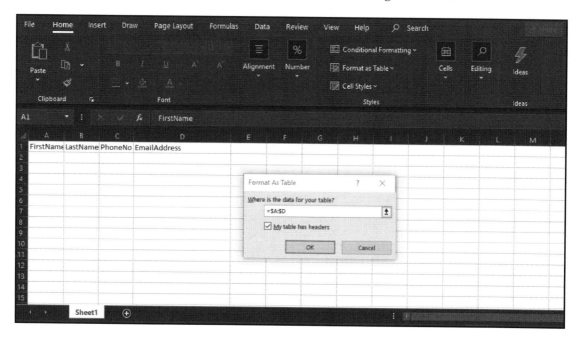

Select **OK** and your table will now be formatted. Give this table the name of the customer. For this example, I'm also adding a new tab with another table.

Make sure you have saved your file, and let's go back to building our canvas app.

Start on the **Data sources** tab to create a new connection to our Excel file. Remember that this file is stored on our personal OneDrive.

Expand **Connectors** in the left navigation, as in the following screenshot:

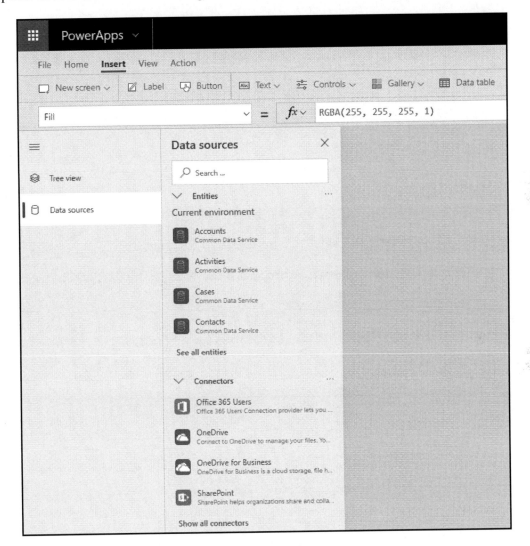

If OneDrive does not show in the quick connectors list, select **Show all connectors** and find the personal OneDrive option. Select **OneDrive** and select the option to add a new connection.

The **Connect to data** wizard starts and allows you to set up a connection to your OneDrive, as presented here:

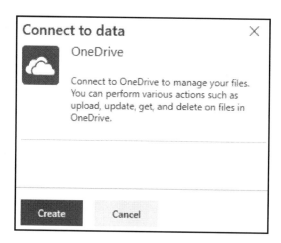

Log in when prompted. You are next prompted to browse and select the Excel target file. Remember we called it Customers.xlsx.

The next step is to select the table we want to use as the data source. The following screenshot shows the selection with the table named **Customers** as an option. Therefore, it's important to give the correct name to the tables in Excel. Here, we see the wizard selection screen:

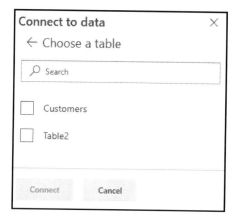

Select the table and then choose **Connect**. Now, your newly created connection will appear in **Data sources** under the **In your app** expanded section, as in the following screenshot:

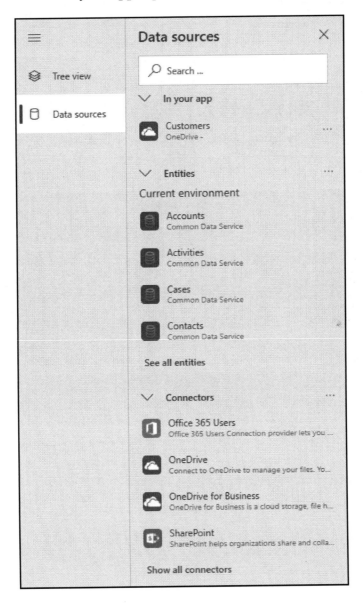

In order to display the contents of our Excel table, let's add a form to the screen design:

1. Select **Insert** from the menu.
2. Find the **Forms** option.
3. Select **Edit** to insert an editable form. Your design should look as in the following screenshot:

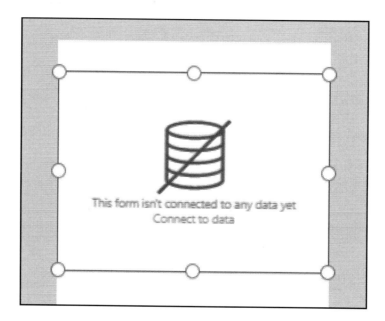

From the **Properties** blade on the right side of the screen, for **Data source**, select the **Customers** connection we created earlier. In **Fields**, select **Edit fields** to define which fields we want to have displayed on this form.

Your selection should look as shown here:

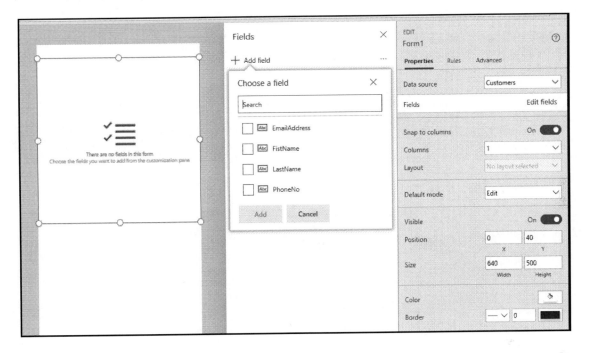

You can choose to select some or all the available fields. If you only select the first and last name, along with the email address, your form will look as in the following screenshot:

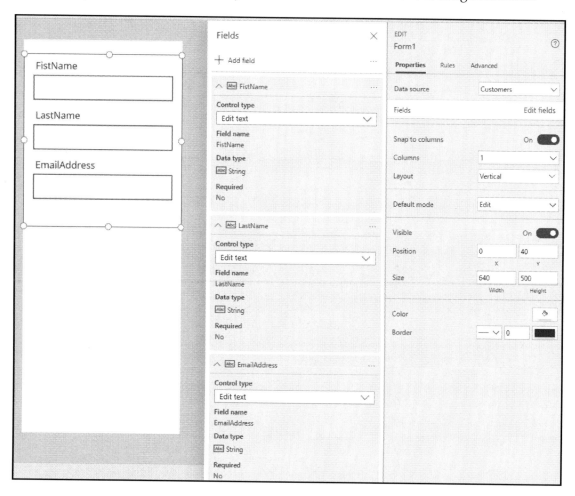

Make sure also to set **Default mode** to **New**. This will open the form by default with a blank form, allowing the user to add a new record.

From the **Insert** menu at the top, select to also add a button to the form. We'll call this button Submit.

Now comes the fun part. Let's wire this all together. With the **Submit** button selected, find the function definition and type in the following statement:

```
SubmitForm(Form1)
```

The following screenshot shows the entire configuration:

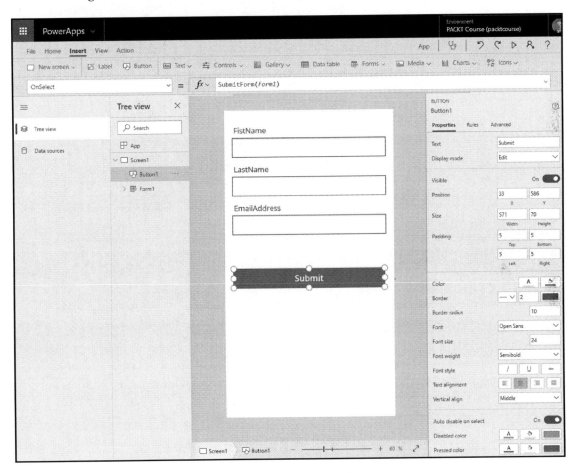

You can now run the application by finding the play button at the top-right side of the editor. The application will present the following screen to a user:

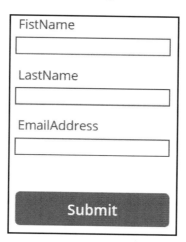

Enter some values in the form and click on **Submit**. Once done, check the Excel file to confirm the data you entered is added. My file looks like so:

This was a very simple example. With a large number of connectors and the functionality available to add various controls and create formula-like actions, you have the ability to create new canvas apps as complex or as simple as you need.

Don't forget to save your application by going to **File** | **Save as** and giving the app a name. Select **Save** when done:

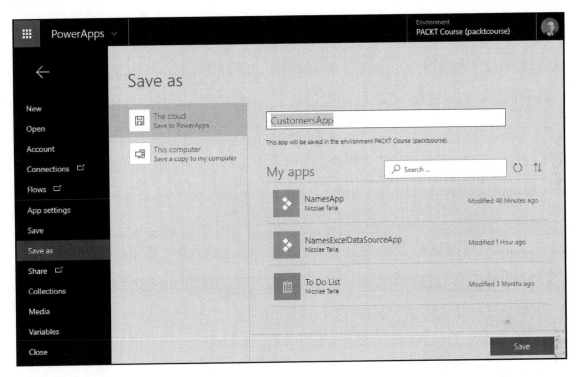

Microsoft provides extensive documentation on creating, maintaining, and extending canvas apps. I would recommend starting from the Power Apps maker documentation, available at `https://docs.microsoft.com/en-us/powerapps/#pivot=homepanel=maker`.

Creating a model-driven app

As opposed to canvas apps, where the app maker has complete control over the application layout, in model-driven apps, the focus is on leveraging predefined components to create a **Line Of Business (LOB)** application. Some of the benefits of this application type include the following:

- Leverage a component-focused application design, with a responsive layout that remains consistent across multiple devices.
- The design of the apps is similar to creating a configuration in Dynamics 365.
- Applications can be packaged and distributed as solutions.

There are three major steps in creating a model-driven application. They are as follows:

- Business data modeling
- Business process definition
- Application composition

A model-driven application will leverage CDS. You can leverage the default entities available with CDS, as well as add your own custom entities. Once you have the data model complete, you can move on to defining the specific business processes. You do this through business process flows and business logic. Finally, when you have these pieces in place, you can define the user interface using the app designer.

Let's build a simple application and see how these pieces fall together to form a model-driven application:

1. In the maker portal, available at `https://make.powerapps.com`, select the **Create** option from the left-side navigation. From the options presented, select **Model-driven app from blank**, as shown in the following screenshot:

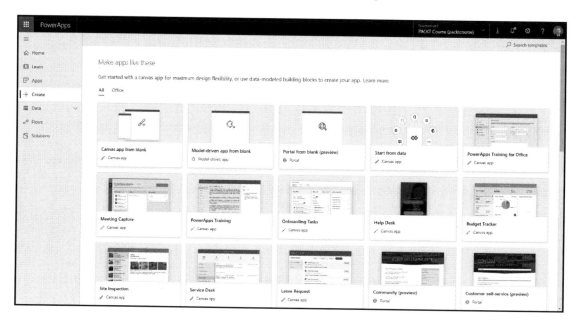

2. This starts the wizard, allowing you to commence working on your application. Select **Create** on the pop-up window:

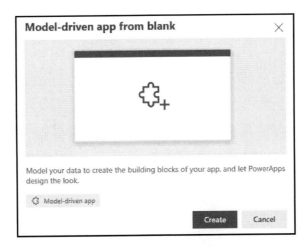

The wizard continues with the definition of the app name and properties. The following screenshot shows the app definition screen of the model-driven application:

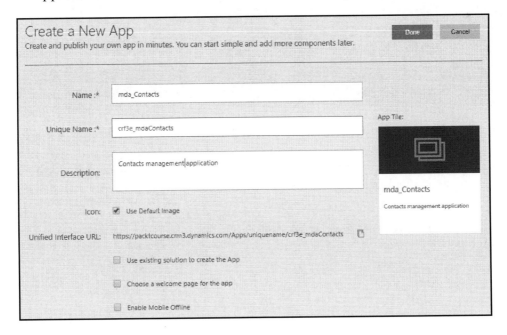

3. When you have completed all the fields, select **Create** to generate the new application.

From this point on, you should be familiar with the interface, as this is the exact same interface as the one we use to configure apps in Dynamics 365. You are presented with the app designer, which allows you to configure the site map, which is the application navigation, the various dashboards, and business process flows, as well as adding the various entities to be used in the application. The following screenshot shows the app designer on a newly created blank model-driven app:

The main components of the designer include the top menu bars, with options to save, validate, and publish, along with the application menu with options to add, edit, and remove items from the application. The main designer window includes the standard view of all components making up the application.

Finally, on the right side, we find the options to add various components to the application, as well as edit and modify component properties.

Let's start by first adding the **Contact** entity to our application. Select the **Entities** option from the **ARTIFACTS** listing. This presents you with a listing of available entities from CDS, as seen here:

Here, you can select an entity by browsing to it from the available entities listing, or by searching for a particular entity.

Searching for and selecting the **Contact** entity adds it to the application, as reflected on the main application screen. The following screenshot shows this action:

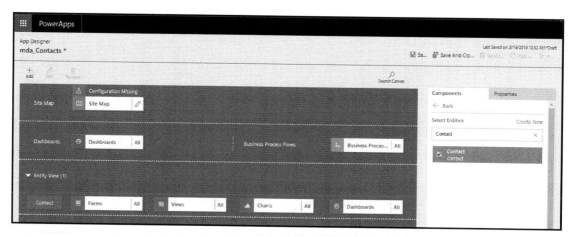

You can use this approach to add multiple entities at the same time. Observe, though, that, along with each entity, we are bringing in all the entity definition elements. Here, we make a very important decision. Do we need to carry in our application all these elements? We can go and edit, for example, the list of views. Selecting **Views** on the designer window shows, on the right-side blade, the Contact views available. You can leave the **All** checkbox selected to add all the elements or choose them one by one. It is recommended to only keep in the application the elements that are strictly needed.

The next screenshot shows this selection choice:

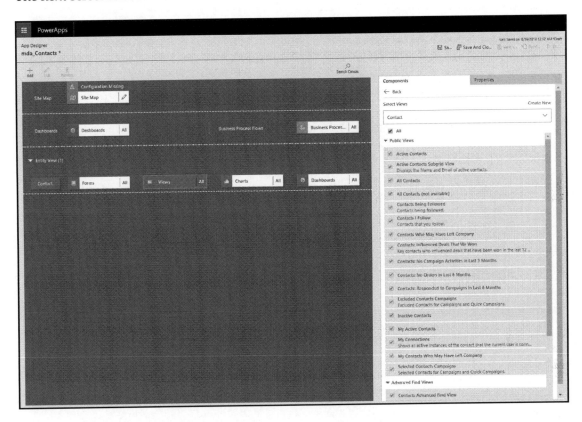

Looking at the site map, we can observe a warning presented by the app designer, along with the **Configuration Missing** message. This is because a certain level of validation takes place as you design your application. The screenshot here shows this message:

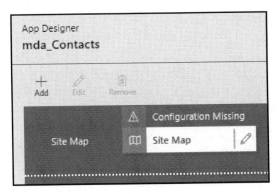

You will see this message on a newly created app since we have not defined the site map properties yet. Select the pen icon to the right of the site map. This presents you with a site map designer screen, as seen here:

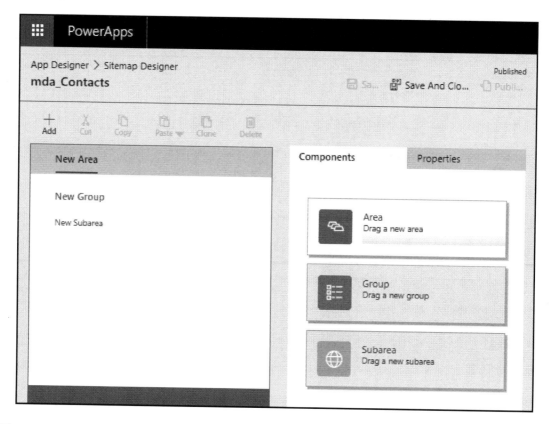

Here, you can start defining the application navigation. Observe the similarities with the configuration for Dynamics 365. You define the three major elements:

- **Area**: The main navigational category; a container for the other elements.
- **Group**: One or more groups can be defined per area, allowing you to categorize subareas.
- **Subarea**: The individual entity links.

You can drag any of these elements to the navigation or edit the existing elements. Selecting the new area's top elements allows us to edit its properties, as in the following screenshot. We have edited the title to show **Customers**:

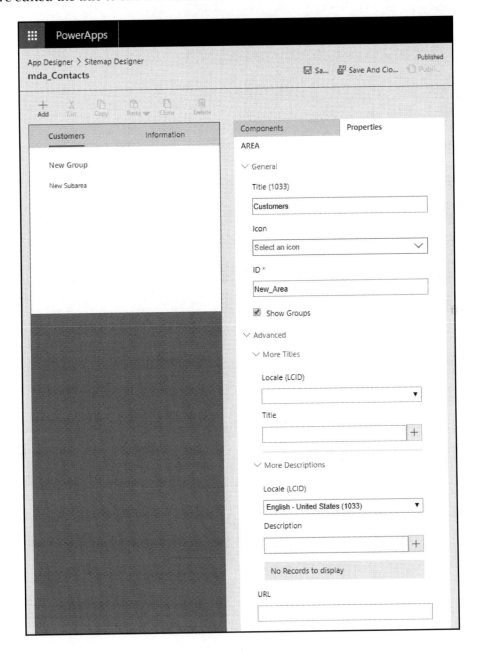

When defining the subarea, which points to an actual entity in CDS, we have a slightly more complex list of properties. We need to select the type, including options for **Entities**, **Dashboards**, **Web Resources**, or **URLs**. Selecting an entity allows selecting the data store entity to be linked to, as in the following screenshot:

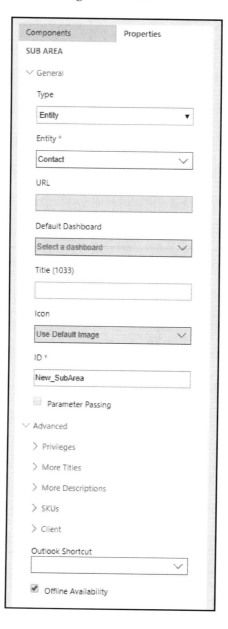

When satisfied with the configuration of your new site map, select the option to save. Note that once you are ready to present the new navigation, you must select **Publish** from the top navigation to move the site map from draft mode to published. The following screenshot shows the final published site map:

Once you return to your app designer, you should save and validate the app. If any other validation errors are encountered, select and resolve each one before publishing the app.

When done designing the app, publish it to make it available to the organization. You do that from the same top-right menu, as shown here:

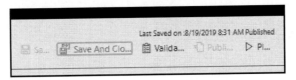

Finally, test your application by selecting the play option on the far right of this menu. Your newly created application will open in a new browser window and will present you with the familiar Dynamics 365 user interface:

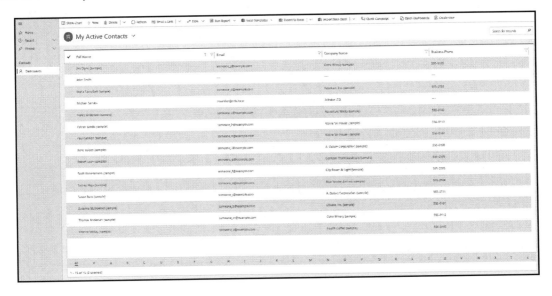

Congratulations! Now you have created a Power Apps model-driven app, albeit a very simplistic one.

For additional details and to learn more about creating model-driven apps, check the Microsoft documentation, available at `https://docs.microsoft.com/en-us/powerapps/` `#pivot=homepanel=maker`.

Understanding CDS

CDS is a relatively new paradigm created by Microsoft. It describes a storage mechanism for data in the cloud. This data is to be used and shared across multiple business applications.

CDS is currently at the core of Dynamics 365. The entire former CRM stack, now comprising of separate applications for Sales, Customer Service, Marketing, Field Service, and PSA, share the same CDS.

Within CDS, data is stored in a set of entities. From a programming perspective, you can think of comparing it to classes. Each entity represents an object type. Some common entities are **Account**, **Contact**, **Lead**, and so on.

You can think of entities as tables in a database or sheets in an Excel spreadsheet. The entity defines the model, the columns of the table. The individual records make up the data stored in these entities.

While CDS includes some standard entities that are typically used and shared across multiple applications, you can always create your new custom entities.

The licensing model covers in different ways the use of custom versus standard entities.

Power Apps application makers can create new applications leveraging the data model in CDS. There are two distinct licenses available for Power Apps. Plan 1 is geared primarily toward user creating canvas apps, while plan 2 is geared toward more complex needs, including model-driven apps with custom code and workflows.

For those learning to use Power Apps, there is also a Community plan, which is free. The licensing guide, refreshed with every biannual release, provides all the licensing details you need. At the time of writing, the most current licensing guide is the one released in August 2019 and is available for download at `https://go.microsoft.com/fwlink/p/?LinkId=866544`.

Where CDS differs from a normal database is in its ability to model a business definition for your organization in a much easier way. This model is easy to manage, through a visual interface and no code. Security is also applied by default, and you must manage permissions to allow users access to your data.

CDS is based on a rich set of metadata. This allows the creation of entity relationships and defining specific data types.

Most importantly, CDS powers a rich set of applications. From the custom application, you can create either a canvas app or model-driven apps; to Dynamics 365 solutions, CDS is at the core. You get to choose how complex your apps are, and if you need to create apps through the provided visual tools or you want to develop custom code applications, CDS can span across all these models and allows great flexibility.

Along with the data model, you can leverage a large set of connectors. These connectors allow integration with other LOB applications. There are hundreds of these connectors available, and you can extend and build your own connectors for specialized applications. Some of the most common available connectors include connectors to all the Microsoft applications, along with connectors to some of the most popular third-party applications. For example, if you want to integrate with tools such as Twitter, Slack, Wunderlist, Google Drive, or other storage platforms, as well as various blogging platforms and others, chances are there's already a connector built.

The power of this platform comes from its ability to connect with a large number of already-existing applications, as well as the ability to customize connectors for new ones. There are over 200 connectors available, and that number is growing rapidly.

The following screenshot shows only a few of the available connections supported by the existing connectors:

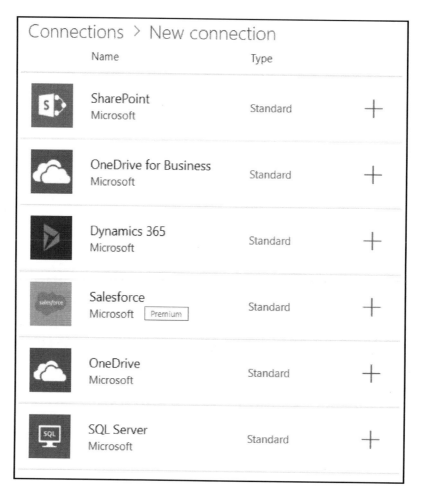

Further to the existing connectors Microsoft is also offering a set of application templates based on the various existing connectors. When you select to create a new application, you can choose to use CDS at the core, but also leverage other connectors. You can select from various application templates, as shown in the following screenshot:

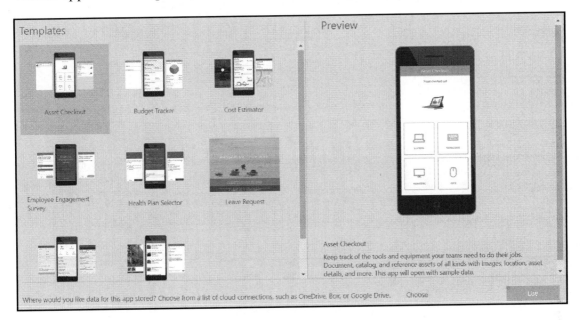

Along with Power Apps creation, if you choose to leverage Flow, it also takes the advantage of the existing connectors and possibly CDS. When creating flows, you can choose to tap into these services supported by the connectors. The following screenshot shows a list of the most popular services available:

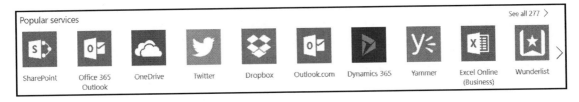

Flow actually takes this approach even further, by providing templates for connectivity. The next screenshot shows some of the connectivity templates available:

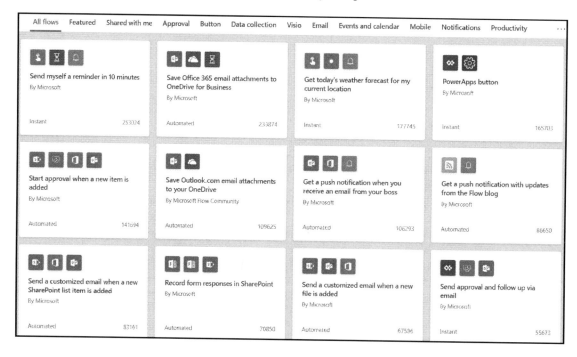

As mentioned, CDS is all about structuring data based on entities. Navigate to the maker interface, available at `https://make.powerapps.com`.

Once you log in, you can find the listing of available entities by going into **Data** | **Entities**. The following screenshot shows you the navigation elements:

Selecting the **Entities** option presents you with a listing of all the entities, as in the following screenshot:

Entities

Entity ↑ ⌄		Name ⌄	Type ⌄	Customizable ⌄	Tags ⌄
Account	⋯	account	Standard	✓	Master
Address	⋯	customeraddress	Standard	✓	Standard
Appointment	⋯	appointment	Standard	✓	Productivity
Attachment	⋯	activitymimeattachment	Standard	✓	Productivity
Business Unit	⋯	businessunit	Standard	✓	Standard
Contact	⋯	contact	Standard	✓	Master
Currency	⋯	transactioncurrency	Standard	✓	Standard
Email	⋯	email	Standard	✓	Productivity
Email Template	⋯	template	Standard	✓	Standard
Fax	⋯	fax	Standard	✓	Productivity
Feedback	⋯	feedback	Standard	✓	KB
Knowledge Article	⋯	knowledgearticle	Standard	✓	Standard
Letter	⋯	letter	Standard	✓	Productivity
Mailbox	⋯	mailbox	Standard	✓	Configuration
Organization	⋯	organization	Standard	✓	System
Phone Call	⋯	phonecall	Standard	✓	Standard
Position	⋯	position	Standard	✓	System

Clicking on any of the available entities allows you to see the definition, with the available fields and data types, as well as other metadata. The following screenshot shows the **Account** entity fields and properties:

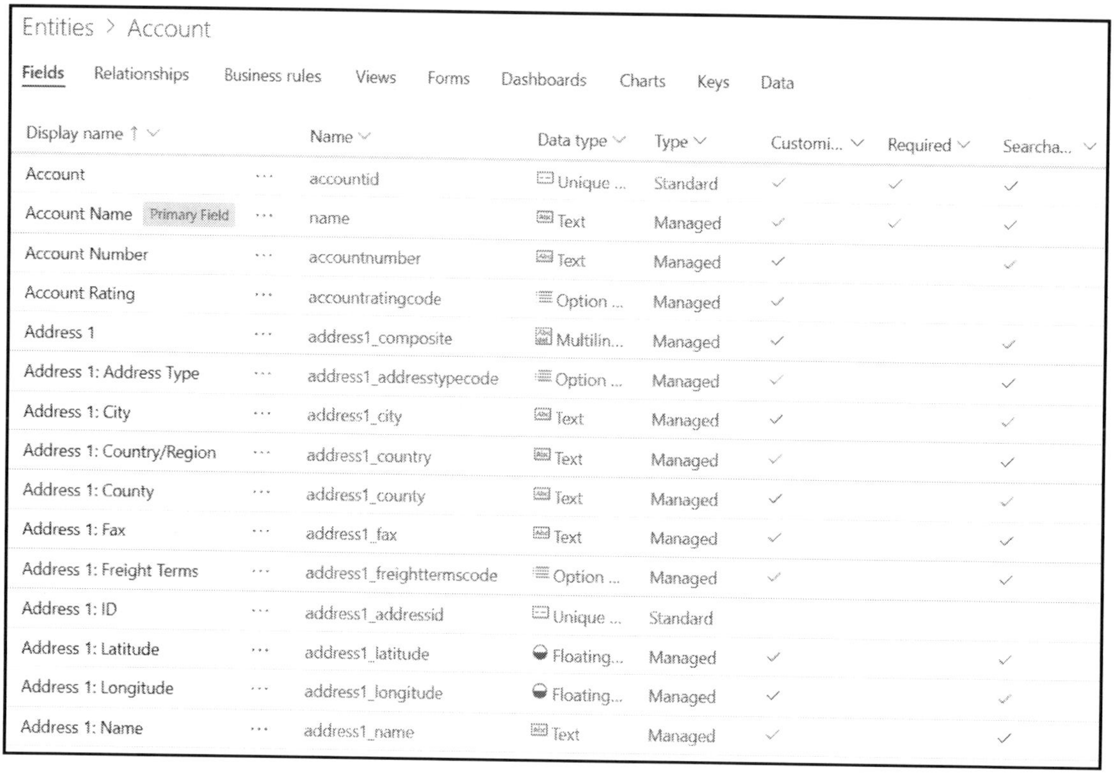

Entities > Account

Fields	Relationships	Business rules	Views	Forms	Dashboards	Charts	Keys	Data

Display name ↑ ∨	Name ∨	Data type ∨	Type ∨	Customi... ∨	Required ∨	Searcha... ∨
Account ⋯	accountid	Unique ...	Standard	✓	✓	✓
Account Name Primary Field ⋯	name	Text	Managed	✓	✓	✓
Account Number ⋯	accountnumber	Text	Managed	✓		✓
Account Rating ⋯	accountratingcode	Option ...	Managed	✓		
Address 1 ⋯	address1_composite	Multilin...	Managed	✓		✓
Address 1: Address Type ⋯	address1_addresstypecode	Option ...	Managed	✓		✓
Address 1: City ⋯	address1_city	Text	Managed	✓		✓
Address 1: Country/Region ⋯	address1_country	Text	Managed	✓		✓
Address 1: County ⋯	address1_county	Text	Managed	✓		✓
Address 1: Fax ⋯	address1_fax	Text	Managed	✓		✓
Address 1: Freight Terms ⋯	address1_freighttermscode	Option ...	Managed	✓		✓
Address 1: ID ⋯	address1_addressid	Unique ...	Standard			
Address 1: Latitude ⋯	address1_latitude	Floating...	Managed	✓		✓
Address 1: Longitude ⋯	address1_longitude	Floating...	Managed	✓		✓
Address 1: Name ⋯	address1_name	Text	Managed	✓		✓

From the top ribbon, selecting the option to add a field allows you to extend the entity definition through a simple user interface, and with no complex SQL statements or other code. The following screenshot shows the **Add field** side blade properties:

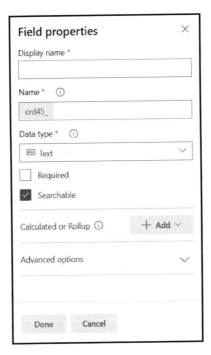

To make things even easier, on the top ribbon, you also get an option to edit data in Excel. The ribbon is shown here:

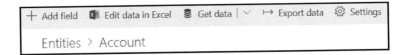

The ability to directly interact with the data, using the same user interface, makes it so much easier to manage your current applications. Once you have your data in Excel, you can make easy modifications, do bulk edits, and then use the **Get data** option to bring those updates into your CDS.

One big advantage of working in CDS, and this is something that former CRM customizers are already familiar with, is the ability to work with solutions. You can manage solutions by navigating from the left-side navigation to **Solutions**. Here, you will find all your existing solutions already deployed in the environment, as well as the ability to create new solutions, import solutions, publish customizations, as well as get the solution checked, which does an analysis of the solutions selected and provides recommendations on things to review and improve in your existing customizations. The following screenshot shows the **Solutions** area, along with some of the standard solutions installed in this environment, and the ribbon options for managing solutions:

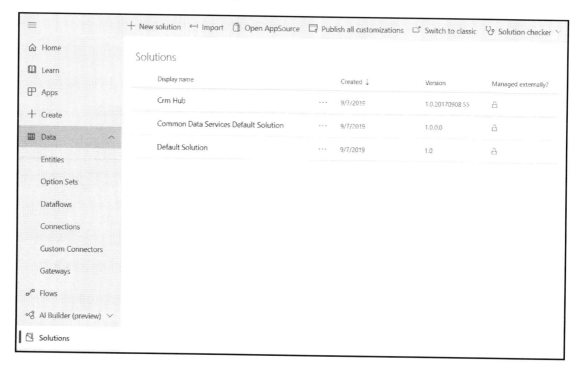

This is also the new interface used by the Dynamics 365 solution manager, in case you switched from the classical interface to the modern one.

Extending the ellipsis on a solution provides you with additional solution management options, as shown in the following screenshot:

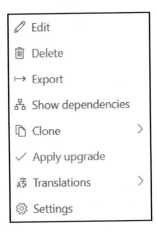

These should also be familiar options for solution management that you have seen while customizing any former CRM system.

Now that we have seen how to create both canvas and model-driven apps, let's look next at how we can present the data to external users through the use of Portals.

Leveraging Power Apps Portals

Power Apps Portals, or Portals for short, is a relatively new feature added in 2019. At the time of writing, this feature is still in preview, but for those that have used the CRM Portal features, it should look familiar.

Basically, we now have the same portal functionality that has been available in Dynamics 365 brought over to the masses in Power Apps. This opens a new world of possibilities, by allowing us to create applications leveraging CDS and exposed to the public through a simple-to-implement portal.

This tool is also targeted at makers – non-developers. Applications with an external-facing website can be exposed to non-organization users, leveraging various identity mechanisms or anonymously. The **Content Management System (CMS)** features of the portal, along with the ability to leverage the other Power Apps tools, now allows the easy creation of various low- to medium-complexity apps with no developer experience needed. A very powerful feature indeed.

Navigating in the Power Apps maker interface to **Create**, you will find the option to create a portal application from blank, as in the following screenshot:

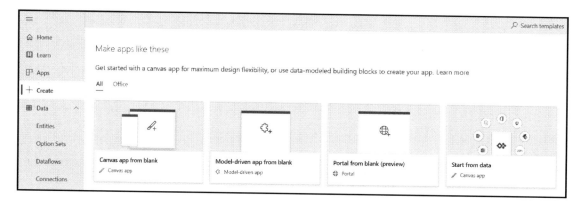

Selecting the **Portal from blank (preview)** option triggers the portal creation wizard, as shown:

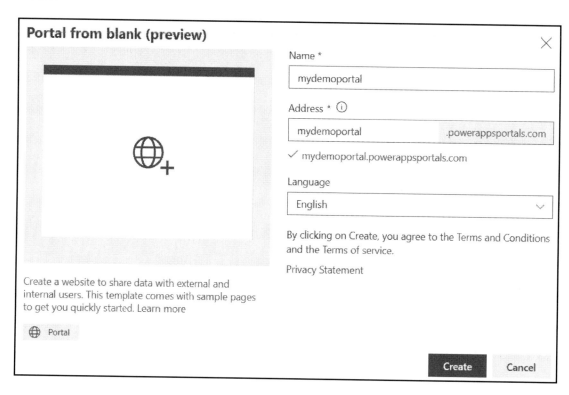

Select a unique name that gets validated and follow the wizard steps to complete the setup. Once you click on **Create**, the portal provisioning process starts, and you are notified of the status, as shown:

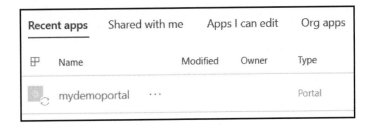

You can check the status of the provisioning process by navigating to **Apps**. Here, you will find the portal grayed out while it's provisioning, as in the following screenshot:

This process will take a couple of minutes, so grab a coffee while you wait.

> There are several portal solutions offered, including a community, a customer self-service, a partner, an employee self-service, and, recently added, a customer portal option. A portal from blank allows us to start from scratch with minimal unnecessary configurations.

When done, you are able to navigate to the portal solution by selecting it from the **Apps** screen, or expanding the ellipsis and selecting **Browse**.

You are taken to a new portal branded with the default template, as in the following screenshot:

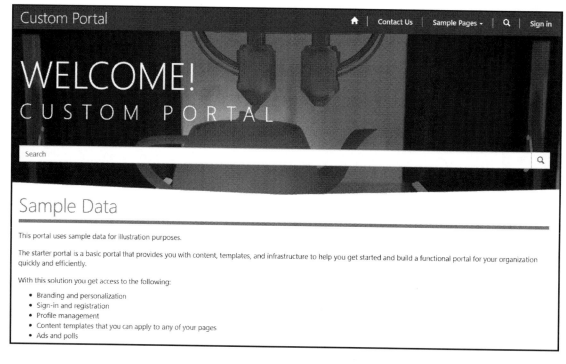

From this point on, you can start customizing and extending the portal. I recommend you see the documentation on portal customization available at docs.microsoft.com.

Let's have a look next at some automation options available through the creation of flows in Power Automate.

Leveraging Microsoft Power Automate flows

Have you ever used IFTTT on your mobile device? If so, then Flow will look familiar, but a lot more useful. Microsoft Power Automate flows allow you to create automation rules and integrate various applications and services. Flows can be triggered automatically or manually and execute within your application or across multiple applications. The most basic example is an approval process, where you need email notifications, user actions, and the ability to store the result set.

As I mentioned before in this chapter, while discussing CDS, Flow is the glue that ties together various aspects of an application.

Within the maker experience in Power Apps, you can navigate from the left navigation to **Flows**, as in the following screenshot:

Here, you are presented with a listing of exiting flows that you or your team has already created and shared, or the ability to create a new flow.

Selecting **New** from the top ribbon presents the following options, as in the following screenshot:

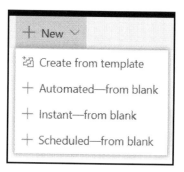

If you select the **Create from template** option, and then choose **See more templates**, you are presented with a listing of available quick templates that you can leverage to quickly create a flow. Some of them leverage Microsoft products, while others span across other applications, such as various social networks or third-party tools. The following screenshot shows but a small example of the templates available:

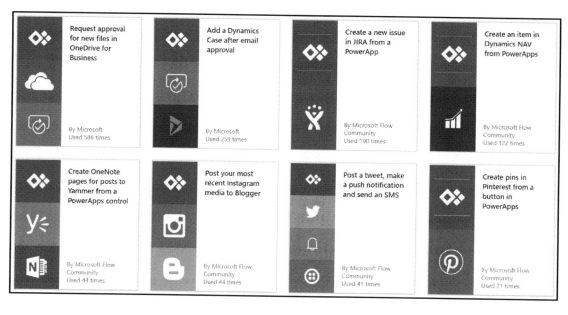

Choosing to build a flow from blank allows you to select the specific properties through a wizard interface. The first selection is the ability to choose a trigger for your flow. This is typically an action in an application or a request to an endpoint that is exposed. The following screenshot shows this selection wizard step:

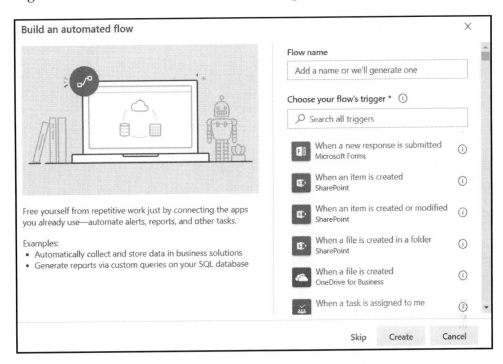

Depending on the selection, your first step is populated in the user interface. You will need to select the specifics of the trigger. For example, if I define my trigger to be the creation of an account record in CDS, my trigger will look as in the following screenshot:

Click on **+New Step** to define the following actions. Let's say we want to wait for 5 minutes before executing the next action. We can search for the **Delay** action and define in this step the delay properties, as shown:

Let's add a new step afterward. We want to send an email with some of the account information. Select **+New Step** again. Select from the options or search for `Mail`. Find the **Send an email notification** option and select it.

Here, we need to populate the specifics. You can leverage the **Dynamic content** option to read information from the account that was just created. We want to send the email to the primary email address on the account. Your selection looks as in the following screenshot:

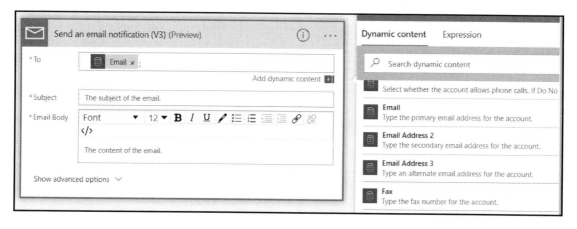

Same with the subject – we want to add some text and the newly created account number. In the body, leveraging the same approach, we can provide some of the information we collected for validation. Your complete email form could look something as in the following screenshot:

Once you are satisfied with your newly created flow, make sure to save it. At a high level, the flow we just created looks as in the following screenshot:

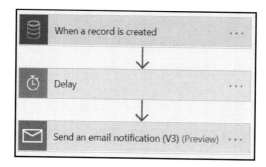

Select the **Flow Checker** option at the top right to validate that the steps created are logically correct. Your output should show no errors, and hopefully no warnings either.

The following screenshot shows the output for the flow we just created:

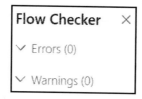

Finally, with the flow created, it's time to test it. Select the **Test** option from the top-right ribbon. Since this is the first run, you can only choose to perform the trigger manually. Select **Save & Test**:

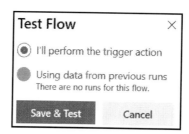

Now, to trigger the test, add an account record to your CDS. You will see the status of your flow in the running state until complete, as in the following screenshot:

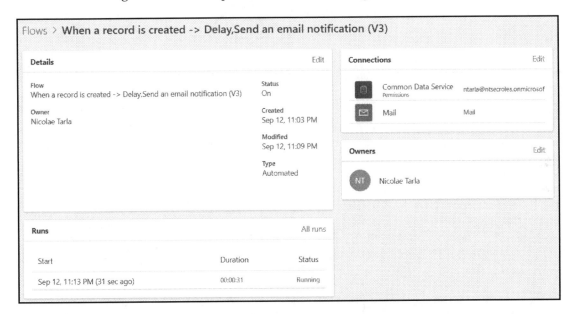

Finally, when the run completes, you will find the status updated. If all is good, your status should show **Succeeded**, as in the following **Run history** window:

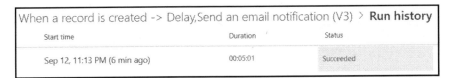

Check also for an email notification with the details provided. It should look as in the following screenshot:

Now we have a fully functional flow that notifies the new account owner when a record was added to CDS. It's all done through configuration alone, without a single line of code. This means that any user with permissions can do this.

Now that we have come to the end of this topic, let's summarize what we have learned in this chapter.

Summary

Throughout this chapter, we learned how to create a small, targeted application with great flexibility and speed. We learned that the no-code/low-code approach really pays off and has an important role in any business.

We looked at the various personas involved with the process of creating and using Power Apps, the process to create Power Apps, the types of available Power Apps, including canvas and model-driven apps, the role CDS plays in the bigger scheme of things, the ability to create public web-based solutions leveraging portals, and finally, how to tie it all together by leveraging **Flow**. (currently known as **Power Automate**)

In the next chapter, we're moving on to core configuration and customization concepts. With an understanding of the core applications, and the ability to build additional apps, we now have the necessary toolset to see how we can get more out of this great flexible platform.

Customizing Dynamics 365 **9**

In previous chapters, we looked at the various applications available in Dynamics 365 Customer Engagement. The platform includes features for Sales, Customer Service, Field Service, **Project Service Automation (PSA)**, and the new Marketing applications. Usually, though, we tackle a new project that falls outside of these applications. Yes, it might integrate with one or more of these applications, leveraging some or all of their functionality, but the scope is so different that it does not fall within any of these functional offerings. Or maybe we just need to extend one of the existing applications with new functionality and modify its existing functionality – who knows?

In any case, having the ability to modify, configure, and customize the platform is what makes it so much more valuable. You can think of Dynamics 365 as a rapid development platform where you can use either no code or little code to build something totally new.

This chapter will focus on introducing a couple of new concepts. We will spend some time building your knowledge and understanding of the following topics:

- Solution package
- Entity elements
- Business versus custom entities
- Extending entities
- Recording images
- Entity forms, quick view, and quick create forms
- Entity views and charts
- Entity relationships
- Composite fields
- SLAs and the timer control
- Geolocation

We will continue our journey by reviewing the customization options and finding out how can we extend the core system to fit new business requirements. Keep in mind that an application is only good if it supports your business. If it becomes too cumbersome to use, it starts too slowly, or blocks your business, then it will lose on the user adoption front and fade into the unknown.

So, let's dive right in!

Exploring the solution package

When talking about customizations for Microsoft Dynamics 365, one of the most important concepts is the solution package. The solution package is a container for all customizations. This packaging method allows customizers to export customizations and reimport them into other environments, as well as group-specific sets of customizations by business functionality or project cycle. Managing solutions is an aspect that should not be taken lightly because, down the road, a properly designed solution packaging model can help a lot or create difficulties.

As mentioned previously, solutions are used to pack a set of features together. They are used to extend the core functionality of the platform through grouped sets of features.

Solutions that contain only Dynamics 365-specific configuration or features can be imported directly into Dynamics 365 using the default solution management framework and the interface provided. For complex solutions that contain both Dynamics 365 solution components as well as other external components, an installer solution is required. One such example is if you provide a custom solution that includes customization of Dynamics 365 to store additional data, as well as maybe a portal or any other kind of application to allow this data to be captured through the use of the standard API. For such a solution, an installer application can be created to deploy all customizations together. This type of scenario is outside the scope of this book and requires a development group or qualified partner to assist with this.

Solutions are created specific to a version of the Dynamics 365 platform. At the time of writing, the Dynamics 365 platform is at version 9.1. There are several previous versions. Usually, a solution exported from a specific version can be imported into the same version or a newer version of the platform. As a rule of thumb, try to keep the solutions within two versions of the exported version in order to minimize the impact of changes introduced by newer versions. The platform is smart enough to enforce version control and does not allow you to load a solution that's too old into a recent platform version. You typically have to go through an incremental upgrade process.

In the next section, we'll look at the components of the solution package, followed by some more aspects related to it in the subsequent sections.

Components of a solution package

Solutions are comprised of a few core components. These components are created using the customization tools available or the APIs provided. These components are part of the following applications:

- Solution schemas are definitions of system entities, attributes, and relationships. They also include a definition of global option sets.
- User interface elements are items such as the application ribbon, the site map, entity ribbons, the definition of entity forms, as well as web resources.
- Analytics elements include things such as graphs, dashboards, and reports.
- Templates are definitions used for Mail-merge, Emails, Contracts, and Knowledge Base Articles.
- The security model definitions include the various security roles, as well as the definition of field-level security profiles.
- Processes and code elements include the definition of processes, as well as custom code elements. We will not cover custom code elements in this book, but we will have a look at the various process types later.

All these solution components can be included in all solutions. They are defined in a solution exported as a ZIP file.

Opening such a solution file shows the following three XML files:

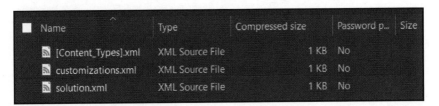

Name	Type	Compressed size	Password p...	Size
[Content_Types].xml	XML Source File	1 KB	No	
customizations.xml	XML Source File	1 KB	No	
solution.xml	XML Source File	1 KB	No	

The first file lists the available customized content types, if any. The solution.xml file contains the following elements:

- Solution definition data
- Version
- Platform version

- Solution name and properties
- Publisher details
- Components
- Missing dependencies

With each solution created, a publisher is required. This is usually the partner or group providing the solution. This information is stored in a publisher entity.

Multiple publishers can exist at the same time, customized on each deployment, but only one at a time can be associated with a solution.

Dependencies are related to solution items. For example, a component could require elements from another entity. This other entity does not necessarily have to be included in the solution. When it is not, a missing dependency is recorded in the solution. When deploying the solution, a check is done on the target system whether determine if the missing dependency is installed on the target by another solution. If it is not found, a missing dependency error is thrown, and the installation is aborted.

The last element of a solution is the `customizations.xml` file. This is the meat of the solution, and it includes all the elements that have been added to the solution. The document is structured by entity but also includes details about the other solution components described earlier.

Analyzing the contents of these `xml` files is beyond the scope of this book, but additional details on working with solutions can be found in the MSDN documentation available at `https://msdn.microsoft.com/en-us/library/gg334530.aspx`.

Next, we will look at the different types of solutions.

Types of solutions

Within the context of Dynamics 365, there are two types of solutions:

- Unmanaged solutions
- Managed solutions

Each of these solution types has its own strengths and properties, and it is recommended that they're used in various circumstances. We'll explore these in the subsequent sections!

Unmanaged solutions

Unmanaged solution is the default state of a solution. A solution is unmanaged while customization work is being performed in the context of the solution. An unmanaged solution is not necessarily intended to be distributed as such. It is a way for developers and system customizers to group their customizations during development. When the work is completed and the unmanaged solution is ready to be distributed, it can be packed as a managed solution.

On an unmanaged solution, the system customizer can perform various tasks. These include the following:

- Adding and removing components
- Deleting components that allow deletion
- Exporting and importing the solution as an unmanaged solution
- Exporting the solution as a managed solution

Changes that are made to components in a particular unmanaged solution are also applied to all unmanaged solutions that include those components.

Deleting an unmanaged solution results in the removal of the container alone, while the unmanaged components of the solution remain in the system.

Deleting a component in an unmanaged solution results in the deletion of that component from the system. To only remove a component from an unmanaged Solution without deleting it from the environment, that component should be removed and not deleted from the solution. This leaves the customization on the platform, and you can add it to another unmanaged solution as needed.

Managed solutions

Once work is completed on an unmanaged solution and the solution is ready to be distributed, it can be exported as a **managed solution**. Packaging a solution as a managed solution presents the following advantages:

- Solution components cannot be added or removed from a managed solution.
- A managed solution cannot be exported from the environment it was deployed in.
- Deleting a managed solution results in uninstalling all the component customizations included with the solution.

A managed solution cannot be installed in the same organization that contains the unmanaged solution that was used to create it.

Within a managed solution, certain components can be configured to allow further customization. Through this mechanism, the managed solution provider can enable future customizations so that aspects of the solution provided can be modified.

Overall, best practice recommends using an unmanaged solution throughout development and converting to a managed solution when promoting to production.

Solution publisher

Besides the solution type, each solution contains a **solution publisher**. This is a set of properties that allows the solution creators to communicate various information to the solution users, including ways to contact the publisher for additional support. The solution publisher record will be created in all organizations where the solution is being deployed.

The solution publisher record is also important when releasing an updated solution to an existing solution. Based on this common record, an updated solution can be released and deployed on top of an existing solution.

Solution layering

When multiple solutions are deployed in an organization, there are two methods by which the system defines the order in which changes take priority: **Merge** and **Top Wins**.

The user interface elements are merged by default. As such, elements such as forms, ribbons, command bars, and site maps are merged, and all base elements and new custom elements are rendered. For all other solution components, the Top Wins approach is taken, where the last solution to bring in customization takes precedence over the solution that was deployed previously.

The system checks for integrity on all solution exports, imports, and other operations. As such, when exporting a solution, a warning is presented if dependent entities are not included. The customizer has the option to ignore this warning.

When importing a solution, if the dependent entities are missing, the import is halted and the import fails. Also, deleting a component from a solution is prevented if dependent entities require it to be present.

For additional details and recommendations regarding solution layering, check out the MSDN documentation available at `https://docs.microsoft.com/en-us/dynamics365/customer-engagement/developer/introduction-solutions`.

Pay close attention to the layering diagram included in the documentation. This should give you a clear picture of how layering various solution types influences the behavior of the resulting environment.

Default solution

Dynamics CRM allows you to customize the system without taking advantage of solutions. By default, the system comes with a default solution. This is an unmanaged solution, and all system customizations applied outside the scope of a solution are applied to it.

The system solution includes all customizations defined within Microsoft Dynamics 365. This solution defines the default application behavior. Most of the components in this solution can be further customized.

Solution segmentation

One of the new great features added to Microsoft Dynamics CRM 2016 is the concept of solution segmentation. For the longest time, we have struggled with situations where a small change to an entity required us to deploy the entire entity definition, and run the risk of overriding changes that were made by newer solutions that were added to the system. This is where solution layering plays an important role in how we customize the system. Segmentation does not completely avoid these issues, but it greatly avoids the risk of possible issues when it is used properly. Let's have a closer look at how this works and what it does.

Let's assume we want to make changes to the account entity and add a new text field to capture the Twitter handle, and a new form called account details. With the new solution segmentation features available, I can now define a solution and include only these items. When deploying this solution, I do not have to worry about overriding any of the other views or field definitions.

When adding only these two items, when opening our solution and adding the account entity, we will be presented with a new intermediary screen:

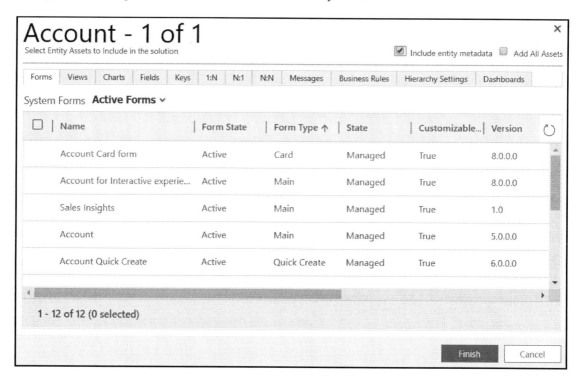

We can now see clearly how easy it is to navigate to the tab containing the type of customization we want to add, find the new field in this case, select it, and click **Finish** when we're done.

Two options to observe are at the top-right of this form. The **Add All Assets** option is unchecked. Checking this option basically puts you back to the solution options we had before this feature was available, where everything related to an entity was included in the solution. There are still cases where we want to select this option, such as for brand new entities that are added with our solution.

The other option is **Include entity metadata**. This option is checked by default and allows us to add all the entity definitions. It is recommended for it to be checked but be aware that it will make the solution file larger. For situations where no changes are done to the entity metadata, and the entity already exists in the target system, this option can be unchecked.

By taking a quick look at the entity that was added to the solution, we can now see the account entity that was added, but in the **Fields** section, we only see the newly added field:

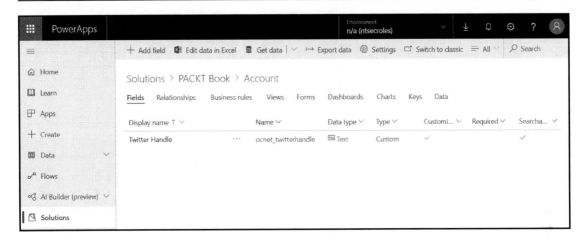

Everything's going well so far, but what if you already have an entity added to a solution and you just need to add a new custom element? No problem. From the solution definition, select the entity. Now, on the top ribbon, you will find an **Add Field** option. This allows you to do just that.

The **Add field** option opens a blade from the right called **Field properties**, where you can define the properties of the new field. The following screenshot shows this option:

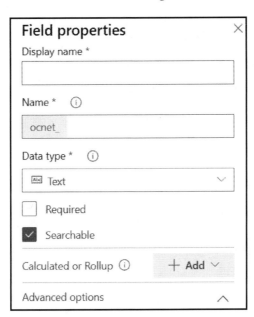

Expanding **Advanced options** shows you additional configurable properties, including a field description and, depending on the field data type, other properties.

Solution cloning and patching

Another great feature that's been added since the 2016 version of Dynamics 365 is the ability to create advanced scenarios when working with solutions. For the last few versions, Microsoft allowed us to associate version numbers with our solutions, but the solution package model was not aligned to the capabilities of proper versioning.

Starting with the 2016 version of Dynamics 365, we can take advantage of proper versioning and have more checks and bounds as to which items are incremental. But before we dig into cloning and patching, let's look at the standard versioning model provided. We've always seen recommendations to start versioning with a format of 1.0.0.0. This is basically a set of four numeric values. Over time, various standards have been released for versioning. One example includes a major version, a minor version, along with an alphanumeric string denoting the release type (alpha, beta, and so on). Another model includes the major and minor versions, followed by another numeric field denoting the change version.

The newer model strives to cover the complexities of newer software solutions. We've moved from three to four numeric values. Depending on the school of thought followed, they can denote *either* of the following:

- Major.Minor.Build.Revision
- Major.Minor.Maintenance.Build

There are other ways to create sequence-based software versioning, some of which are combinations of these described approaches.

With Dynamics 365, the onus to increment and confirm the version being used is still with the customizer creating and packaging the solution.

Solution cloning in Dynamics 365 has the ability to create a new version that increments the major and minor versions. As a process, this is done by selecting the **Clone solution** option on the expanded **Solutions** menu:

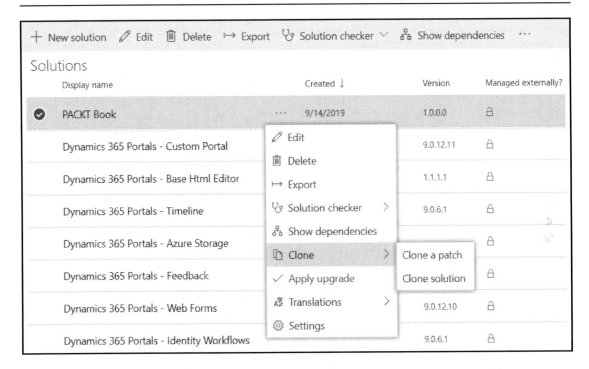

Selecting the **Clone solution** option brings up the following **Clone to solution** screen:

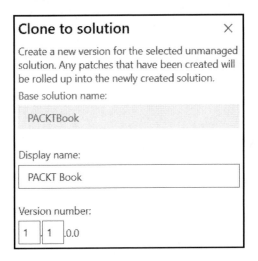

As you can see, when cloning a solution called PACKT Book, we can modify **Display name** if needed, as well as the major and minor version numbers.

One important aspect to understand is that cloning a solution basically creates a brand new solution, including the original solution and all the patches applied to it. The original solution, as well as the existing patches that are included, are then removed from the organization. Make sure you save the original solution and patches as needed before proceeding with cloning.

Solution patching is quite different in terms of behavior. It is triggered by clicking the **Clone a patch** menu option.

A patch is used for a small change or fix that has been released in-between regular release cycles. This, in most cases, is restricted to a small component being modified, and it is where we take advantage of solution segmentation. We can only include the definition of a field that changes properties, a view that is modified, and so on.

Once the **Clone to patch** command has been issued, the following window allows us to define the patch properties:

Clone to patch ✕

Create a patch for the selected unmanaged solution. A patch contains changes to the existing solution.

Base solution name:

PACKTBook

Display name:

PACKT Book

Version number:

1.0. | 1 | . | 0 |

Just like before, **Display name** can be edited as needed. However, only the last two versioning digits can be edited now.

You can create and deploy as many patches as needed before moving on to the next version.

One thing you will observe is that if the solution definition's xml file mentioned earlier in this chapter is opened, a reference to the base solution will be kept in the patch definition.

We will look at modifying entities next.

The elements that make up an entity definition

Within a solution, we work with various entities. In Dynamics 365, there are three main entity types:

- System entities
- Business entities
- Custom entities

Each entity is comprised of various attributes, while each attribute is defined as a value with a specific data type. We can think of an entity as a data table. Each row represents an entity record, while each column represents an entity attribute. As with any table, each attribute has specific properties that define its data type.

The system entities in Dynamics 365 are used internally by the application and are not customizable. They also cannot be deleted.

As a system customizer or developer, we will work mainly with Business entities and Custom entities. Business entities are the default entities that come with the application. They are customizable and can be extended as needed. Custom entities are all new entities that are created as part of our system customizations.

Aspects of customizing an entity include renaming the entity; modifying, adding, or removing entity attributes; and changing various settings and properties. We'll look at all these in detail in the subsequent sections.

Renaming an entity

One of the ways we can customize an entity is by renaming it. Selecting an Entity in the solution and then choosing the **Settings** option on the ribbon brings up the **Edit entity** blade on the right. The **Display name** field allows us to change the name of an entity. The **Plural display name** field can also be updated accordingly.

When renaming an entity, make sure all the references and messages are updated to reflect the new entity name. Views, charts, messages, business rules, and even certain fields could reference the original name, and they should be updated to reflect the new name that's been assigned to the entity.

The following screenshot shows the **Edit entity** options for the **Account** entity:

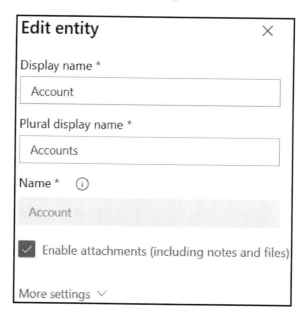

Pay close attention when modifying the properties of the default **Name** field of an entity. This is usually a required field. While it can be marked as not required and hidden from the form, the drawback to this approach is that this field is used in lookups to this entity. As such, if this field is not populated, your lookup will only show a multitude of blank record references. A better approach is to either re-label this field and use it to store record-specific distinct data or to hide it and create a process that automatically populates some specific information about each record. This way, all lookups will reflect the data in this field correctly and you will not run into any other issues.

Changing entity settings and properties

When creating and managing entities in Dynamics 365, there are generic entity settings that we must pay attention to. We can easily get to these settings and properties by navigating within a solution to an entity and selecting the **Settings** option from the ribbon. As we've just seen, you get an option to update the **Display name** and **Plural display name** fields, but also an option for **More settings**. If we expand that, we will see the following screen:

Further expanding each of those sections reveals a set of configurable properties for the entity. There's a total of five categories, with specific properties for each. We'll look at them in the subsequent sections.

Description

The **Description** area allows us to provide entity description text, in a multi-line text input area. The following screenshot shows this section expanded for the **Account** entity:

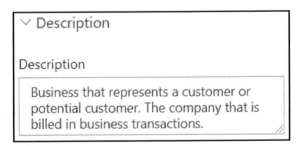

Let's look at the next option available under **More settings**.

Entity type and ownership

The **Entity type and ownership** section provides the definition of the type, as well as ownership configuration. Once an entity has been created, these settings can't be edited anymore. Pay attention to how you configure these options when creating a new entity. The following screenshot shows this section when creating a new entity:

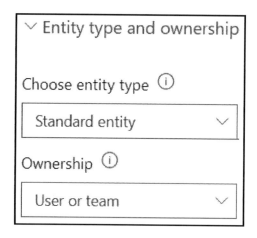

Regarding the entity type, you have a choice between defining this as a **Standard entity** or an **Activity entity**. **Ownership** can be configured as **User or team** or **Organization**. Depending on the **Ownership** type selected, the configuration of security roles will vary. Organizational owned entity records do not enforce the same security capabilities as user or team owned entities.

Collaboration

The **Collaboration** section holds configurable properties for enabling special entity properties such as activity tasks, connections, mail-merge, queues, and others. The following screenshot shows this section expanded:

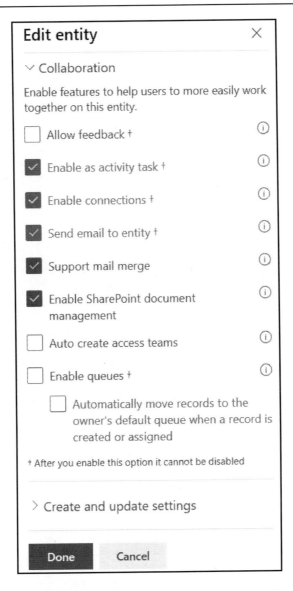

For additional details on each feature, you can simply select the information icon presented to the right of each element.

Note that some of these settings, once enabled, can't be disabled. This is because the entity definition is committed and you will need to remove and recreate the entity to modify these options. They are clearly marked with a cross (†) sign next to the name.

Creating and updating settings

This section deals with the ability to enable quick create forms, which are simplistic overlays that allow you to create a quick record from within another record; enable or disable duplicate detection, a feature used to notify a user when attempting to create a record that might already exist in the system; and finally. enable change tracking, which is used by Flow. The following screenshot shows this section expanded:

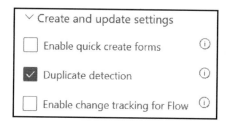

Now, let's understand the last option available under more settings.

Dynamics 365 for Outlook

Finally, this section allows you to control whether this entity is supported in offline mode in Outlook. This is a feature leveraged by the Outlook client to allow users to take data offline, such as when flying, making changes while offline, and then synchronizing the changes once back online.

The following screenshot shows this section expanded:

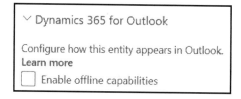

Now that we've seen the configurable general entity options, we need to understand where these options and properties might vary. We'll do that by looking at the differences between various entity types in Dynamics 365.

Business versus custom entities

As mentioned previously, there are two types of customizable entities in Dynamics 365:

- Business entities
- Custom entities

Business entities are customizable entities that are created by Microsoft and come as part of the default solution package. They are part of three modules: Sales, Service, and Marketing. Custom entities are all the new entities that are created as part of the customization and extending process. Let's look at them in detail.

Business entities

Business entities are part of the default customization provided with the application by Microsoft. They are either grouped into one of the modules of functionality or spread across all of them. Examples of business entities include, but are not limited to, Account, Contact, Lead, Opportunity, Case, and so on.

Most of the properties of Business entities are customizable in Dynamics 365. However, there are certain items that are not customizable across these entities. These are, in general, the same types of customizations that can't be changed when creating a custom entity. For example, the entity's internal name cannot be changed once an entity has been created. In addition, the primary field properties cannot be modified once an entity has been created.

The display name of an entity can be modified for the default value. This is a very common customization. In many instances, we need to adjust the default entity name so that it matches the business that we are customizing the system for. For instance, many customers use the term organization instead of account. This is a very easy piece of customization that can be achieved by updating the **Display Name** and **Plural Name** fields. While implementing this change, make sure to update the entity name across other properties as well, as a lot of them use the original name of the entity by default. Some examples include view names and forms.

Custom entities

All new entities that are created as part of customization and are implemented in Dynamics 365 are known as **custom entities**. When creating a new custom entity, we have the freedom to configure all the settings and properties as needed from the beginning. We can use a naming convention that makes sense to the user and generate all entity elements from the beginning by taking advantage of this name.

During creation, we must pay close attention to some properties that cannot be changed once enabled. These include enabling **Business Process Flows** on the entity; enabling **Notes**, **Activities**, and **Connections**; configuring the entity to support **Queues**; as well as defining the entity's primary field properties.

A custom entity can be assigned by default so that it's displayed in one of the main applications or displayed in the **Settings** and/or the **Help** section.

If a new module is created and custom entities need to be part of this new module, we can achieve this by customizing the application navigation or by creating new apps. While customizing the application navigation might not be such a straightforward process, tools have been released to the community that make this job a lot easier and more visual. The default method that's used to customize this navigation is described in detail in the SDK, and it involves exporting a solution with the navigation configuration, modifying the XML data, and reimporting the updated solution.

With the evolution of the platform and the introduction of the apps concept, we can now simply select the entities and entity elements that make up our business set of functionality and roll them together into an app by using a simple configuration wizard. No more editing XML files and messing with the overall platform navigation!

Note that, while we've seen most of the new management interface, for a certain function that has yet to reach parity, you might have to switch to classical mode. You can do this by selecting a solution or a solution element and finding the **Switch to classic** option on the ribbon. The following screenshot shows this option on the ribbon, at the solution level:

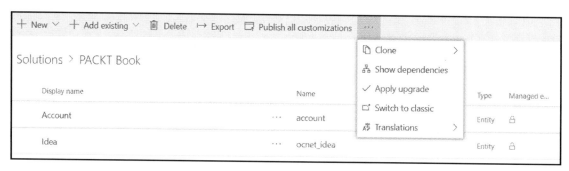

This puts you back into the old, familiar interface for managing the solution components. The following screenshot shows the same solution in the classical interface:

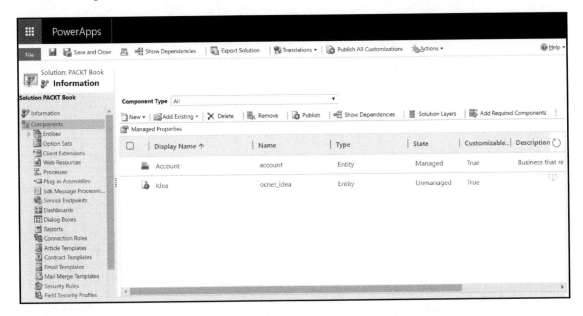

Now that we're in the solution view, let's look at modifying entity properties, and extending these to create new functionality.

Extending entities

Whether we are looking to extend a customizable business entity or a custom entity, the process is very similar. We extend entities by creating new entity fields, forms, views, charts, relationships, and/or business rules. The following screenshot shows these options for the account entity where we added the **Twitter Handle** custom field:

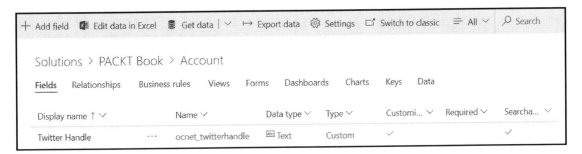

We will look at each of these options in detail in the remaining sections of this chapter.

Recording images

When creating a new record in Microsoft Dynamics 365, we have the ability to define an image for the record. One example is that, when storing accounts, you can capture the company logo as an image associated with the record. You can do this by clicking on the image container to the left of the title, as shown in the following screenshot:

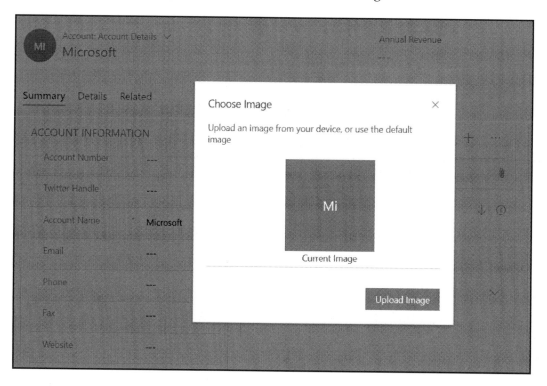

This brings up a modal window that allows you to upload your custom image. When complete, your account records will display the provided logo in front of the account name on the form:

Having a record-specific logo is great as it creates a more personal experience for your users. Next, we'll learn how to set up the forms that present data, as well as how to quickly and easily create new related records or view them.

Quickly viewing and creating entity forms

The most common customization that's made to the Microsoft Dynamics 365 platform is the ability to modify an entity form. We can add, remove, and hide fields and sections on the form, as well as implementing logic to make the form behave in a dynamic fashion. First, let's look at a standard form and the components that are part of it.

The entity form

With the current version at Dynamics 365 v9.1, most of the updated entities now have four different types of form types. These are as follows:

- The main form
- The quick view form
- The quick create form
- The card form

We will look at each of these form types in detail in the subsequent sections. Various other forms can be created on an entity, either from scratch or by opening an existing form and saving it with a new name. When complex forms need to be created, in many circumstances, it is much easier to start from an existing entity form rather than recreating everything.

The main form

The main form is the default form associated with an entity. This form will be available by default when opening a record. There can be more than one main form, and they can be configured so that they're available to various security roles. A security role must have at least one form available for the role. If more than one form is available for a specific role, then they will be available to be selected by the user. Forms available for various roles are called **role-based forms**. As an example, HR could have a specific view of an account that shows more information than a form available to a Sales role.

When editing the main form of an entity, it will look like the following custom entity form:

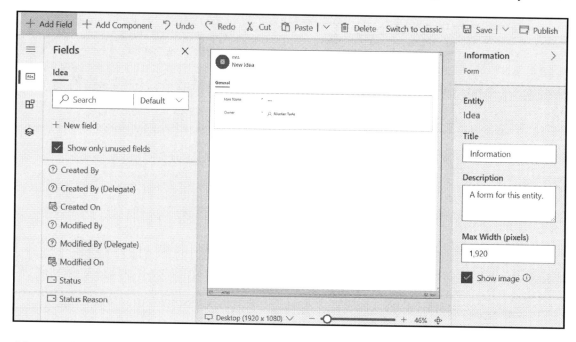

Observe the center of the screen, which shows a preview of the form. You can zoom in or out as needed, and you interact with this area by dragging and dropping various elements from different locations onto the form.

The form editor presents a **What You See is What You Get (WYSIWYG)** approach, with the ability to drag and drop elements, create new sections, and drag elements to rearrange them on the form. We have seen this approach in various tools since the inception of the internet. On the left-hand side, we can work with creating and managing data fields, while on the right-hand side, we can view contextual information about the selected elements. As mentioned previously, the central area provides the form design area.

The quick view form

The quick view form is similar in functionality to the quick create form but is used once a record has already been created. The only difference between the quick view form and the quick create form is when they are displayed to the user. As far as extensibility is concerned, we have the same customization options available. The reason why we have two different forms, in this case, is because we can display different information to the user based on when he/she is looking at the data.

The quick create form

The quick create form is a shortened version of the main form, in which only a limited number of fields are made available for the user to fill in. The idea is that only a few fields are mandatory and must be included for us to open a record in the system. Later, a user can come back and populate additional information as needed. A quick form will open over an existing form and closing it will leave the user on the original form. As such, a user can quickly create new records without navigating away from the current record.

The quick create form gives us more flexibility than the main form, while still presenting a trimmed-down version of it.

The card form

Finally, the card form is a mini stylized form available for specific visual representations. It includes a minimal number of fields and is typically used for presenting details in a larger context. For example, a card form can be used to present a primary contact information block on an account record form.

With that, we've looked at the entity form and some of its types. Next, we'll learn how to customize them as per our needs.

Customizing forms

In Dynamics 365, forms are comprised of various elements. We have various layout elements, including tabs and sections, iFrames, sub-grids, spacers, and various field types. At the lowest level, we have data fields, which can be placed within some of the previously mentioned containers. We'll look at each of these elements in detail in the subsequent sections.

Tabs

A **tab** is the highest level available in terms of grouping elements visually on the form. A tab can be set to open by default when it's expanded or collapsed. Clicking on the tab name of an open form allows the user to expand or collapse it. This makes navigating a form easier.

Tabs can also be opened, closed, and hidden programmatically by using certain business rules or scripts. For example, if the value of a field is set to a certain value, then we show another tab; otherwise, we keep it hidden.

The following screenshot shows the layout options available for a custom entity default form:

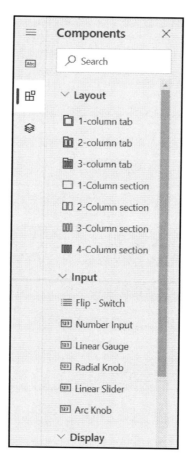

Tabs can be created with various predefined layout options. When editing the form, on the toolbar, we are presented with the options to create a one-, two-, or three-column tab.

Once a tab has been inserted into the form, the layout can be further customized. You can change the originally selected layout and adjust the width of the columns as needed. This is all done by double-clicking the tab on the form in edit mode. A **Tab Properties** window will appear. On the **Formatting** tab, you will be presented with the following layout options:

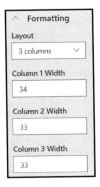

Next, we'll understand the sections element.

Sections

Sections is a sub-grouping element that is used for further designing your forms. Creating a tab with three columns will automatically generate three new sections aligned side by side. We can then add an additional section to each of the columns from the tab.

A section's layout can also be customized to present information in multiple columns. The layout options are presented by double-clicking the section in edit mode. This opens a **Section configuration** blade. In the **Display options** section, **Section label** and **Name** are mandatory fields. Other section configuration options include the ability to lock and hide the section, as well as managing the label's visibility. These are presented in the following screenshot:

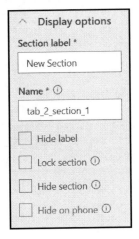

In addition, we can customize the formatting of the form section by setting the number of columns available. This option includes configuring one to four columns, as shown in the following screenshot:

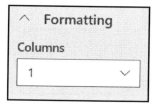

When customizing the form layouts, pay close attention to the amount of data presented horizontally, and make sure that, on a lower resolution, it does not result in unexpected line-wrapping. Items laid out might look perfect at a higher resolution, but on lower resolution screens, the fields might get wrapped, resulting in a layout that is not ideal for the user. The responsive layout definition allows form elements to be wrapped, but you might find the order of the elements is not what was needed when moving to a smaller resolution layout.

iFrames

iFrames are a feature that allows us to bring external pages or web resources into a form. Using this approach, we can introduce custom HTML elements into entity forms. This allows us to extend the system with custom elements. A good use for this is taking advantage of custom forms formatting, as well as dashboard elements and reports.

Pay attention to the formatting of iFrames. The risk is that bringing in forms with a format larger than the actual iFrame will result in scroll bars.

The iFrame concept was never very successful, and only seldom implemented. In the new user interface, the configuration does not even present iFrames as a configurable option. To use this, you must switch back to the classic configuration.

It is not recommended to use iFrames in the configuration anymore.

Sub-grids

In Dynamics 365, sub-grids allow us to display listings of related entity records. They are based on existing views, with specific filters added. For example, on an account entity, we can have a listing in a sub-grid showing all the contacts related to the current account:

A sub-grid is bound by the same limitation as the iFrame, where if the view is larger than the allocated space on the form, we will be presented with scroll bars. This makes the user experience less friendly.

As far as options for configuration, for sub-grids, we can adjust the entity and view being referenced, as well as the ability for the user to change the view in the respective sub-grid. All these settings are available from the **Subgrid properties** blade on the right-hand side, as shown in the following screenshot:

Typically, you will want to make sure the **Show related records** option is selected as that will provide a filter that only shows records related to the current record. Otherwise, what would be the point of showing all contacts in the system when looking at a particular account?

We'll have a look at creating and using data fields next.

Fields

Fields are the building blocks of forms. They are used to collect and display record data. In Dynamics 365, fields are defined with various data types. Just like the data residing in the database, each field is defined with a related data type, and some specific fields include formatting properties.

The data types that are used in Dynamics 365 are as follows:

- **Text**
- **Whole Number**
- **Date and Time**
- **Floating Point Number**
- **Decimal Number**
- **Currency**
- **Multiline Text**
- **Lookup**
- **Two Options**

Some of these options have sub-categories, as shown in the following screenshot:

The **Advanced settings** area is content-aware and provides different options, depending on the field data type selected. As such, the following screenshot shows the options for a **Whole Number** data type configuration:

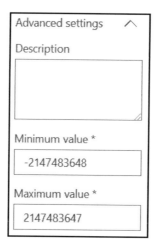

There are certain similarities between some of these data types. For example, the **Single Line of Text** and the **Multiple Lines of Text** data types capture all characters and are differentiated only by the total number of characters allowed. **Two Options** is like option set but captures only two possible options. They are also rendered differently on the form.

 Note that some options are only available in classic mode, such as the **Option Set** type. If you want to add an Option Set with more than two options, at the time of writing, you must switch to classic mode to define the field.

Under each of these data types, there are various options for formatting the data. For example, for the **Text** option, the data can be left as a string of characters limited by the length of the field defined, or it can be formatted as one of the following options: email, text, text area, URL, ticker symbol, or phone.

The **Whole Number** data type can be formatted as a regular whole number set to **Duration**, **Time Zone**, or **Language**.

Duration is stored in the database as a value representing the total number of minutes. On the form, the field is represented as a dropdown with the suggested option of 1 minute all the way to 3 days. The field is also smart enough to interpret user input. For example, typing in 60 (minutes) resolves automatically to 1 hour. The duration formats supported include the following options: x minutes, x hours, x days. You can also enter values such as x.x hours.

The **Time Zone** formatted field displays a list of selections in the format of (GMT-08:00) Pacific Time (US and Canada) or (GMT-12:00) International Date Line West. In the database, these values are stored as numbers.

The **Language** field displays a list of all the languages provisioned in the current organization. These values are presented as a dropdown. On the database end, the selection is stored as a number using LCID codes. These codes are four- or five-digit codes and all the values are available from the MSDN documentation.

The **Currency** data type allows us to select currency precision. We can select from zero to four-digit precision, as well as **Pricing Decimal Precision** and **Currency Precision**. **Pricing Decimal Precision** is a global value defined in the system settings. **Currency Precision** applies the precision defined by the currency being used by the record.

The **Date and Time** data type allows us to select whether we intend to display the date and time or the date only. We also can select whether the Date and Time is representative of the user's local configuration or whether it is time-zone independent.

The **Lookup** data type allows us to select the related entity where values are being selected. For example, a lookup field allows us to select the parent account of a contact by presenting a window that allows us to search for the specific account record.

Global options sets

Global options sets, as the name implies, are groups of values defined at a global level. They can be shared on various entities and forms and are kept in sync across all the locations where they are used. Changing the values in a global options set results in the change being applied to all the locations where they are used.

> Whenever possible, you should use a global option set for when you need to use the same values in multiple places in your application.

Global options sets are not located and customizable in the solution in terms of the entity where they are being referred to, but rather in a separate category in the solution called Option Sets. Here, we can manage all existing and new global option sets.

The Option Set definition window is presented in the following screenshot. This is where we define an Option Set with three values:

When referencing one of these on a form, you create a new field, just like you would create any other field. Set **Data type** to **Option Set**. After doing this, you'll be presented with the option to select one of the pre-defined global option sets. The following screenshot shows adding the custom Option Set we created on the account form:

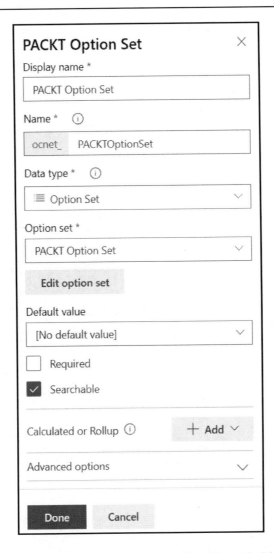

Once you select the Option Set to be used, you can edit it if needed by selecting the **Edit option set** button. Keep in mind that any changes will be reflected in all the locations where this global option set is being used. Also, you can select the **Default value** for this Option Set. This is the value that will be automatically selected when no option is selected by the user.

Expanding the **Advanced options** area allows you to provide a detailed description of this Option Set in the respective form where it has been added.

Spacers

Spacers are used for formatting. Because forms are generated by adding fields and ordering these fields on the form, in certain instances, we need to leave blank spaces for clarity. As such, a spacer will take the same space as a regular field, but no actual data will be present.

With the move to the new responsive user interface, the use of Spacers is rendered almost non-essential, and you can only find the spacers configuration in the classic interface.

Other inputs

While some options have been dropped in the new user interface, new controls are now available to enhance the user experience. These can be found on the form editing window, under the **Add Components** option. A new category called **Input** is available and provides some out-of-the-box options. The following screenshot shows these options in the **Components** dock:

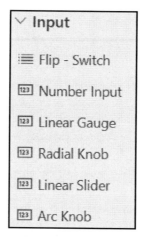

These are highly visual elements that take advantage of the new user interface capabilities. For example, if you select the **Radial Knob** option, you'll see the following:

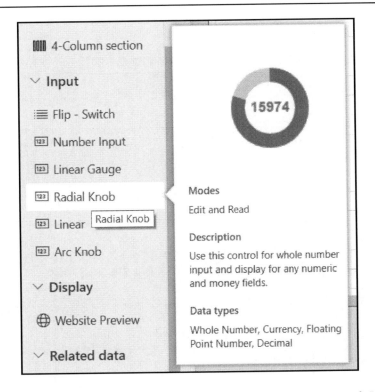

The way we present data helps users make more sense of what's presented. When looking across a larger subset of data, views and charts can enhance this experience. We'll look at this next.

Presenting data to the user

Entity views and charts are essential components to be used when presenting data to users. While views are more data-oriented, charts tend to be more visual, and are used more in the overall analysis of data. To bring these elements together, dashboards are used to present the final aggregations of views and charts.

We'll look at these components in detail in the subsequent sections.

Views

Entity views are queries that are saved against system data. These queries apply filters to the present subsets of data as needed. Views also contain formatting details regarding how the data will be displayed, their columns, and their order. Views can be defined programmatically or in XML. When using XML, the views can be exported, modified, and reimported back into Dynamics 365. You can export an entity using an unmanaged solution, modify the entity properties in the XML definition file, and then repackage and reimport the solution into your organization.

An entity view is a saved query available globally throughout the organization. Each entity can have multiple views, with various filter conditions and formatting.

Each entity can have various types of views. They can serve various purposes, and include the following: **Advanced Find Views**, **Associated Views**, **Lookup Views**, **Public Views**, and **Quick Find Views**. Also, each entity will have one **Default Public View**.

Just like any other record in Dynamics 365, **Public Entity Views** can be created, updated, retrieved, deleted, and deactivated.

You can start creating a new view in a solution by adding an entity to the solution, navigating to **Views**, and clicking on **Add view**:

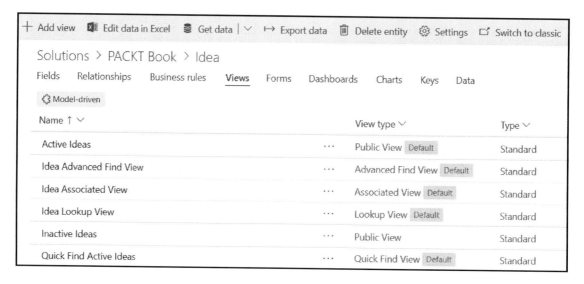

On the view properties wizard, define the **Name** and **Description** fields. Once done, click on **Create**, as shown in the following screenshot:

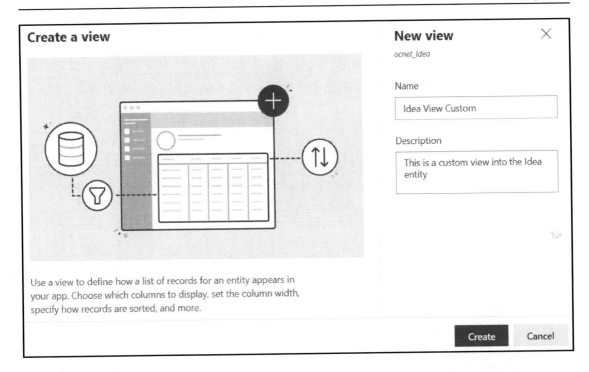

You can customize the columns, sorting, and filtering properties on a view. For columns, you can add various fields from the current entity or fields from related entities, as shown in the following screenshot:

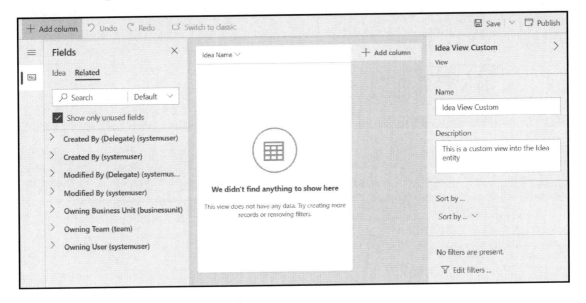

Editing filters allows you to define filtering criteria for the view. Using a very simplistic wizard-based interface, a system customizer can easily create and enhance the filters that have been applied to a view. The following screenshot shows the **Edit filters** window:

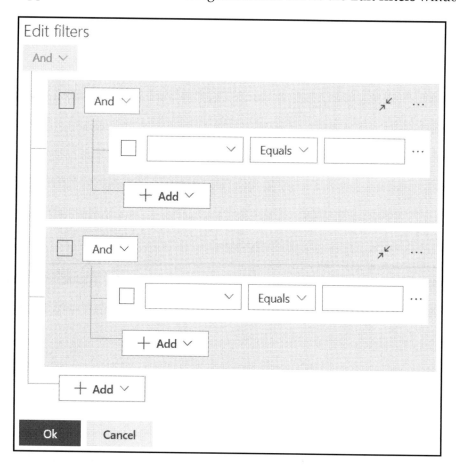

Sorting configuration allows a customizer to choose sorting columns and the order of sorting for each. You can select the columns to use sorting from the view.

You can also select sorting or filtering by choosing the preferred sorting order or the **Filter by** option, as shown in the following screenshot:

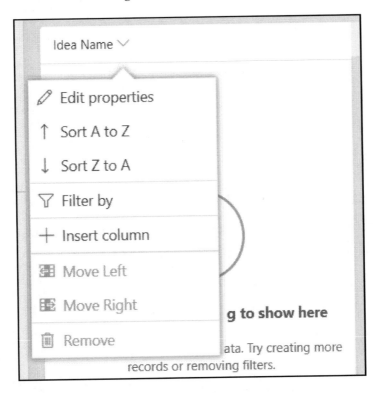

Selecting **Edit properties** allows you to define a fixed width for the respective column. This is important for minimizing the user's effort to expands columns to see all the text.

Finally, you are also presented with options to rearrange the order of columns by moving them either left or right, or removing certain columns from the view. These options are available depending on the column type and the total number of columns. A view must always have at least one column of data.

Typically, you want to keep the **Name** column as this provides a link you can use to navigate to the respective record.

Charts

Once we have a view customized, we can move on and create a chart. **Charts** are visual representations of views that are created in the system.

Within the solution you're using for customization, navigate to the entity you want to add a Chart to. Find the **Charts** tab and select it. The ribbon will now present you with an option called **Add chart**. If any charts exist for this entity, they will be displayed here in the main section, as shown in the following screenshot:

Creating a chart is a selection-driven process, and the classical interface is still used for this functionality. The following screenshot presents the chart creation window:

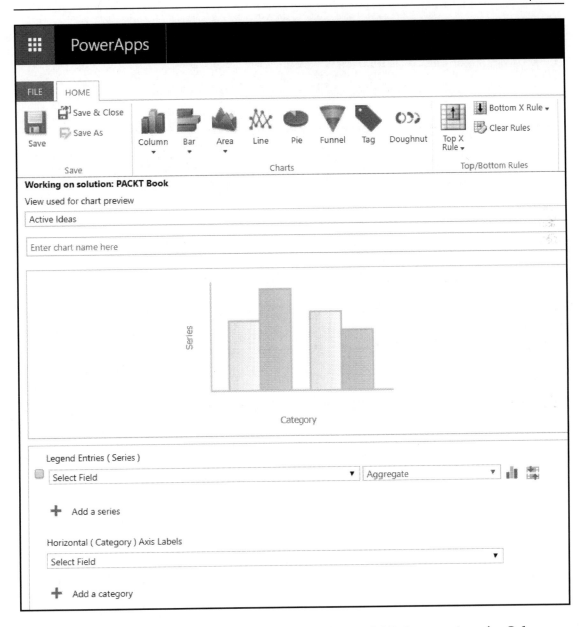

From this view, we can choose the type of Chart to be used. We have options for **Column**, **Bar**, **Area**, **Line**, **Pie**, and **Funnel** charts. In addition, we have support for **Tag** and **Doughnut** charts.

All charts are based on a view. When creating a chart, the first item we need to select in the definition of the chart is the view that's used to collect the records that will drive the chart data. The steps for this are as follows:

1. Select one of the entity views available from the dropdown.
2. The next step is to name your chart and verify the preview. You have options to adjust the series used in generating the chart, add new series, define and add categories, as well as to define a description for the chart.
3. Once we have created the chart(s), we can see them by navigating to **View**. We can also start adding these charts to dashboards.

Now that we have looked at views and charts, we need to understand how are they presented as a final aggregation, together. We will do that next.

Dashboards

A dashboard is a special type of entity form in Dynamics 365. It is comprised of several columns. Each of these areas can present one chart, while the bottom area of the dashboard, by default, presents a selection of streams.

The following screenshot shows us configuring a dashboard for a custom **Idea** entity:

In addition to entity-specific dashboards, Dynamics 365 allows us to create dashboards that show data across multiple entities. These dashboards are created in the context of the solution, but unrelated to an entity.

In these dashboards, you can add multiple components, including charts, views, iFrames, web resources, and other elements. The following screenshot shows the creation of such a dashboard:

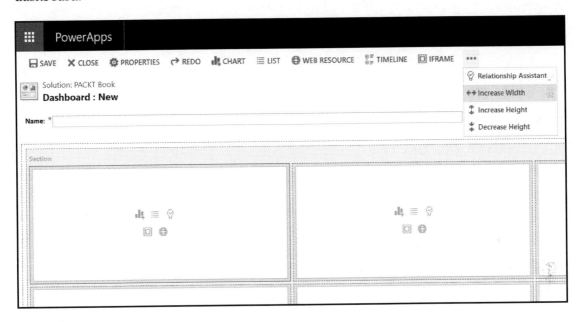

In Dynamics 365 there are two types of such dashboards:

- Organization-owned dashboards
- User-owned dashboards

The difference between these two types is in their behavior:

- **Organization-owned dashboard**: An organization-owned dashboard, once created, must be published to make it available to the organization. As such, it cannot be assigned or shared. It is created as part of a solution and published with the solution.
- **User-owned dashboard**: A user-owned dashboard is a dashboard created by a user. As such, the user owns the dashboard, and they can assign or share it with other users.

A generic dashboard looks like this:

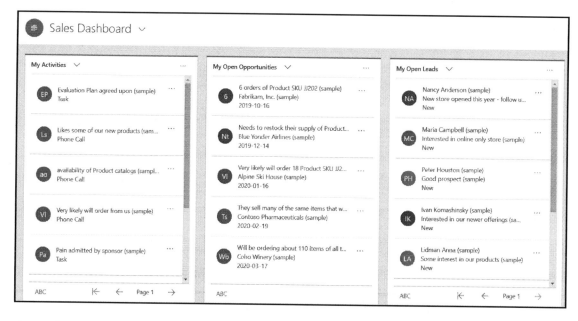

As we have seen so far, presenting data in an easily readable way is important for understanding and making decisions. But most of the time, this data relies heavily on relationships. We'll learn how to define these relationships in the next section.

Defining entity relationship types

Entity relationships are used to represent relationships between various Dynamics 365 entities. The customization tools included with Dynamics 365 make it easy for system customizers to create new entities, modify existing entities, and create relationships between them.

Entity relationships define associations from one entity to other entities or to itself. A new relationship is represented as a new table relationship in the database.

The simplest example of an entity relationship is the creation of a lookup to an entity. This creates a one-to-many relationship between the two entities. This allows you to associate multiple child records with a parent record.

Within Dynamics 365, there are three types of relationships, as follows:

- One-to-many
- Many-to-one
- Many-to-many

We'll look at these types of relationships in the subsequent sections.

One-to-many (1:N) and many-to-one (N:1) relationships

One-to-many kind of relationship defines an entity record that can be associated with many records of a different entity. The difference between 1:N and N:1 is the direction of the relationship.

When viewing a primary entity record, you will see a listing of the related entity records defined by the relationship.

Defining a custom 1:N relationship involves defining the following parts: relationship definition, lookup field, and relationship behavior. We use this relationship to define a lookup value on a form, with one entity referencing a record of another entity. The following screenshot shows the definition of a one-to-many relationship:

The **Type of behavior** field is important to understand as it defines certain aspects of data integrity. For example, we can define a relationship to automatically remove child-related records when a parent record is removed, thus not leaving behind active orphaned records. In addition, it can prevent records from being removed if they have related records. Internally, this is referred to as cascading configuration, and includes options for **cascading all**, **none**, or **active only**, along with **remove link**, **restrict**, and **cascade only user-owned record**.

The next relationship type is many-to-many, which is denoted by N:N.

Many-to-many (N:N) relationships

N:N relationships are special types of relationships that depend on an intersect entity to create a relationship. This allows us to relate many primary entities to many child entities.

When viewing the record of the parent or child entity, in an N:N relationship, you can see a listing for any record of the related entity.

Creating a new many-to-many relationship involves defining the parent and the child entity and naming the relationship:

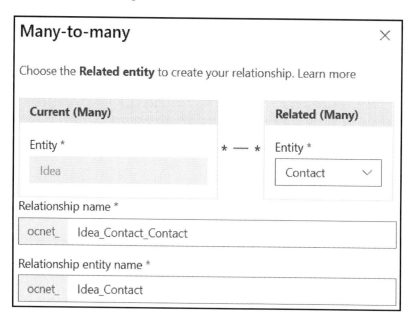

N:N relationships do not generate a hierarchy between related entities. In such a relationship, you do not define lookups or behaviors. The relationship is reciprocal.

The intersect entity is generated automatically by the system, and it is not customizable. As such, you cannot add custom fields to it.

When creating entity relationships, close attention should be paid to the relationship behavior settings. These influence how the relationship behaves and how changes are cascaded to the related records. For example, a parental relationship cascades all changes to the related records.

For more details on relationships, take a look at the information box provided next to **Type of behavior**, as shown in the following screenshot:

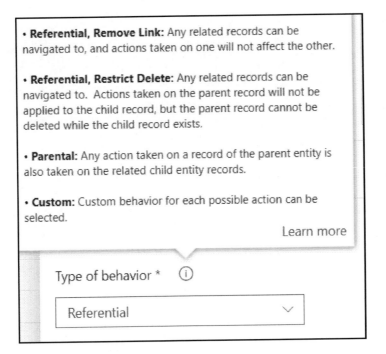

A list of all relationships defined on an entity will be presented, along with clear information about the relationship type, the entities involved, the type, and the internal relationship name. Pay attention to the naming of these relationships; sometimes, you will end up with repeating sections in a name, as shown in the following screenshot for the **Idea** relationship. You should try to keep the names as clean as possible by renaming the default name:

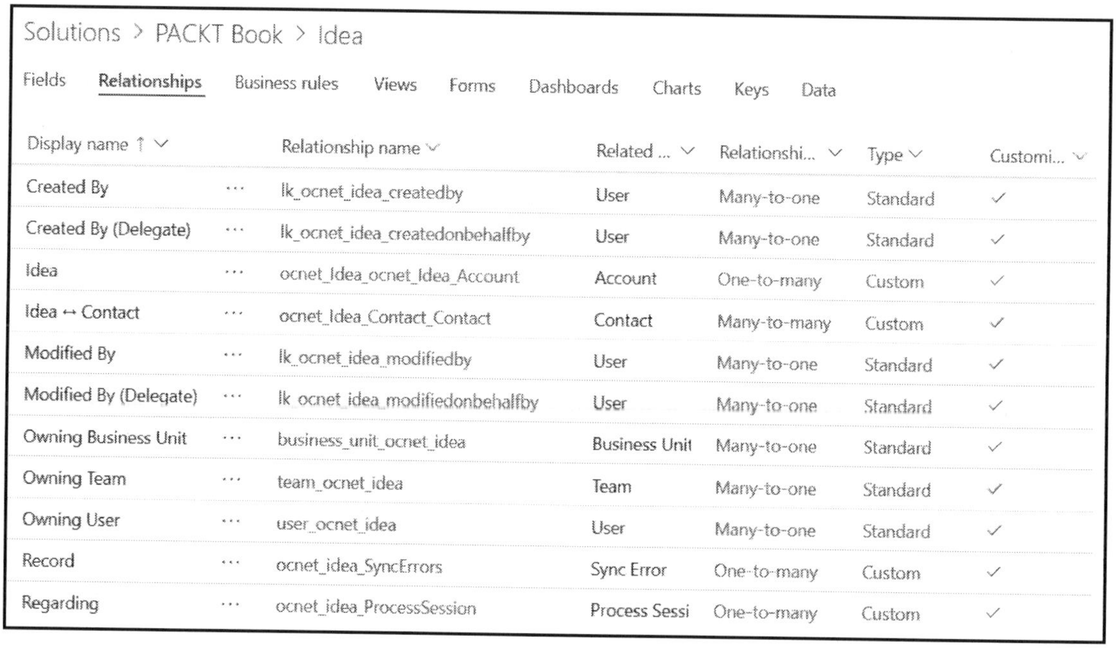

Solutions > PACKT Book > Idea

| Fields | Relationships | Business rules | Views | Forms | Dashboards | Charts | Keys | Data |

Display name ↑ ∨		Relationship name ∨	Related ... ∨	Relationshi... ∨	Type ∨	Customi... ∨
Created By	···	lk_ocnet_idea_createdby	User	Many-to-one	Standard	✓
Created By (Delegate)	···	lk_ocnet_idea_createdonbehalfby	User	Many-to-one	Standard	✓
Idea	···	ocnet_Idea_ocnet_Idea_Account	Account	One-to-many	Custom	✓
Idea ↔ Contact	···	ocnet_Idea_Contact_Contact	Contact	Many-to-many	Custom	✓
Modified By	···	lk_ocnet_idea_modifiedby	User	Many-to-one	Standard	✓
Modified By (Delegate)	···	lk_ocnet_idea_modifiedonbehalfby	User	Many-to-one	Standard	✓
Owning Business Unit	···	business_unit_ocnet_idea	Business Unit	Many-to-one	Standard	✓
Owning Team	···	team_ocnet_idea	Team	Many-to-one	Standard	✓
Owning User	···	user_ocnet_idea	User	Many-to-one	Standard	✓
Record	···	ocnet_idea_SyncErrors	Sync Error	One-to-many	Custom	✓
Regarding	···	ocnet_idea_ProcessSession	Process Sessi	One-to-many	Custom	✓

Now that we've learned how to relate separate entities, let's go to the entity level and learn how the specific fields of an entity can be configured in order to optimize presentation and data collection.

Working with composite fields

Composite fields are another feature introduced with Dynamics CRM 2013. They group a set of fields together, resulting in optimized screen real estate usage. An example of a composite field is the **Full Name** field, which is comprised of a first, middle, and last name. Once the user selects one of these composite fields, a *fly-out* is presented. Each field can be edited separately as permissions allow.

The following screenshot shows the definition of the **Full Name** field:

While some of these composite fields have been removed from the new UI in favor of individual fields, some are still used in other aspects, such as for presentation on certain views, or for integrations into other applications that only support a composed value made up of multiple fields. One such example is when integrating with ERP, where the expected street address must be a single field, rather than multiple fields available in Dynamics 365.

We can build our own composite fields and use things such as Flow to populate them based on changes made to base field values. That way, we can replicate the functionality and use this approach for various business needs.

In order to minimize the amount of custom code we have, we can use calculated fields. The next section looks at how to configure and use this feature.

Using calculated fields

Calculated fields were introduced with Dynamics CRM 2015. The purpose of these fields is to provide automatically calculated field values based on other existing firm field values. Before version 2015, we used a lot of customization to generate this behavior. In addition, all change requests involved reaching out to the development team again and processing a change request, as well as the associated hoops.

Calculated fields bring the ease and usability found in Excel to Dynamics CRM. The process also does not require a developer anymore, and any Power user with permission to edit the system can create these fields. as well as rollup fields, which will be described next.

To create a calculated field, you create a field in a solution just like you would any other customization. On the **Field properties** form, look for the calculated or rollup definition. From the dropdown, select **+ Calculation**. Once you make this selection, a rules definition window will pop up, as shown in the following screenshot:

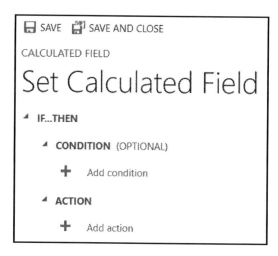

The interface to configure calculated fields is very intuitive. You will be presented with an **IF...THEN** condition. You set up your conditions and, after validating these conditions, the configured Actions will be executed.

This interface is common across multiple configurable elements. You will become very familiar with it when using not only calculated fields, but also rollup fields and, to some extent, business rules.

When working with calculated fields, it is important to understand that, depending on the data type of the field selected, various functions are presented. For example, a **Floating Point Number**, **Multiple Lines of Text**, or **Lookup** data type cannot be used as part of a calculated field. For the ones that accept this option, functions around working with date and strings are available. Some of these include adding and/or removing days, months, years, concatenating strings, and so on. To do actual numeric calculations, you can generate formulas just as you would in Excel, with some limitations. You will have to write the formulas manually since automated generated functions such as sum, sin, and others are not pre-defined.

Once the field has been added to a form and the changes have been published, navigating to the respective form will show the newly added calculated field with a lock icon next to it. This represents the fact that the field is updating automatically and thus is non-editable.

Taking advantage of rollup fields

In the same category as calculated fields is rollup fields. Generating this type of field is quite like adding calculated fields. The purpose of rollup fields is to aggregate data from multiple child records. This addition is extremely helpful as it reduces a lot of previous code complexity when performing such actions. An example is calculating the number of closed opportunities in the last 6 months. In the previous version of Dynamics 365, before rollup fields were available, this scenario was handled by a developer creating this functionality custom through code. Now, this can be replaced with simple customization.

Adding a rollup field is an option made available to only certain field data types. The ones that do not accept rollup fields are as follows:

- **Single Line of Text**
- **Option Set**
- **Two Option**s
- **Image**
- **Floating Point Number**
- **Multiple Lines of Text**
- **Lookup**

Selecting a data type that supports rollup fields allows us to set the field type as rollup, as shown in the following screenshot:

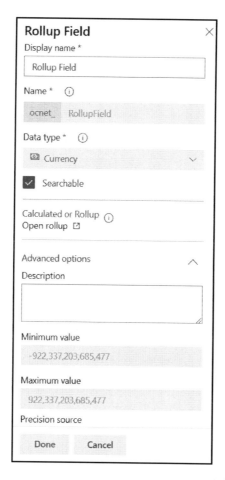

Select **Open rollup** to configure the behavior of the newly created **Rollup Field**. This presents the already familiar interface that we've seen already for calculated fields.

On the configuration screen, **SOURCE ENTITY** is usually pre-selected based on the entity we started the configuration of the field from. We get to select **RELATED ENTITY** and the **AGGREGATION** type, as shown in the following screenshot:

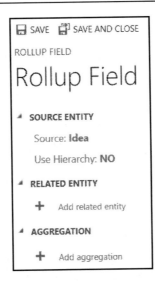

When creating a Rollup Field, the value is automatically calculated every 12 hours by default. The first run is not, in fact, on the field creation, but rather 12 hours after creation. This is highlighted in a message that's displayed at the bottom of the Rollup Field editor window on a yellow background, as shown in the following screenshot:

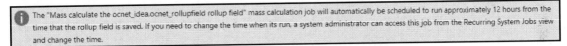

The final Rollup Field, once added on a form and published, will present a lock icon, just like calculated fields, along with a representation of a calculator.

Observe the option to manually refresh the value. This will trigger an immediate refresh, which basically allows a user to manually refresh a rollup field value when they know a change has been made to a value.

An invalid formula will be flagged by the system. On the actual form, a field with an invalid formula is presented with an exclamation mark. You must fix the formula and republish the correct values.

Several good examples of using rollup fields include the ability to configure calculations of estimated revenue for all opportunities on an account, a hierarchy of related accounts, or a value of leads generated by a campaign. Of course, there are many more scenarios where this feature is valuable.

One important aspect of managing the services offered to our customers, while keeping expenses under control and creating a profitable business model, is the ability to honor service agreements. Dynamics 365 provides **Service-Level Agreement (SLA)** configurable features to serve this purpose. The next section looks at this feature and the configuration required.

When to use SLAs and the timer control

This functionality in Dynamics 365 allows us to define the level of support and commitment to respect this agreement. SLAs allow us to track performance for client services in accordance with set expectations. We can define measurable metrics to push to the service team, as well as timely warnings with regard to various support scenarios.

In Dynamics 365, SLAs work in conjunction with entitlements if need be. Alternatively, SLAs can be defined across an organization. When used with entitlements, we define various levels of entitlements for groups of customers. These entitlements define the related SLAs, and all services and interactions with these customers are regulated through these new SLAs.

One simple example is to define company XYZ Inc. as a Gold-level customer. Our Gold-level customers receive special treatment. Their inquiries and requests must be fully addressed within a time frame of 24 hours. Thus, XYZ Inc. is entitled to this. A representative of this company opens a case with us with regard to a product they have purchased. The product turns out to be defective and needs to be replaced. Because of the current entitlement, we need to dispatch a technician to replace the defective product within 24 hours. Once the case is opened, the SLA is associated with the case. The timer control is triggered and starts counting down from 24 hours. We could also have notifications at the 12-hour mark, to remind the service team to review the case if no action was performed on it.

We had the ability to achieve this with custom code before Dynamics CRM 2013. With the Dynamics CRM Online Spring 2014 update and the CRM 2013 Service Pack 1 on-premise version, Standard SLAs were introduced. It evolved over the next few versions and enhanced SLAs were added.

Standard versus enhanced SLAs

Enhanced SLAs followed after standard SLAs and added a few additional features. These include features such as the following:

- **Ability to pause an existing SLA**: An SLA can be paused by the user if needed, to reflect waiting for input from a customer. While the SLA is paused, the time is not counted against the entitlement.
- **Ability to create success actions on an SLA:** We can trigger specific actions when a case has been resolved, resulting in a successful SLA. These actions could include both external and/or internal communication.
- **Default SLA tracking on cases**: With enhanced SLAs, the default case forms include a timer control, not requiring us to make this customization.

 Since SLAs are configured at the organization level, they are not classed as components of a solution. SLAs are configured in each environment individually and can't be exported as part of a standard solution package.

To customize SLAs, navigate to **Settings | Service Management**. In the **Service Terms** section, you will find the configurations for both **Service Level Agreements** and **Entitlements**:

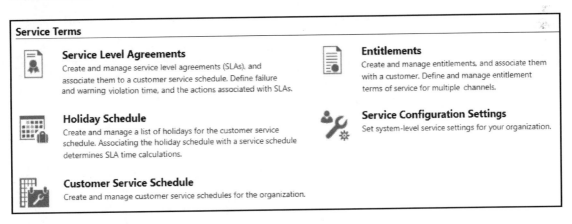

Let's navigate to **Service Level Agreements** and see how we can create our first SLA. We will pick a very simple SLA example.

On the **All Service Level Agreements** view, select the **New form** option on the ribbon. This brings us to the new SLA wizard form, which is where we provide the SLA's **Name** and the **Entity** enabled for the SLA. Typically, this is the case entity:

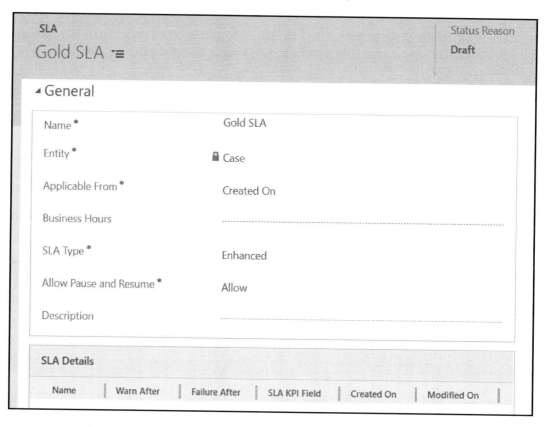

Here, we must define, as a minimum, the **Name**, **Applicable From**, **SLA Type**, and **Allow Pause and Resume** fields.

The **Applicable From** field defines the starting time when the timer commences the count. The default value is **Created On**, which represents the time when the case with the associated SLA was created. If this is not necessarily the time when you want the SLA to commence, there are other values that are available, as follows:

- **Modified On**
- **Follow Up By**
- **Record Created On**
- **Resolved By**

- **First Response By**
- **Escalated On**
- **Last On Hold Time**

SLA Type is where you select the type of SLA you intend to create.

Observe that with the introduction of enhanced SLAs, this is the default value in this field.

Allow Pause and Resume tells the system exactly that. The default is set to **Allow**, but it can be changed on SLA creation.

Setting up **Business Hours** allows the SLA to be aware of working schedules, and only counts against these schedules. For an organization that does not run 24/7, this is an important configuration.

Once the SLA has been created, the following fields can't be changed anymore:

- **Applicable From**
- **SLA Type**
- **Allow Pause and Resume**

If the configurations you have made are not correct, then you'll need to correct them. To correct any of these fields, you must recreate the SLA from scratch.

Note that an SLA is not available and applicable until it is activated.

Once Activated, an SLA can be applied to specific records, or it can be set to default through the available ribbon buttons.

The **SLA Details** form represents the specific **Key Performance Indicators (KPIs)** or metrics for the respective SLA. You can also define the success and failure actions related to this SLA.

The default new SLA Details form we've created, called **New SLA Item**, looks as follows:

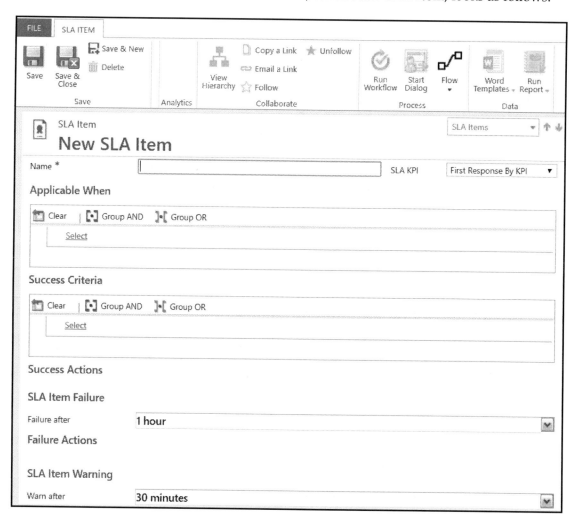

The SLA KPIs are trackable performance indicators. These can be selected from the dropdown at the top of the form. The two values we can choose from are as follows:

- **First Response By KPI**
- **Resolve By KPI**

By default, there are only two predefined values. If you need to track other KPIs, you must create new case fields of the lookup type that refer to that KPI instance entity.

You can add as many SLA items as necessary, and you can order them as needed. The condition in **Applicable When** defines when an SLA item is triggered.

Only the first SLA item that matches the condition in **Applicable When** is applied.

SLAs have behind-the-scenes corresponding workflows that get triggered. When activating an SLA for the first time, the corresponding workflow is also created based on the definition of the SLA. From a permission standpoint, when you have permission to trigger actions in an SLA, you must have the same permissions to perform the actions in the workflow.

Not all actions available in workflows are also available when defining the failure and warning actions. Only the following actions are available:

- **Send Email**
- **Create Record**
- **Update Record**
- **Assign Record**
- **Change Status**

When defining the **Applicable When** and the **Success Criteria** clauses, if no AND or OR grouping is defined, the system defaults to AND grouping.

To be able to define the failure actions and warning actions, you must first save **New SLA Item**. You must define at least a **Success Criteria** for the SLA to make any sense. This validation is automatically performed by the system. Clicking on **Save** before having the Success Criteria defined results in the following warning:

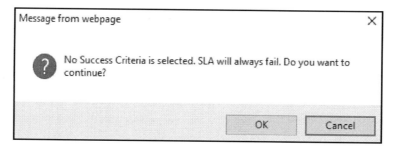

Defining success actions, as well as failure and warning actions, is done in a very visual way as well – by selecting from the **Add Step** dropdown provided:

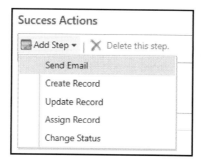

Here, you have the ability to define multiple steps as needed. If a step is not required anymore, it can easily be removed by selecting it and clicking on **Delete this step**:

Working with SLAs during maintenance periods is a task to be considered carefully. When performing bulk data updates that trigger SLAs where you don't want the SLAs to be triggered, you must disable the SLAs for the organization and re-enable them once the maintenance work has been completed.

How SLAs are applied

SLAs are applied upon Case creation if enabled, either by default or triggered by an entitlement. The SLA is reapplied if any of the **Applicable When** fields are updated. This could potentially result in failure or warning actions being retriggered. You can prevent this behavior by adding a custom tracking flag field and adding it to the **Applicable When** condition. This will check whether the flag was raised already, and not trigger the actions a second time.

SLAs can also be applied on demand or by using workflows. To apply an SLA manually to a Case, you must add the **SLA** field to the Case form, as shown in the following screenshot:

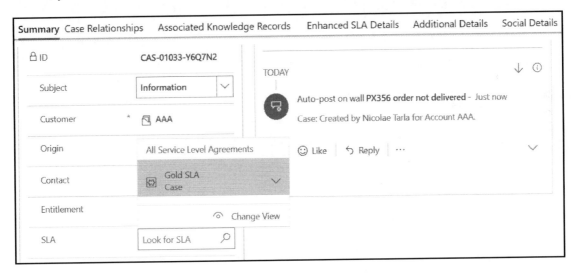

This allows the user to manually select an SLA to be applied to each case. Adding this Enhanced SLA to an existing case makes the **Enhanced SLA Details** section of the Case form light up with SLA-specific information.

We will look at available geolocation features in the next section, including how to enable these features and the other mapping options available, along with Bing Maps.

Enabling geolocation and mapping

Geolocation has been available for a few versions now. While not greatly popular, out of the box, we can map elements on a Bing map. We can, for example, map the locations of various offices and warehouses for a client, or extend the mapping capabilities to show the location of all customers in a specific serviced area. There are, however, a few small configurations required to enable it.

To use this feature in Microsoft Dynamics 365, you must enable it from **System Settings**. Some previous versions had this enabled by default, which caused additional customization requirements to hide it when not in use.

Navigate to **Settings** | **Administration** | **System Settings**. Scroll down on the **General** tab until you find the **Enable Bing Maps** section. Set **Enable Bing Maps** to **Yes**:

Once enabled, check which address fields it is using. For the out-of-the-box account, for example, **Address 1** is used as the source:

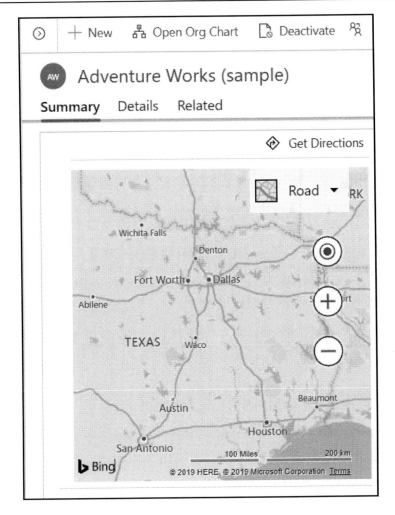

Make sure that, when using this feature, the required licensing is in order. Bing Maps has its own licensing model in place.

Additional geolocation features can be built on other platforms, such as Google Maps, but most of them have a licensing cost associated with them.

One other option you can use when customizing this functionality is Open Street Map. This is available at `http://www.openstreetmap.org/`.

This is a freely available set of mapping data that's licensed under the *Open Data Commons Open Database License* by the **OpenStreetMap Foundation** (**OSMF**). Unfortunately, there is no customizable module that can be added to your organization. You will require a partner to help you build this integration.

Next, we will look at a scenario to build a practical understanding of the lessons from this chapter.

Creating a new solution package scenario

As we have seen throughout this chapter, all new configurations extend the standard functionality of the platform and are packaged into a solution package.

For this scenario, your user must have either the System Customizer or Administrator role.

This section presents a simplified scenario to bring together all the material presented throughout this chapter. We will create a new entity for product rating, with several rating fields, and package it into a solution called **product rating**. In Chapter 13, *Core Administration Concepts*, we will see how to handle permissions for a user to access this new functionality. So, let's get started.

Creating the solution package

Begin by navigating to the Power Apps maker portal, at https://make.powerapps.com.

By default, you will be directed to the home page, as the starting point for any configurations. If you have multiple environments, make sure to select from the top right of the screen the environment that hosts your Dynamics 365 instance, as seen in the following screenshot:

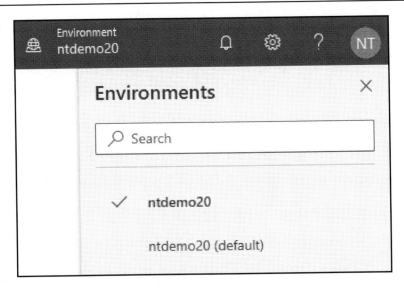

With the correct environment selected, now navigate on the left navigation area of the screen to the **Solutions** option. You will see listed here all the installed solutions for your currently selected environment. Select **New solution** from the ribbon, as shown here:

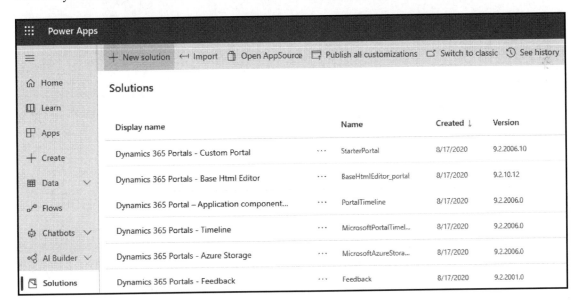

When the section opens, define the solution properties, including the **Name** and **Display name**, **Publisher**, **Version**, and under **More options**, a **Description** of your solution, as shown in the following screenshot:

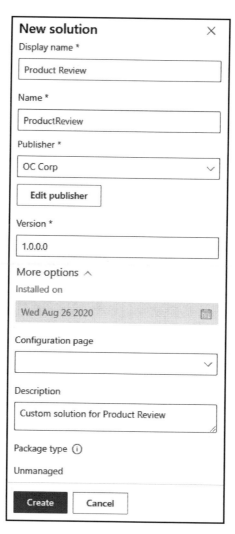

Click **Create** when done to generate the solution package structure. Your newly created solution will appear now listed under the listing of solutions. Once you click on the solution name, you are taken to a blank page with a message of **No components found**. That is expected as at this point, we only have a shell, an envelope if you will. We need to start adding content to this solution package.

Creating a new entity

The ribbon presents options to create new elements or add existing elements to our newly created solution package, as shown here:

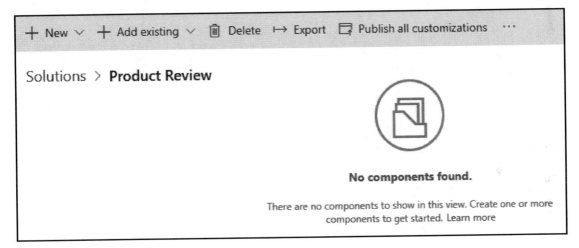

For this scenario, we will add a new entity to capture product reviews. So, let's select **+ New** on the ribbon, and select the **Entity** option from the fly-out.

In the same way, we defined the solution package properties up here, we are now presented with the entity definition area. Fill in here the name and display names for the entity and the primary field. You can choose to enable attachments if you want documents attached to data records, but for this scenario, we are not taking advantage of this option. The following screenshot shows the entity creation area:

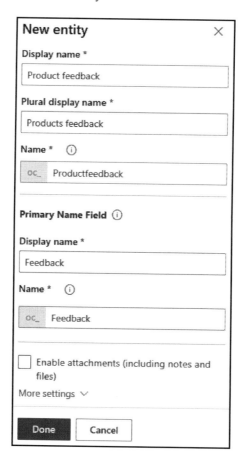

Do note the **More settings** area. It is collapsed by default, but once expanded it presents several more sections with configurable elements. Besides providing a description for the entity, you should choose the **Entity type and ownership** section and define the **Ownership** setting. When using the **User or team** option, you have more granular control over security, while choosing the **Organization** option gives you a more generic access model. We will leave our custom entity set to **User or team**, as we will configure security in the scenario presented in Chapter 13, *Core Administration Concepts*.

Select **Done** when ready to create this new entity.

The screen refreshes and presents us with the entity properties. As you can see from the following screenshot, once the entity is provisioned, it comes along with quite a lot of defined properties:

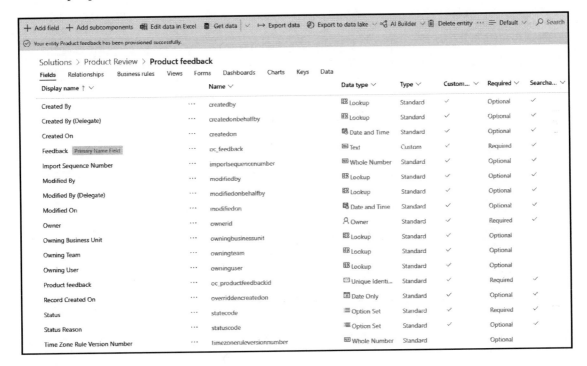

In the next section, we will look at how to extend the newly created entity.

Extending the entity

We want to add two custom fields to our entity. First off, we need a reference to the product. We do this by selecting the **Add field** option on the ribbon and defining the new field as a **Lookup** field to the **Product** table, as seen here:

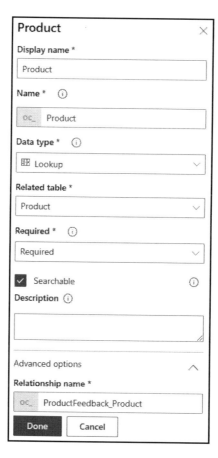

If you have not pre-defined the relationship to the product, make sure to expand the **Advanced options** area, and review the default relationship name given. In most cases, you should rename this relationship to clean up repetitive or weird naming results. The relationship typically reflects the solution-defined prefix along with the names of the two entities it relates to.

Click **Done** when ready.

The second field we will add is a product rating. We want to present the user with three options: **Low**, **Average**, and **Great**. In the **Option set** dropdown, set and define the three options, as seen in the following screenshot:

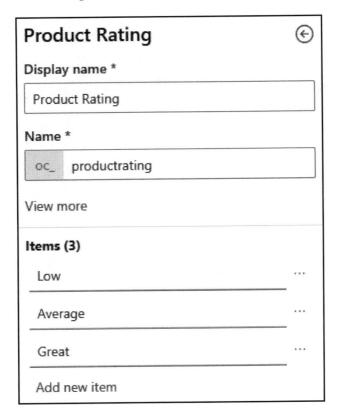

Select **Save** to store the option definitions and return to the field definition. Set the field as required and select **Done** when complete. The following screenshot shows the entire configuration:

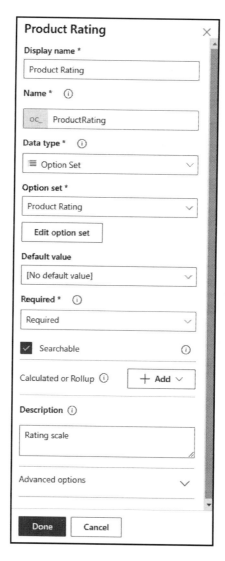

Let's save our progress so far by selecting the **Save Entity** button at the bottom of the entity screen.

From the tabs at the top, we can choose **Relationships** and see the newly created relationship between Product Feedback and Product.

Let's see next how to edit the main form of our entity and add the newly created fields.

Configuring the entity form

For the newly created fields to be of any use, we need to add them to a form. Select the **Forms** tab and click on the **Main form**. This opens the Power Apps form editor window. Drag the two custom fields to the form, as seen in the following screenshot:

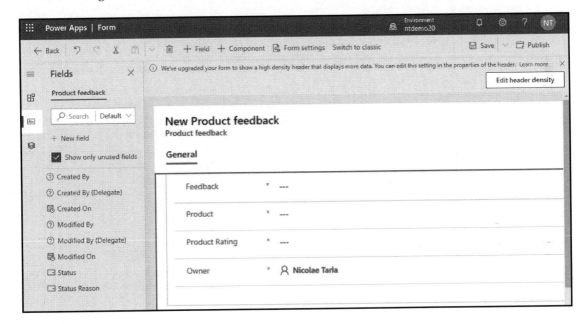

Click **Save** to commit the changes and then click **Publish** to make them available in the environment.

Selecting **Back** on the ribbon takes us back to the previous listing of forms.

You can now configure additional properties as needed, including creating custom views, business rules, charts, and dashboards, as well as see and edit the data records for this entity.

Homework: Add additional fields of various data types, create a new view, and define a chart and dashboard for this entity. Use the Microsoft documentation available at docs.microsoft.com to guide you through the additional configuration options.

As we have seen in this scenario, we created a new custom solution, added a new entity to our solution, and configured two custom fields and the main form of our entity. This provides the basics of extending the platform.

You should continue experimenting with additional entities, field types, forms, charts, and dashboards.

Summary

Throughout this chapter, we learned how to create a small targeted application with great flexibility and speed. We learned that the no/low code approach really pays off and has an important role in any business.

While building the application, we covered concepts around solutions and solution packages, as well as configuring entities and relationships. We also looked at some of the functionality around enforcing SLAs and geolocation.

In the next chapter, we'll move on and look at the core configuration and customization concepts available in Dynamics 365. Now that we have an understanding of the core applications and the ability to build additional apps, we have the necessary toolset to learn how to get more out of this great, flexible platform.

10
Building Better Business Functionality

In the previous chapters, we looked at the various applications available for Dynamics 365 Customer Engagement. These include Sales, Customer Service, Field Service, **Project Service Automation (PSA)**, and the new Marketing applications. Often enough, though, we tackle a new project that falls outside of these applications. Yes, it might integrate with one or more of these applications, leveraging some or all of their functionality, but the scope is so different that it does not fall within any of these functional offerings.

In the previous chapter, we learned how to extend functionality through configurations, how to capture additional data points, the different data types, the roles of views and charts, creating relationships, and the concept of **Service-Level Agreements (SLAs)**. With all that knowledge in the bag already, let's spend some time in this chapter looking at the next step. All those small components must work together and make a system that maps your business needs.

Throughout this chapter, we will focus our attention on the following core concepts:

- Understanding processes
- Dialogs (deprecated and replacement options)
- Learning about workflows
- Understanding real-time workflows
- Using Flow instead of workflows
- Leveraging actions
- Configuring business rules
- Learning about Business Process Flows
- Leveraging Excel
- Learning about document templates
- Leveraging search correctly

By the end of this chapter, you will be able to understand the capabilities available to allow you to extend the platform's core functionality through configuration. There are complex point and click configuration capabilities that allow us to add great value to the application, and understanding these options will make you a better Power user.

This chapter focuses on processes, allowing for the configuration of various user guidance and automation features, as well as various ways of working with data. From exporting data for analysis and updating data in bulk to printing data formatted with templates, the user is in full control. Finally, a multitude of ways to search and retrieve the needed data puts any and all information at the fingertips of any user, making it very easy and friendly for any data to be found and retrieved with great ease.

Let's get going.

Understanding processes

In the context of Dynamics 365, processes is a generic category that covers a few functional features grouped together. A process is any type of automation introduced as part of customizing the system, and it involves multiple actions grouped together. As such, some examples of processes supported by the platform include dialogs (deprecated), workflows, actions, and Business Process Flows.

In the context of customizing Dynamics 365, processes are created and grouped as part of one or more solutions. Within the solution, processes are listed as a separate category and are accessible on their own configuration tab.

The core platform comes with a set of processes already defined. If we open a solution and go to **Add Existing** on the ribbon, one of the options presented is **Process**. The following screenshot shows a list of existing processes that can be added to your solution:

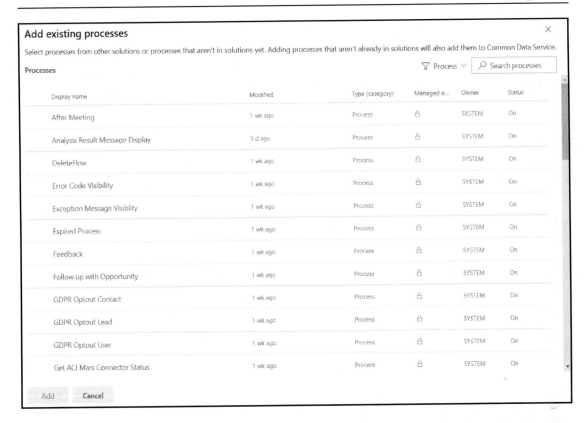

For a classic representation, we can also drop into Classic mode by expanding the ellipsis (...) on the ribbon and selecting **Switch to classic**, as depicted in the following screenshot:

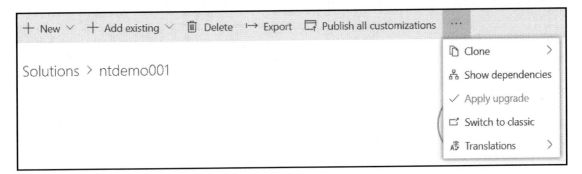

This takes us to the **Solution management** screen, which has a separate classification for **Processes**, as shown in the following screenshot:

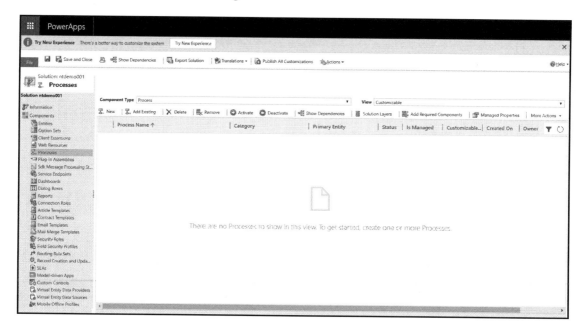

Working within a solution, we can add **New** or **Existing** processes, **Remove** processes, or completely delete them. Other options include **Activate** and **Deactivate**. Any process, to be available to users, must be activated. While a process is activated, it cannot be removed and/or deleted.

When working with many processes customized in a solution, you can order the view of the processes by any of the columns available, either ascending or descending. You can also apply filters to sort and reduce the number of processes displayed in this view. This will help a lot when retrieving a specific process from many customized items.

Processes can have defined, specified dependencies. As such, a process could be related to another process, in a parent or child relationship. A process can have one or more child processes, depending on the complexity of the business requirements. Splitting a large process into parent and child processes is a good practice to help manage functionality in smaller and more manageable chunks, or to avoid repeat customizations of the same steps in multiple processes.

There are three ways to create processes in Dynamics 365:

- The most common method used by Power users and administrators is interactively through the user interface. The process builder in Dynamics 365 is a pretty robust and simple to use tool that allows us to build custom processes with no code. This is quite appealing to Power users who can customize aspects of the system without having to call for support from a development team and wait for the features to be implemented.
- Another method is by creating custom processes using code. This method is targeted at developers and uses workflow-related classes from the **Software Development Kit (SDK)**. This is a very developer-focused approach, and it involves planning, designing, developing, testing, and deploying custom code solutions. Usually, this approach involves a strict deployment process and tends to involve various teams in producing properly packaged solutions.
- Finally, the last method to create processes is by importing already developed processes from other environments or solutions. These processes come packaged in a solution. They can be either internally created or can come from an external source such as a system customizer or **Independent Software Vendor (ISV)**.

Taking advantage of the flexibility in relating processes, coupled with the various options to create new processes, we now have great flexibility in guiding users through the necessary steps to complete an action.

In the next section, we will look at the alternatives used for dialogs after they become deprecated in Dynamics 365.

Using alternatives for dialogs

Dialogs were one of the common customizations applied to Dynamics 365 to guide a user through specific steps. They were commonly used in call center scenarios, where a fixed script must be followed while interacting with a customer, and data is being captured at each step.

They are still available in the current version of Dynamics 365 but have been marked as deprecated. This means that no new functionality will be added, and they will be removed from the platform in a future version. With that being said, there are many organizations still using this functionality, and time is allowed for these customers to upgrade to the new functionality.

A **dialog** is a type of process used to create an interactive data entry form that guides the user step by step through a scenario. This process relies on continuous user interaction and requires user input to run through to completion.

A dialog presents the user with an interface that's similar to a wizard. The user can make an appropriate selection at each step of the dialog, and then progress through all the steps to completion.

A dialog is usually launched by the user, or it can be customized to be triggered by an action on the form.

The new Unified Interface has already removed the ability to launch a dialog, and the Microsoft documentation marks dialogs as being removed with the October 2020 release wave. This functionality is to be replaced with two alternatives, as recommended by Microsoft. These include Business Process Flows and Canvas Apps. We will take a look at both alternatives for replacing this functionality.

Replacing dialogs with Business Process Flows

Business Process Flows will be described later in this chapter, in the *Business Process Flows* section.

At a high level, a Business Process Flow is meant to guide a user through various steps, thus mapping a real-life business process on the platform. We'll find out more details later in this chapter, but it suffices to say that starting such a process is done from a specific entity record and by walking through the steps in a sequential order. The main difference is that, while a dialog needed to be run and completed in one session, the Business Process Flow can be started, left off at a certain stage, and continued at a later time.

Replacing dialogs with Canvas Apps

Canvas Apps provide the necessary flexibility to capture and guide a user through steps designed to map an existing Business Flow. The app can be integrated into a record form and used to guide a user directly from within a record. It is an interactive component that can also be triggered as an app on its own, if designed as such. This allows its flexibility to be used without it even being in your Dynamics solution. However, this can trigger certain things to happen, such as the creation of new records or updates.

We talked in more detail about Canvas Apps in `Chapter 8`, *Dynamics 365 Customer Engagement and Power Platform,* when we looked at the Power Platform and the various types of apps available. Remember that we said a Canvas App is not necessarily related to the underlying **Common Data Service (CDS)** but can also leverage other platforms as a data storage mechanism through connectors? To replace dialogs, a Canvas App will have to leverage CDS and be built in a format that makes sense so that we can integrate it into a platform record form.

 For more documentation on replacing dialogs, see the Microsoft documentation available at `https://docs.microsoft.com/en-us/flow/replace-dialogs`.

Another important type of Process on the platform is the workflow. This allows automation to be implemented. We'll look at the available options for using workflows in the next section.

Learning about workflows

A workflow is another type of process that can be defined within the Dynamics 365 platform. This process is also used to model and automate business processes. Workflows run in the background. They are triggered automatically based on certain triggers on the entity forms or based on specific conditions, or they can be started manually by a user. Starting a workflow manually is done by navigating to a record and selecting the **Run Flow** option on the ribbon. Then, within the **Run Workflow** section, you need to find the specific workflow to be run:

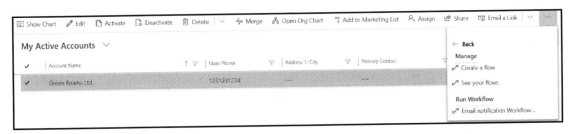

Note that Flow is now the preferred and recommended way to create automation, and Workflows can only be created by dropping into the Classic solution interface. Workflows created through the Classic interface are presented in the Unified Interface for workflows marked as on-demand processes.

For workflows to be available in this view, a few conditions must be met – the workflow has to be enabled, the workflow has to be targeted at the entity we are trying to run the workflow against, and the workflow must be an on-demand workflow. No child workflows can be selected to be run this way, nor can workflows be set to run in the background.

Workflows can be created in a similar fashion with dialogs, by using the Dynamics 365 process builder wizard, by creating them in custom code, or by importing them from other solutions. In addition, workflows can be created declaratively. This process does not involve writing any code, and you do not have to compile them. Using this approach, you declare the workflow definitions using a language called XAML. This is a declarative markup language used mostly to simplify creating user interfaces for .NET applications. This approach is only supported in the on-premise version and is not commonly used.

While workflows can perform almost the same operations as custom coded plugins, there are certain situations where a workflow is recommended over a plugin. These include situations where the business logic needs to be updated regularly by non-developer users, or when we need to start a process manually.

Workflows can be distributed from one environment to another as part of a custom solution. There are, however, some considerations to be aware of. If your workflows reference specific entity instances, the unique IDs of the entity will differ in a new environment, unless they are part of the deployment you push not only to platform configuration but also to static data records. Dynamics 365 only resolves system user and currency records based on the full name property, while all other entities do not get resolved. For this reason, if you deploy workflows as part of a solution to another environment, you must verify them after deployment to make sure all the workflows are enabled. Workflows, where the aforementioned condition is encountered, will remain in Draft status and will require the user to perform a deployment to correct the references and reactivate the workflows.

Just like dialogs, workflows are in a Draft state while they are being worked on. Once you are ready to make them available to users, you must activate them. Upon activation, the workflow subscribes to specific events and listens for them to be triggered. Once triggered, the workflow creates a new asynchronous operation and adds it to the asynchronous service queue. As such, workflows are running asynchronously.

 Asynchronous operations can be suspended and restarted by users.

Running a workflow asynchronously allows Dynamics 365 to queue execution and process operations later. This allows the platform to manage resources efficiently and allows long-running processes to be paused and resumed as needed.

Using the asynchronous service, long-running processes can be safely paused and resumed while the state is being saved. This allows the system to restart without losing the process state. This takes advantage of the persistence service by saving the state. This also allows a process that crashed to restart from the last persisted point.

Another type of workflow is the real-time workflow. We'll look at this in the next section.

Understanding real-time workflows

Real-time workflows are, by nature, very similar to regular workflows in Dynamics 365. The creation process is identical to regular workflows. This type of workflow was introduced with Dynamics CRM 2013 and involves making a change on the backend regarding how the information is processed. These processes are not queued, but they execute immediately or in response to a message.

Real-time workflows execute in the same stage as synchronous plugins. They can execute before, after, or during the main operation. They can also be ranked within a stage, the same as plugins.

These workflows can run either in the context of the current user or the workflow owner. When running a workflow manually, it only runs in the context of the current user.

A limitation of real-time workflows is that it cannot contain any delay or waiting periods for activities.

A real-time workflow can be converted into an asynchronous one and back into real-time. The workflow must be in the Draft state to be modified.

So far, we've seen the standard processes available on the platform. But in addition to the workflows we've just seen, now, we can offload some of the work to a new feature. In the next section, we'll look at how we can use Flow (Power Automate) to achieve similar results.

Using Flow instead of workflows

As described in Chapter 8, *Dynamics 365 Customer Engagement and Power Platform*, Microsoft Flow allows for various automation processes to be built. One of the connectors allows Flow to tap into CDS, and thus act upon various records in Dynamics 365.

Since Flow is much more flexible and provides a more modern interface for building automation and executing various processes against Dynamics 365 and other systems, it is now the preferred method of automating processes. Classical workflows are still supported in Dynamics 365, but due to the greater flexibility of the Flow platform, we should consider building Flows where possible.

One of the advantages of Flow is that it comes with the ability to transform data in the process. As an example, workflows allow you to populate data with specific values based on various conditions. But in a satiation where you need to compose a field context from the values of multiple other fields, a Flow is a much better alternative. In addition, various expressions are available with Flow, including math functions, conversion functions, logical functions, and others. While in a workflow some of these could have been created through additional configurations, others are just not available.

Flows created in the context of a solution, with the new modern solution interface, are present just like workflows in a folder within the solution called Workflows. The following screenshot shows the **Workflows** folder, which contains the definition of a Classic workflow in XAML format, as well as a new Flow in JSON format:

Name	Type	Compressed size	Password p...	Size	Ratio
EmailnotificationWorkflowDEMO-5580EA07-4CCE-4977-BEFD-356C480B56BC.xaml	Windows Markup File	3 KB	No	32 KB	94%
Whenarecordiscreated-Updatearecord-A7C07A6E-B4EA-E911-A812-000D3A0C24F7.json	JSON Source File	1 KB	No	2 KB	62%

So, the real question here is, when do you use Workflow versus Flow? And it's a valid question. To answer this, I would recommend looking at the following criteria.

It is preferred to use workflows when answering yes to the following questions:

- Is the entire process integrated within your current Dynamics 365 instance?
- Does the action need to take place in real time or near-real-time?
- Does the process generate an email linking back to a record in Dynamics 365?
- Is this going to be an on-demand process? Note that both Flows and Workflows can now be triggered on-demand, but Flow is accessible on-demand only in the Unified Interface.

Alternatively, we should use Flows when the answer is yes to the following questions:

- Do we need to send emails from system accounts or non-user accounts?
- Do we want to use a non-Microsoft, non-Office 365 email service provider?
- Do we need to create push notifications or use SMS services?
- Do we want to create a more complex and robust approval workflow?
- Do we want to create light integrations to other external platforms or tools?
- Do we want more advanced scheduling capabilities?
- While not often used, and not really recommended, do we want to delete records?
- Do we want to use other tools for data capture, but have the data transferred automatically into our Dynamics 365 instance?

This is only a high-level decision option, and in time, experience will help you make these decisions easily.

Using actions

Actions are a special type of workflow in Dynamics 365. They were introduced with Dynamics CRM 2013 and are used to define custom messages. Actions are used to add new functionality to the organization web service or to combine multiple organization web service message requests into one.

The basic actions in most systems are defined by verbs such as Create, Update, and Delete. Dynamics 365 systems add Assign to this list. Through actions, we can define additional functionality such as Escalate, Approve, Schedule, Route, and so on. By combining processes based on these core actions, system customizers can create new actions for specific business needs.

These actions are defined by implementing workflows. The action workflows are registered in the core operation of the execution pipeline.

Actions are supported in both on-premise and online Dynamics 365 organizations, but just like workflows, when defined using declarative XAML, they are only supported in Dynamics 365 on-premise and **Internet-Facing Deployment (IFD)** scenarios.

One main difference between actions and regular workflows is that actions can be declared as global, where they are not associated with a particular entity. Also, actions can be triggered by client-side scripts.

 Actions always run in the context of the calling user.

One aspect to be aware of when defining actions is that they are not supported by offline clients. If the expectation is that offline access is required for certain actions, a more creative approach must be taken and, possibly, plugins may be used.

Actions can be created in two ways – through the process builder, just like any workflows and dialogs, or through custom code. The first approach is targeted mostly at Power users, as a no-code approach, while the latter requires a developer to be involved in the creation of the action definition. Note that in order to create actions, you must use the Classic interface for solution management. At the time of writing, the new user experience does not include this functionality.

Just like workflows and dialogs, actions can be added to a packaged solution and transferred to another environment.

The process to create action through the process builder is quite simple:

1. In the context of a solution, navigate to **Processes**.
2. On the processes listing view, select **New** to create a new process.
3. In the **Create Process** window that pops-up, define the required fields and select **Action** from the **Category** drop-down.
4. For the entity definition, you can create an action against a specific entity, or a **global** action, as shown in the following screenshot:

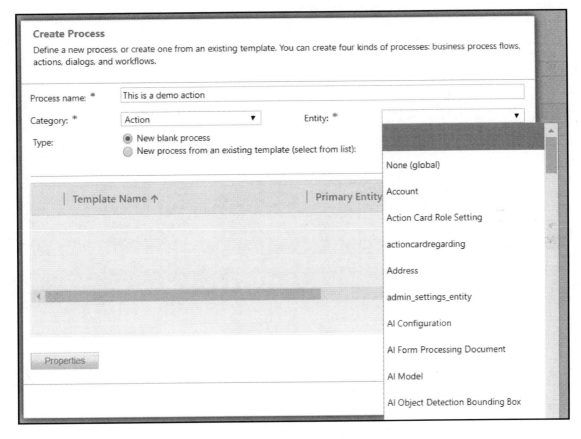

5. With the selections in place, you are ready to create the new action.
6. Then, select **OK**.

Creating an action, from this point forward, is quite like creating a workflow. The main difference is the ability to define a multitude of arguments for various data types, as well as the direction of these arguments. The following screenshot shows the six arguments that are created, with five input arguments and one output argument:

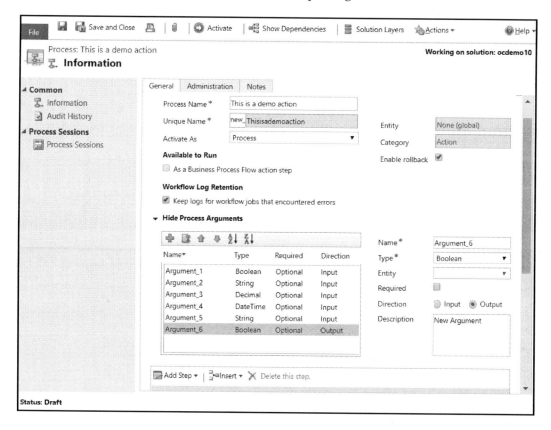

The **Enable Rollback** configuration on the action creation screen allows us to define when we disable the rollback feature. There are situations when code runs out of scope for CRM. These actions cannot be rolled back, so we can disable this option in the action configuration form.

 Using actions allows us to run custom business logic using server-side events.

Now that we've covered the available processes, let's focus on business rules. These allow a Power user or administrator to define the user experience in real time.

Using business rules

Business rules were introduced with Dynamics CRM 2013 to assist Power users in creating validation rules without any coding skills. As such, this is a very powerful feature that's been added to the system customizer's toolbox.

Lots of customizations include various validation rules. From field-level validation to showing or hiding form fields based on values selected in other fields, business rules allow Power users to implement a variety of rules in a pseudocode format. No code is required as the whole creation of business rules is wizard-based.

While this is a step in the right direction, business rules will not replace JScript completely. For complex validations and the implementation of complicated rules, you will find that certain limitations will still require a JScript developer to be involved.

The main difference between workflows and business rules is the location where the process runs. Business rules are primarily meant as client-side logic, and the result is expected to directly and immediately influence the user's interaction with the system.

The most common application for business rules involves the following processes:

- Set or clear a field's value
- Set the required or not required level on a field
- Enable or disable fields
- Show or hide fields
- Validate field data
- Show error messages to users

Business rules are included in a solution at the entity level. This way, they can be deployed from one environment to another.

> Business rules can be applied not only to the main entity form but also quick create forms.

When creating business rules, you can set the scope to either a specific form or to all forms. Selecting **All Forms** applies the business rule to all main and quick create forms for the entity. You can't select only specific forms.

Creating a new business rule involves the following steps:

1. From the solution package that holds the customizations, navigate to an entity and select it. From the tabs at the top, select the **Business rules** tab. This will show any business rules that have already been created on this entity, if any, as shown in the following screenshot:

2. In the business rules grid, select **New** to create a new business rule. You will be presented with a new window that allows you to customize the business rule definition. The following screenshot shows a rule that's been configured to check for a blank field and set the required field if it's blank, or locked, once populated:

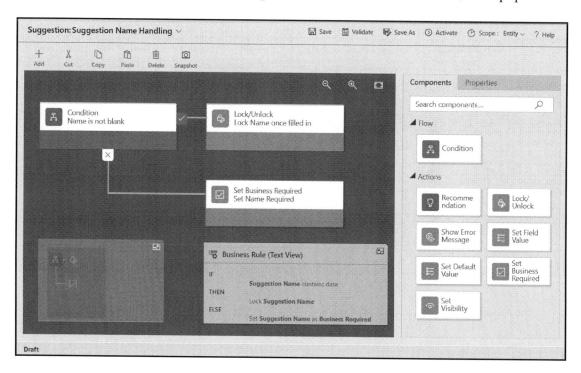

3. Provide a name for your new business rule. Make sure the name is descriptive enough to allow other users to customize the system in the future so that they quickly understand the purpose of this business rule. In this example, the name given is **Suggestion Name Handling**. Selecting the drop-down arrow next to the name allows you to expand the section where you define the **Name** and **Description** details for your business rule. As a best practice, you should not only provide a descriptive name but also a description.

4. Next, configure the conditions for execution. Here, you can set various conditions by selecting the **Components** tab from the right blade and selecting the **Condition** box. Note that, by default, your first condition is populated as a new Business rule, which always starts with a condition. At a minimum, you must always include an action for the condition met branch.
   Other components you can leverage include the standard functionality around locking or unlocking a field, setting a field value, setting a default value, and setting the visibility of a field or business requirements.
   Operators used within the condition include most of the common conditions, such as **equals**, **does not equal**, **contains**, and **does not contain**, **begins with** and **does not begin with**, **ends with** and **does not end with**, and **contains data** and **does not contain data**. The following screenshot shows the options available in the **Properties** tab for setting up a condition:

5. Once you have defined the conditions, we can move on to defining the actions. We can configure one or more actions, as required. All actions will be executed in order on a specific path.

   Adding an action is done similarly to adding a condition, by simply dragging one of the actions from the **Components** window onto an **Add** box in the visual designer. The following screenshot shows dragging the **Set Visibility** action onto the condition success path, after the **Lock/Unlock** action:

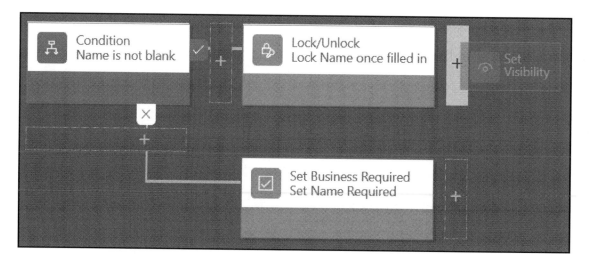

Starting with Dynamics CRM 2015, a new option has been added to actions. Now, we can also set a default value for a field.

Through these pre-configured actions, we can generate and display a defined error message, we can set a field's value either as a fixed value or the value of another field, we can set a field as business required or not, set a field's visibility, and lock or unlock a field.

As we can observe, some of the limitations include not being able to set a field as Business Recommended or set the value of a field to a calculated value. For these situations, we still need to revert to JScript or use a Flow.

6. Finally, provide a description of the business rule in the description field. This will help future system customizers determine the reasons for creating this business rule, as well as business logic. You can also track the updates performed while customizing the system from here.

7. Once your business rule has been fully customized, save it. To make it available to users, you must activate it. Later, if you need to modify it, you must deactivate it before any modifications can be done.
   While saving your business rule, it may happen that your business rule changes and the configuration is validated. You can also trigger a validation by selecting the **Validate** option on the ribbon, as shown in the following screenshot:

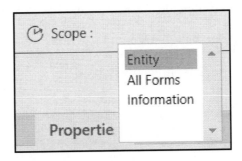

You can create a business rule based on another existing business rule by performing **Save As** and modifying the new rule as required.

One other important aspect of customizing business rules is defining the scope. The default value is **Entity**, but you can select to scope this rule to a specific form. The options available are shown in the following screenshot:

When using business rules to customize a system, you must be aware of the order of execution. First off, all system scripts are executed, followed by custom scripts on the form, and then the business rules logic. When multiple business rules execute against the same fields, the business rules are applied in the order in which they were activated. The oldest activated business rule is applied first.

Now that we understand the business rules capabilities, let's look at some of the limitations.

Understanding the limitations of business rules

While business rules are a very handy customization option for Power users, we must take into consideration the following limitations:

- Business rules do not run on record save. They are triggered by the `OnChange` message of the field, or by the `OnLoad` form.
- If a field associated with a business rule is removed from the form, the business rule will not run. No error message is presented to the user or logged in the system.
- The interaction of business rules is limited to form fields only. No other elements can be manipulated through business rules.
- When performing a field value change using business rules, the `OnChange` event is not triggered. As such, if you have scripts set to run on the `OnChange` event of that field, they will not run when the value is updated by a business rule.
- Certain whole number fields cannot be used in business rules. They include Time Zone, Duration, and Language, and they are not presented in the rule editor.

Nevertheless, business rules are an important advancement that has been added to the system. They enhance the ability of non-developer system customizers to create rules through a visual editor and implement logic with no code.

Another great feature of the platform is the ability to visually guide a user through the steps necessary to accomplish a task. We'll see how that's done in the next section.

Learning about Business Process Flows

Starting with the 2013 version (Microsoft Dynamics CRM 2013), Microsoft introduced Business Process Flows. They are a feature similar in design to other processes but provides very different capabilities to the system. Business Process Flows provide users with a visual way to guide a system user through a predefined business process to get work done.

The user experience is greatly enhanced and streamlined. They provide visual guidance through a predefined business process, highlighting the user interaction with the system and defining the steps and the requirements at each step in order for a user to complete a process. These processes can easily be customized through a wizard-based, no-code approach. They also allow a user to select the process type to be used when performing an activity.

Business Process Flows are used to define a process and the required steps for users to take to achieve the desired outcome. Each step is visually indicated through graphical representation on the record and includes a list of required fields at that step. A user can navigate through the defined steps, determine what needs to happen at each step, and make decisions regarding the best approach to take to complete a process. Users also can advance the process to a new step if certain business requirements are met.

The following screenshot shows an example of a pre-defined Business Process Flow in the Lead to Opportunity Sales Process:

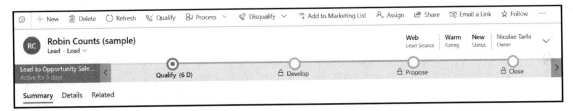

This is one of the processes defined as standard in Dynamics 365 and provides a good representation of the potential of Business Process Flows on the platform. All existing Business Process Flows can be customized to match existing business requirements, and new processes can be created from scratch.

The main purpose of Business Process Flows is to reduce the amount of user training by enhancing the system's ability to guide the user through a set of predefined steps.

Business Process Flows can be configured to support sales methodologies specific to each business and group, as well as service-response processes. You can also customize Business Process Flows for any other business requirements involving standard or custom entities defined in your Dynamics 365 environments.

Following a specific predefined business process flow greatly reduces the potential number of mistakes a user can make when performing his or her duties and allows users to quickly and efficiently correct these mistakes. This results in increased customer satisfaction and better, more standardized processes.

With the help of Business Process Flows, a system user can easily determine where he or she is in the process, what needs to be done next, and what has already been completed.

Each Business Process Flow defines a collection of stages and steps. They are visually displayed at the top of the records that have Business Process flows enabled.

Stages are the main groupings and contain a set of steps. They are represented visually by the bubble headers. The current step is highlighted and marked with a target symbol. The completed stages are represented with a bubble checkmark. The current stage selected is marked with a slightly darker, grayed-out background. A user can navigate to past or future stages by clicking on the forward or back arrows at the ends of the Business Process Flow bar.

Opening any of the past or current stages presents the user with a list of the most important action items that must be completed, as shown in the following screenshot:

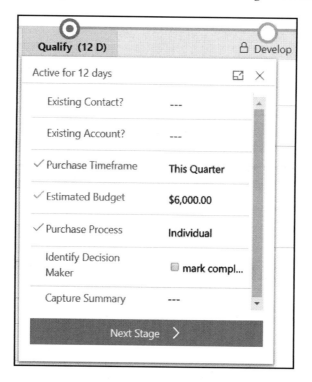

Opening a future stage, depending on whether it is a stage related to the current entity or a stage in a new entity, will present a slightly different view. If the same entity is covered by the respective future stage, then actions are presented; otherwise, a grayed-out area with an **Inactive** label is presented, as shown in the following screenshot:

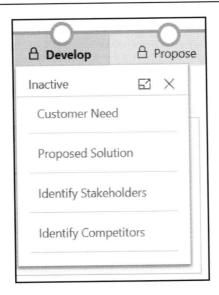

You typically advance to the next stage by either performing a required action that automatically advances the process to a new stage or by clicking on the next stage button, represented by an arrow to the right of the Business Process Flow area.

Within each stage, the completed steps are represented with a green checkmark in front of each field, while the remaining steps are blank and unfilled. Blank fields are visualized with three lines.

Business Process Flows provide a streamlined experience for capturing user input at each defined stage. A complete solution can mix Business Process Flows with other system processes to enhance and validate the user interactions with the system, thus creating a complex scenario with absolutely no involvement from developers. As such, Power users can create and add to the system's complex business requirements and scenarios while maintaining them, without having to rely on a development group or partner.

The data captured in the Business Process Flows stage data fields is also replicated on the form fields, where other custom processes or customizations can be triggered to execute validation or any other type of customized process. This gives us the ability to not only visually guide users but also validate that the work performed is correct and in line with the current company business processes, requirements, restrictions, and SLAs.

Business Process Flows can set field values for fields that are not present on the form. As such, the form can be kept simpler, while still collecting all the necessary information on the record.

The order of execution is very important when designing Business Process Flows. Other processes that are initiated by changes that have been made to Business Process Flow fields are only triggered when the data in the form is saved.

The platform includes a multitude of default Business Process Flows for the various solutions. Depending on whether you are using only Sales, only Customer Service, or a combination of the two, your list of Business Process Flows will vary.

At their core, the solutions started with the following three Business Process Flows:

- Lead to Opportunity Sales Process
- Opportunity Sales Process
- Phone to Case Process

As you can see from the naming, these pertain to either the Sales solution or the Customer Service solution. A couple of new processes have been added since and serve as additional functionality to several modules. A good example is a set of **Business Process Flows** (**BPFs**) around the management of Knowledge Articles. These include the following default BPFs:

- New Process
- Translation Process
- Expired Process

When creating and working with Business Process Flows, they can span across one or multiple entities. Processes can be created to begin in an entity and continue through other entities to completion. For example, you can start a Business Process Flow at the Opportunity record level and progress through to Quote, Order, and Invoice. You can also return in the last step to update the Opportunity record with the conclusion of the process.

There are a few considerations when working with BPFs. These include items such as the following:

- There are a limited number of entities a BPF can span across. You will want to keep your process limited to a maximum of five different entities.
- The users running through a BPF must have proper permissions to all the entities involved in a BPF; otherwise, you will encounter permission errors that will block the user from completing the process.

From a user perspective, we can define which Business Process Flow is required when working with a specific record. As a customizer, multiple Business Process Flows can be created for the same entity. When creating a new entity record, the user can select which Business Process Flow applies to the scenario being used.

Note that up to 10 Business Process Flows can be activated per entity.

In Dynamics 365, Business Process Flows can be associated with specific security roles. This way, specific users can be restricted from using specific Business Process Flows. This functionality is like restricting forms by using a security role. The default business Process Flow that's assigned to an entity is the oldest one to be activated on the entity that the user has permissions to use.

When multiple Business Process Flows are activated on an entity, the user can choose which one to use. He or she can choose **Process** from the ribbon and select **Switch Process**. Next, they can follow the on-screen steps to change to a different Business Process Flow. Upon changing the process, the newly assigned process starts at the first step, even if the previously completed steps appear to match the ones in the original process.

If a user opens a record with a Business Process Flow assigned that he or she does not have permissions for, the Business Process Flow will be displayed but will be disabled. Thus, the user cannot modify anything on the process itself.

Another limitation of Business Process Flows is in the number of stages available. For performance and usability reasons, a Business Process Flow cannot contain more than 30 stages.

Also, Business Process Flows are only available for entities that use an Update form. This limits the use of Business Process Flows to custom entities and the following standard system entities: Account, Appointment, Campaign, Campaign Activity, Campaign Response, Competitor, Contact, Email, Fax, Case, Invoice, Lead, Letter, Marketing List, Opportunity, Phone Call, Product, Price List Item, Quote, Recurring Appointment, Sales Literature, Order, User, Task, and Team.

For custom created entities, Business Process Flows must be enabled on the entity definition. Once this option is enabled, it cannot be disabled. Thus, next, we will look at creating Business Process Flows.

Creating Business Process Flows

Creating Business Process Flows is quite like creating any other process in Dynamics 365, but the process definition is quite different. We will start by navigating to the solution that will store our customizations.

 We should always create customizations in the context of a custom solution. This allows us to group our customizations and create portability to another environment, for instance.

Note that at the time of writing, the modern solution management interface does not allow us to create new processes. We must drop into the Classic interface for these customizations. We do this as follows:

1. Start by expanding the ellipsis (**...**) menu on the modern solution management window and select **Switch to classic**.
2. Select the **Processes** section on the left navigation area. This section will display all existing processes that have been customized in this solution. This includes not only Business Process Flows, but also workflows, dialogs, and actions. In the **Processes** view, we can easily see the status of each customized process. We can also sort and filter by any of the columns in the view:

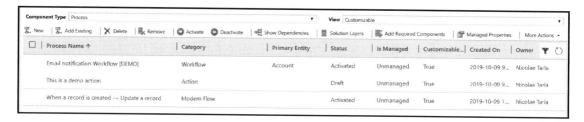

Process Name ↑	Category	Primary Entity	Status	Is Managed	Customizable...	Created On	Owner
Email notification Workflow [DEMO]	Workflow	Account	Activated	Unmanaged	True	2019-10-09 9...	Nicolae Tarla
This is a demo action	Action		Draft	Unmanaged	True	2019-10-09 9...	Nicolae Tarla
When a record is created -> Update a record	Modern Flow		Activated	Unmanaged	True	2019-10-09 1...	Nicolae Tarla

3. Select **New** from the ribbon to create a new Business Process Flow. This triggers the **Create process** window, as shown in the following screenshot:

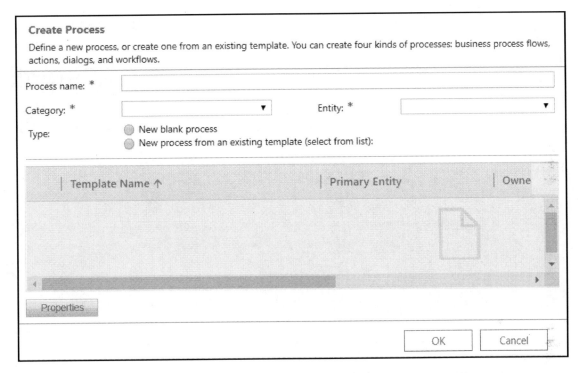

4. Populate all the required fields, specify a name for the process and the entity it's being applied to, and from the **Category** drop-down, select **Business Process Flow**. If a template is created in the system, you can use the template as a starting point for your new process. Observe that, now, processes can be targeted at either the Classic interface or Unified Interface only. With the Classic interface on its way out the door, we should only select the Unified Interface option, unless we're still servicing instances where the transition to Unified Interface has not happened yet. Click **OK** when you're done.

5. The next window presents us with the options to define the Business Process Flow stages and steps, as well as generic properties. This leverages the updated builder, which presents us with a more graphical and simplistic way of creating the logic for this process. The following screenshot shows a simple, predefined process:

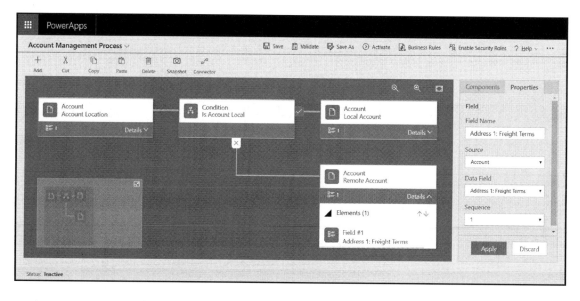

In the previous screenshot, at the very top, we can see the process name we defined. We can click on the down arrow next to the name to expand the process' **properties** window, where we can define the description of the process.

While the description is not mandatory, it is always a good idea to describe the processes you create. It will be a lot easier to maintain the system in the future, as well as easier for the support team to figure out which process does what in the system.

At the same level but to the right, we find the control to manage this process. We can **Save** the process at various stages during creation, or we can open an existing process and select **Save As** to create a new process based on the current one. This makes things easier when we need a new, slightly modified, process.

The **Validate** option allows us to perform an initial check on the process. While this does not validate that the logic we're implementing is correct, it does check to make sure the configuration is at least complete and will not result in a process failure due to missing configuration.

Once we are done with configuring our process, we must **Activate** it to make it available to users. Furthermore, we can restrict access to this process by **Enabling Security Roles**. This way, we can make this process available to only a subset of users in the enterprise that is part of a specific role.

Finally, we can configure business rules that are scoped to this process alone. Business rules are specific to the entity targeted and can work only for a specific Business Process Flow. This way, we can execute a specific set of logic in a business rule targeted by the currently running process.

Further down on this window, we will find the **Actions** ribbon. Here, we will find the options to **Add**, **Cut**, **Copy**, **Paste**, and **Delete** various options in the process. The **Snapshot** button allows you to take an image of the configured process. This is very handy when you want to document your configurations.

Underneath the ribbon, and taking central place, is the editor window. Here, you define the components that make up your process logic in a visual way, and you have the ability to zoom in and out to see the bigger picture or drill into the details. A preview block is available as an overlay to show you where you are in the process when you've zoomed in too much.

Finally, on the right-hand side of the screen, you have the **Components** and **Properties** sections. You drag components from the **Components** tab and place them into your process while defining the specifications of each selected component on the **Properties** tab. For example, the following screenshot shows you the **Properties** configuration for a **Field** defined on a component:

Once you have your process defined, select **Enable Security Roles**. This brings up a window where you can select to enable a process for everyone, or just for specific security roles. Selecting the option to **Enable only for the selected security roles** allows you to select from the existing security roles and choose the ones that will have access to this process, as shown in the following screenshot:

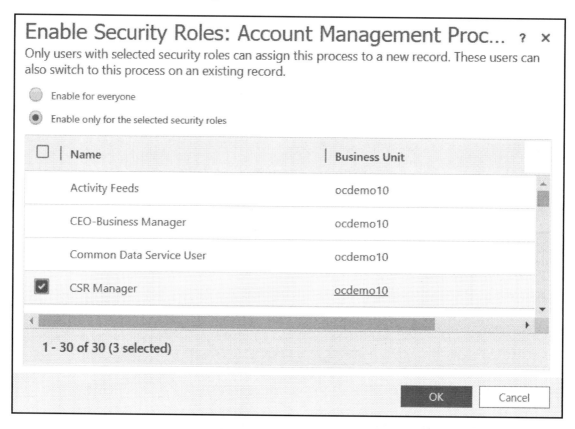

One other important customization option that's presented to Power users is the ability to create a new Business Process Flow from an existing one. You can open an existing process and click on **Save As** on the ribbon. This action triggers the validation of the process before the save occurs. The following screenshot shows a copy that's been created from the original Account Management Process:

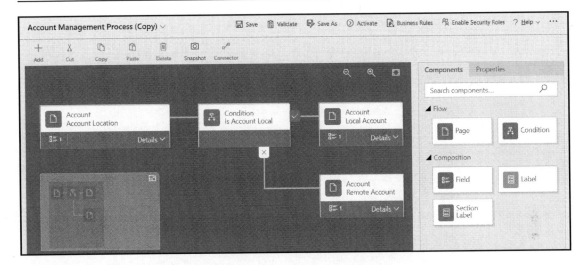

Once validated, it creates a copy of the existing Business Process Flow and allows you to change the Process Name and then modify any of the stages or steps to suit your new business requirements. The new process is saved by appending (Copy) to the end of the name. Make sure to rename this process as needed once you start editing it.

In order to automate more functionality, you can capture a stage change and perform an action. We'll look at this in the next section.

Triggering workflows on Business Process Flow stage change

The beauty of Business Process Flows is that they allow a system customizer to declare workflows that are triggered by a change of stage in a Business Process Flow. The whole configuration lies with the custom workflow, and the workflow can be added or removed later without affecting the original Business Process Flow.

To achieve this functionality, we will look at the following steps:

1. First, edit an existing Business Process Flow, or create a new one. On a specific step, from the **Add** option on the ribbon, select **Add Workflow**, as shown in the following screenshot:

2. In the **Workflow** definition, select what triggers your workflow. The available options include **Stage Entry** and **Stage Exit**, as shown in the following screenshot:

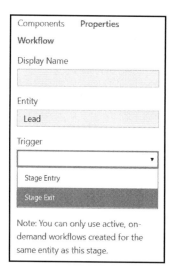

3. Finally, in the **Workflows** area, select the workflow you intend to trigger, as shown in the following screenshot:

4. When complete, select **Apply** and continue customizing the Business Process Flow. Your final designer window should reflect the triggered workflow in the customized stage, as follows:

With both the Business Process Flow and the workflow now published, you can test and see that each process step change that's made in the Business Process Flow now triggers the workflow to execute.

> Note that you can trigger either a synchronous or asynchronous workflow this way.

Now, let's move in a different direction. The greatest value of Dynamics is its ability to tightly integrate with the Office suite of applications. We'll look at using Excel within Dynamics 365 in the next section.

Leveraging Excel

Dynamics 365's tight integration with the Office suite of applications has always been one of the strengths of this platform. Each new version is built on top of existing features, thus adding new ways to interact with it. This brings the tools closer to the platform and makes the platform a core service for client applications.

The modern Dynamics 365 platform now leverages even more Office features, with the ability to tightly work with Office 365 and, in particular, Excel.

While we had the ability to export data to Excel for further analysis and have the data ready to be reimported in a blink of an eye, with the tight integration with Office 365, now, client applications can be substituted by their online versions. For details on online apps, see the main Office landing page at `https://www.office.com/`.

With these capabilities, we can render Excel data directly in a record in Microsoft Dynamics 365. When working with Excel, instead of spending time and clicks switching between applications, a system user can stay on the same record page and analyze data in Excel in the same view. All changes that are made to the data this way are being captured and saved back in the platform. Excel now becomes another user interface, tightly integrated into the Dynamics 365 interface.

To further enhance these features, we can use **Excel templates** to format data, present it graphically in the context of the Dynamics 365 record and analyze changes and their impact in real-time.

The ribbon presents the new **Excel Templates** options next to the former **Export to Excel** options, as shown in the following screenshot:

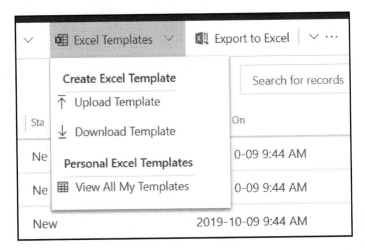

Excel is also a great tool for bulk updates. We can leverage an export to Excel to take some data, modify fields in bulk, and then reload the updated data. This is a very handy approach for many users dealing with data quality or that have to update the end-of-day status of a set of records.

In the next section, we're going to look at leveraging document templates for generating nicely and printable formatted output.

Learning about document templates

Document templates is a feature that was added to the platform a few versions back. As seen previously, we can use templates for Excel files. We can also create templates for Word documents. These templates can be created outside of the system and uploaded or generated while working in Dynamics 365.

You use document templates to arrange and present data in a printable format as needed. For example, you can have a Word template that allows you to print a formatted invoice so that you can send it to a customer.

From any ribbon option where we are presented with the **Templates** menu, we can trigger the template creation process by navigating to **View All My Templates**, as shown in the following screenshot:

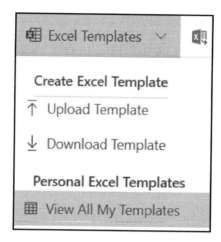

This presents you with a view of all available templates. You can create a new template by selecting the **New** option on the ribbon. You have a choice between Excel or Word templates. Selecting one option triggers an overlay window where you can select the **Entity** and **View** to start from, as shown in the following screenshot:

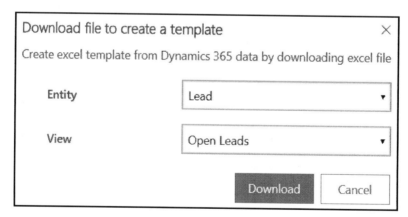

Clicking on **Download** allows you to download a template with data from the system.

The opposite is also true, where you can choose to upload a template created outside of the system.

You can use this approach to move templates from one instance to another by modifying it and reimporting it into another organization. Alternatively, you can update the existing organization by uploading the modified template back into the original instance.

In addition, with the template exported, you can now take advantage of the various graphs and rendering options in Excel to create more interactive templates that can be used for extensive analysis. Keep in mind that you should probably consider using **Power BI** if you intend to generate more robust visual representations of the data.

With new templates generated, let's look at how to leverage these templates to generate output documents.

Document generation templates

Document generation templates have also been added to Microsoft Dynamics 365. While with older versions we had to create either custom reports or various programmable processes to be able to generate branded and well-formatted documents such as a Quote or an Invoice, now, we can do all that with a single click. Once the templates have been generated and loaded into your organization, they are made available to users.

From a record where you want to generate a document based on a template, navigate to the extended ribbon options and find the **Word Templates** option, as shown in the following screenshot:

Here, you can either create a new word template if permissions allow you to, or you can use an existing one if available. The following screenshot shows the available options:

Selecting the default **Invoice Summary** template triggers an export to Word. If you save the document and open it, it will be formatted like so:

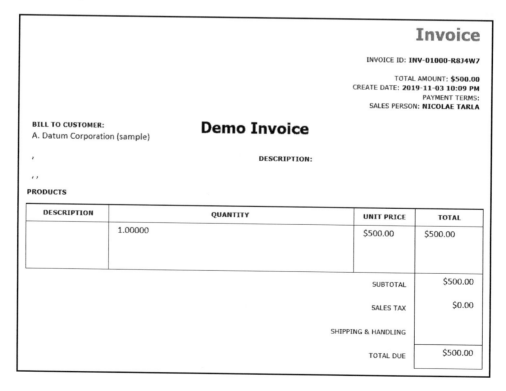

Note that once a document has been generated, it can be downloaded and saved, printed, shared, or emailed to other users or clients.

> You can always format this template so that it includes branding and a new layout, as needed by your business.

These bypass the rather complex process of using the old Office Mail Merge functionality and makes it a lot easier for the platform users to generate modern documents on the fly.

In the next section, we'll focus our attention on the platform's search capabilities.

Leveraging search correctly

Search has been at the core of this platform from its early days. It has evolved with the platform, and today, it provides extensive features that greatly enhance the user experience and usability.

There are various ways to search in Microsoft Dynamics CRM 2016, as follows:

- Searching in a view
- Searching across the entire organization
- Advanced Find
- Search using voice on mobile
- Relevance Search

> For all searches, the results are returned based on the fields we have already defined as searchable. For any data in fields not marked as searchable, no match will be identified.

Each one presents a different set of data, and each one has a best scenario where it can be used. Let's look at each one individually and see what their strengths are.

Searching in a view

One of the simplest ways to search in Microsoft Dynamics 365 is to search in a view. This is available from any entity view and is presented at the top-right-hand side of the view, as shown in the following screenshot:

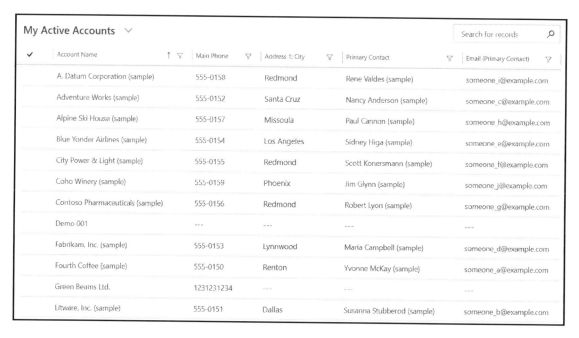

The search box, when not selected, is marked with the **Search for records** text.

This type of search is performed against the entity whose view are we seeing. The results are always security trimmed, meaning we only see the records we have permission to see.

Searching across the entire organization

To perform a search across the entire organization, on the top ribbon, we are provided with a different search option. This is represented by a magnifying glass symbol, as shown in the following screenshot:

The platform now takes a page from other solutions, such as SharePoint, and presents the user with a Search page with several configurable options. Here, you select the Search type first, followed by the search box, and finally the filter definition. The following screenshot shows this page:

Note that from the Search type drop-down, you can select between **Categorized Search** or the newer **Relevance Search**. The following screenshot shows these two options:

This search capability is available pretty much anywhere in the system, and it performs a search across multiple entities and returns the results grouped by the entity, as shown in the following screenshot:

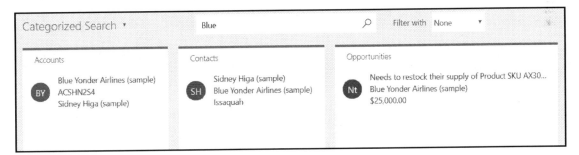

We will look at Advanced Find next.

Understanding Advanced Find

Advanced Find is a feature that allows us to retrieve data. It can also be used as the starting point for creating a new view.

We can access Advanced Find from the top ribbon, to the right of the Search box. The icon for Advanced Find looks like a funnel.

Selecting this brings up a new window where you can configure the target and parameters of your search. You define the entity you search against in the **Look for** drop-down, as well as an existing view if you want to search using an existing view. If not, your search will be performed across all the records for the selected entity. The following screenshot shows the default **ADVANCED FIND** window:

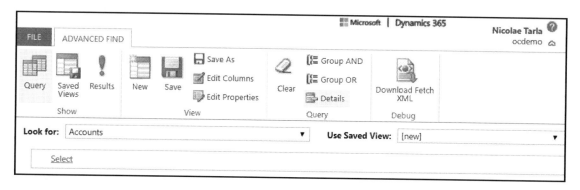

In the following section, you start defining the conditions and filtering parameters. Click on **Select** and choose a field, then define a condition. For example, if we want to retrieve all **Accounts** with an **Account Name** containing the text **Blue**, our search filters will look as follows:

As you can see, on the ribbon, in the Query area, we have the option to group our defined condition either as **AND** conditions or **OR** conditions. We can configure an **AND** condition along with an **OR** condition, as shown in the following screenshot:

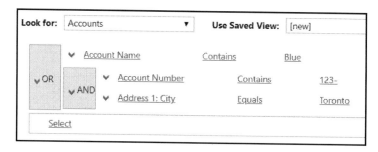

Click on the **Results** ribbon button to see how your search parameters behave. Once you are satisfied, you can save this search as a new view. Clicking on **Save** brings up the following screen, prompting for a **Name** and a **Description**, as shown in the following screenshot:

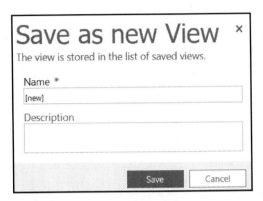

The **Edit Columns** button allows us to select which columns are displayed and define the order in which they are shown. You will be presented with a new window, where you can configure how the results are sorted, use the options for adding or removing columns, and add arrows to move the selected column to the right or left, as shown in the following screenshot:

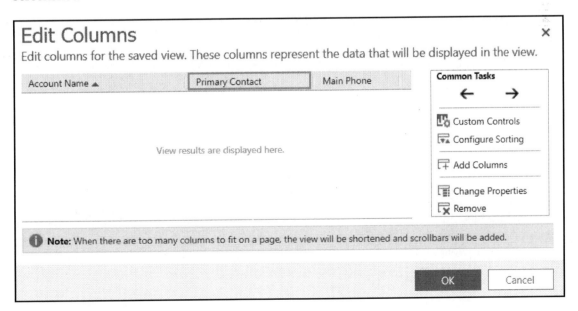

Selecting a column, and then choosing **Change Properties** from the options to the right, allows us to modify how a particular column is displayed. Here, we have the ability to enable presence for a column, if it refers to an active system user and presence is enabled on the platform, as well as reference a **Web Resource** or a **Function Name**.

Finally, we can define the standard width for a column in pixels. This makes a column with a fixed width, different from the default of **150px**. The following screenshot shows the column configuration options:

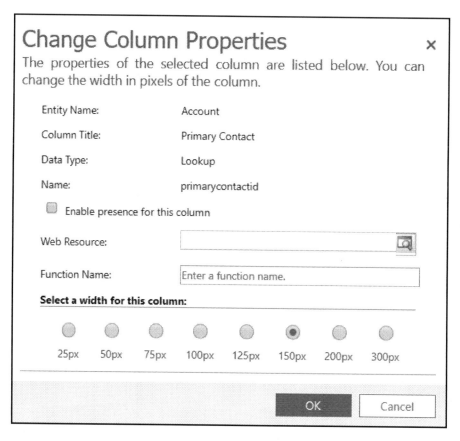

The **Custom Control** option allows us to define where a certain column is displayed, as well as the format. With the Unified Interface, we have the ability to leverage rich controls to display data. We can now define a specific column so that it has a visual representation that's different from the standard text box, for example.

The following screenshot shows the windows used to select the controls, where the column is rendered, as well as the properties for a particular control:

Finally, when working on a mobile device, you have yet another search option. The next section looks at leveraging voice for search on mobile devices.

Searching using voice on mobile

With the extended support for mobile, on the Windows platform, we now have the ability to use Cortana, the mobile digital assistant, to interact with the Dynamics CRM platform. A series of commands have been customized for support and integration with CRM. Some of these include the following actions:

- Opening a record
- Showing a view
- Searching for an item
- Creating a new record

To find a record in CRM, the Cortana command is as follows:

```
CRM find <item> called <name>.
```

For example, to retrieve a contact called James, we would ask Cortana, *CRM find* contact *called* James.

For more details on the available commands for Cortana integration with Dynamics CRM, see the following URL in the CRM Help & Training guide: `https://www.microsoft.com/en-us/dynamics/crm-customer-center/use-cortana-voice-commands-in-crm-for-phones.aspx`.

Understanding Relevance Search

The Relevance Search feature was added to the platform starting with Dynamics 365 version 8.2.

In some ways, it is similar to **Categorized Search**'s capabilities as it performs the operation across multiple record types.

This feature is not enabled by default on the platform. Hence, if your organization does not provide this option, you must enable the feature through administration.

In order to enable Relevance Search, you must be a System Customizer or an Administrator. You must then navigate to **Settings | Advanced Settings | Administration | System Settings**.

On the pop-up window, on the **General** tab, scroll done until you find the **Setup Search** area. Here, you must select the checkbox to **Enable Relevance Search**, as shown in the following screenshot:

Once you enable this feature, you must configure the entities available for indexing. You do that by selecting the **Select** button, just below the **System Settings** window.

Note that once you enable this feature, the platform will use an external indexing engine. The configured data will flow outside your organization.

You can **Add** or **Remove** entities as needed. By default, the system pre-selects a set of the most common entities to search across, as seen in the following screenshot:

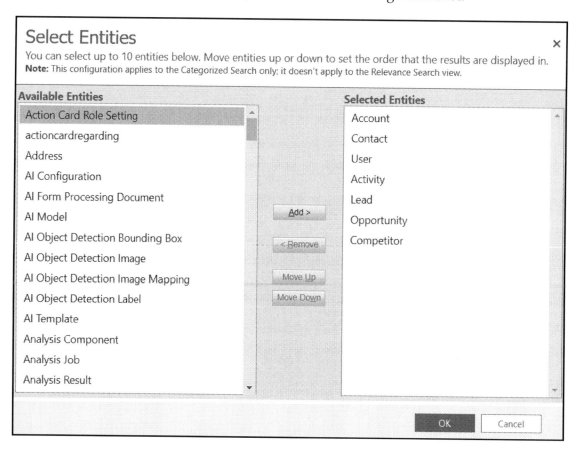

With your configuration complete, you can now return to your search area by selecting the magnifying glass icon on the ribbon. On the **Search** page presented, for the search type, instead of the default **Categorized Search**, select the **Relevance Search** option. Observe how the screen layout changes:

Performing a search now presents us with a list of results, as well as various filters and details on the left column. The following screenshot shows the results that are returned from such a search:

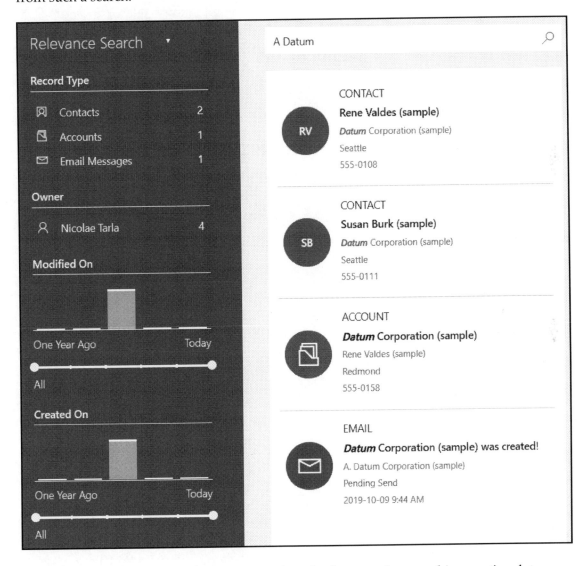

You can now filter not only by record type but also by record ownership, creation date, or the date when a record was last modified. The card format for the results makes it more visible and clearer to the user when trying to retrieve the correct data.

If you try adding custom entities to **Relevance Search**, but they don't appear to be available, this is most likely because custom entities need to be configured so that they can be synced to an external search index. You can achieve this by selecting a custom entity and modifying its properties. At the time of writing, this option is only available through the Classic interface for solution management. In your standard modern user interface, select **Switch to classic**. Here, select the entity and select the **Managed Properties** option from the ribbon.

On the pop-up window, scroll to the bottom and find the option called **Can enable sync to external search index**. Make sure this is set to **True**, as shown in the following screenshot:

Now, you should be able to add this entity to your index and retrieve search results from this entity with no problem.

When returning the results through **Relevance Search**, you will find the fields are returned in a specific order. This is because the results are based on the **Quick Find** view configuration. If you want your field results to be displayed differently, you must edit the entity's **Quick Find** view, as shown in the following screenshot:

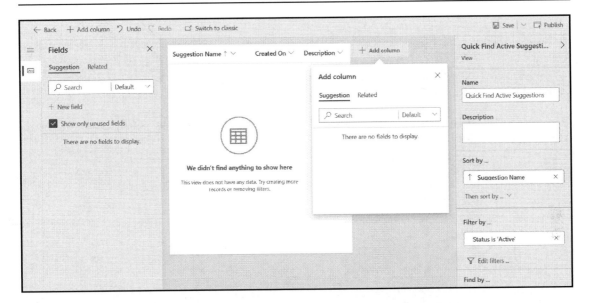

Note that, at the time of writing, the new interface only allows you to configure the **View** columns. For the **Find** columns, you must drop back to the Classic interface.

The difference between the **View** and **Find** columns stems from the fact that, while you should be able to search for data within multiple columns to retrieve a particular record, you might want to display only a subset of those columns to a user. The following screenshot shows the Quick Find view configuration in the Classic interface, with both options available in the right **Tasks** window:

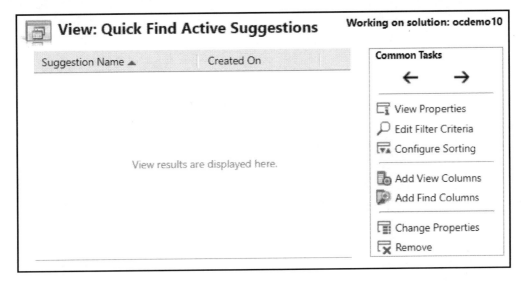

A user has the ability to configure their own personal preferences when it comes to Relevance Search. Navigating to **Set Personal Options**, on the **General** tab, in the **Select the default search experience** section, allows a user to configure their preferred default search as either **Relevance Search** or **Categorized Search**. Alternatively, you can choose the last search option available.

The **Facets and Filters** option allows for further filtering at the user level. A user can select up to four facet fields for each entity they can search across.

As we've seen so far, there are many great capabilities we can use to extend the platform and provide much more functionality to a business. We can easily map various requirements and configure solutions with no code.

Summary

Throughout this chapter, we learned about the various processes available with the Dynamics 365 platform. We looked at the use of various templates, as well as the platform's capabilities to leverage Office 365 features. Finally, we looked at the various search capabilities across the platform.

This entire set of functionality allows you to configure platform behavior that will make a user's life easier. From visual guidance through the steps needed to achieve the result, coupled with automation capabilities and tight integration with Office applications, the users' life has now become much easier, leaving them with time to focus on the creative aspect of the business.

In the next chapter, we will tackle the concept of integrations by looking at the available out of the box configurable integration options.

Section 4 - Integrations

An independent, non-integrated platform does not have that much value. In this section, we will look at the integration capabilities available, leveraging configuration, Microsoft services, and third-party tools.

This section comprises of the following chapters:

- Chapter 11, *Out-of-the-Box Integration Capabilities*
- Chapter 12, *Custom Integration Capabilities*

11
Out-of-the-Box Integration Capabilities

The previous chapter walked through the Dynamics 365 platform's capabilities with regard to mapping business capabilities and processes. Such configuration and customization capabilities allow businesses to design and map complex business flows. Leveraging these various configuration capabilities, we cannot only map processes but also trigger actions from cascading processes.

While mapping business processes on the platform is essential for the success of an organization, there are many instances where external data or platforms are used in conjunction with the Dynamics 365 platform to add value. This chapter will focus on the out-of-the-box capabilities of Dynamics 365 to integrate and leverage other platforms in business processes.

The following topics will be covered in this chapter:

- Configuring email integration
- Dynamics 365 App for Outlook
- Server-based SharePoint integration
- OneDrive for Business
- OneNote
- Virtual entities
- Sales insights
- LinkedIn's Sales Navigator

These topics only look at configurable integrations available on the platform.

Configuring email integration

Email is still the most used method of business communication. As such, it is a core component of the Dynamics 365 platform. Dynamics 365 integrates with Office 365 to leverage email functionality.

Integrating email functionality into Dynamics 365 is a simple matter of configuration. We find the email configuration area under **Advanced Settings** | **System** | **Email Configuration**. The configuration screen looks like what you see in the following screenshot:

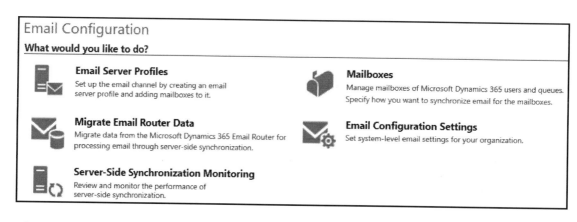

This section of the **Settings** area allows us to configure the type of email integration used and to manage the various integration points and methods.

The **Email Configuration Settings** section allows us to configure global settings for email. This leads us back to the **System Settings** area. Here, we can select an email processing option, whether it's server-side synchronization or via the old email router option. In addition, we can select the default server profile to be used, as well as the email handling options for either incoming or outgoing email messages. The configuration area under the **Email** tab looks as follows:

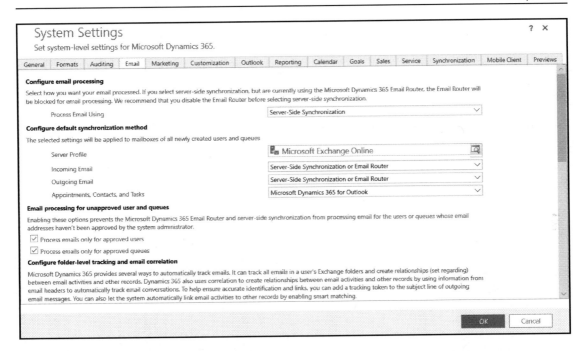

We'll be looking at the details and available configurable options in **System Settings** in the final chapter, when we will discuss platform administration.

The **Migrate Email Router Data** area, found under **Settings | Email Configuration** as shown in the preceding screenshot, allows us to move our configuration from the email router to server-side synchronization. For this functionality to work, you must have the old email router available, as well as the new server-side synchronization, enabled and configured; also, the organization must be using HTTPS.

The **Active Email Server Profiles** section allows us to configure one or more profiles for email handling. We can configure both the **Exchange** and **POP3-SMTP** servers for integration with Dynamics 365. This allows us to cover the configuration for various types of email servers, including public email services from third-party providers. We can have as many profiles configured as needed. These profiles can be for any of the following configurations:

- Exchange Server (Hybrid)
- Exchange Online
- POP3/SMTP Server
- IMAP/SMTP Server

The following screenshot shows the listing of active email server profiles. This includes the default Microsoft Exchange Online profile, which stores the configuration for connecting to Office 365 Exchange, as well as a custom profile created for POP3/SMTP:

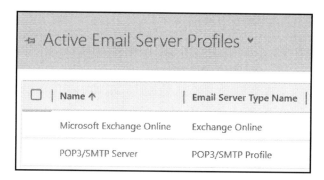

For Exchange configuration, as long as the Exchange server is in the same domain as our Dynamics 365 environment, we can use the **Auto Discover Server Location** option, which simplifies the configuration process.

For each profile created, we need to configure the authentication rules, either by using specified credentials, Integrated Windows authentication, or anonymity where supported. We can also specify the same or separate credentials to be used for incoming and outgoing emails.

Once a profile is created, we can manage related mailboxes from within the profile or separately.

The **Mailboxes** area allows us to manage individual mailboxes separately. For each mailbox, we can configure the synchronization method using an already-created email server profile or by including a specific setting for incoming and outgoing emails, as well as appointments, contacts, and tasks. When an email server profile is not being used, we can specify the use of Microsoft Dynamics for Outlook, server-side synchronization, an email router, or a forward mailbox as needed. We can do this for both incoming and outgoing messages. For the other items to be synchronized, including appointments, contacts, and tasks, the only available options are Microsoft Dynamics CRM for Outlook or server-side synchronization.

Note that the email router option does not support synchronizing appointments, contacts, and tasks.

Once a mailbox is configured and the email is approved, we can test and enable the mailbox by clicking on **Test & Enable Mailbox** in the ribbon:

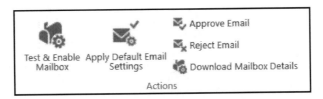

This runs a validation process and returns status messages regarding the success of your configuration. The process to test the configuration runs asynchronously, which can result in a slight delay before the actual result is displayed. You will first be prompted that the test has been scheduled. Once it's complete, you will get the results.

Added with Dynamics CRM 2016, the **Server-Side Synchronization Performance** area allows administrators to monitor the performance of this functionality, as well as allowing them to review various messages. It is a dashboard that collects details on mailboxes, errors, and processing statuses. When coupled with Microsoft 365 licenses or Exchange Online licenses, this functionality is available for the platform.

Configuring Dynamics 365 App for Outlook

Added with Dynamics CRM 2016 Online, the CRM app for Outlook, now renamed Dynamics 365 App for Outlook, allows us to surface Dynamics 365 details directly into **Outlook Web Access (OWA)**. When accessing Outlook directly from the browser, now we are presented with a view into Dynamics 365, if configured, and we have the ability to track information and interact with the Dynamics 365 functionality without the need for the Outlook client to be integrated.

This functionality provides features that allow online clients to work with Dynamics 365 records and data using the Outlook web experience. Contextual information is surfaced using Dynamics 365 App for Outlook directly into the user's inbox.

Dynamics 365 App for Outlook makes it easy to manage contacts and track emails directly from within the message interface.

The most important features of Dynamics 365 App for Outlook include the following:

- Access data from within your inbox
- Track emails from within a browser
- Link emails to an existing platform record
- Convert emails into a new platform record

 Dynamics 365 App for Outlook is currently available only for Dynamics 365 Online. It is based on Exchange Online and server-side synchronization, as well as specific privileges in the system.

To push Dynamics 365 App for Outlook, navigate to **Settings | Dynamics 365 App for Outlook**, as seen in the following screenshot:

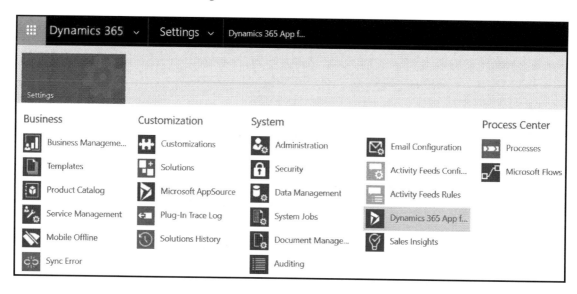

This triggers the configuration wizard. Here, you are reminded of the configuration needed on the user profiles to be able to use this feature. Check the **Automatically add the app to Outlook** checkbox, then click on **Save**. The following screenshot shows this screen:

Getting Started with Microsoft Dynamics 365 App for Outlook

Microsoft Dynamics 365 App for Outlook is an Office add-in that you can quickly add to your users' mailbox so they can track communication and review Dynamics 365 for Customer Engagement applications' information in Outlook.

> ⓘ **Note:** For users to be eligible for Dynamics 365 App for Outlook, they need to:
>
> 1. Have server-side synchronization set up on their mailbox for incoming emails and for appointments, contacts and tasks. Learn more Verify that the mailboxes are tested and enabled.
> 2. Have the **Dynamics 365 App for Outlook User** security role. Learn more

Documentation

Review the Dynamics 365 App for Outlook requirements here.

Explore the Dynamics 365 App for Outlook user guide here.

You can customize Dynamics 365 App for Outlook to control the list of entities that appear in the Regarding lookup and add a custom entity to the quick create menu.

Are your users not seeing the default Dynamics 365 App for Outlook dashboard? View this information to troubleshoot.

View the server-side synchronization dashboard to get a quick look at the health of mailboxes, which could affect user eligibility for Dynamics 365 App for Outlook.

Questions? Review the troubleshooting guide.

☐ Automatically add Dynamics 365 App for Outlook to all eligible users. See more

    Save

Once done, you can identify the users for whom you want this feature deployed. As mentioned previously, you need to make sure the requirements are met so you can add this feature.

In order to give a user permission to use Dynamics 365 App for Outlook, in the respective security role a new role, navigate to the **Business Management** tab, and in the **Privacy Related Privileges** section, find the **Use Dynamics 365 App for Outlook** setting. Enable it from here, as seen in the following screenshot:

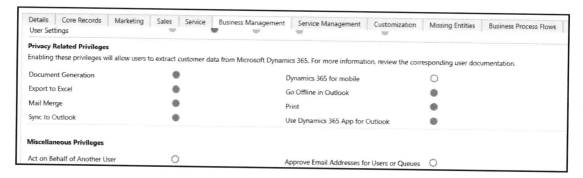

Once your users are configured properly, selecting **Add App** for all eligible users triggers the configuration for users, and their statuses are presented in a list:

Once enabled, a user navigating to their inbox is presented with a view like the one in the following screenshot:

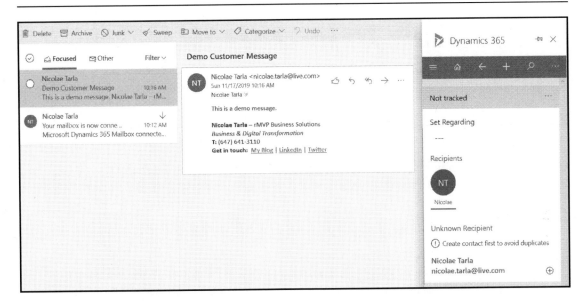

TIP

If the Dynamics 365 window is not displayed, expand the ellipsis at the top right of the message and select **Dynamics 365** from the options presented.

Now we can start working with this message, by tracking it or creating a new contact. Once we have a contact created and the message tracked, we can see additional details regarding the contact and the activities existing in the organization. We can also navigate directly to related records from this interface, thus making it much easier to get a complete picture of a customer interaction history.

Let's look in the next section at leveraging SharePoint integration for document management.

Configuring server-based SharePoint integration

In the world of business, documents are at the core of most processes. From email attachments to network shares, documents are a central aspect of any business process.

Historically, sharing documents has had some challenges, especially with regards to collaboration.

Tools have now been created that allow multiple users to work on the same document. Document management was born from the need to work collaboratively on the same document.

SharePoint is such a tool, and it allows not only collaboration on the same document, but also versioning, metadata associated with a document, access control, and security through enterprise policies, retention, and other features. As such, this is a mature enterprise product with lots of features.

Within Dynamics 365, before SharePoint integration was available, documents were simply attached to a record's **Notes** field. While this works as a quick-and-dirty solution, it misses the mark on several aspects. Some of the most important of these aspects are these:

- Inability to search
- No true versioning controls
- Database usage and cost, as documents are stored in the Dynamics database
- No collaboration ability, as you would have to download the original document, make modifications, and upload a new version when done

With that in mind, the need for a true document management system is obvious. Marrying the two Dynamics 365 and SharePoint platforms is simply the next logical step. This provides all the benefits of a true document management system while offloading documents from the Dynamics 365 system.

Configuring Dynamics 365 SharePoint integration

SharePoint integration is simply a matter of configuration when dealing with Dynamics 365. All the configuration options are collected under **Advanced Settings** | **System** | **Document Management**, as shown in the following screenshot:

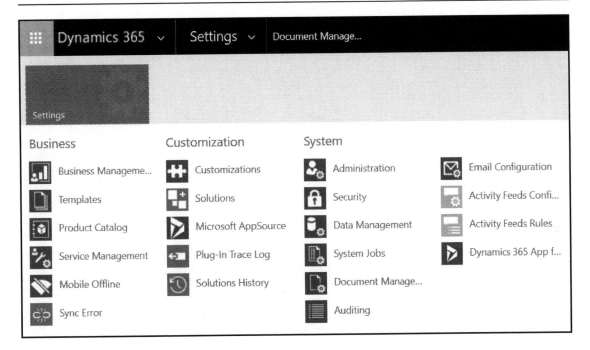

This brings us to the landing page shown in the following screenshot:

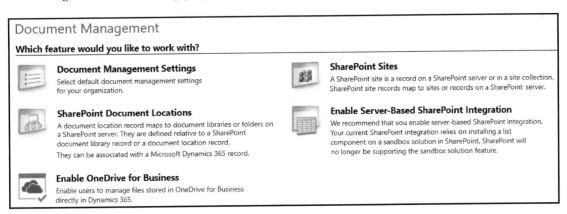

Here, we can set up the integration with SharePoint, as well as with OneDrive for Business, as we'll see in the next section.

To configure SharePoint to store our documents, we must have a SharePoint site configured for this purpose. Note that the integration configuration will allow us to define the structure in which documents are arranged on that site. We'll be looking at the structure once we have this integration configured and functional.

Let's start the configuration:

1. First, let's navigate to **Enable Server-Based SharePoint Integration**. This starts the configuration wizard with the following screen:

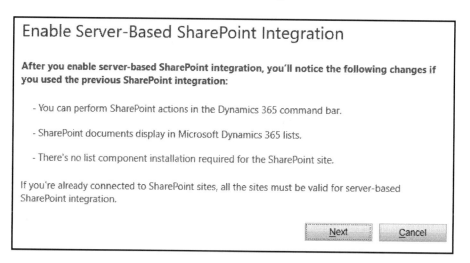

2. Click the **Next** button to begin. On the following screen, you choose whether you will be configuring against SharePoint **Online** or **On-Premises**:

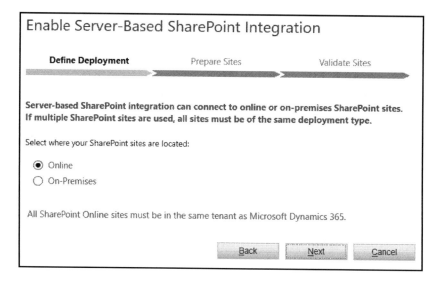

3. Since we're configuring Dynamics 365 Online, we're going to set up against SharePoint Online. Click on **Next**.

Note that SharePoint Online must be in the same tenant as your Microsoft Dynamics 365 Online instance.

4. On the next screen, specify the URL to your SharePoint site, as seen in the following screenshot:

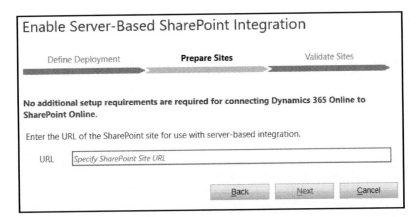

5. Clicking **Next** takes you to the validation screen. A process runs in the background to make sure the provided URL points to a valid site and that permissions are in place. The screen looks like this:

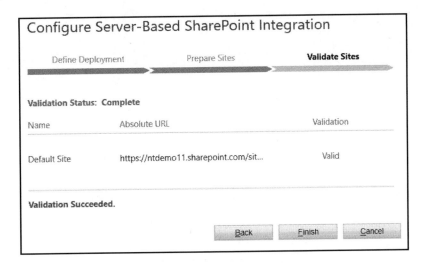

6. If everything is okay, you'll get a status of **Valid**. Click **Finish** when complete.

When the screen refreshes, the **Document Management** area will look like the following screenshot:

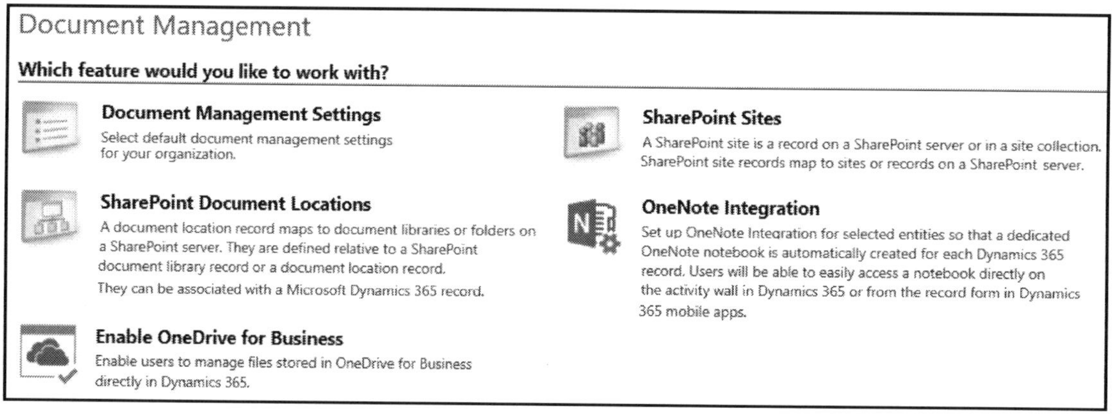

Document Management

Which feature would you like to work with?

Document Management Settings
Select default document management settings for your organization.

SharePoint Sites
A SharePoint site is a record on a SharePoint server or in a site collection. SharePoint site records map to sites or records on a SharePoint server.

SharePoint Document Locations
A document location record maps to document libraries or folders on a SharePoint server. They are defined relative to a SharePoint document library record or a document location record. They can be associated with a Microsoft Dynamics 365 record.

OneNote Integration
Set up OneNote Integration for selected entities so that a dedicated OneNote notebook is automatically created for each Dynamics 365 record. Users will be able to easily access a notebook directly on the activity wall in Dynamics 365 or from the record form in Dynamics 365 mobile apps.

Enable OneDrive for Business
Enable users to manage files stored in OneDrive for Business directly in Dynamics 365.

Observe that now you can start configuring OneNote Integrations. This leverages SharePoint integration as the note files are stored on SharePoint. We'll be looking at this configuration in a later section.

With the server-Based SharePoint integration configured, the next step is to configure and enable the entities that will leverage the document management functionality:

1. Select the **Document Management Settings** option. This opens a new wizard:

2. Here, select the entities and again provide the URL to the SharePoint site. The reason you must provide the SharePoint site URL here is so that you can configure multiple sites to be used.

Select only the entities you need to leverage document management. Note that the more entities are configured, the more load will be applied to the system.

3. Click **Next** to move on to the next configuration screen, which looks like this:

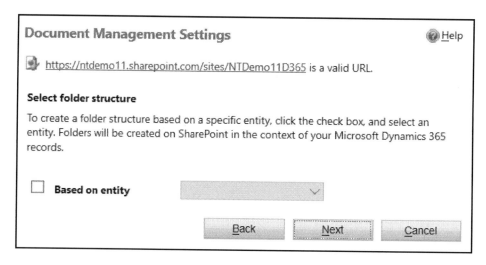

4. Here we see that the URL provided has again been validated and is correct. The next area we define is the folder structure on SharePoint. To create a folder structure based on an entity, we select the **Based on entity** checkbox and select the root entity from the dropdown. Click on **Next** when done.

5. You will get a prompt as seen in the following screenshot. Click **OK**:

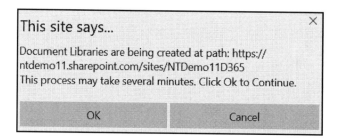

The next screen provides a status update as the structure is configured on the SharePoint side. It should show **Succeeded** as the status for all entities, as shown in the following screenshot:

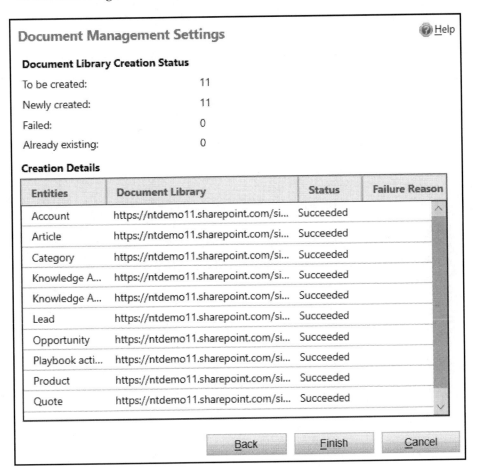

6. Click on **Finish** to close the wizard.

Navigating to **SharePoint**, we can look at the site contents and see the structure created, as presented in the following screenshot:

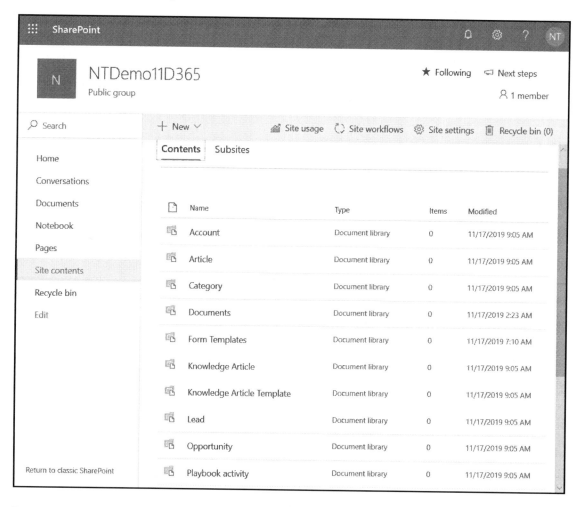

In your Dynamics 365 instance, navigating to a record, we find the **Files** tab. Selecting it, we see the library of documents available on SharePoint. The following screenshot shows the library of documents associated with an account in Dynamics 365:

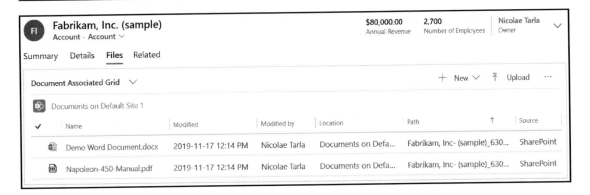

From here, you can upload documents or create new documents. You can create a custom folder structure, and various document types, as depicted in the following screenshot:

Selecting the ellipsis expands a new navigational menu, where you can choose to edit the locations available for document storage and open the document location in SharePoint. The following screenshot shows this menu expanded:

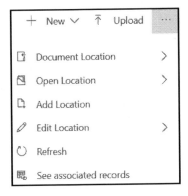

Selecting **Open Location** allows a new window to be opened directly to the folder in SharePoint, as seen in the following screenshot:

Account > Fabrikam, Inc- (sample)_630C1F6F4E09EA11A814000D3A0C21EB				
	Name ∨	Modified ∨	Modified By ∨	+ Add column ∨
📄	Demo Word Document.docx	26 minutes ago	Nicolae Tarla	
📄	Napoleon-450-Manual.pdf	26 minutes ago	Nicolae Tarla	

Navigating up to **Account** in SharePoint, you get a list of all accounts in Dynamics 365 that have associated documents. The following screenshot shows this list with a single account where we added documents. Once we add documents to more accounts, this list will expand accordingly:

Account				
	Name ∨	Modified ∨	Modified By ∨	+ Add column ∨
📁	Fabrikam, Inc- (sample)_630C1F6F4E09EA1...	33 minutes ago	Nicolae Tarla	

Observe that the integration is configured by default to create folders for each account. It also adds a suffix to the folder name with a unique ID used for referencing.

From the SharePoint view, you can edit documents the same way you would work with any other SharePoint document, along with all the document management features available with this platform.

Now that we have SharePoint integration configured, let's next have a look at configuring OneDrive for Business.

Configuring OneDrive for Business

Another option for managing documents from Dynamics 365 is to leverage OneDrive for Business. While both OneDrive for Business and SharePoint provide cloud document storage, the intent of how these should be used is quite different.

Note that files stored in OneDrive for Business default to private, unless specifically set up for sharing. This is a major difference that should be taken into consideration.

As such, when considering which file storage is better and how to use these options, we should think of OneDrive as a personal storage mechanism. We can store files in OneDrive when they are in *draft*, and before we are ready to share them with the rest of the organization. This is a good holding place for work in progress, associated research documents used in producing a final version, and other assets. We can structure these as related to a specific Dynamics 365 record, in preparation for creating a final document to be shared with the rest of the organization.

Configuring OneDrive for Business in Dynamics 365 is simply a matter of enabling this feature. Let's see how:

1. In the **Settings** | **Document Management** area, select the **Enable OneDrive for Business** option. This brings up an overlay window where we can enable this functionality, as seen in the following screenshot:

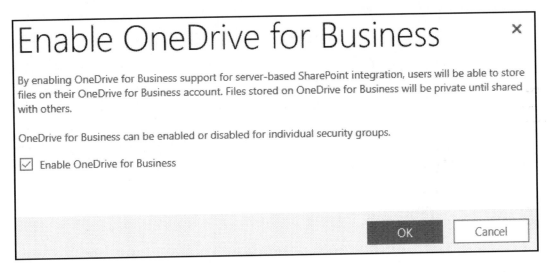

2. Select the checkbox and click **OK** to enable this feature.

3. Once enabled, you are presented with a new option on the **Document Management** screen to configure folder settings, as seen here:

4. Selecting this option allows us to configure the default folder name for Dynamics 365 documents stored in OneDrive on a new overlay window. By default, they are placed in a folder named CRM, but you can change that to a custom value, as seen in the following screenshot:

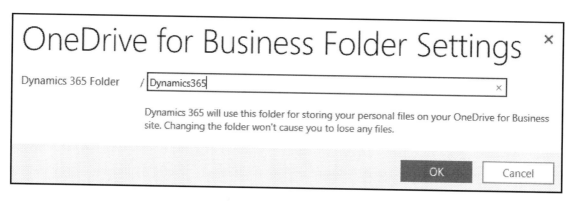

5. Click **OK** when done.
6. Navigating back to our account, on the **Files** tab, we are now prompted by a notification that we can now use multiple locations for document management, as seen in the following screenshot:

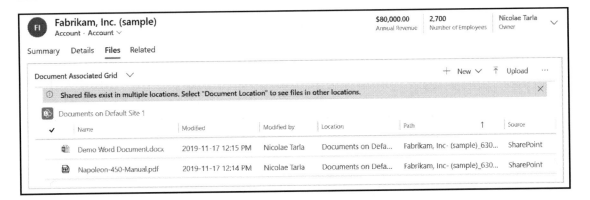

7. Expand the ellipsis menu and select **Document Locations**. This presents all the available options, as seen here:

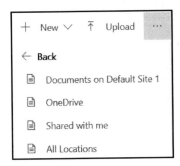

8. Observe that OneDrive is now an available location for documents. Select **OneDrive** to navigate to that respective location. If this is the first time you're browsing to OneDrive from Dynamics 365, you are prompted with the following message:

You can choose here to change the default configuration for the documents folder in OneDrive or leave it as is and continue.

9. After a moment, the *documents* view changes to show you all documents in OneDrive, as seen in the following screenshot. Observe that the SharePoint icon at the top of the list has now been replaced with **OneDrive**:

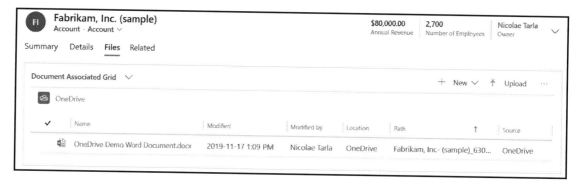

10. You can add and edit documents here in the same way you do it on SharePoint. Selecting **New** | **Word document** brings up a screen to define the document name, as seen here:

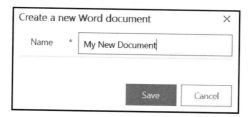

11. Once you give it a name and select **Save**, you are taken to Word Online, where you can edit the document:

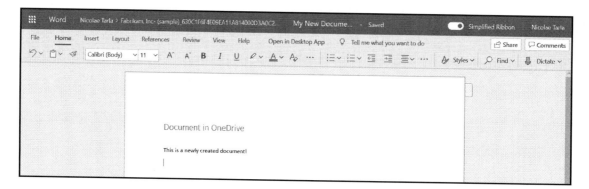

This document is automatically saved, and it shows in the list of documents in Dynamics 365:

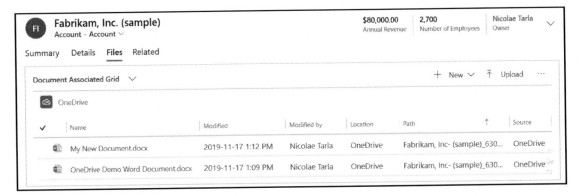

12. Now you can start preparing your client-specific documentation in this area and move it to SharePoint when ready to share with the rest of the organization. You can switch the view to show all documents by expanding the ellipsis menu and selecting **Document Location | All Locations**, as shown here:

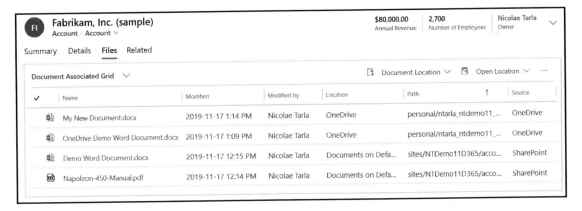

Note in this view the **Source** column, which shows for each document whether it's on OneDrive or on SharePoint. Also, the **Location** column shows documents on OneDrive or any of the SharePoint locations available.

Looking at your OneDrive, you will see the folder location for all Dynamics 365 documents, and a similar structure to what was configured in SharePoint. The documents we're looking at are under **Dynamics 365 | Account**, followed by the account name with the ID suffix:

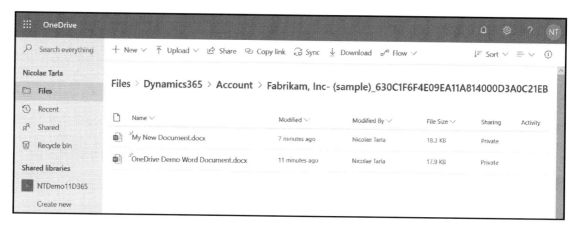

Let's look next at another feature that leverages SharePoint integration, that is, OneNote.

Integrating OneNote

OneNote is a free-form information gathering and structuring tool. You can collect and structure various notes, images, and other information as needed.

As such, this could be a very useful tool for gathering additional details about customers. OneNote can easily integrate with Dynamics 365 through a simple configuration.

 To configure OneNote for Dynamics 365, you must have SharePoint integration configured and in place.

You configure OneNote integration from the same **Document Management** tab under **Settings**. Select the **OneNote Integration** option to start the configuration process. This presents an overlay window:

OneNote Integration Settings   ⓘ <u>Help</u>

Turn on OneNote integration for the entities you select.
Only entities that are already enabled for document management are listed.

☐	**Entities**
☑	Account
☐	Article
☐	Category
☐	Knowledge Article
☐	Knowledge Article Template
☑	Lead
☑	Opportunity
☐	Playbook activity
☑	Product
☐	Quote

The OneNote notebook for each Dynamics 365 record will be automatically created and be available in all Dynamics 365 apps. To access a notebook, a user navigates to the form and chooses the OneNote tab (in the activity wall). Note that section groups in a OneNote notebook aren't supported.
This doesn't replace the current Notes feature, but gives users another way to access notes stored in OneNote.

                <u>Finish</u>   <u>Cancel</u>

This screen is similar to the configuration for SharePoint. Select the entities that will leverage the OneNote functionality, and select **Finish** when done. This enables OneNote for the selected entities.

Back in Dynamics 365, on our **Account Files** tab, select the **OneNote** option from the **New** dropdown. You are prompted to give a name to the notebook that is being created when accessing this feature for the first time:

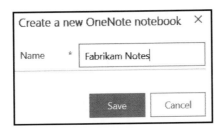

Once you click **Save**, you are directed to the OneNote notebook in the online editor:

Back on your account's **Files** view in Dynamics 365, the newly created OneNote file named **Fabrikam Notes.one** appears in the list of all document:

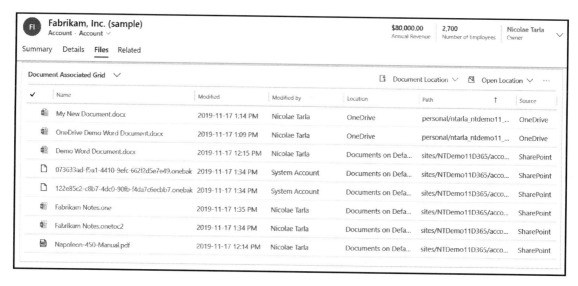

And with that, we've seen how we can leverage document management platforms and track notes against a specific Dynamics 365 record. Let's look at what virtual entities are and how they enhance the platform's functionality in the next section.

Leveraging virtual entities to present external data

Virtual entities are a feature that was added to Dynamics 365 with version 9. Their sole purpose is to allow the presentation of data from external sources in Dynamics 365 in a read-only manner. This feature is to be used in two main scenarios:

- Data resides in an external system – most probably a legacy system – and needs to be presented to users in Dynamics 365
- Data is highly sensitive and should not be stored in Dynamics 365, but needs to be taken into consideration in typical scenarios handled by Dynamics 365

For these situations, virtual entities are created to simplify the process of presenting this data.

In Dynamics 365, virtual entities are custom entities that appear as regular entity records to users. These records are available in all clients, and an entity behaves similarly to any other custom entity. The data is presented in a read-only manner.

To configure virtual entities, there are two steps to be completed:

1. Defining a data source
2. Configuring a new virtual entity

Let's look at each step in detail.

Defining a data source

A data source is a record in Dynamics 365 storing a URI to an OData v4 endpoint. This is our source of data.

Navigate to **Settings** | **Administration** and find the **Virtual Entity Data Sources** area, as seen here:

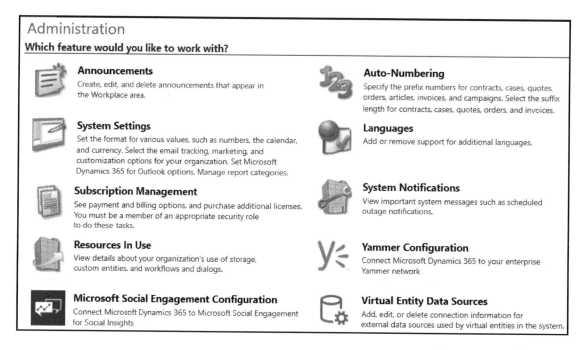

Select it and you are presented with a list of all registered **Data Sources**:

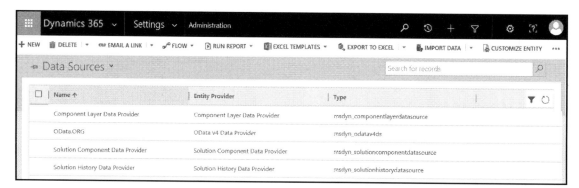

Select **New** to create a new data source record. In the record definition, you must give it a **Name**, as well as the URL to an OData v4 endpoint, as seen here:

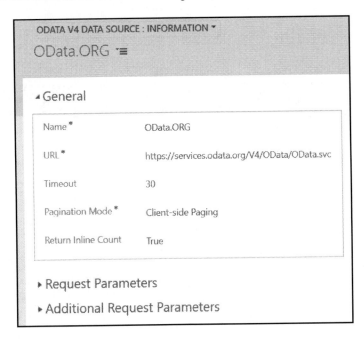

You could define additional request parameters if needed, as required by the endpoint used. For endpoints that require parameters, this allows simple configuration options to present filters or references to specific record IDs.

Click **Save** when complete. Now we have a data source created and we are ready to define the virtual entity.

Configuring a new virtual entity

Creating a virtual entity is like creating any other custom entity. Navigate to a solution and select the option to create a new entity. On the **Entity Definition** screen, give a **Display Name** and **Plural Name**. To the right, select the **Virtual Entity** checkbox. Observe how the screen changes to capture some specific information, as seen in the following screenshot:

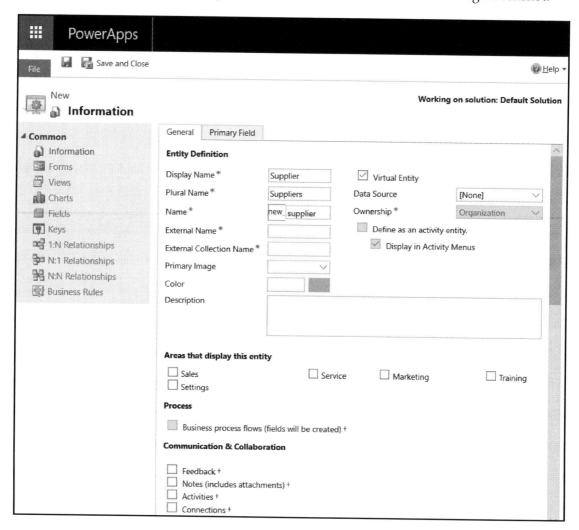

Observe that **External Name** and **External Collection Name** are now new and required fields.

We can get this information by navigating to the Service URL and looking in the response for the `Suppliers` collection, as seen in the following screenshot:

```
<?xml version="1.0" encoding="ISO-8859-1"?>
<service m:context="https://services.odata.org/V4/OData/OData.svc/$metadata" xmlns:m="http://docs.oasis-open.org/odata/ns/metadata" xmlns:atom="http://www.w3.org/2005/Atom"
xmlns="http://www.w3.org/2007/app" xml:base="https://services.odata.org/V4/OData/OData.svc/">
  - <workspace>
      <atom:title type="text">Default</atom:title>
    + <collection href="Products">
    + <collection href="ProductDetails">
    + <collection href="Categories">
    - <collection href="Suppliers">
        <atom:title type="text">Suppliers</atom:title>
      </collection>
    + <collection href="Persons">
    + <collection href="PersonDetails">
    + <collection href="Advertisements">
  </workspace>
</service>
```

Once you click **Save**, the virtual entity is created and the data is validated. If you browse to the fields, you will now find two fields created, a **Name** field and an **ID** field. Looking at the service metadata, we have some additional fields we want to capture, as shown in the following screenshot:

```
<?xml version="1.0" encoding="ISO-8859-1"?>
- <edmx:Edmx xmlns:edmx="http://docs.oasis-open.org/odata/ns/edmx" Version="4.0">
  - <edmx:DataServices>
    - <Schema xmlns="http://docs.oasis-open.org/odata/ns/edm" Namespace="ODataDemo">
      + <EntityType Name="Product">
      + <EntityType Name="FeaturedProduct" BaseType="ODataDemo.Product">
      + <EntityType Name="ProductDetail">
      + <EntityType Name="Category" OpenType="true">
      - <EntityType Name="Supplier">
        - <Key>
            <PropertyRef Name="ID"/>
          </Key>
          <Property Name="ID" Nullable="false" Type="Edm.Int32"/>
          <Property Name="Name" Type="Edm.String"/>
          <Property Name="Address" Type="ODataDemo.Address"/>
          <Property Name="Location" Type="Edm.GeographyPoint" SRID="Variable"/>
          <Property Name="Concurrency" Nullable="false" Type="Edm.Int32" ConcurrencyMode="Fixed"/>
          <NavigationProperty Name="Products" Type="Collection(ODataDemo.Product)" Partner="Supplier"/>
        </EntityType>
      + <ComplexType Name="Address">
      + <EntityType Name="Person">
      + <EntityType Name="Customer" BaseType="ODataDemo.Person">
      + <EntityType Name="Employee" BaseType="ODataDemo.Person">
      + <EntityType Name="PersonDetail">
      + <EntityType Name="Advertisement" HasStream="true">
      + <EntityContainer Name="DemoService">
      + <Annotations Target="ODataDemo.DemoService">
      + <Annotations Target="ODataDemo.Product">
      + <Annotations Target="ODataDemo.Product/Name">
      + <Annotations Target="ODataDemo.DemoService/Suppliers">
      </Schema>
    </edmx:DataServices>
  </edmx:Edmx>
```

Let's first start by verifying the already created fields. Select the **Supplier** field. On the field definition, you need to fill in the **External Name** field, as seen in the following screenshot:

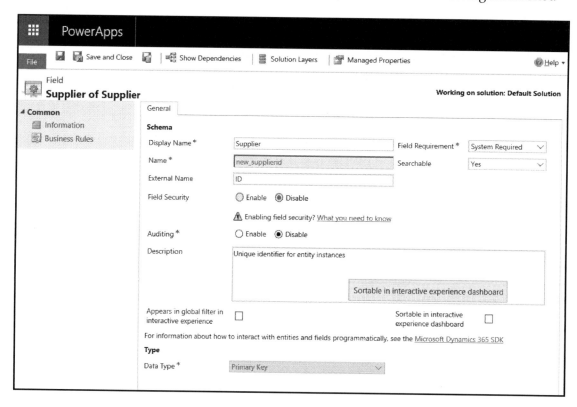

Do the same for the **Name** field.

Next, let's add the remaining fields.

Finally, and very importantly, on the **Data Source** tab, select the previously defined record from the dropdown. If you forget to do this, you will get a **Not Implemented** message as seen in the following screenshot:

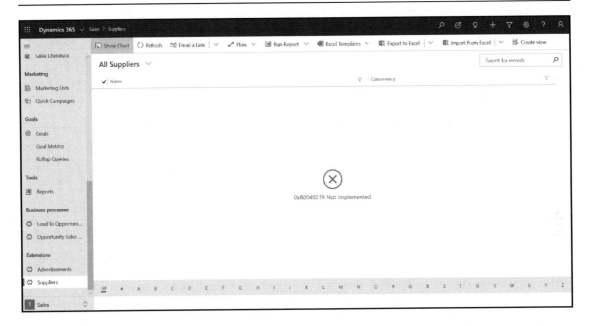

Now, if everything worked out okay, once you refresh your main window, you should be able to navigate to the newly created virtual entity, the same way you would navigate to any other entity on the platform.

You will see a listing of all records returned from the OData endpoint, similar to any other entity records.

When browsing to any of the records, the difference is that all data is read-only. You can use this data in advanced searches, in views, or on dashboards.

In conclusion, virtual entities allow us to bring in external data for consumption in Dynamics 365. With a simple configuration, we can leverage external platforms from within our application.

Let's have a look at some enhancements to aid a salesperson in closing sales smartly in the next section.

Leveraging Sales Insights features

With the second wave released in 2019, Dynamics 365 added Sales Insights. This is a new, AI-driven set of functionality and features that analyze data from sources like your Dynamics 365 Sales along with Office 365 to generate recommendations.

Sales Insights comes in three flavors:

- Free Sales Insights features
- Advanced Sales Insights features
- The Sales Insights application

The features available with each of these offerings are described next.

Free Sales Insights

The subsequent sections describe the features that are available for free with the Sales Insights component of Dynamics 365.

Assistant

Formerly known as Relationship Assistant, this feature analyzes data in your Dynamics 365 system and generates action cards specific to users. An Action Card is a component displayed to users on both web-based applications and on mobile devices. The following screenshot shows an Action Card:

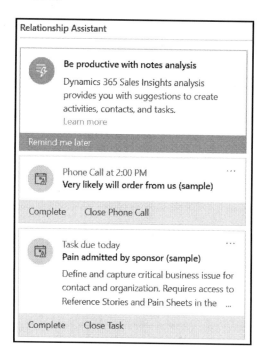

Auto capture

This feature works in conjunction with your Exchange profile to query your email messages and determine the relevance of a use case. This process looks at messages from contacts in your current sales pipeline, along with other activities to determine recommendations for the next course of action.

As an example, when you have a contact already created in your system, and you receive new email messages from that contact, those new messages are surfaced in your contact's profile even before they are tracked. They will appear as untracked messages, as shown in the following screenshot:

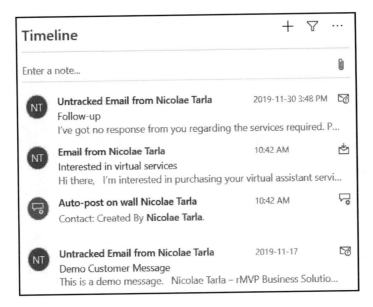

Here, you can choose to track a message directly from the Dynamics 365 interface, without the need to drop back into your email application:

This makes the process much smoother for salespeople, as it reduces the need to alternate between multiple applications.

Email engagement

As the final free feature available with Sales Insights, email engagement assists users in creating effective email messages. Some of the features available include the ability to see when your messages have been opened or interacted with, whether links sent were followed or attachments were opened, or whether a reply was sent. It also assists in determining the best time to deliver messages based on the recipient's time zone definition.

When creating email messages from the platform, the **Email Engagement** section is displayed with options for managing the message delivery options, as seen in the following screenshot:

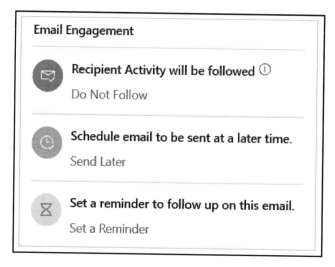

Here, you can define whether the activity will be followed. When an email is set to be followed, all links and attachments are tracked for interaction. This is the default status but can be disabled by selecting the **Do Not Follow** link. In addition, you are presented with the option to schedule the message to be sent at a better time, as well as the ability to create a reminder for follow-up automatically.

There is a background process run every 15 minutes that updates the status in Dynamics 365 and, where necessary, creates new relationship assistant cards with links to the message, related records, and options to generate related activities or manage the alert.

In addition, the email creation form now allows an email attachment to be tracked in order to determine when they were opened, as well as the ability to define and use standard complex templates with branding and extensive formatting. The emails can be edited before sending, in either the designer or directly in HTML format for more accuracy. The **Preview** tab allows you to visualize how the email will be seen on various devices, including desktop, tablets, and mobile devices. The following screenshot shows the entire email creation experience:

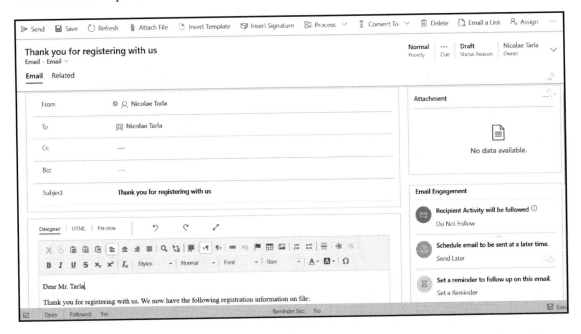

These features make for a more modern experience, both from the perspective of creating messages for customers, as well as for customers experiencing modern communication.

Once an email has been sent to a customer, the status shows the email as sent, and will be refreshed once there is interaction from the customers, as seen here:

When the recipient starts to interact with the messages, updates are presented within your Dynamics 365 record:

Observe how this brings invaluable information to the user, allowing them to have a more meaningful conversation with customers.

Advanced Sales Insights

The advanced Sales Insights features build on top of the free offering and come at a premium. You can choose to purchase this package, which offers the following added benefits:

- Assistant with Studio
- Relationship analytics
- Predictive lead scoring
- Predictive opportunity scoring
- Notes analysis
- Talking points
- Who knows whom
- Dynamics 365 assistant for Microsoft Teams

The action revolves around actionable insight cards. These were previously known as action cards, and now support a much larger set of features as well as the creation of custom actionable insight cards and the ability to define ranking criteria for your cards.

At the time of writing, the following features are still in preview:

- Creating custom insight cards
- Prioritizing individual cards
- Optimizing ranking
- Assigning cards to users by specific roles
- Turning specific cards on or off
- Configuring the flow of a card

These advanced features allow the creation of very specific customizable scenarios to map any business needs.

To enable these features, start by navigating to the **Advanced Settings** area of the application. Under **Settings | System**, find the **Sales Insights** section, as seen in the following screenshot:

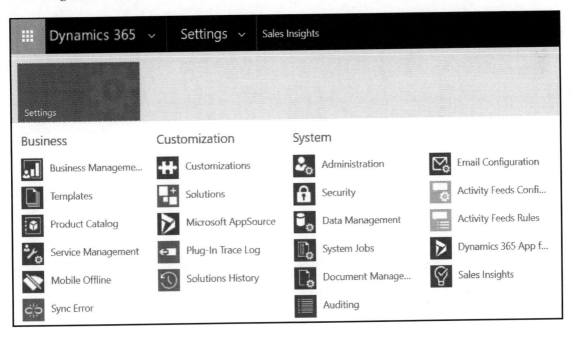

Here, you will find the standard fee **Sales Insights settings**. If you have not enabled this feature yet, do so now. Your screen should look like this:

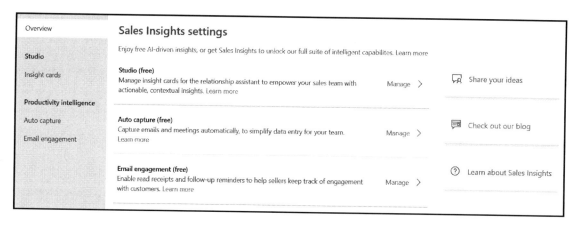

If we start drilling through these features, we can look at **Studio (free)** and see the list of already created cards, with the ability to turn some off, as well as to create new ones:

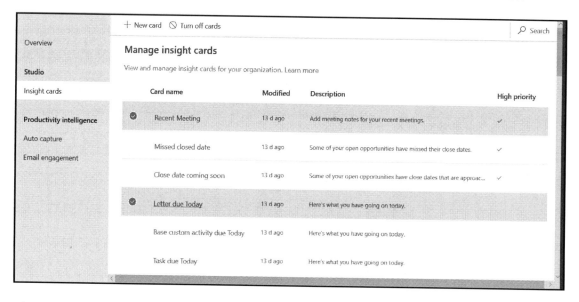

The other options, including **Auto capture** and **Email engagement**, are simple toggles to turn on the features.

Finally, looking further down, we find the section for **Advanced AI with Sales Insights**. If you are running in a demo environment, or if you have not configured this feature yet, you have the option to start a trial of this feature from this screen:

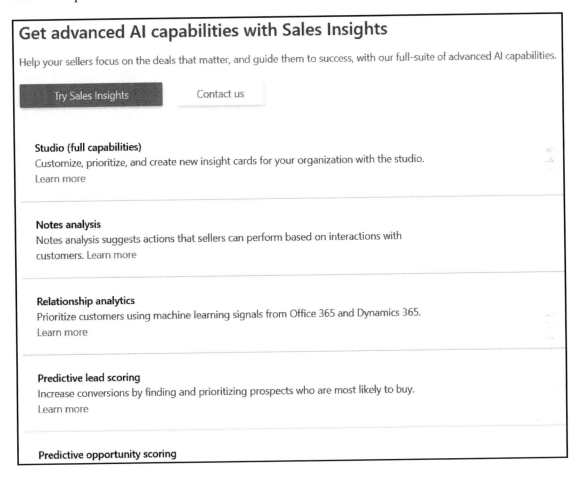

Enabling this feature brings up a notification that your data will be accessible to certain external systems. This is obviously something to be considered, as it could have a major impact on compliance requirements:

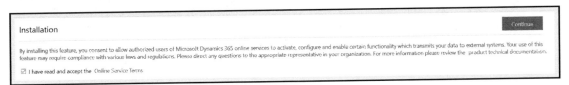

The installation begins and presents several cards describing the application features:

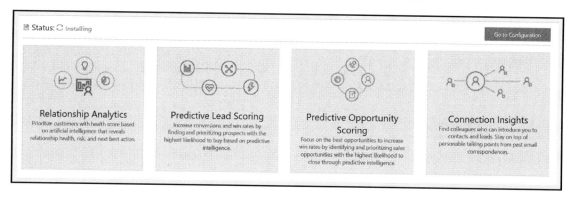

Once the installation completes, you can proceed to configure the features. You do that by returning to the Sales Insights settings. You will observe that Studio is now changed from **Studio (free)** to **Studio (full capabilities)**, and the remaining advanced features have the **Set up** option:

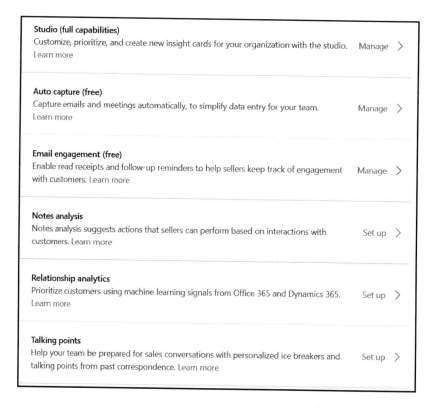

You are now ready to start configuring each of the advanced features individually. For the most part, this is a matter of enabling the feature. Some features, such as Predictive lead scoring and Predictive opportunity scoring, require a sample set of data in order to determine the model. If you do not have sufficient data in your system, you will be prompted.

The Sales Insights application

Finally, the Sales Insights app is the centralized interface for managing all of the smart capabilities enabled with the Sales Insights features.

The first time you launch Dynamics 365 Sales Insights, if you are running this in a trial, you will be presented with a demo version using sample data. This allows new users to familiarize themselves with the available features. Your interface will look like the following screen:

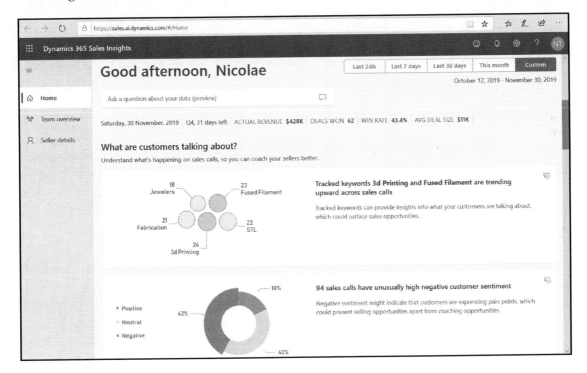

Observe that, using data analysis across your entire organization, including call recordings, your Dynamics 365 for Sales environment, and Microsoft Office 365, builds a set of *insights* that can be used to answer questions about the business using natural language queries. The information can also be used to guide and coach your sales team members, by providing additional insights into the most successful approaches to sales from the top performers, along with analytics about the most trending products and keywords used in conversations. The deals on track analysis can quickly identify potential issues in the pipeline, and the next course of action to prevent a negative outcome.

For sales managers, the **Team overview** area on the left-hand navigation opens up a treasure trove of information about the customer sentiment and team conversation style. This can help in identifying trending behavior and taking action early on. The following screenshot shows this area of the Sales Insights application:

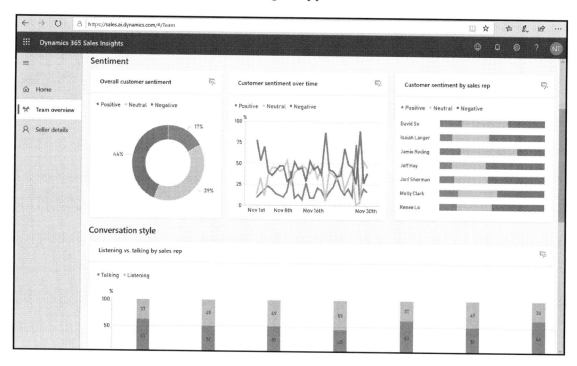

Finally, the **Seller details** area drills down and focuses on a specific team member and their performance indicators. The top area provides an overall personal analysis of conversation style, followed by some specific insights aggregated with data across the organization, as seen in the following screenshot:

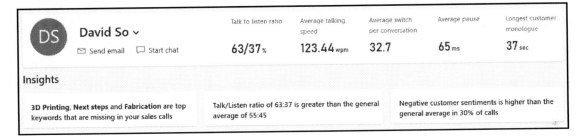

The following area shows various statistics visualized for easy understanding:

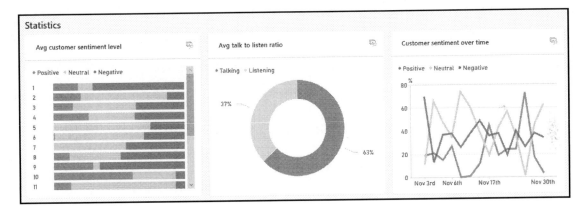

Finally, the **Call history** area, presented in the following screenshot, details the activities as they relate to specific records, and allow the user to drill down into the conversation transcripts:

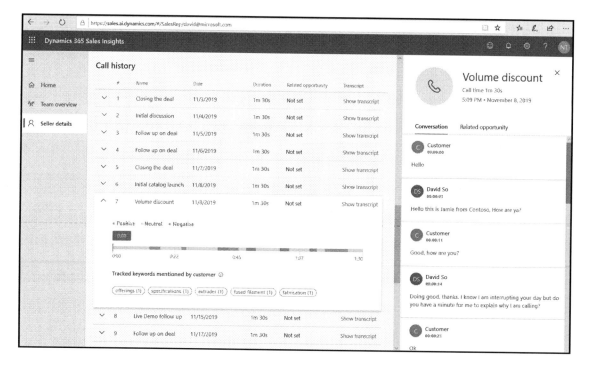

Further to this analysis, pre-configured for your organization, administrators can configure additional keywords and competitors to track in the team conversations, configure retention plans for data, and manage additional environments and conversation intelligence to mine call data.

Note that, for best results, you must have a proper sales management hierarchy defined in your organization. This analysis relies on this configuration being in place. It relies on a tree-like organizational structure.

Let's next look at the Sales Navigator extensions for LinkedIn.

LinkedIn Sales Navigator

Microsoft made a major acquisition when purchasing LinkedIn. In conjunction with Dynamics 365, this creates a huge advantage over its competition. As one of the most established professional networks, LinkedIn is a treasure trove of information that can be used to enrich and enhance business processes with data on contacts, accounts, and relationships.

To enable this functionality, the user configuring the platform must be a system administrator, and the proper subscriptions must be available. These include either a Microsoft Relationship Sales subscription or one of the Sales Navigator licenses including LinkedIn Sales Navigator Team or LinkedIn Sales Navigator Enterprise.

 Note that, as of the spring 2019 wave, the default solutions for LinkedIn are not installed out of the box; the administrator performing the configuration must install these.

Starting the initial configuration

To start the configuration, navigate to **Settings** | **Business Management** and select the **LinkedIn Sales Navigator** option, as seen in the following screenshot:

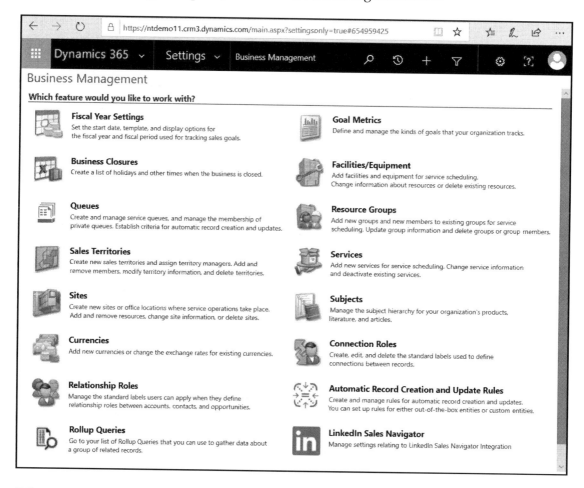

When prompted, choose **Enable Sales Navigator integration**, as well as the **Photo refresh** feature, which allows profile pictures to be synchronized with LinkedIn images. The following screenshot shows this configuration screen:

Now that we are equipped with the initial configuration, let's learn about the LinkedIn Sales Navigator controls.

LinkedIn Sales Navigator controls

The Sales Navigator solution brings several controls for Unified Interface. These can be grouped into the following categories:

- LinkedIn Sales Navigator Lead controls
- LinkedIn Sales Navigator Account controls

Let's look at the controls available within each of these categories.

LinkedIn Sales Navigator Lead controls

The Lead controls present the user with information about a specific member profile. These controls comprise several sections, and are configurable to show or hide each of them:

- **Top Card**: Presents retrieved information from LinkedIn about a person/contact. This control also provides messaging capabilities, as well as the ability to create a Lead directly in Sales Navigator.
- **News (Icebreakers)**: Displays highlights for the respective contact.
- **Connections (Get Introduced)**: Retrieves the common connections that you can use to obtain an introduction.
- **Related Leads**: Retrieves and displays potential Sales Navigator leads related to the target contact.

An alternate version of these controls is available as Lookup controls.

LinkedIn Sales Navigator Account Controls

The Account controls pull information about an organization profile on LinkedIn. These controls include the following modules, which are configurable to show or hide as needed:

- **Top Card**: Presents retrieved information from LinkedIn about an organization. This information includes organization name, industry, location, and other information.
- **News**: Presents the latest news about this organization.
- **Connections**: Pulls together a list of contacts for this organization.
- **Recommended Leads**: Queries and retrieves recommended potential leads.

An alternate version of this control is available, where the name of the entity is used as an organization name.

Overall, these controls can be integrated into a record form, as shown in the following screenshot:

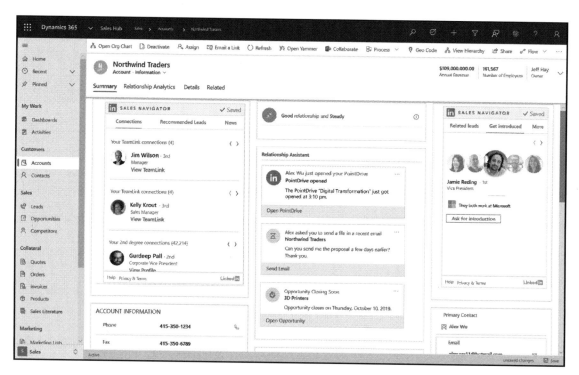

We've now covered the LinkedIn Sales Navigator controls. Next, let's see how to add controls to entity forms.

Adding controls to entity forms

By default, once you have the solutions installed, you must define where you want the controls presented on the record forms.

Note that the LinkedIn Sales Navigator controls are designed to bind to a matching field used to map to the profile on LinkedIn. Once a match is created, the record **Global Unique Identifier (GUID)** is associated and used in future queries.

 The system allows us to correct an incorrect match by leveraging the search interface.

Adding the controls to a form is done in a similar fashion to adding any custom controls. You should be working within a solution when performing these customizations.

Start by opening your custom solutions. Add the respective entity's main form where you want the control added, as shown in the following screenshot:

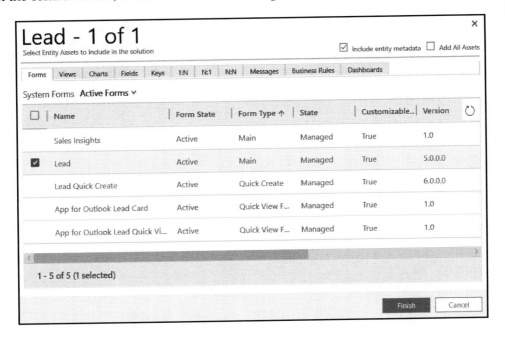

On the added form, select the **Last Name** field, which is the binding field. Choose the option on the ribbon to edit the field:

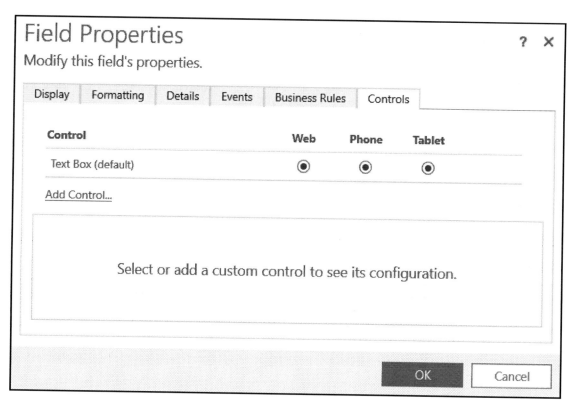

Select the option to **Add Control**, and find the respective **LinkedIn Sales Navigator** control, as seen in the following screenshot:

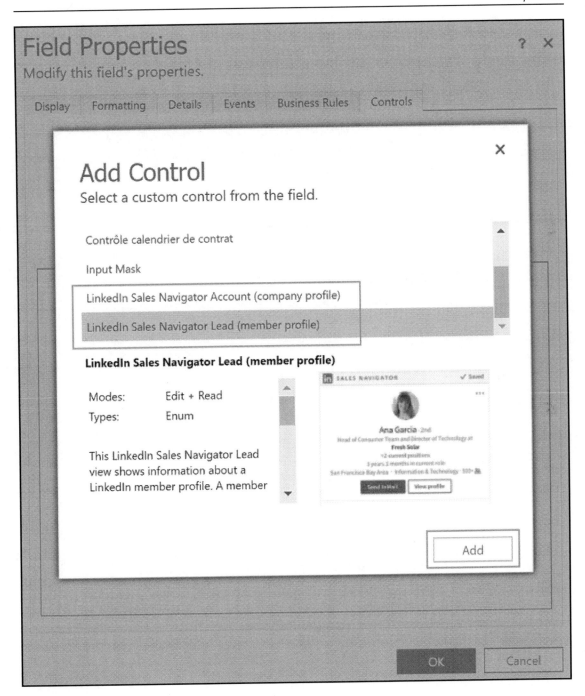

With the control added to your form, now you can proceed to configure the control. With the control selected, in the control configuration area, select a field for mapping, and define the mapping details as shown in the following screenshot:

When done, publish the solution changes and observe the control on the respective record forms. You are now ready to use the LinkedIn functionality integrated with Dynamics 365.

Summary

Throughout this chapter, we learned about several configurable integrations, including the ability to leverage email from Dynamics 365 along with the reverse scenario, using Dynamics 365 from the Outlook web app. Next, we looked at integration with SharePoint and OneDrive for Business for document management as well as leveraging virtual entities to present data from an external system in a read-only form within Dynamics 365.

Later on, we looked at some additional sales-specific enhancements, leveraging the Sales Insights solution for AI-driven functionality, as well as the LinkedIn Sales Navigator feature, allowing us to enrich our platform data and make more relevant decisions.

In the next chapter, we'll be looking at several custom integration approaches available. These are driven by several of Microsoft's Azure services and are, for the most part, configurable. We will tackle more complex integrations and leveraging other external tools there.

12
Custom Integration Capabilities

So far, we've covered the core platform, the applications available, as well as related services that integrate with Dynamics 365 through configuration only. These are services that, while they might come at a premium, are meant to function alongside the platform for increased usability and overall value.

This only takes us so far. In the current market, with an aggressive push toward Digital Transformation, we often see multiple platforms, the best of the breed, working alongside each other. We create modular systems that tightly integrate, but can easily be swapped and replaced by new or better components at any time.

In order to have a complete ecosystem, we need more than just a set of tools meant to work with each other. We need the capability to integrate with other systems.

In this chapter, we will look at a few tools available from Microsoft to serve this purpose, as follows:

- Power Automate, part of Power Platform
- Azure Logic Apps, for true Enterprise integration
- PowerApps Data integration, for easy, configurable data integration

Each has its strengths in various scenarios, as we'll see throughout this chapter.

This chapter will not look at other third-party tools, but the following two are worth mentioning here:

- KingswaySoft: A well-known integration tool based on **SQL Server Integration Services (SSIS)**

- Tibco Cloud Integration: Based on the former Scribe Software integration tool

 These two products are the de facto tools for integration and are the most popular tools available. Choosing one over the other depends primarily on the skill set available to support the tool selected. There is a learning curve with either of these, and I have seen organizations using either successfully. Unfortunately, I have also seen some instances where these tools are used side by side in the same environment. This is a result of bringing together, through acquisition, a new group with a different use for the second tool. I would recommend standardizing on only one toolset, especially when the needs are very similar. This will reduce the need to support two different tools with the different skill set requirements, thus making your life a lot easier down the road.

Now, let's begin this chapter by exploring how to use Power Automate.

Using Power Automate

With the rebranding taking place in 2019 Wave 2 release, Microsoft Flow is now Power Automate. It remains part of the Power Platform, alongside Power Apps, Power BI, and Power Virtual Agents. It is meant to work alongside **Common Data Service (CDS)** and **Common Data Model (CDM)**, as well as a multitude of other applications. A rich set of out-of-the-box connectors allows this integration. We can also create new custom connectors as needed, for platforms that are not in the list of existing connectors.

The following screenshot shows some of the available connectors:

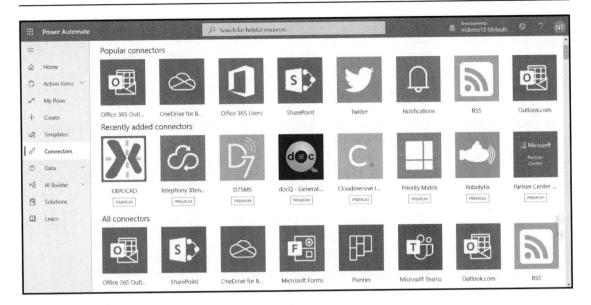

First, let's understand what Power Automate (Flow) is.

Power Automate – Flow reborn

Power Automate allows us to boost productivity by automating mundane organizational processes. In a way, if you are familiar with **IF This Then That** (**IFTTT**), which has been around for a very long time, there are many similarities. You create the if/then processes in a simple visual interface. The main difference is that where IFTTT focuses more on actions than on hardware, Power Automate has a distinct focus on business processes and works closely in the context of a business environment. It allows us to connect various cloud services, automate interactions between those services, and triggered actions to be performed when an event occurs.

We provided an introduction to the Flow functionality at the end of `Chapter 8`, *Dynamics 365 Customer Engagement and Power Platform*. Throughout this chapter, we will be focusing on several common scenarios, and we will see how we can have data flow from one application to another through simple automation. Some of these scenarios include the following:

- Notifications
- Managing approvals

Now that we have some understanding of what Power Automate is, let's learn about Power Automate connectors.

Power Automate connectors

The Power Automate (Flow) system relies heavily on connectors. They are the bread and butter of this platform and are what allows for the rich set of functionalities across various platforms. These connectors allow your application to interact with other platforms. A large library of existing connectors is provided, and many third-party connectors are provided by partners. In addition, when connecting to an application that does not have an existing connector in the store, you can create your own custom connector or have a partner build one for you.

When logging into `https://flow.microsoft.com` with the proper credentials, you will be presented with the main landing page for Power Automate, as shown in the following screenshot:

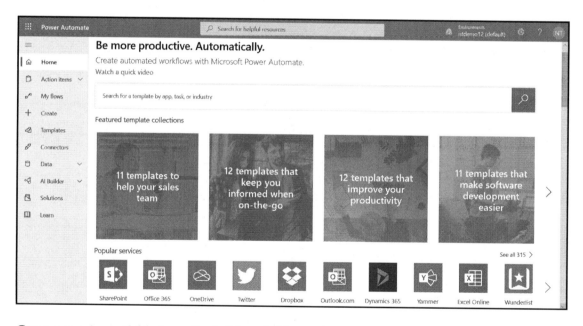

Connectors is available from the left-hand side navigation. You can choose to browse through the various categories, such as **Popular Connectors**, **Recently Added Connectors**, and **All Connectors**. Alternatively, if you know the connector type you are looking for, you can search for it directly from the top search bar.

Note the distinction between regular connectors and Premium connectors. The ones marked as Premium have specific licensing requirements associate with the users executing the process.

In addition, you will find several versions of certain connectors. For example, the Dynamics 365 connector is the first generation, which was later replaced by the Common Data Service connectors. As Dynamics 365 is at the core of the Common Data Service, this now makes sense, but it might not be that obvious from the get-go.

Next, we will look at the templates that are available in Power Automate.

Power Automate templates

Along with the connectors available, we also have access to a series of templates that have been created to simplify certain process creation activities.

By navigating from the left-hand side to **Templates**, we will find a series of flows, along with categories and the ability to search for a specific flow, as shown in the following screenshot:

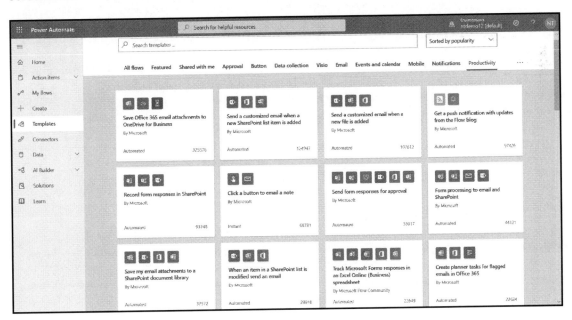

Running a search for Dynamics 365 brings up a set of results that rely on connecting to one or more of the Dynamics 365 solution offerings. The following screenshot shows the top results for this search:

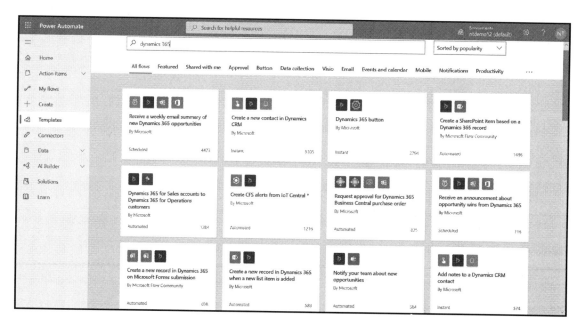

One common integration flow we will find in the results presented is the **Dynamics 365 for Sales accounts to Dynamics 365 for Operations customers** template. Selecting this template brings us to the following page, where we create the connections to the environments we are pointing to:

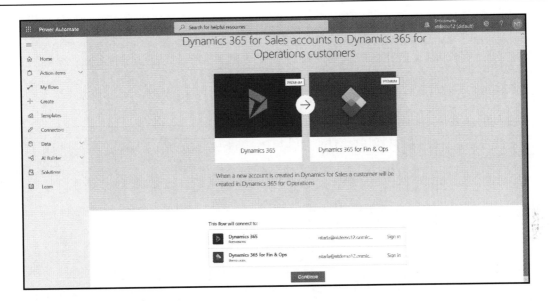

Once you sign in to both the source and target environments, you can enable the template and have all new accounts created in **Dynamics 365 for Sales** synchronized as Customers on the ERP side. Observe that, in this instance, both connectors being used are Premium connectors.

Once configured, you can configure the condition and actions further. The following screenshot shows the configuration window:

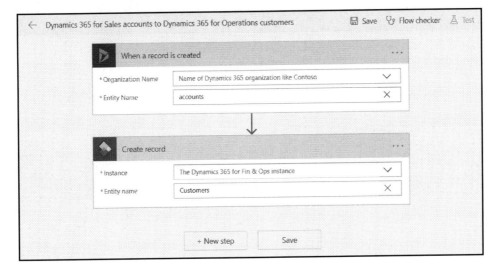

We can extend this template with additional functionality, add conditional decisions, and create a brand-new flow based on one of the existing templates. You can have flows that are triggered in various scenarios. For example, you can have a flow running on a schedule for actions that need to be triggered hourly or daily. You can also have flows that are triggered automatically by an action. These are flows that could be triggered when data on a record is created, changed, or removed. Finally, another triggered flow could be an on-demand flow. This is a flow that's triggered by a user action directly, and it only runs when a user decides to activate it through the user interface. In the next section, we will learn how to use conditional controls.

Conditional decisions

Let's start with the existing template we looked at previously and modify it to create a totally new flow:

1. Start by selecting the **Create record** box. Select the ellipsis to the top-right of the **Create record** box and select the **Delete** option from the drop-down, as shown in the following screenshot:

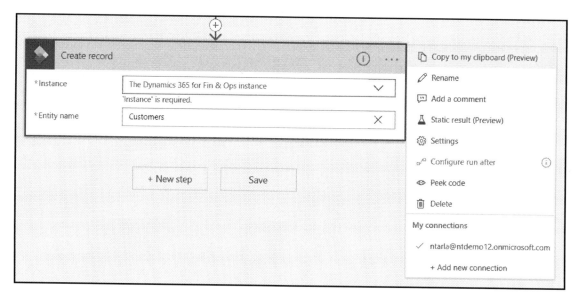

2. You will be prompted with a confirmation window. Select **OK** to confirm deleting this step, as shown in the following screenshot:

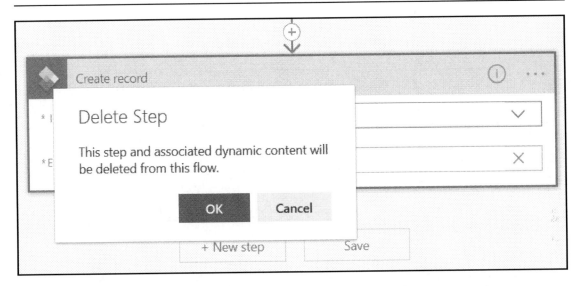

Now, our flow only has a trigger action, as shown here:

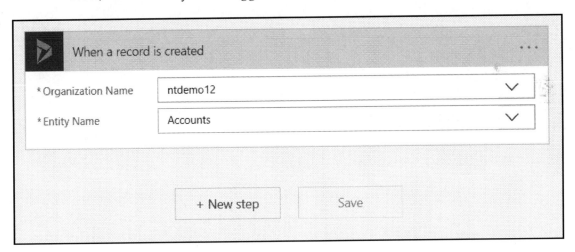

At this point, we will decide what to do when a new account is created in the Dynamics 365 for Sales application. Let's proceed with a conditional statement next, in order to determine the next course of action.

3. Select the **+ New step** button. Here, we can choose an action, as shown in the following screenshot:

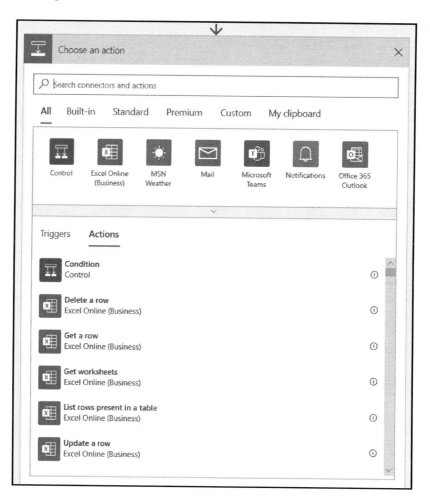

4. Let's select **Condition Control** from the **Actions** area. The configuration for this action is presented in the following screenshot:

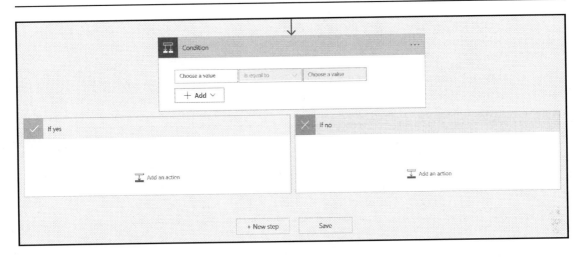

First, we need to configure the condition, followed by the actions for when the condition is met or not.

5. Clicking on the **Choose a value** text box presents us with a dynamic content window, which brings forward a set of available fields in the source Account entity. Here, we can configure conditions using **And/Or** conditions to create a more complex statement. The following screenshot depicts a condition where the main address' country is `Canada` and the provinces are either `Ontario` or `Quebec`:

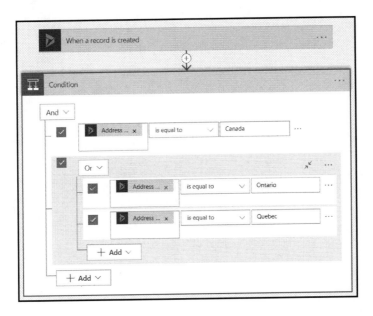

6. With the condition in place, we can now configure the actions that will be performed. For when the condition is met, in the **If yes** box, add an action to notify a user of this. Select the **Add an action** option in the respective box.

7. From the presented options, select the **Mail** option. The **Send an email notification** option will be presented, as shown in the following screenshot:

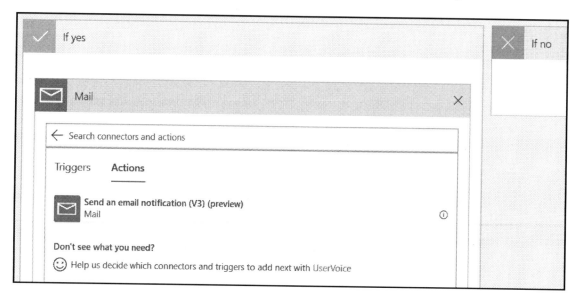

8. Once you select this option, you will be prompted to accept the terms and privacy policy. Once you select **Accept**, you can now configure the email notification message, as shown here:

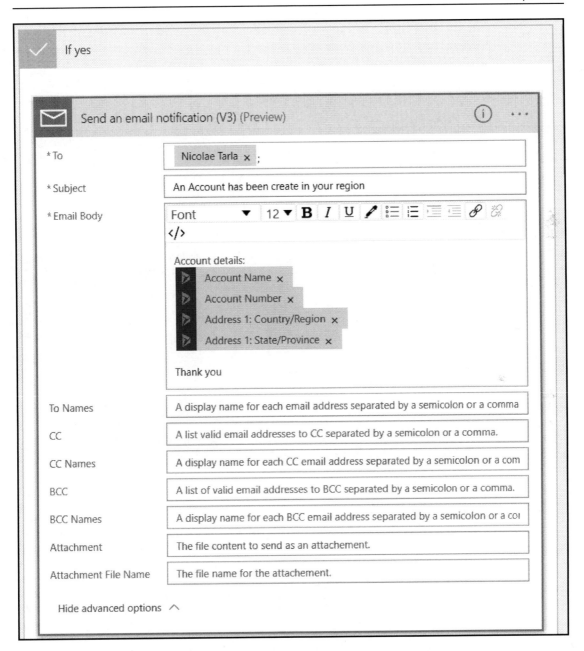

It's pretty straightforward to include data from the record by leveraging the **Dynamic content** window, as shown here:

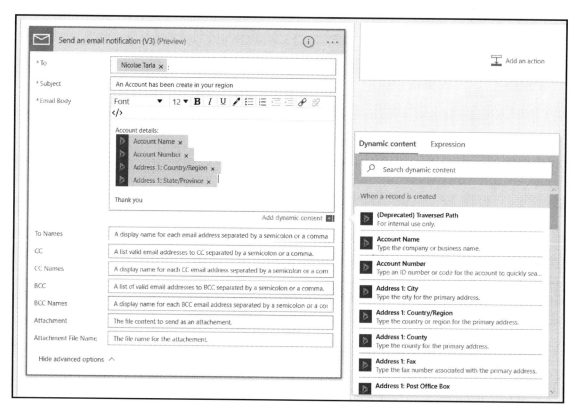

We can leave the **If no** branch with no action, or we can configure other actions as needed.

9. When complete, save your newly created Flow. When you changed an existing template so much, it's always a good idea to go back to the Flow description and modify its name and description to reflect the new functionality. You can see that in the following screenshot:

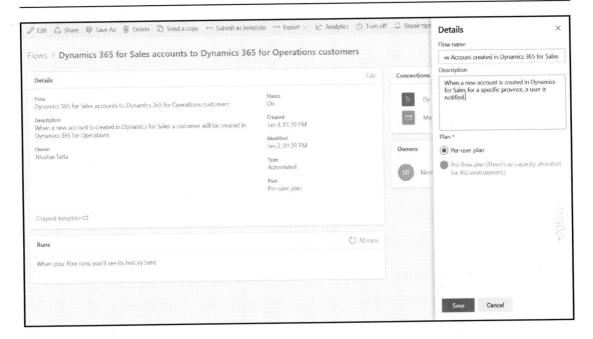

The main status, along with details on **Flow**, **Runs**, **Connections**, and **Owners**, is presented in the following screenshot:

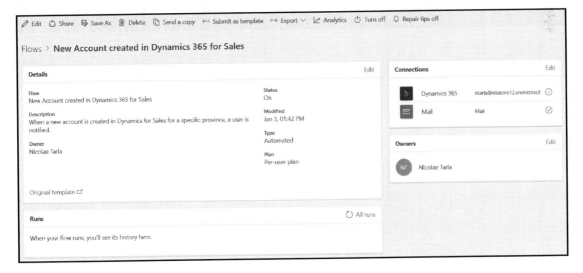

Now that we have seen a simple notification workflow, let's look at a scenario that adds more complexity. Imagine you have a business process that requires approval from a manager. We can check for won opportunities and notify the user's manager so that they approve the deal.

For this scenario, we will create a new Flow from scratch. This way, we can understand the individual steps and the creation process:

1. Let's begin from Power Automate by navigating to **Create** from the left-hand side navigation. Select the option for **Automated flow**, as shown in the following screenshot:

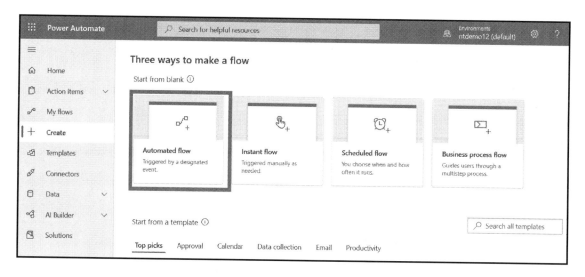

2. For the flow definition, let's name it Opportunity Approval and select a trigger for **When a record is updated**, as shown in the following screenshot:

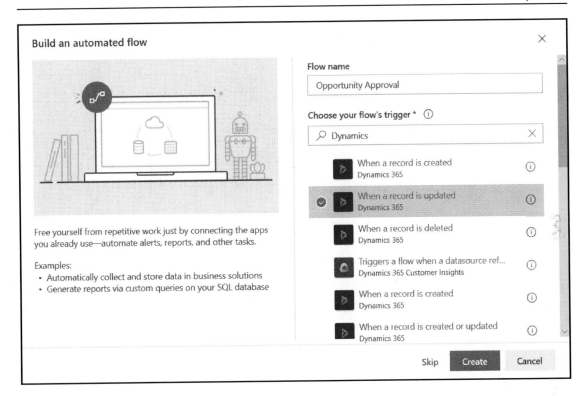

3. Once you select **Create**, the Flow is created, and the trigger is added to the canvas. We can now configure the organization and the Opportunity entities, as shown in the following screenshot:

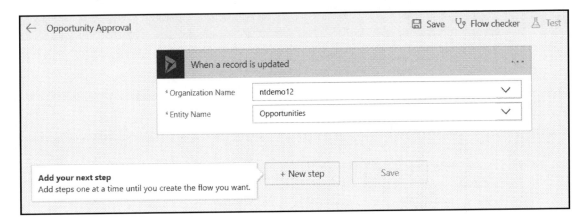

4. In order to trigger an approval, we need to add a step for **Start and wait for the approval**. This allows us to generate the approval process via email. Configure the approval properties like so:

5. Here, we choose an Approval type of **Custom Responses – Wait for one response**. This will allow the first approver to move the process forward. From the Response options, we add the two options for Approved or Rejected. These are custom values, and they could be anything.

6. Next, configure the email properties, including **Title**, **Assigned to**, and the body of the email. We can assign the approval rights to a specific person or persons, or we can infer, if needed, the manager of the user triggering the process. In the body of the email, we get the dynamic values from the record that was created and embed them into the content.

   We can configure some additional options, including a link to the record if needed, and other non-mandatory properties.

7. With the Approval in place, we can add a decision tree and act upon the response from the approver. Add a **Condition** using the reference values, where the **Outcome** of the approval is **Approved**. On the **If yes** branch, send an email notification for the **Approved** value, while on the **If no** branch, send a message for **Rejected**, as shown in the following screenshot:

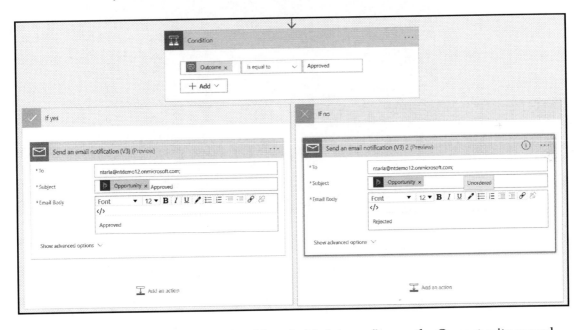

For the sake of completeness, you should probably have a flag on the Opportunity record and update that flag, according to the approval response, by adding another action to each of the conditional branches.

Leveraging mobility with the Dynamics 365 platform

The beauty of the approach shown in the preceding section is that we now have full mobility support for approvals. Using a mobile device, we can easily retrieve the respective email on a mobile device and continue the process on that device. The following screenshot shows the approval email presented on a mobile device:

Furthermore, when using the mobile Power Automate app, we can see the active approvals that have been collected on the **Approvals** tab, as shown here:

We can also perform some administration from the same application if permissions allow. From the **Flows** tab at the bottom, we can see the available flows in the environment. After selecting a Flow, we get to see the options to enable or disable the flow, edit it, its **Run history**, and other details, as shown in the following screenshot:

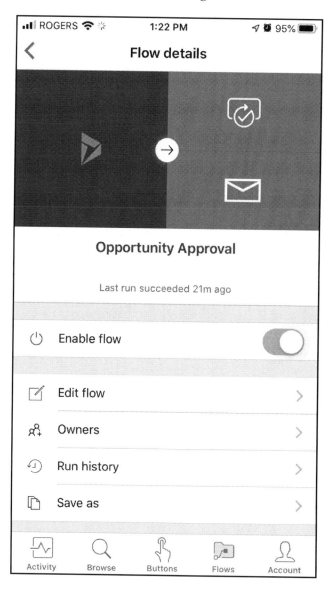

Selecting **Run history** shows us the statuses of all the previous runs, as shown here:

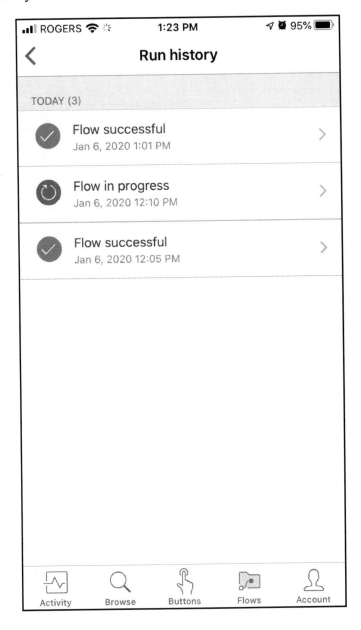

Finally, we can trigger an approval directly from the application, just like we did from an email. Navigate to **Activity** on the bottom tab, go to **Approvals** on the top tab, and select one of the active Flow runs. The screen presented allows you to either approve, reject, reassign, or add comments, as shown in the following screenshot:

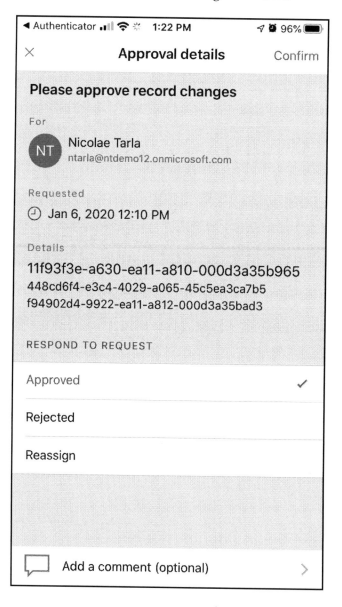

As you can see, for the mobile warrior, all the required functionality is available in a mobile app.

Next, we'll look at the security configurations for our Power Automate Flows.

Enforcing security through configuration

From a security perspective, Flows are owned by a specified user. Managing owners is done from the Power Automate admin interface by selecting a Flow and either selecting **Edit** on the **Owners** card or selecting **Share** on the ribbon. This presents the **Owners** management interface, along with the **Embedded Connections** listing and management, as shown in the following screenshot:

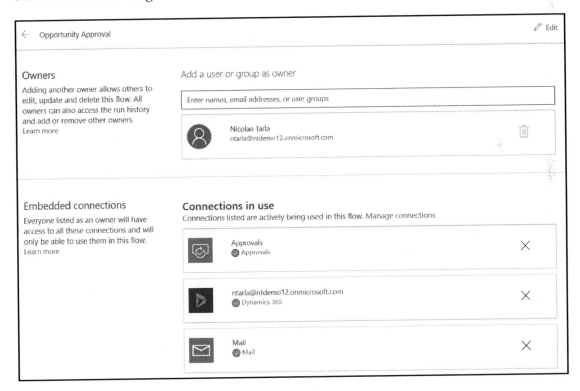

Typically, a Flow will run in the context of the user triggering the execution. For Flows with more flexibility with regards to using other accounts, consider creating a Team Flow. This allows shared connections to be used in the flow in which they were created.

You can manage the available connections as an administrator by navigating to **Data** from the side navigation and finding **Connections**. The following screenshot shows this interface:

You can further drill down into one of the connections to see additional details, along with information about which app or Flow is using this connection, as shown in the following screenshot:

Connections > **Approvals**

Details   Apps using this connection   Flows using this connection

Connector name

 Approvals

Description

Enables approvals in workflows.

Status

Connected

Owner

Nicolae Tarla

Created

1/3/2020, 5:36:16 PM

Modified

1/3/2020, 5:36:16 PM

Now that we've configured several connectors, let's recap some of the best practices when using connectors.

Recommendations on using connectors

The subsequent sections provide a short list of quick recommendations when working with some of the available connectors for Power Automate. This is by no means an exhaustive list, but rather just some things to consider when selecting a specific connector for a Flow.

Using the CDS Connector instead of the older Dynamics 365 Connector

With the Dynamics 365 platform leveraging the **Common Data Service (CDS)**, the connector for Dynamics 365 has been updated. You should be using the CDS connectors going forward, rather than the older version of Dynamics 365 connectors. The following screenshot shows the CDS connectors available:

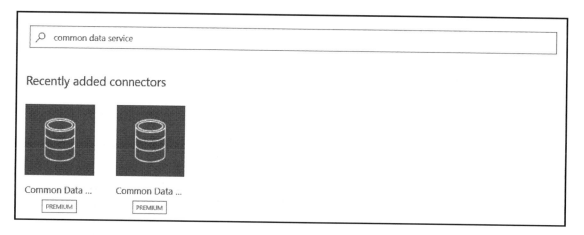

Using the right CDS Connector for the job

When looking at the CDS connectors, the search results will show you two different connectors. These are as follows:

- Common Data Service (current environment)
- Common Data Service

Their functionality and use are slightly different. The most important difference is their availability for different Services, where the second option is available not only for Flow and PowerApps but also for Logic Apps. We will touch on Logic Apps in the next section.

When it comes to available actions, the first option takes the cake, with a larger variety of available actions to be performed. Some distinct advantages include the ability to create queries using FetchXML for filtering a subset of data returned, as well as the ability to leverage AI models.

Personal automation versus Application Lifecycle Management (ALM)

Based on some of the properties described in the preceding section for these connectors, it makes sense to identify which connectors make more sense to be used when configuring personal automation, versus a more organizational approach.

Typically, you should be using the Common Data Service connector either for personal automation or when building a simple scenario that could be exported for use with Azure Logic Apps at a later date.

Alternatively, for ALM, it makes more sense to use the Common Data Service (current environment) connector as it will update the connections based on the environment it is deployed to.

Also, from a Solution awareness perspective, the Common Data Service (current environment) connectors can only be used with Flows that are part of a Solution. The Flows that use the Common Data Service connector can be part of a Solution, but it is not mandatory.

Azure Logic Apps shares some of the inner workings of ALM while being targeted at large enterprises. We'll look at this in more detail next.

Leveraging Azure Logic Apps for enterprises

As we saw previously, Power Automate is a good option for integrating certain scenarios. But for true enterprise scenarios, a more robust toolset is needed. This is where Azure Logic Apps comes into play.

Sharing similar inner workings to Power Automate, Azure Logic Apps allows for both no-code and code-based integrations. The tool allows true developers to create robust solutions, with full source control support. There are certainly simpler scenarios that can be ported directly between the two platforms, but you will soon reach the threshold where you will be forced to choose one path over the other. We'll discuss such scenarios in the subsequent sections.

Logic Apps and Power Automate – similar but different

Let's begin by looking at some of their similarities. To an extent, the user interface and the ability to build integrations is quite similar. The following screenshot shows how the **Logic Apps Designer** interface is quite similar to that of Power Automate's:

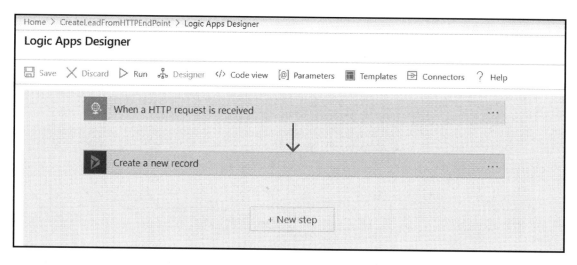

Furthermore, for certain Power Automate Flows, if built using connectors that support Logic Apps, you can export these Power Automate Flows so that they can be imported in Logic Apps. You can do that from Power Automate's Flow interface, by selecting **Export | Logic Apps template (.json)** from the top ribbon, as shown in the following screenshot:

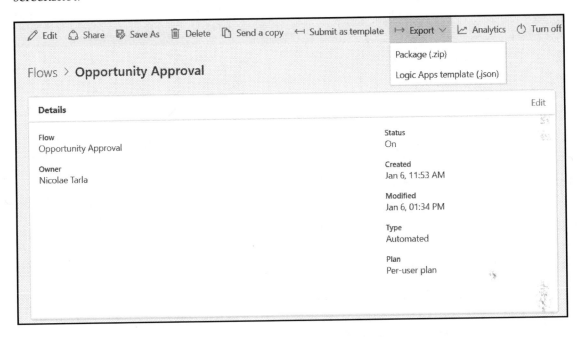

From a creation perspective, though, the similarities end at the point where true code creation is needed. Developers will quickly adopt Logic App's robust capabilities, allowing them to create complex scenarios with true development skills and tools.

When to use Logic Apps

As mentioned previously, Logic Apps is a more robust option. Some of the advantages include the ability to create and manage parameters, as well as the ability to use code. Once you have a Logic Apps solution, you can drop into the code view, as shown in the following screenshot:

```
Home > CreateLeadFromHTTPEndPoint > Logic Apps Designer

Logic Apps Designer

💾 Save    ✕ Discard    ▷ Run    🔗 Designer    </> Code view    [@] Parameters    ▦ Templates    🔲 Connectors    ? Help

 1  {
 2      "definition": {
 3          "$schema": "https://schema.management.azure.com/providers/Microsoft.Logic/schemas/2016-06-01/workflowdefinition.json#",
 4          "actions": {
 5              "Create_a_new_record": {
 6                  "inputs": {
 7                      "body": {
 8                          "_address1_addresstypecode_label": "Default Value",
 9                          "_address2_addresstypecode_label": "Default Value",
10                          "_budgetstatus_label": "",
11                          "_customerid_type": "",
12                          "_industrycode_label": "",
13                          "_initialcommunication_label": "",
14                          "_leadqualitycode_label": "Warm",
15                          "_leadsourcecode_label": "",
16                          "_need_label": "",
17                          "_ownerid_type": "",
18                          "_preferredcontactmethodcode_label": "Any",
19                          "_prioritycode_label": "Default Value",
20                          "_purchaseprocess_label": "",
21                          "_purchasetimeframe_label": "",
22                          "_salesstage_label": "",
23                          "_salesstagecode_label": "Default Value",
24                          "_statuscode_label": "",
25                          "confirminterest": false,
26                          "decisionmaker": false,
27                          "donotbulkemail": false,
28                          "donotemail": false,
29                          "donotfax": false,
```

This allows enterprises to leverage source control, among other benefits.

Just like creating a Flow in Power Automate, though, you start with a trigger from a set of existing configured triggers and a set of connectors. A lot of the triggers and connectors are common across Logic Apps and Power Automate. You can always build your own custom connectors for situations where there is no existing solution available.

Some other benefits of Logic Apps include the ability to connect between cloud and on-premise solutions, leverage enterprise messaging standards, monitor and troubleshoot enterprise-level integrations, better scalability, as well as the ability to leverage BizTalk for integrations. BizTalk Server was positioned as an application integration server for on-premise deployments. It is now a robust enterprise solution, and at the time of writing, the latest version was released at the beginning of 2020.

Of course, all this power and flexibility comes at a cost, and the licensing for Logic Apps tends to result in a more expensive operational cost compared to using Flow.

Logic Apps has also a steeper learning curve. An entire book can be written on this topic, but I would recommend starting your learning journey from the documentation provided by Microsoft at https://docs.microsoft.com/en-us/azure/logic-apps/.

Finally, note that Logic Apps is one of the many Azure services available. It is primarily a consumption-based service.

When you make a choice between Power Automate Flows or Logic App, you can think of Power Automate as the go-to tool for simple operations, such as an approval process on a SharePoint Document Library, while Logic Apps is more tuned for advanced integrations where enterprise-level DevOps and modular security requirements are in place. These products allow you to start simple and expand complexity levels later, transitioning to an enterprise-grade Logic App later on.

Microsoft has recognized that not all integrations are triggered by an action and that not all need to follow this specific format. Part of the Power Platform, the data integration service was born to support a simple approach to mapping fiends in tables across platforms in a very visual manner. We'll look at leveraging this data integration service in the next section.

Leveraging the Power Apps Data Integration service

For integrating data with the Common Data Service, a simple point and click tool has been built into the Power Apps platform. The Data Integrator is a direct integration service that leverages connections to bring data to and from several platforms into the Common Data Service.

While it does leverage the connectors configured through the Power Apps connections, the templates revolve mainly around transferring data between the Dynamics ERP offering and the Sales product, between Salesforce and Dynamics 365 for Sales, or for integration to various SQL databases. The plan is to extend these connections, but at the time of writing, the capabilities are much more restrictive than the previous integration options presented.

The service has been available since 2017, but it is still at a stage where a lack of more robust controls is impacting the usability. We will be looking at some of the drawbacks throughout this section.

The Data Integrator is built by leveraging M-based connectors and leverages the Power Query capabilities. This allows some basic data filtering to be put in place, and simple data transformation.

The concept of integration is based on both sources and destinations. From a supported platform perspective, Sources include the following platforms:

- Dynamics 365 for Sales
- Dynamics 365 for Finance and Operations
- CDS for Apps
- Additional connectors leveraging Power Query

On the opposite end, the following destinations are available:

- Dynamics 365 for Sales
- CDS for Apps
- Dynamics 365 for Finance and Operations

The following diagram describes this:

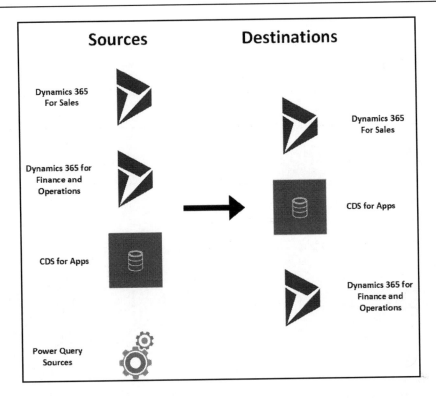

Process-based integrations are supported through scenarios such as Prospect to Cash. This provides direct synchronization between Dynamics 365 for Sales and Dynamics 365 for Finance and Operations. The flows presented as part of this template include synchronizations of the following entities: Accounts, Contacts, Products, Sales Quotations, Sales Orders, and Sales Invoices. This set of templates allows for the Sales processes to take place in the Sales platform, while the fulfillment operations take place on the Finance and Operations platform.

Additionally, templates have been provided for Field Service integrations and Project Service Automation integrations, following a similar set of integration project templates.

Simple no-code integrations

The Data Integrator has been created from scratch for the Power user as a citizen developer. No code is required in order to create integrations, but an understanding of the source and destination platforms is definitely required.

At the core of these integrations, we leverage connections to the various endpoints, connection sets that group several connections required by an integration template together, and integration templates that describe the entities and mappings required.

We will explore the connections, connection sets, projects, and templates in the following sections.

Data Integrator connections

As mentioned previously, the integration projects we created rely heavily on connections. We create these connections by navigating to the Power Apps Maker portal, available at `https://make.powerapps.com`.

Here, from the left navigation, navigate to **Date**. Underneath, find **Connections**. The following screenshot shows this area:

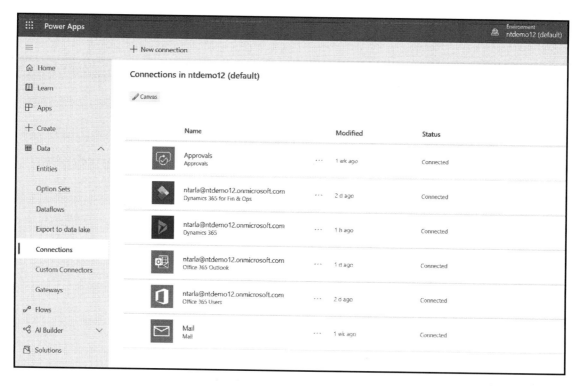

As you can see, we already have a couple of connections from the previous examples. Let's add a new connection and see the steps:

1. Start by selecting the **New connection** option from the ribbon. This takes you to a selections screen that contains the available connections you can configure. We can use the top-right search box to find a specific connection we are looking for, as shown in the following screenshot:

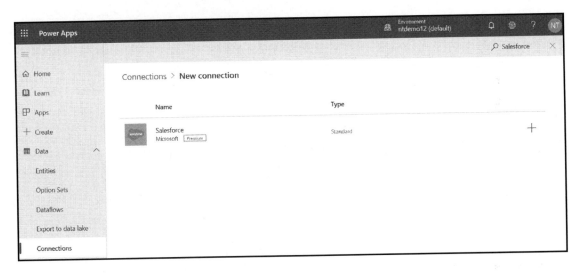

2. Click on the connection. You will be prompted to configure the connection API version, as shown in the following screenshot:

3. The next screen prompts you for the credentials to log into the connection platform. Once you provide these, the new connection will validate and show up in the list of connections available, as shown here:

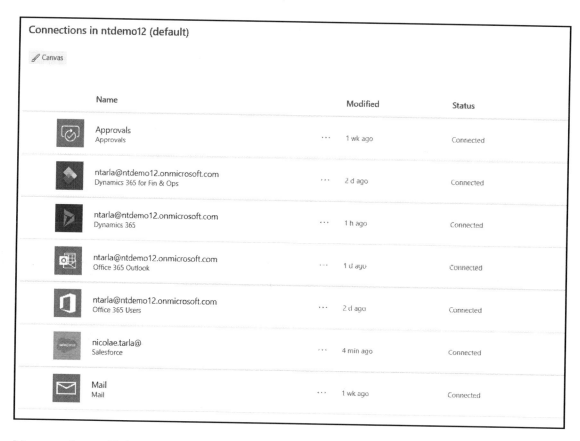

Now, we have all the needed connections in place. Next, we'll look at grouping these connections for a specific project.

Data Integrator connection sets

Since connections are presented on a shared interface, we can now move on to the Power Apps admin center to continue our work on the Data Integrator:

1. Navigate to `https://admin.powerapps.com`. Here, in the left navigation area, select **Data integration**, as shown in the following screenshot:

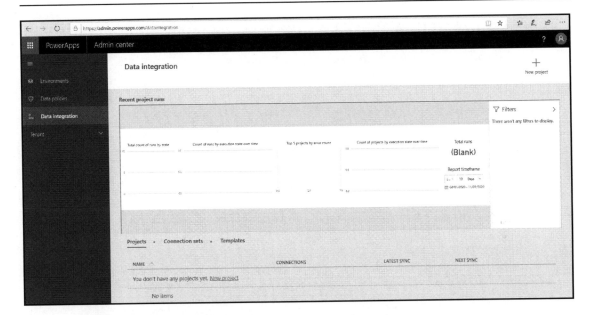

2. First off, before creating a project, we need to define the **Connection sets**. Find the respective link to the right of **Projects**, just under the dashboard. Upon clicking this option, you will be presented with an option to **Add connection set**, as shown in the following screenshot:

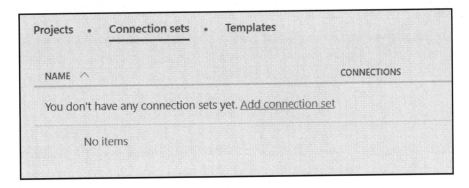

3. Select this link. Then, in the pop-up window that appears, configure your connection set by providing a name, the connections for the source and destination, as well as the organization names, as shown here:

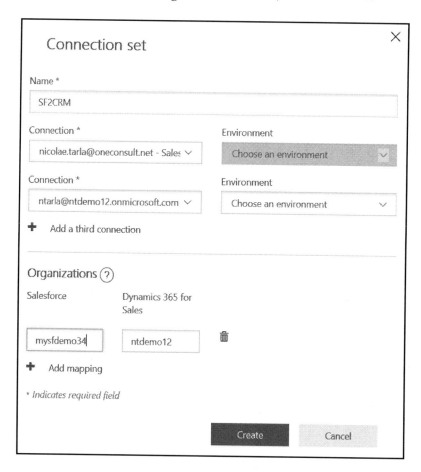

4. Click **Create** when you're done. We can manage our connection by selecting the ellipsis to the right of connection records, and either **Delete** the connection when it's not in use or **Export** it into another environment, as shown in the following screenshot:

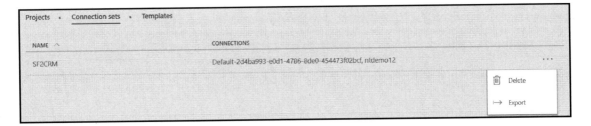

We are now ready to create an integration project.

Data Integrator projects

With connections and a connection set defined, we are now ready to create a data integration project:

1. Navigate back to **Projects** under the previous dashboard. We will be presented with an option to create a **New project**, as shown in the following screenshot:

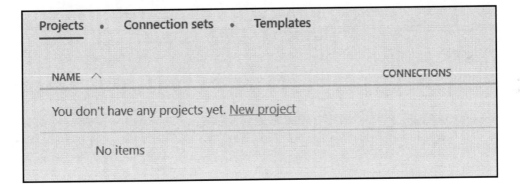

2. On the next wizard screen, give the project a name, select a project template from the templates provided by Microsoft, and click **Next**, as shown in the following screenshot:

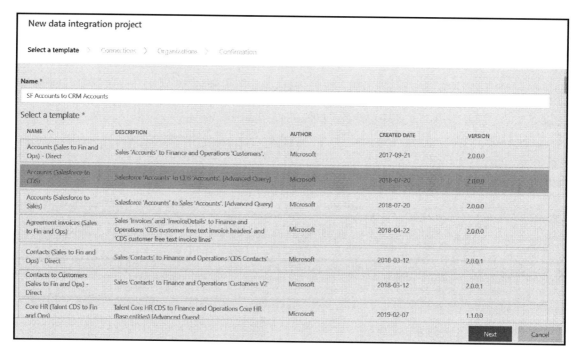

3. On the next screen, select the connection set we created earlier in the *Data Integrator connection set* section (SF2CRM). Once you've selected a connection set, you will be presented with information about the connections in the set, as shown in the following screenshot:

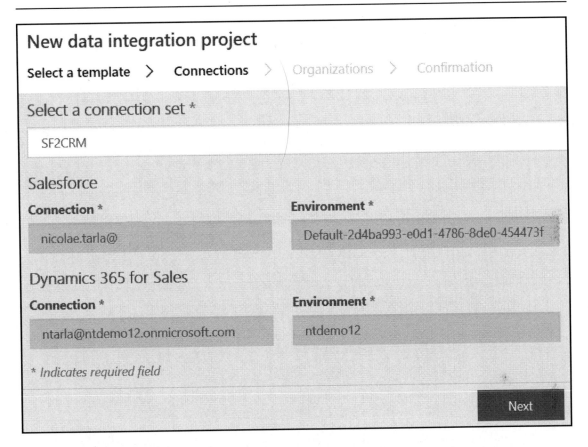

4. Click on **Next** and select the **Organizations** group, as shown here:

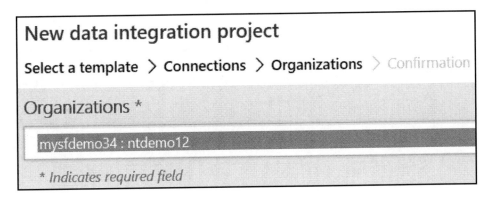

5. Finally, click **Next** again on the last screen and **Create** at the end. You will now have your first data integration project in place, as shown in the following screenshot:

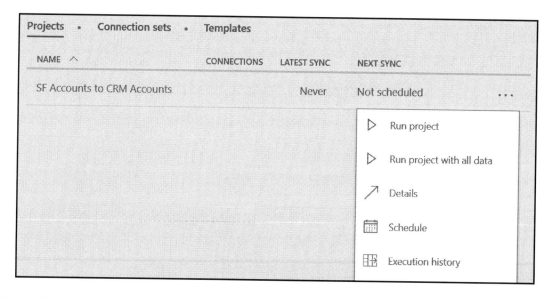

Expanding the drop-down menu on this project reveals several options you can use to run the project (either incremental or with all data), see details on the project configuration, schedule automated runs for this project, and see the execution history.

Selecting **Run project** takes us to the run screen, which updates automatically to present the execution status. When errors occur in the project, you will be presented with a status to reflect this, as shown in the following screenshot:

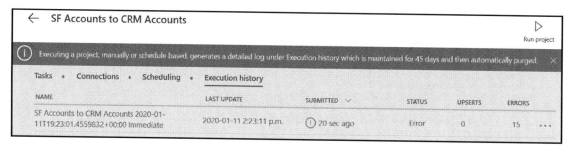

You can now drill down into the execution job, and again into the specific task to see what the error is, as shown here:

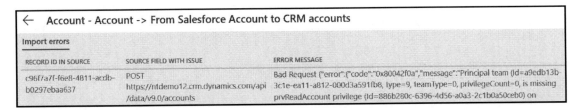

Most of the time, the error message that's logged here will be enough to determine what the issue is and how to correct it. Once you've fixed the permission issue, everything should run correctly.

Navigating to the **Tasks** tab allows you to modify an existing task or create a new one, as shown in the following screenshot:

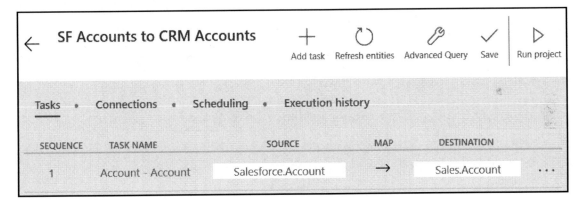

Opening a task presents us with a simple mapping table, where we can define the
SOURCE and **DESTINATION** field equivalents, as shown here:

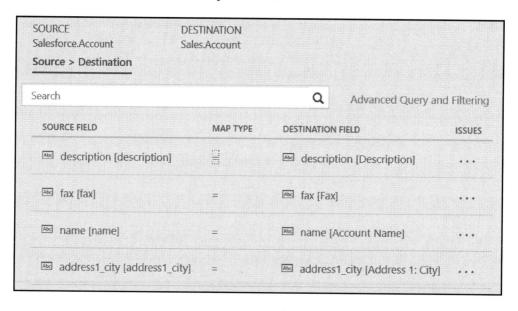

Selecting the **Advanced Query and Filtering** link allows us to enable capabilities around
putting a filter in place, on the source data, so that only specific records are synchronized.
Be careful as enabling this feature does not allow you to disable it afterward.

Clicking on **Map Type** for a certain map presents us with an option to add a transform rule,
as shown in the following screenshot:

Selecting the option to **Add transform** allows us to map specific values from the source to
specific values from the target when these values differ, as well as to select a default value
map when nothing is populated in the Source.

Once you fix all errors, run your project again until you get a successful run. In certain situations, a warning is an expected outcome. This includes situations where, when moving data to an ERP system, for example, line item records with a zero value can exist in Dynamics 365 for Sales but will not be written in ERP.

Finally, as you complete more runs of multiple integration projects, the dashboard will update to reflect the results, as shown here:

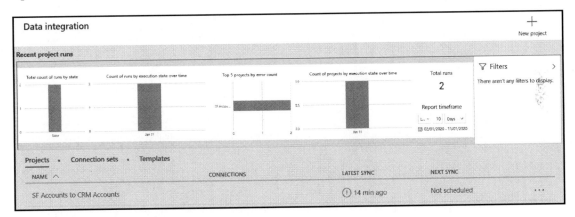

Next, let's learn about data integration templates in more detail.

Data Integrator templates

As we have seen so far, several templates are provided by Microsoft. But you will most definitely want to create your own custom templates and export these to other environments.

This is possible from the **Projects** screen, by selecting a project and expanding the ellipsis (...) drop-down menu. At the bottom of the list, we have options for saving a project as a template and exporting it, as shown in the following screenshot:

Saving a project as a template allows us to define a **Template name**, a **Description**, and whether this template will be shared across the entire organization, as shown in the following screenshot:

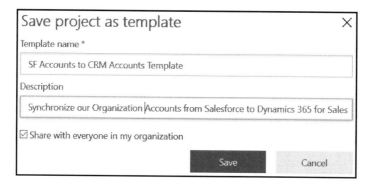

Now, our template is available in the list of templates when creating a new project, as shown here:

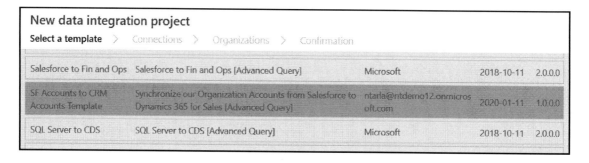

Similarly, when exporting and reimporting this template into another organization, it will be presented in the new environment in the same manner.

Benefits and challenges of data integration

As we have seen so far, data integration is a simple approach to direct integration between a source and a target system. Its relative short learning curve allows PowerApps users to create integrations between various platforms and migrate data across applications. The scheduling and monitoring tools available are satisfactory for most situations, and debugging issues can be relatively easy, with explicit messages provided right in the interface.

But alongside these benefits, there are also some drawbacks. For instance, for complex data transformations that are required during integration, we should definitely consider a more advanced tool or a design that combines tools such as Flow for transformation in conjunction with the Data Integrator.

Summary

Throughout this chapter, we looked at some of the options available for integrating various platforms and data across applications. We started our journey with a look at Flow, as part of the renamed and extended Power Automate platform. We then looked at Azure Logic Apps and its similarities with Power Automate. Finally, we looked at the PowerApps Data Integrator and its ability to move data across platforms.

At this point, we should have a good understanding of the available integration options. We now know that Power Automate provides low-code/no-code integration options, while Azure Logic Apps provides a more developer-focused approach. Now, we also understand that, with the Power Platform, Microsoft is providing data integration capabilities based on provided and configurable templates for the Dynamics family.

In the next and final chapter in our journey, we will look at the administration capabilities of Dynamics 365.

5

Section 5 - Administration

In this final section, we'll be looking at the administration capabilities provided by the platform. Some important aspects include the optimal operation of the platform from a performance perspective considering data quality, and extension management.

This section comprises the following chapter:

- Chapter 13, *Core Administration Concepts*

13
Core Administration Concepts

Over the course of the previous chapters, we have looked at the various applications that are available with Dynamics 365, how to extend the platform through configuration, the business functionality, and the ability to map existing business processes, as well as configurable out-of-the-box and other integration capabilities. In this final chapter, we are looking at the administration capabilities for this platform.

Administration is essential not only for a pure administrator role, but also for a power user or developer. Understanding the core administrative concepts will allow you to create better configurations and understand the core platform better, as well as communicate better with resources when acting in an administrator role.

In this chapter, we will be looking at some of the available administrative configurations, the features available with the classic administrative interface, and the new Power Apps administrative console for solution management and some of its new features, as well as some of the configurations that are not yet available through the new solution administrative interface. The following concepts will be covered in this chapter:

- General administration concepts
- The Settings page
- Other administrative options

This is by no means an exhaustive description of all the administrative options available in Dynamics 365—a whole book can be dedicated to this topic. In this chapter, we will try to give a quick overview of the available functionality, as well as highlight the most commonly used configuration options that an administrator of the system will work with on a day-to-day basis.

Introducing the Settings area

Just like any other platform, Dynamics 365 requires constant care and attention. An administrator of the system is tasked with monitoring the system, analyzing its performance, and intervening where necessary to make improvements.

In a standard, out-of-the-box configuration, all the system management options are collected in the **Settings** page. You can reach this from the Apps screen or from within any of the applications by navigating to the *cog* icon on the top-right of the screen and selecting the **Advanced Settings** option from the dropdown, as shown in the following screenshot:

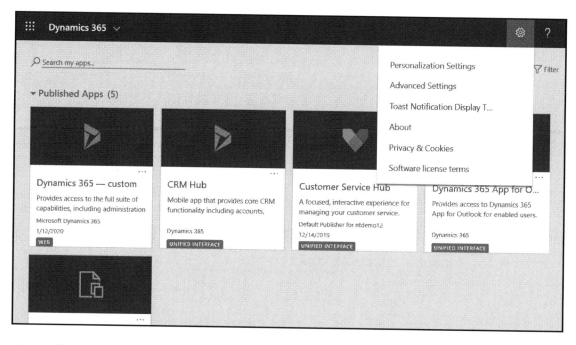

This will take you to a new window where environment configurations are presented. With the move to the Unified Interface and the tight integration with the Power Platform, the administration interface has been revamped and now has a more modern look, with structured main categories and expandable sections, as shown here:

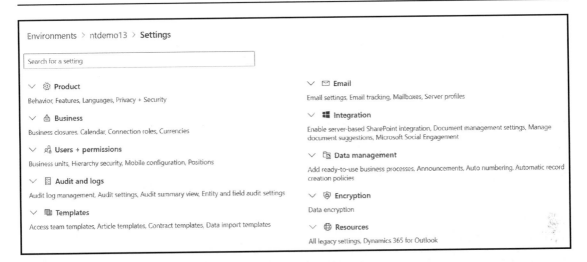

This new structure retains some similarities to the classic interface, but it introduces better navigation and grouping. The following screenshot shows the classic interface for those who remember the previous versions of the platform:

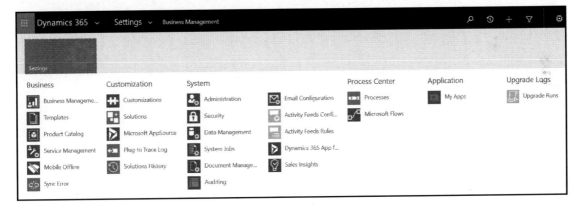

Note that you can still access the classic **Settings** area by expanding the **Resources** area and selecting **All legacy settings**, as shown in the following screenshot:

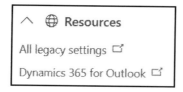

Let's have a look at the **Settings** area in more detail next.

Exploring the Settings area

The **Settings** page is now structured in 10 main groupings of configurable options. Underneath each heading, you can see the main configurable options for the respective categories. This description is not always a complete listing of all the options, and you will need to expand each category to gain access to the full set of configurable settings.

Let's look at each area separately and understand what the available configurable options are.

Product

The **Product** configuration area is structured around four main categories, as shown in the following screenshot:

Let's look at each of the options available in the **Product** configuration area in the subsequent sections.

Behavior

The **Behavior** area includes generic settings that apply across the environment. Some of these were covered in the System Settings area in the old interface, and include the items shown in the following screenshot:

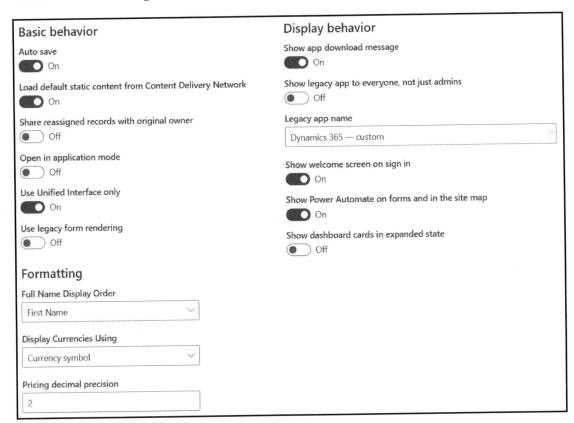

Here, we define basic behaviors, such as whether auto save is enabled across the platform, and whether only the Unified Interface is allowed to be used.

The formatting area presents options to configure how we want the names to be displayed, as shown in the following screenshot:

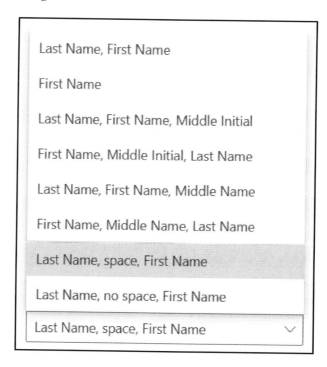

We can also define the currency display as well as the precision required. While the precision is typically set at two decimal points, you can change it as needed.

Finally, the **Display** behavior section allows us to define whether certain elements such as messages and the legacy app are presented to all users, change the label on the legacy app from the default **Dynamics 365 – custom** to a more meaningful name, and change features such as Power Automate or the default state for dashboard cards.

As an example, to understand how these configurations directly affect the user experience, if we enable the option to Show Power Automate on forms and in the site map, then the users will see a record ribbon with the option to trigger a Flow, as shown in the following screenshot:

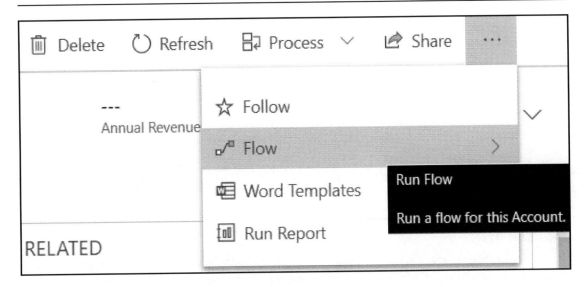

For your reference, as we said earlier, some of these settings correlate to the classic web interface, as shown in the following screenshot:

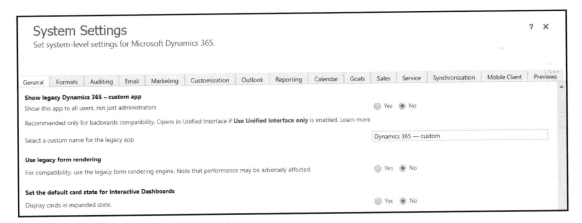

As we are moving to the Unified Interface, with the scheduled date of December 2020, we will be focusing our attention going forward on the administrative options presented in the modern Power Platform Admin center and will not be referring to the classic web interface.

Another great aspect of the Power Platform Admin center is the fact that each category of the settings now links directly to the official documentation. As such, if you encounter a configuration feature whose purpose you are not sure of, you can quickly find the answers needed.

In the **Behavior** configurations area, right at the top, under the navigation breadcrumb, you will find a **Learn more about Behavior** area, as shown here:

Environments > ntdemo13 > Settings > **Behavior**

Learn more about Behavior ⧉

Following that link takes you straight to the documents that describe each feature and its intended use.

Features

The **Features** area provides us with the ability to control whether certain special features are enabled and how they behave. Some of these include the ability to enable the modern AI Builder models, embed various elements, such as Power BI and Bing Maps, set communication preferences, and so on. The following screenshot shows this area:

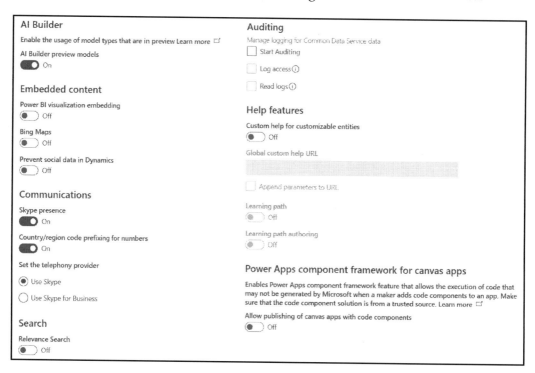

Some of the new elements, in addition to what was available through the classic web interface, include the ability to enable the AI Builder and allow the publishing of canvas apps with code components. Note that these features also link to the respective documentation in Microsoft Docs for each by selecting the **Learn more** link in the description.

The **Communications, Search, Auditing,** and **Help features** configurations have been available on the platform for several versions now, and for the most part, they are quite self-explanatory. The **Communication** area allows for the configuration of the integration with Skype or Skype for Business. In **Search**, you have the option to turn on **Relevance Search**, which is an AI-driven feature that requires your data to flow to Azure. The **Auditing** section allows the generic enabling of this feature for the entire platform, while the **Help** section allows you to configure a custom **Help** feature, potentially leveraging a **learning management system** (**LMS**) and pointing the application to that platform.

The **AI Builder** features are a relatively new addition to the platform and include several models, such as the Business Card Scanner feature and the ability to extract invoice data from a picture. As new models are released, they go through a preview phase before being made generally available. Allowing the preview models enables users to access new models before they are made generally available. Note that this is enabled by default, but should be disabled in production environments where you want to control what's made available to users in order to minimize risk.

Other features will come disabled by default, such as the Power Apps component framework for canvas apps. If you click the **Learn more** link, you will quickly find out why this feature is not enabled. This is an experimental feature, as shown in the important message at the top of the documentation page, as shown here:

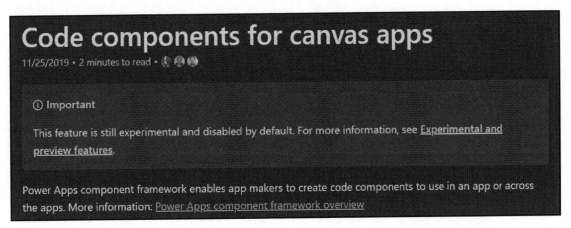

Languages

The **Languages** area is still being transitioned. At the time of writing, the link from **Settings** takes you to a new window showing the classic **Language Settings** area. Here, you have a choice to select the languages that you want to enable within your organization, as shown in the following screen:

Language Settings

Select the languages to enable for your organization, and then click Apply.

Language ↑	Language Code	Status	Version
Arabic	1025	Disabled	0.0
Basque (Basque)	1069	Disabled	0.0
Bulgarian (Bulgaria)	1026	Disabled	0.0
Catalan (Catalan)	1027	Disabled	0.0
Chinese (Hong Kong S.A.R.)	3076	Disabled	0.0
Chinese (PRC)	2052	Disabled	0.0
Chinese (Taiwan)	1028	Disabled	0.0
Croatian (Croatia)	1050	Disabled	0.0

Selecting one or more languages and clicking **Apply** enables the respective languages in your environment. Users with profiles configured with a different primary language will see default labels and fields translated in their language.

As we get closer to transitioning data to the Unified Interface, it is expected that all administrative features will be moved to the Power Platform Admin center.

Privacy + Security

The **Privacy + Security** area shows options governing the presentation of **Privacy** statements, attachment handling, and blocking on the platform to reduce security risks, as well as the settings governing **Session Expiration** and **Inactivity timeout**, as shown in the following screenshot:

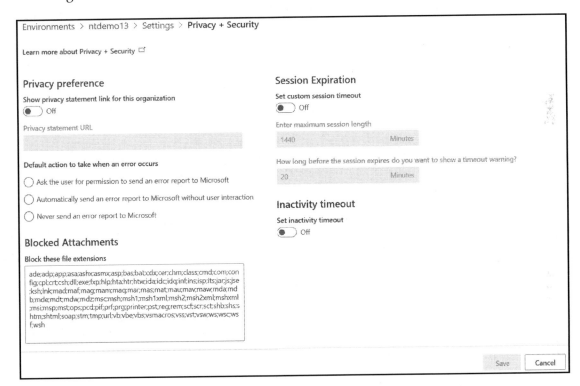

It is good practice to verify the extensions allowed on the platform, as this dictates the types of documents that can be attached to note fields on various records. Blocking extensions for common executables and files, which are known to potentially carry viruses minimizes the risk of exposing users to harmful documents.

It is also good practice to enable and define **Session Expiration** times and **Inactivity timeouts**. Your organization might have standards around how these options should be configured.

The next available configurable option under the **Settings** area is **Business**.

Business

The **Business** area groups together settings for general business functionality. As mentioned earlier in this chapter, the expanded settings can include more than the options described in the area description. This is a good example, as expanding it presents us with the options shown in the following screenshot:

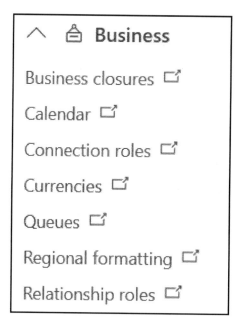

The options available in the **Business** area are elaborated in the subsequent sections.

Business Closures

The **Business Closures** section allows us to define the standard holidays for each year, as well as certain company-specific closures. Usually, these settings are configured at the beginning of a year. These settings work in conjunction with the Service module and integrate into scheduling activities.

Once the business closures are configured, we can export them to Excel or print them.

Scheduling a new Business Closure involves the definition of a name for the record, as well as start and end dates and times, if required. The following screenshot shows the configuration of an organization celebration closure:

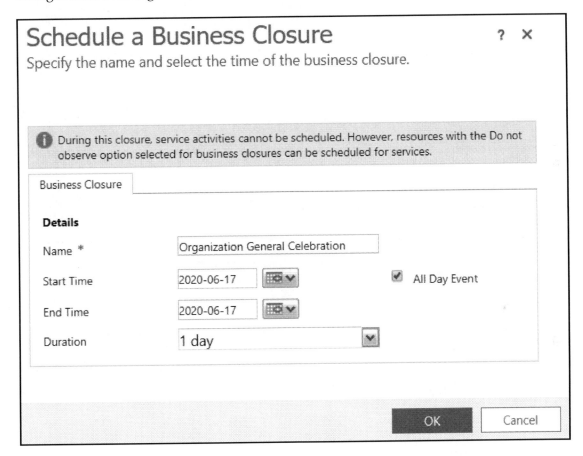

You can schedule business closures to span across hours, full day, or multiple days. This can also be used for seasonal businesses, where they could potentially be closed during certain seasons. An example is a landscaping company that does not include winter services like snow removal, and only performs work from spring to fall.

Calendar

The **Calendar** area is where we define the organization's fiscal year settings. This is one of the configurations that should be done at the beginning, and it seldom changes.

In this area, we configure the fiscal year start date and the period, as well as formatting options for display throughout the system, in the **How to display** area.

Chances are that, once you've initially configured these settings, you might not have to touch them again for a very long time, if ever.

The following screenshot shows these configuration options:

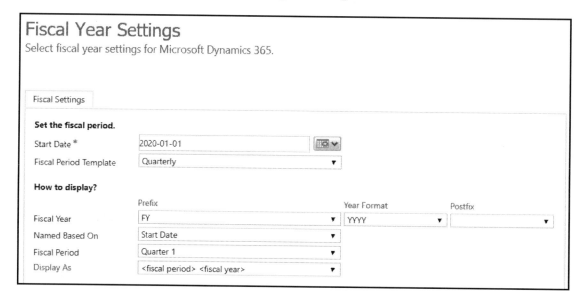

Connection Roles

The **Connection Roles** area allows you to view and define new connections. The connection roles are used for defining relationships between entities based on the specifically defined roles that are assigned.

The following screenshot shows some of the out-of-the-box defined connection roles:

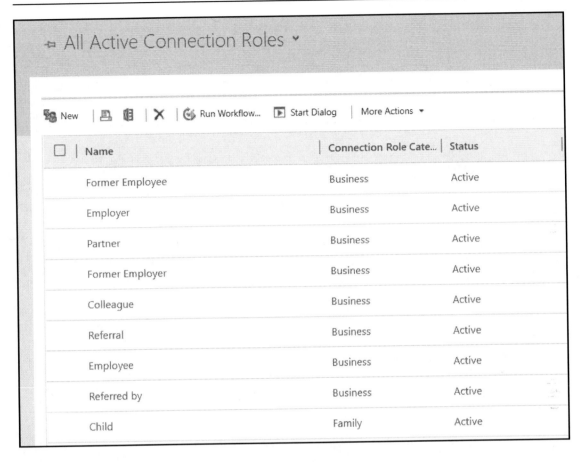

You can apply connection roles in three different ways:

- Apply the same connection role to both the source and the target records.
- Apply a connection role from the source record to the target record only.
- Apply reciprocal roles, which is a role from a source to a target and a related role from a target to a source entity.

The screen to define a new connection role is shown in the following screenshot:

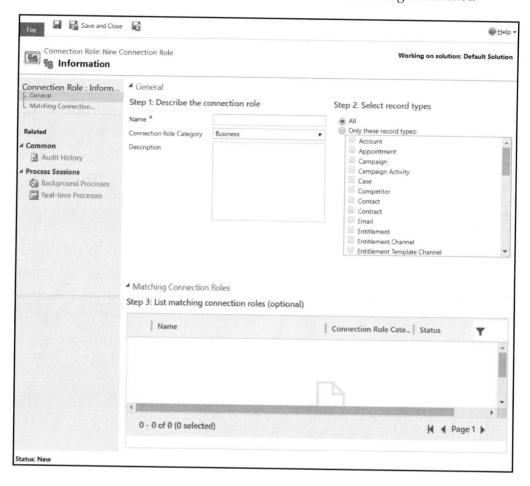

Currencies

The **Currencies** section is where we define the additional currencies used by the system. Each system will have a base currency defined upon the creation of the Organization. On top of this base currency, we can define as many new currencies as needed. For example, if we have retail stores in two different countries, then in addition to the base currency for one of the countries, we can define an additional currency for the other covered country. This allows sales personnel from the other country to track sales in that country's currency. The conversion is done automatically by the system using the conversion rate that is defined.

The following screenshot shows the currencies available with an Organization:

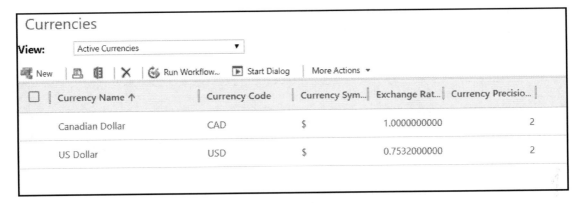

You define a new currency by selecting a specific country, which includes the currency symbol and precision configuration, and defining a conversion rate to the base currency, as shown in the following screenshot:

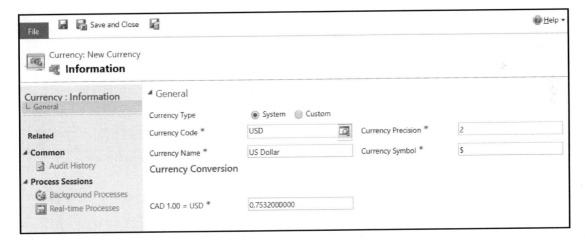

Note that the currency conversion rate must either be maintained manually by an administrator or custom code must be used to create an automation.

Queues

The **Queues** area allows us to manage system Queues. By default, Queues are created for users and teams in the system, but they can be created for all customizable entities in Dynamics 365.

Queues can be either public or private. Queue Items residing in private Queues are only accessible to members of that Queue.

 We can store multiple Queue Item types in a Queue. We can have items for entities such as Cases, Tasks, and Emails in the same queue.

In addition to the standard information regarding the item placed in the Queue, Queues also store information about the user that is working on each queue item.

A very important aspect of automating Queues is the ability to enable workflows and audits for Queues. This helps with automating processes in order to validate specific business processes and rules. The processes are automated around processing various Queue Items, improving productivity, and tracking progress. Auditing allows us to report on changes at various stages in processing Queue Items.

 Starting with the introduction of Service Pack 1 for Dynamics CRM 2013, improvements to managing Queues access now allow for private Queues.

The following screenshot shows a listing of Queues that are available in a simple Organization:

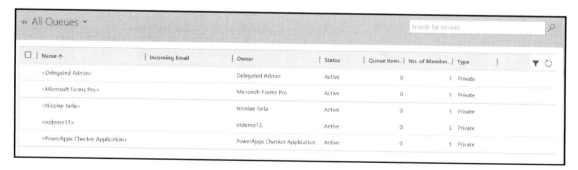

	Name ↑	Incoming Email	Owner	Status	Queue Item...	No. of Member...	Type
	‹Delegated Admin›		Delegated Admin	Active	0	1	Private
	‹Microsoft Forms Pro›		Microsoft Forms Pro	Active	0	1	Private
	‹Nicolae Tarla›		Nicolae Tarla	Active	0	1	Private
	‹ntdemo13›		ntdemo13	Active	0	3	Private
	‹PowerApps Checker Application›		PowerApps Checker Application	Active	0	1	Private

Regional Formatting

At the time of writing, the **Regional Formatting** area takes you to the classic **System Settings**. As we get closer to the transition date to the Unified Interface, this area will undoubtedly receive an update.

Relationship Roles

The **Relationship Roles** section allows us to manage the labels that define relationship roles. This type of relationship existed in previous versions of Dynamics CRM before the introduction of Connections and is retained in the system for backward compatibility. The Connections are much more versatile and should be used for all new customizations.

One of the major limitations of Relationship Roles is that they are only available to define relationships between Accounts, Contacts, and Opportunities.

This feature has been marked as deprecated from the next version of Dynamics 365.

Now, let's turn our attention to the next option available in the **Settings** area, **Users + Permissions**.

Users + Permissions

The Users + Permissions section groups together typical user management settings, as shown in the following screenshot:

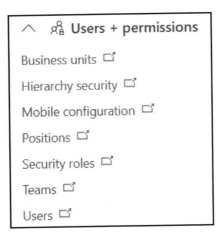

Let's explore these user management settings one by one in the following sections.

Business Units

The **Business Units** area allows us to customize various Business Units and their relationships. Within every Dynamics 365 Organization, there is one main Business Unit created upon the creation of an Organization. Additional Business Units can be added as children of this main Business Unit or as children of its children.

With the Business Unit structure, we can create a tree structure of parent–child Business Units. The purpose of using Business Units is mainly for security modeling. As part of configuring security roles, permissions allow you to configure access as follows:

- None Selected
- User
- Business Unit
- Parent: Child Business Units
- Organization

Your typical business unit configuration screen looks like the following screenshot:

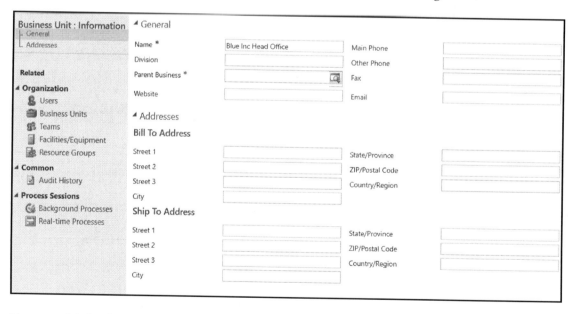

You can think of Business Units as separate containers of data. Security will allow you access through one of the configurations for either the entire organization, the current Business Unit, or the current and all child Business Units. This model will allow separation where required—for example, between a finance department and a sales group.

Hierarchy Security

The Hierarchy Security is an extension of the default security model in Dynamics 365 that allows the use of business units, security roles, sharing, and teams to create a more comprehensive and easier-to-manage security model. This offers a more granular way of configuring access to specific records and record types.

This model allows for the configuration of either a Manager hierarchy or a Position hierarchy. These two models differ based on the location of resources within the various related Business Units.

While a Manager hierarchy closely mimics the typical tree-like structure of a traditional organization, the Position hierarchy allows for mapping more modern and dynamic organizations.

Mobile Configuration

The **Mobile Configuration** area allows for configurations that are related to the mobile experience, in particular to mobile offline capabilities. The following screenshot shows the **Mobile Offline** setup area:

Microsoft Dynamics 365 has been supporting various mobile experiences for a few versions now, from the original mobile page, which was nothing more than a stripped-down basic form designed for small screens that had reduced functionality, to newer and more robust specific mobile applications that allow us to work not only with various mobile screen sizes, but also provide support for various mobile platforms. We now have applications for the most common platforms, including Windows Phone, iOS, and Android, for both phones and tablets.

This mobile application interface has been streamlined and standardized, and now it presents a familiar experience across all devices and platforms. With the move to the Unified Interface, a new responsive experience has been provided that adapts to various screen sizes and devices.

Various profiles can be managed independently, defining properties for multiple groups of users. Within each profile, we can define the entities available for offline access, as shown in the following screenshot:

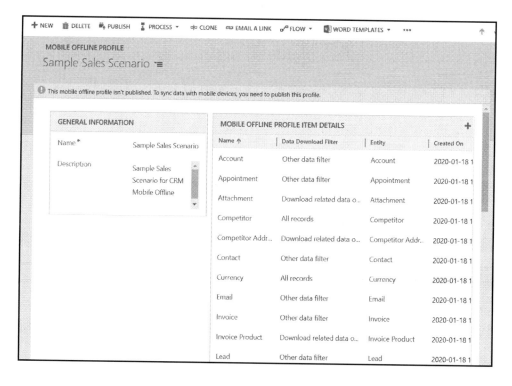

Positions

The **Positions** configuration area allows us to define an Organization's structure, with related roles. The following screenshot shows a subset of related roles configured for an Organization:

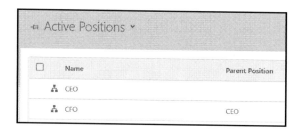

Security Roles

The **Security Roles** area is where we define specific roles and permissions. There is a tight relationship here with the **Business Units** configuration. The following screenshot shows a sub-set of default Security Roles on the platform, along with the Business Units they belong to:

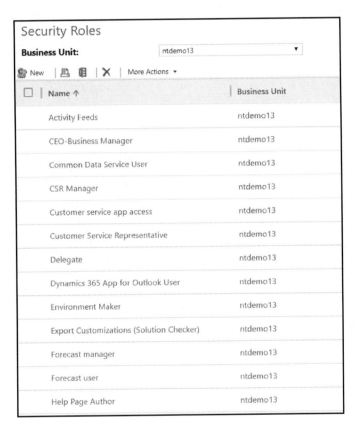

We can create as many Security Roles as needed, and we can assign one or more security roles to a user. The final permissions are determined by merging all permissions allocated through all the Security Roles assigned to a user.

Security Roles can be assigned to either a user or a team. Assigning a Security Role to a Team will give all Team members the same permissions as the Team.

All Security Roles are assigned to a Business Unit or a Team. Once one or more Security Roles are assigned to a Team in the context of a Business Unit, they exist for that Team, and are available for the current Business Unit and its child Business Units if they are so configured.

From a configuration perspective, when the intention is to carry Security Roles with a solution, you should create them in the top-most parent Business Unit, and cascade them to the child Business Units. This ensures the availability of the roles throughout the various Business Units.

Teams

The **Team** section allows us to define and manage Teams in the system. Defining a Team involves naming the Team, assigning it to a particular Business Unit, defining who the Team administrator is (by default the user creating the team), and determining and assigning the Team members. Once a Team is created, going to **Manage Roles** allows us to associate one or more Security Roles to the Team.

The Teams configuration screen is shown in this screenshot:

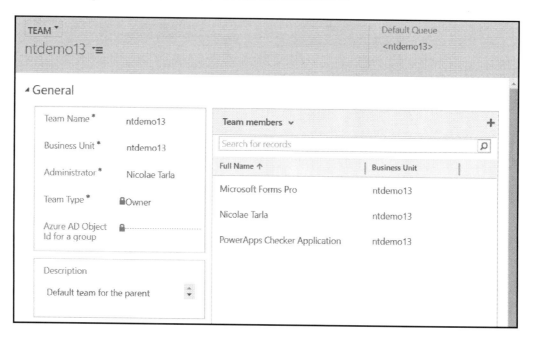

Users

Finally, at the lowest level, user management is the ability to define and manage the users that will be able to access the platform.

We have a large variety of views available to view the **users** listing, with various filter options already created for us to use. We can see users by their status, by ownership, by roles, by relationship, Team, or social relationship. This area is also the entry point for adding new users to the system, disabling users, or updating their information.

A user-management screen is shown in the following screenshot:

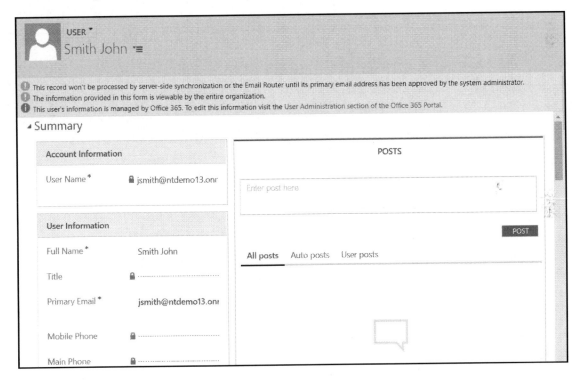

In order to be able to track and make sure that users do not take destructive actions on our solution and data, auditing is essential for any application. The next section will introduce you to the auditing capabilities available.

Audit and logs

The **Audit and logs** area allows a system administrator to peek at the platform performance, look at the jobs that have been triggered and their status, and manage the auditing capabilities of the platform. The following screenshot shows the configurable options available:

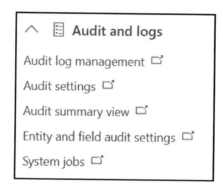

Let's look at these options one by one in detail in the following sections.

Audit log management

The **Audit log management** allows us to view a listing of all the logs, with the start and end dates. For managing space, we can remove older logs from this view.

Active management of logs is crucial, as it can result in unnecessary space consumed, thereby increasing the overall cost. Dynamics 365 has a consumption-based pricing model, and unnecessary data should be purged from the system or extracted to another system in order to keep costs under control.

Audit settings

The **Audit settings** area allows us to enable auditing across the entire organization. In order to leverage the auditing features, you must first enable auditing globally, followed by specific entity-level configurations.

Dynamics 365 allows extensive auditing down to the field level. This can be enabled on any Organization. Careful attention should be given to how much we need to audit, as this excessive auditing can have a negative impact on both performance and data storage. The more you audit, the more space you will require for the audit logs.

Audit summary view

The **Audit summary** area allows us to investigate the audit trace logs, filter by specific categories, as well as manage the history of changes.

Entity and field audit settings

The **Entity and field audit settings** link takes us back to the default solution management. You can configure auditing at the entity level, as mentioned previously.

> You should be configuring the entity-level auditing within your configuration solutions, and not at the default solution level.

System Jobs

System Jobs, also known as asynchronous operations, are a way to create and manage the execution of asynchronous system operations. These operations include the execution of workflows, running plugins asynchronously, and other background jobs. These operations are managed in the database through records in the async operation entity.

The following screenshot shows a listing of the most recent System Jobs in an environment:

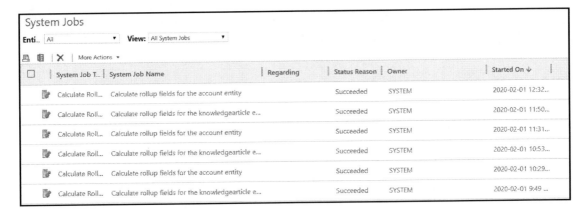

You can filter the view of jobs by entity, and by using the predefined System Jobs views available. These include a listing of all jobs, as well as jobs by status. This makes it easier to find a job you are looking for.

Opening a job, we can see status details about the owner of the job, as well as the time it was created and completed. For jobs that fail and are set to automatically retry, we also have a retry count presented in the job details. The following screenshot shows this view:

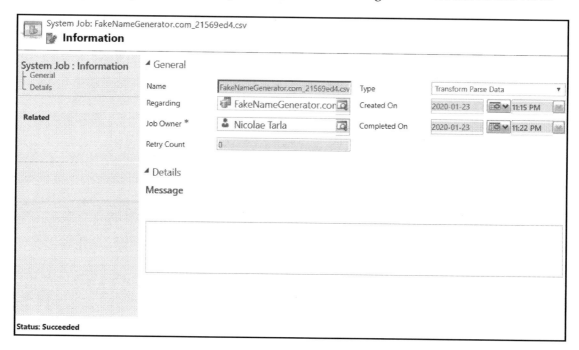

In the System Jobs view, expanding the **More Actions** dropdown presents us with additional commands to manage the jobs. The following screenshot shows these options:

You can also export the list of jobs to Excel for further analysis.

Having data is one thing, but being able to visualize it in a way that makes more sense to a human is essential. The next section looks at various template options for creating such visualizations.

Templates

The **Templates** area collects options for managing various entity templates, document templates, email signatures, and templates, as well as mail merge templates. The following screenshot shows these options:

These options are described in more detail in the following sections.

Access team templates

The **Access team templates** area allows the creation of configurable permission sets for a specific entity. The following screenshot shows the configuration of one such template:

Article templates

The **Article templates** section allows us to create simplistic templates for knowledge-base articles through a wizard-based interface. We can create various sections within a template, and we have limited options to modify the text properties.

An article template must be activated before it can be used to generate new knowledge-base articles.

Contract templates

The **Contract templates** area allows us to manage and create templates defining support contracts. Here, we can define the frequency for billing, service level, working hours/schedule, and the type of allotment. We can have contracts limited by the number of cases, time, or coverage dates.

By default, a single Service Contract template is created in the system. We can remove it, modify it, or create new ones as needed.

This feature has been marked as deprecated from the next release.

Data import templates

The **Data import template** area allows us to download standard entity templates. We can then populate these templates with data and use them to import this data into the system.

Document templates

The **Document templates** area allows for the creation of various templates to be used for printable documents through a wizard-based process. We can have both Excel- and Word-based templates. The following screenshot shows a listing of the default templates that are available out of the box:

	Type ↑	Name ↑	Status	Modified On	Modified By
	Microsoft Excel	Campaign Overview	Activated	2020-01-18 1:50 ...	SYSTEM
	Microsoft Excel	Case SLA Status	Activated	2020-01-18 1:50 ...	SYSTEM
	Microsoft Excel	Case Summary	Activated	2020-01-18 1:50 ...	SYSTEM
	Microsoft Excel	Pipeline Management	Activated	2020-01-18 1:50 ...	SYSTEM
	Microsoft Word	Account Summary	Activated	2020-01-18 1:50 ...	SYSTEM
	Microsoft Word	Campaign Summary	Activated	2020-01-18 1:50 ...	SYSTEM
	Microsoft Word	Case Summary	Activated	2020-01-18 1:50 ...	SYSTEM
	Microsoft Word	Invoice	Activated	2020-01-18 1:50 ...	SYSTEM
	Microsoft Word	Invoice Summary	Activated	2020-01-18 1:50 ...	SYSTEM
	Microsoft Word	Opportunity Summary	Activated	2020-01-18 1:50 ...	SYSTEM
	Microsoft Word	Order Summary	Activated	2020-01-18 1:50 ...	SYSTEM
	Microsoft Word	Print quote for customer	Activated	2020-01-18 1:50 ...	SYSTEM
	Microsoft Word	Quote Summary	Activated	2020-01-18 1:50 ...	SYSTEM

Available Templates View

Email signatures

The **Email signatures** area allows an administrator to define standard signature templates for the email sent through the platform. You can filter the default view by either personal signatures or all system signatures, depending on the permission.

Email templates

Just as with document templates, you can define standard templates for emails that are automatically generated by the platform. You can include a reference to the record field data in these templates in order to personalize the messages.

Mail merge templates

The **Mail merge templates** area allows us to upload mail merge templates created with Microsoft Word. Here, we can define the template properties, including the associated entity, the language, and the base Word document to be used.

 Mail merge has been marked as deprecated from the next version.

The next section will focus on configuring email integration and leveraging various options for a richer user experience.

Email

The **Email** area collects the configurations concerning global email settings, email tracking, profiles, and mailboxes. The following screenshot shows the expanded area and the available options:

Let's explore these options in the following sections.

Email settings

The **Email settings** area includes configurations for security, notifications, attachment global limitations, server synchronization options, and specific form options for emails. The following screenshot shows these options:

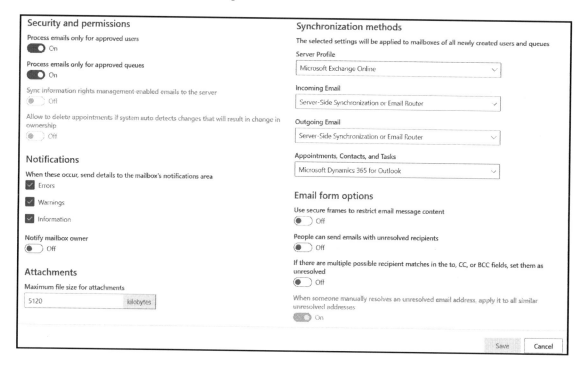

The synchronization methods rely heavily on the definitions of email server profiles.

Email tracking

The **Email tracking** area provides the necessary configurations for tracking email communication within the platform. The use of correlations and tracking tokens is controlled from here, as well as the definition of the preferred token format.

Folder-level tracking can be enabled where supported by leveraging Exchange folders.

In addition, tracking between people can be enabled as single or separate activities.

The following screenshot shows the available configuration options in this area:

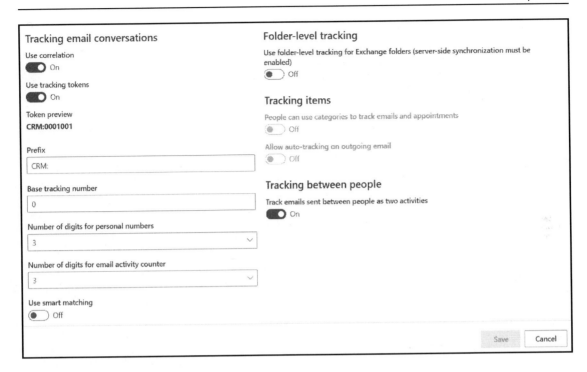

Mailboxes

The **Mailboxes** area allows us to manage individual mailboxes separately. For each mailbox, we can configure the synchronization method to either use an Email Server Profile already created or include a specific setting for incoming and outgoing emails, as well as appointments, contacts, and tasks. When an Email Server Profile is not being used, we can specify that it should use Microsoft Dynamics for Outlook, server-side synchronization, email routers, or a forward mailbox as needed. We can do this for both incoming and outgoing messages. For the other items to be synchronized, including appointments, contacts, and tasks, the only available options are Microsoft Dynamics CRM for Outlook or server-side synchronization.

Note that the email router does not support synchronizing appointments, contacts, or tasks.

Once a mailbox is configured and the email is approved, we can test and enable the mailbox by clicking on the ribbon on **Test & Enable Mailbox**:

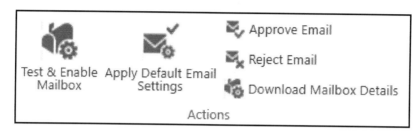

This runs a validation process and returns status messages regarding the success of your configuration. The process to test the configuration runs asynchronously, which can result in a slight delay before the actual result is displayed. You will first be notified that the test has been scheduled. Once it's completed, you will get the results.

Server profiles

The email server profiles allow us to configure one or more profiles for email handling. We can configure both Exchange and POP3-SMTP servers for integration with Dynamics 365. This allows us to cover the configuration for various types of email servers, including public email services from other third-party providers.

For **Exchange** configuration, if the Exchange server is in the same domain as our Dynamics 365 environment, then we can use the **Auto Discover Server Location** option, which simplifies the configuration process.

For each profile created, we need to configure the authentication rules, either by using specified credentials, Windows-integrated authentication, or setting it as anonymous where this option is supported. We can also specify the same or separate credentials to be used for incoming and outgoing emails.

Once a profile is created, we can manage related mailboxes from within the profile or separately.

The next section will delve into the configurable integration options, where we get to leverage other Microsoft-provided features and solutions to enrich the user experience and the platform functionality.

Integration

The **Integration** area brings together the configuration section for the most common integrated platforms. The following screenshot shows the available options:

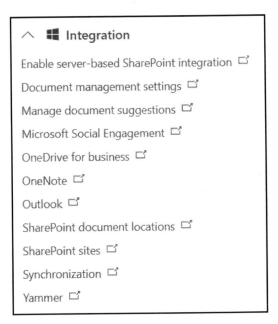

A subset of these options is commonly configured with most deployments. Let's look at these and discover what options are provided:

- **Enable server-based SharePoint integration**: As covered in `Chapter 11`, *Out-of-the-Box Integration Capabilities,* SharePoint integration provides advanced document management and versioning capabilities to the platform. This is one of the integrations that is configured in the majority of deployments.
- **Document management settings**: This relates to the SharePoint configuration and defines the entities for which SharePoint libraries will be created.

- **Manage document suggestions**: The document suggestions functionality is driven by similarity rules defined in an environment. With these settings, we can also enable the ability to suggest documents from an external source.
- **Microsoft Social Engagement (MSE)**: MSE has been discontinued; this area is still present for backward compatibility reasons.
- **OneDrive for Business**: The functionality of OneDrive for Business relies heavily on SharePoint integration and was covered in `Chapter 11`, *Out-of-the-Box Integration Capabilities*.
- **OneNote**: This is another feature that relies on the SharePoint configuration, and allows OneNote functionality within Dynamics 365.
- **Outlook**: This option points to the configurations related to the Outlook integration functionality. We can configure synchronization intervals for email and address books.
- **SharePoint document locations and SharePoint sites**: These areas hold additional configuration options for mapping existing document locations and sites into your Dynamics 365 instance.
- **Synchronization**: This area extends the standard Outlook configuration by capturing rules for appointments, contacts, and tasks, as well as resource bookings for Field Service functionality.
- **Yammer**: The Yammer network has been discontinued as a standalone network and is now fully integrated as part of Office 365. This area allows for the configuration of integration to Yammer to extend the capabilities of your standard Sales team.

The next section will delve into the many aspects of managing the most important part of any platform—its data.

Data management

The **Data management** section collects a set of configurations that are related to various data-management activities, including managing data jobs, importing and exporting data, and some automation. The following screenshot shows the available options:

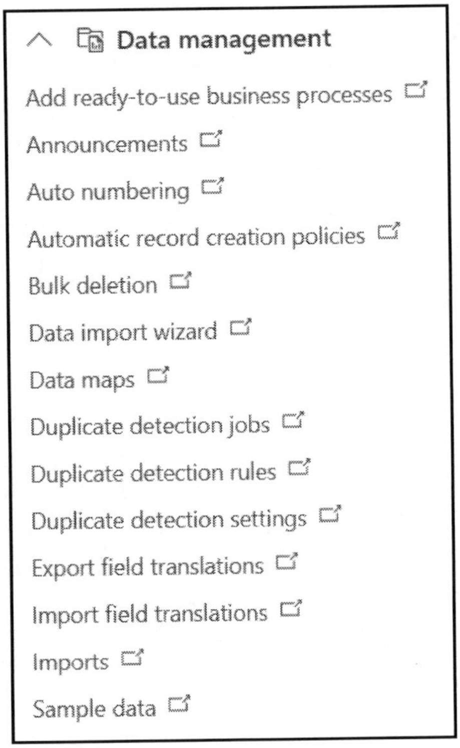

∧   ▣ **Data management**

Add ready-to-use business processes ⬀

Announcements ⬀

Auto numbering ⬀

Automatic record creation policies ⬀

Bulk deletion ⬀

Data import wizard ⬀

Data maps ⬀

Duplicate detection jobs ⬀

Duplicate detection rules ⬀

Duplicate detection settings ⬀

Export field translations ⬀

Import field translations ⬀

Imports ⬀

Sample data ⬀

Let's explore some of these options available in the **Data management** section in more detail in the following sections.

Auto-numbering

Auto-numbering allows the definition of standard numbering formats for entities such as Contracts, Cases, Quotes, Orders, Invoices, Campaigns, Articles, Categories, and Knowledge Articles. The following screenshot shows the formatting options for the Orders entity, which defines a three-letter prefix, followed by a number and a random six-character suffix:

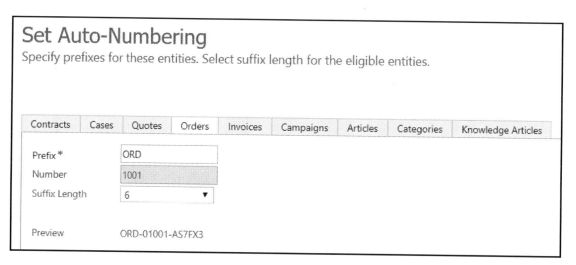

Automatic record creation policies

The **Automatic record creation policies** area allows for the customization of autocreation rules. Based on the settings provided, we can generate new records from incoming emails, based on valid entitlements and activities related to a resolved case. We can also configure automatic responses notifying customers that the provided information was successfully captured and queued for action.

The following screenshot shows some of the conditions available, as well as the channel selection option:

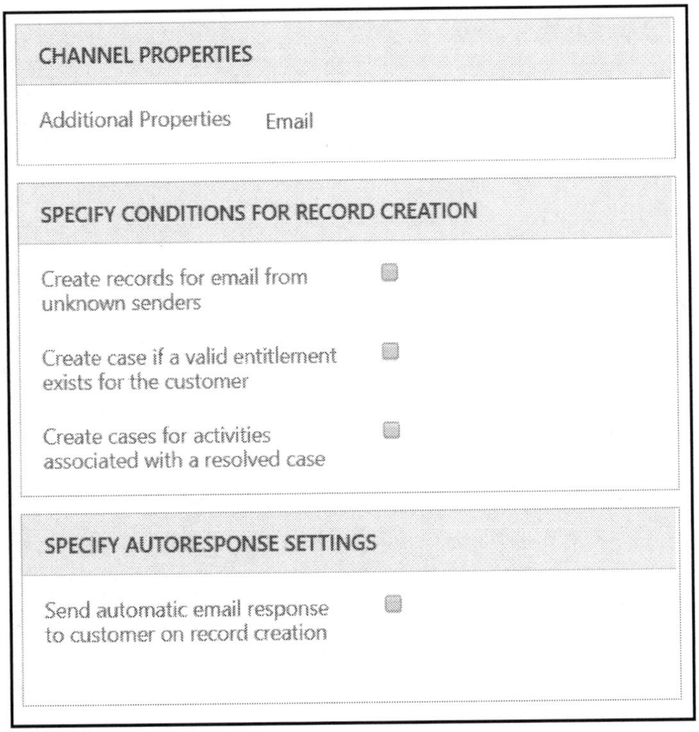

CHANNEL PROPERTIES

Additional Properties   Email

SPECIFY CONDITIONS FOR RECORD CREATION

Create records for email from
unknown senders

Create case if a valid entitlement
exists for the customer

Create cases for activities
associated with a resolved case

SPECIFY AUTORESPONSE SETTINGS

Send automatic email response
to customer on record creation

Defining the creation rules involves defining a set of conditions as well as a set of actions to be executed.

Once rules are created, they must be activated to make them available across the entire organization.

Data import wizard

The data import wizard allows us to manage various data import jobs. We can see the status of an import job, the number of successfully imported records, and the number of failures. Drilling down into a job, we have access to the errors, and the ability to export the failed rows, re-edit them, and re-import them. The following screenshot shows some import jobs with the associated failures:

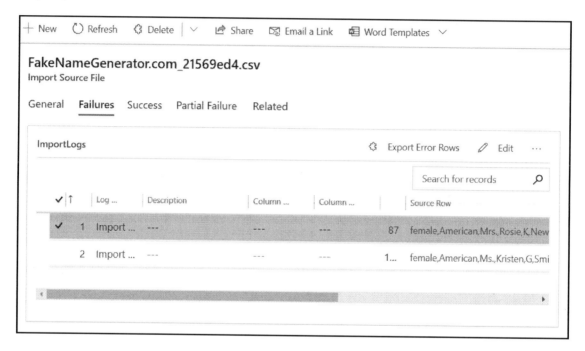

Data maps

The **Data Maps** area allows us to manage the saved maps for data imports. Here, we see a listing of existing data maps. We have a choice of views with filters for active, inactive, and personal data maps, as shown in the following screenshot:

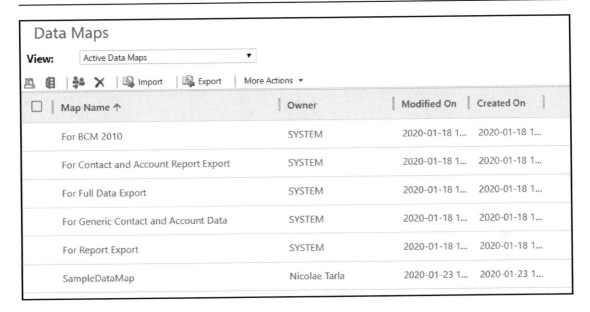

We can import or export data maps, share them, and activate or deactivate existing maps.

Duplicate detection rules

In the **Duplicate Detection Rules** area, we have the ability to enable some of the out-of-the-box rules provided or create new rules and update existing ones. For a rule to be active, it must be published.

When editing rules, you must unpublish the rule first, make the necessary modifications, and then publish the rule again to make it available to all users.

Out of the box, a set of rules is made available, as shown in the following screenshot:

These cover the most common scenarios for duplicate detection, but can be further customized to reflect your organization's needs.

Duplicate detection settings

The **Duplicate Detection Settings** area allows us to enable or disable duplicate detection, and has options for some of the most common scenarios when duplicate detection should run. We can check for duplicates upon the creation and updating of a record, when Outlook goes offline and comes back online, and during the importing of data.

The following screenshot shows this configuration window:

Duplicate Detection Settings
Select default duplicate detection settings for your organization.

Settings

Enable Duplicate Detection
☑ **Enable duplicate detection:**
  Detect duplicates:
    ☑ When a record is created or updated
    ☑ When Microsoft Dynamics 365 for Outlook goes from offline to online
    ☑ During data import

The other, equally important options under the **Data management** section are listed as follows:

- **Add ready-to-use business processes**: This option presents a wizard to allow you to add default business processes. This option is deprecated, and business processes will be moved into Microsoft AppSource. These processes include common Sales, Service, and Marketing scenarios.
- **Announcements**: Announcements are also deprecated. They will be removed in a future major release, but are still available for backward compatibility.
- **Bulk deletion**: This option presents us with a filtered view of system jobs, presenting the delete jobs, their status, and the number of deleted records and failures.
- **Duplicate detection jobs**: The **Duplicate Detection Jobs** area allows a user to see existing duplicate detection jobs, the status of each job, and gives them the ability to create new jobs manually. Here, we have the option to select various views from a listing of six default system views. We can filter by jobs completed, jobs in progress, jobs not started, and recurring jobs. We can also filter by jobs belonging to the current user.

- **Export field translations**: This option allows us to export a package to be used for updating field translations. This is a ZIP archive including two XML definition files. The `CrmFieldTranslations.xml` file contains the defined translations.
- **Import field translations**: Going in the opposite direction, once a translation package has been exported and possibly modified, it can be imported back into an organization. This allows for the easy movement of field translations from one environment to another.
- **Imports**: This area presents a listing of all previous data imports that were executed. You have several views, as shown in the following screenshot:

- **Sample data**: This area allows an administrator to install or remove a set of sample data.

No platform is ready without security, and as part of this, we need to make sure that our data is encrypted. The next section looks at this topic.

Encryption

The **Data Encryption** area presents us with the ability to manage an organization's encryption key. We can check, change, and activate an encryption key here. It is essential that an organization manages its encryption key; any issues here could result in losing access to the organization's data.

The encryption key configuration screen is shown in the following screenshot:

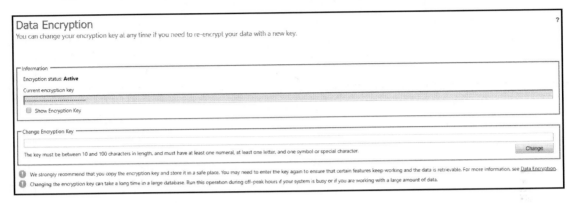

Next in the **Settings** area, let's look at a section that points us back to some of the remaining legacy settings.

Resources

The **Resources** area points us to legacy configurations, including the classic web interface for settings and configurations for Dynamics 365 for Outlook. This area is presented in the following screenshot, but will most likely disappear once Dynamics 365 fully transitions to the Unified Interface:

As a part of the transition to a modern platform, and the changes brought over by the new unified interface, the next section looks at the unified modern experience provided with the new versions of the platform.

Leveraging a unified experience

As part of the move to the unified experience, the entire administration is now moving under the control of the Power Platform Admin center. This creates a centralized location where multiple settings can be grouped together. Multiple environments within the same tenant can be managed together from the same interface, along with features handling **Data integration** and **Data gateways**, various **Data policies**, **Analytics**, and the new **Help** and **support** center. All of the Admin centers are also accessible from this interface. The following screenshot shows this interface:

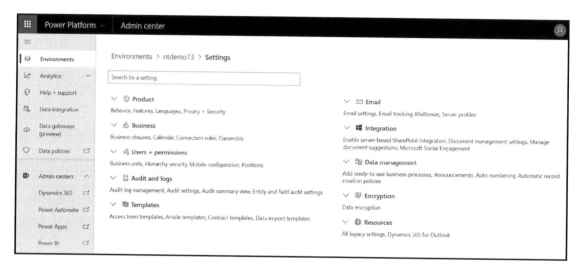

A listing of all of the environments can be shown by selecting the **Environments** option in the left navigation bar as shown in the following screenshot:

By expanding the **Analytics** area, we can look at a summary dashboard, as shown in the following screenshot:

Selecting the **Storage capacity** tab shows us the usage by the environment.

The **Common Data Service** area shows various dashboards describing the environment over a select period of time, as shown in the following screenshot:

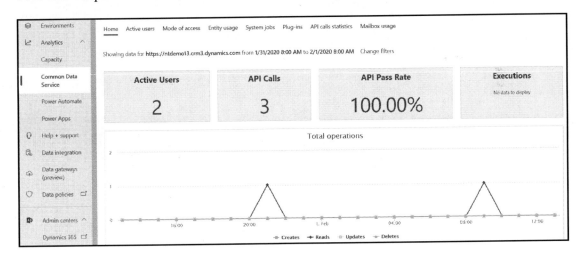

Expanding the **Admin centers** presents us with a link to the classic Dynamics 365 administration console. This opens a new tab in the **Administration Center**, as shown here:

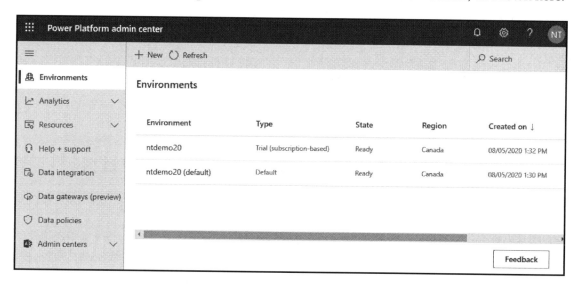

Here, we can see the available environment updates in the **UPDATES** tab.

In the **SERVICE HEALTH** tab, we can see whether there are any health concerns regarding your environment. When there are issues with cloud performance, this section will contain various notifications.

The **BACKUP & RESTORE** tab allows us to see the automated daily backups that take place and enables us to trigger a manual backup. You should always create a backup before pushing new solutions that have an impact on the organization's schema.

Note that most of these features have already been transitioned to the Power Platform Admin portal. For example, the **Environments** area in the **Power Platform admin center** presents the same instances that are available through the classic Administration Center, as shown in the following screenshot:

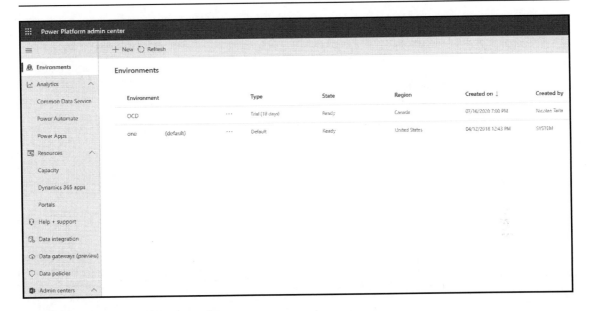

The following screenshot shows the options available for backing up or restoring an environment in the **Power Platform admin center**:

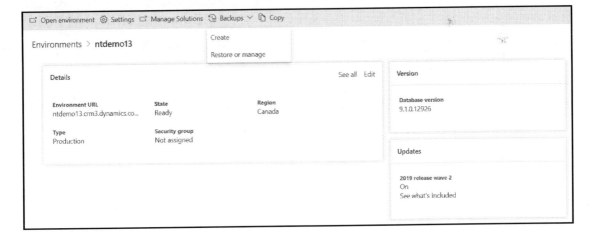

Finally, the **APPLICATIONS** tab allows an administrator to see and manage the installed and available solutions through the **Power Platform admin center**, as shown in the following screenshot:

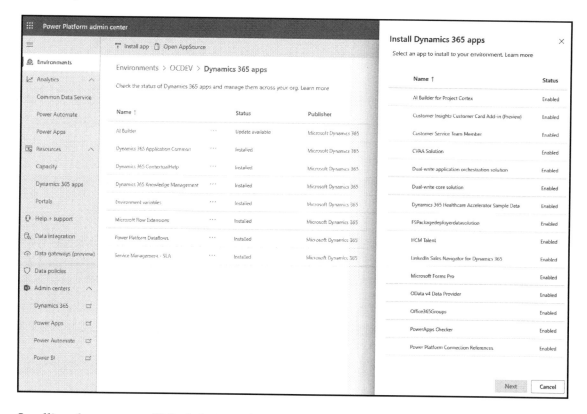

Scrolling down, you will find the **Portal Add-On**. You can choose this option and select **Manage** to deploy a portal for your instance. This will take you to a new tab presenting the **Portal Details** on the **PowerApps Portals admin center**, as shown here:

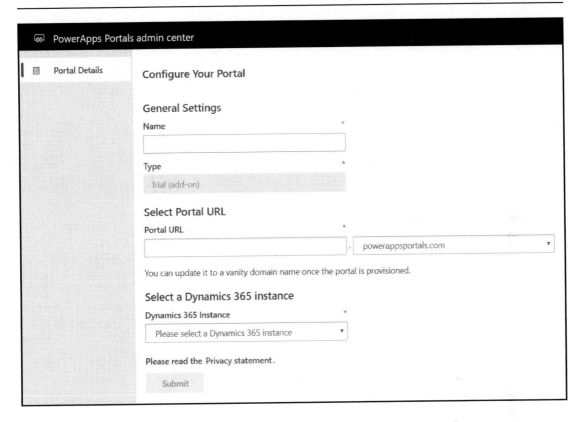

When selecting and validating the configuration, you are prompted to select a name, a URL, an instance, the portal audience type, and the portal type to be deployed.

Here, you will find the standard classic portals, as well as the new **Common Data Service Base Portal** currently in preview, as seen here:

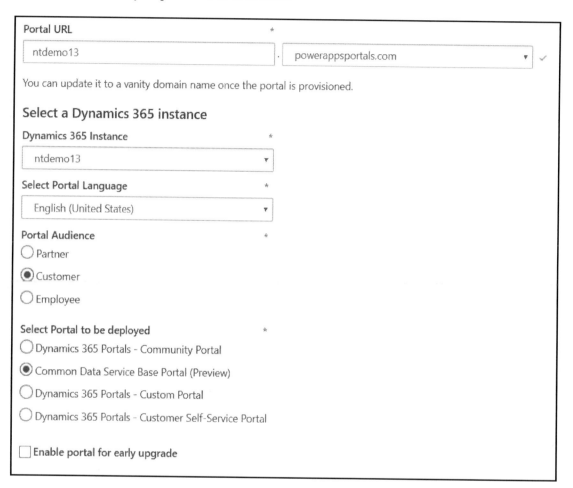

While a portal is being provisioned, you will see the status grayed out in the Power Apps maker portal, as shown in the following screenshot:

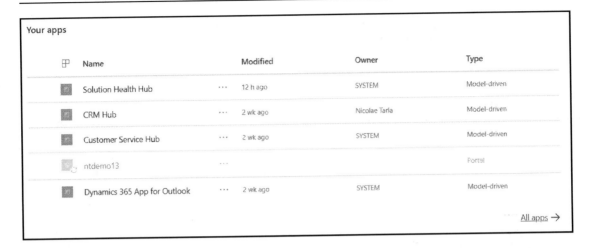

The status is also presented in the **PowerApps Portals admin center**, as shown in the following screenshot:

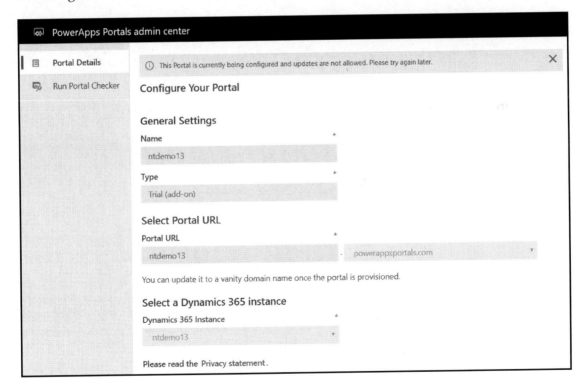

Once a portal is provisioned, you should be able to access it at the URL you have configured during the provisioning process.

The unified experience driven by the Unified Interface is the result of a lot of effort from Microsoft. It brings disparate pieces together, and creates a standard and robust model for future platform evolution and extensions. This is not a matter of *if I want it*, but rather of *when I need it*, which is why transitioning to this interface will be mandatory before the end of 2020. This could require some effort for certain implementations, as certain features are deprecated and replaced by better and more robust solutions for building extensions. Microsoft has given partners and clients enough lead time to prepare the transition process and be ready when the transition time comes. A lot of customers have already taken advantage of this and have migrated to the new Unified Interface.

 If you have not yet migrated to the Unified Interface, time is running out. Plan for this sooner rather than later.

The advantages of this Unified Interface are obvious once you start using the features: a more streamlined user experience, a more robust way to build rich extensions through the use of PCF controls, and a unified common code base to support the entire platform going forward.

In the next section, let's see a practical scenario of managing users.

Managing users scenario

At the end of Chapter 9, *Customizing Dynamics 365*, we saw a scenario where we created a new custom solution and added a new entity with some additional custom fields. Since this is a new custom entity, the existing permissions do not handle giving users access to this new functionality.

In this scenario, we are looking at creating a new security role and assigning it to a user. This will allow the user to access the functionality provided by our customizations. Let us get started!

Creating a new security role

The default security roles provided with the core platform manage and allow access to the standard entities. Whenever we create custom elements, we need to consider the security of those elements and provide access to security.

Typically, security roles are created just like any other configuration, within the scope of a solution. Depending on the complexity of your solution, you could add the newly created security roles to your existing solution, or for a more complex scenario, you can create a specific solution only for the custom security roles. Having a separate solution allows security changes to be implemented independently of the standard configuration.

For the current example, since the configurations are minimal, we will add the newly created security role to the existing solution.

Start by navigating in the Power Apps maker portal to the environment you have used so far. Find the solution we created in `Chapter 9`, *Customizing Dynamics 365*, and open it. Find the **+ New** option on the ribbon, expand **Other**, and find **Security role**. Select it, as shown in the following screenshot:

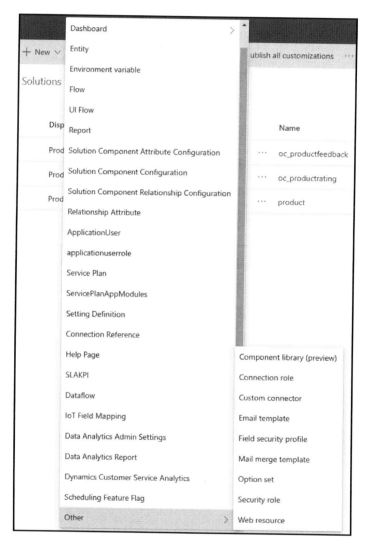

You are now presented with the screen to define properties for a new security role. Provide a **Name** and select the **Business Unit** for this new role. The default **Business Unit** selected is the top parent business unit of your organization.

For our custom role, we have a new entity called **Product feedback** and a relationship to the Product entity. Hence, we need to make sure that the role includes permissions to these entities. We want to have read/write permission to the Product feedback entity as well as read-only permissions to the Product entity.

You will find the Product feedback entity on the **Custom Entities** tab, as well as the Product entity on the **Sales** tab.

For the **Product** entity, select the permissions to **Read**, **Append**, and **Append To**, as shown in the following screenshot:

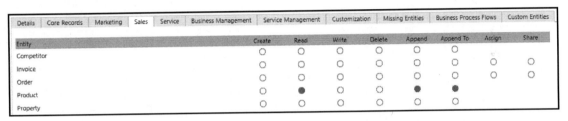

Details	Core Records	Marketing	Sales	Service	Business Management	Service Management	Customization	Missing Entities	Business Process Flows	Custom Entities

Entity	Create	Read	Write	Delete	Append	Append To	Assign	Share
Competitor	○	○	○	○	○	○		
Invoice	○	○	○	○	○	○	○	○
Order	○	○	○	○	○	○	○	○
Product	○	●	○	○	●	●		
Property	○	○	○	○	○	○		

Similarly, for the Product feedback entity we want to give all organization-wide permissions to all **Create**, **Read**, **Update**, **Delete** (**CRUD**) actions on these records. You could choose to restrict these permissions as needed, by selecting, for example, the user instead of the organization so that users will only see their own records. The following screenshot shows this configuration:

Details	Core Records	Marketing	Sales	Service	Business Management	Service Management	Customization	Missing Entities	Business Process Flows	Custom Entities
Process Notes										
ProcessStageParameter				○	○	○	○	○	○	○	○
Product feedback				●	●	●	●	●	●	●	●
Product Inventory				○	○	○	○	○	○		

Note that, alternatively, you could choose to add an existing role and add these additional permissions to that role instead of creating a new role.

Once you save, your newly created security role will appear in the solution components listing, as presented in the following screenshot:

Solutions > **Product Review**							
Display name ∨		Name	Type ∨	Managed…	Modified	Owner	Status
Product feedback	⋯	oc_productfeedback	Entity	🔒	23 h ago	-	-
Product Rating	⋯	oc_productrating	Option set	🔒	-	-	-
Product	⋯	product	Entity	🔒	1 mo ago	-	-
Product Feedback Administrator ↗	⋯	Product Feedback Administrator	Security Role	🔒	27 sec ago	-	-

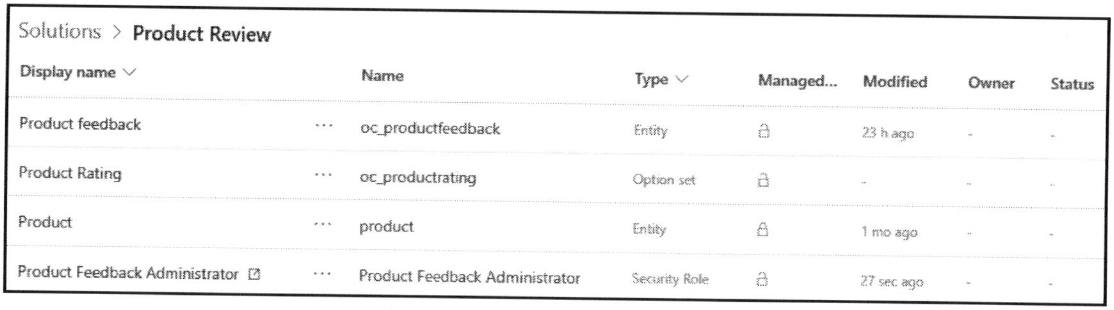

Now that we have a new security role created with permissions to the new entity, we can proceed to assign it to our users.

Assigning a role to a user

For user roles management, we need to navigate to the **Power Platform admin center**, available at: https://admin.powerplatform.microsoft.com.

Once here, select your current environment and select **Settings** on the ribbon. You are presented with the **Settings** area, where you can expand the **Users + permissions** section, as presented in the following screenshot:

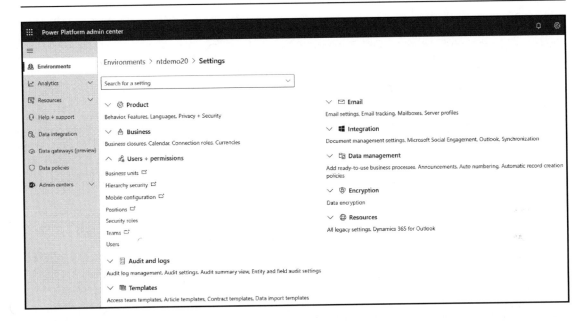

Select **Users**, then select a user to assign this role to. This opens the user details screen, where you can find on the ribbon the option to **Manage Roles**.

On the **Manage User Roles** pop-up scroll through the list of roles until you find the newly created role. In this example, I named it **Product Feedback Administrator**. Select it, as seen in the following screenshot, and click **OK** to assign it:

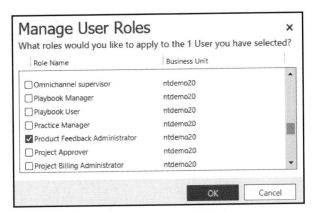

To remove a role, perform these operations in the same order, but simply uncheck the role you want to remove.

Now your user will have the previously assigned permissions, along with the new permissions assigned by our custom security role.

Security works by summing up the permissions granted in all the roles assigned to a particular user. Hence, a user with a Sales role, for example, to which we add this newly created role will have permissions for both the standard Sales functionality and our newly created Product feedback entity.

We have seen in this scenario how to create a new custom security role, define access permissions to specific existing and custom entities, and how to assign this new custom role to a platform user.

User management and security permission management are among the most common administrative scenarios you will encounter during standard platform administration.

Summary

Over the course of this chapter, we had a high-level look at the administration areas of Dynamics 365. While this is not an in-depth presentation of all the available administration options, we touched on most of the important administrative aspects and looked at what each area of the administrative section is dedicated to. Grouping administrative options makes for a cleaner user interface and makes it easier to find the relevant sections and features.

This chapter presented just enough information to get you familiar with the various administration options available with Dynamics 365, and showed you where to find each option. For in-depth information about each of the topics covered, refer to the documentation available from Microsoft at https://docs.microsoft.com/en-us/dynamics365/. This documentation describes the available applications and provides information specific to the on-premise version, the Power Platform, and Power Automate.

Over the course of this book, we have learned about the various applications provided on the Dynamics 365 platform. With the separation of modules, now we have individual applications that govern various functionalities, including Sales, Customer Service, Field Service, Project Service Automation, and Marketing. We also looked at the Power Platform, which is now at the core of the entire Dynamics 365 platform, and how we can leverage it for new custom applications. A couple of our chapters covered configuration, customization, and administration options—namely, Chapter 11, *Out-of-the-Box Integration Capabilities* and Chapter 12, *Custom Integration Capabilities*, which looked at integration options (from the available configurable integration points to custom integrations with other Microsoft-provided and third-party solutions).

This book gave you readers the necessary knowledge to start working with Dynamics 365 and Power Platform. You should have all the necessary understanding to start your career in a citizen developer role, and possibly later into a developer role, if you are so inclined. Development on this platform is heavily reliant on understanding the platform and using configurations where available instead of producing custom code. As such, it is essential for a Dynamics 365 developer to understand the platform and the configurable and customizable options before ever writing their first line of code. This will make for more robust solutions, with easier maintenance overhead.

I truly hope that, over the course of this book, I have provided enough information to make you readers comfortable with this platform and interested in pursuing a career in Dynamics 365 or the Power Platform. Your learning journey is just starting, and this is a platform that evolves at a very fast pace. Continuous learning is essential, but this book has provided the basis for that learning. You might find that in your career, you will focus on one of the applications more than the others. I have encountered consultants with a focus on Marketing, or Field Service, or Sales alone. I think that having an understanding of all of the applications that are available is essential, even if the role you are in at the moment deals with only one of them.

Other Books You May Enjoy

If you enjoyed this book, you may be interested in these other books by Packt:

Implementing Microsoft Dynamics 365 Customer Engagement
Mahender Pal

ISBN: 978-1-83855-687-7

- Explore the new features of Microsoft Dynamics 365 CE
- Understand various project management methodologies, such as Agile, Waterfall, and DevOps
- Customize Dynamics 365 CE to meet your business requirements
- Integrate Dynamics 365 with other applications, such as PowerApps, Power Automate, and Power BI
- Convert client requirements into functional designs
- Extend Dynamics 365 functionality using web resources, custom logic, and client-side and server-side code
- Discover different techniques for writing and executing test cases
- Understand various data migration options to import data from legacy systems

Mastering Microsoft Dynamics 365 Business Central
Stefano Demiliani, Duilio Tacconi

ISBN: 978-1-78995-125-7

- Create a sandbox environment with Dynamics 365 Business Central
- Handle source control management when developing solutions
- Explore extension testing, debugging, and deployment
- Create real-world business processes using Business Central and different Azure services
- Integrate Business Central with external applications
- Apply DevOps and CI/CD to development projects
- Move existing solutions to the new extension-based architecture

Leave a review - let other readers know what you think

Please share your thoughts on this book with others by leaving a review on the site that you bought it from. If you purchased the book from Amazon, please leave us an honest review on this book's Amazon page. This is vital so that other potential readers can see and use your unbiased opinion to make purchasing decisions, we can understand what our customers think about our products, and our authors can see your feedback on the title that they have worked with Packt to create. It will only take a few minutes of your time, but is valuable to other potential customers, our authors, and Packt. Thank you!

Index

C

calculated fields
  using 362, 363
canvas app
  creating 265, 266, 267, 268, 269, 270, 271,
    272, 273, 274, 275, 276, 277, 278, 279
  versus model-driven app 265
Canvas Apps 392
Card Form 335
Cases 115
Charts 352, 354
classical web UI 154, 155, 156
Common Data Model (CDM)
  about 11, 66, 158, 500
  standard core entities 66
Common Data Service (CDS) 11, 158, 290, 291,
    292, 293, 294, 296, 297, 298, 299, 393, 500,
    526
competitor entity 90, 91, 92
composite fields
  working with 360
Connected Customer Service Dashboard 149
Content Management System (CMS) 242, 299
core entities, PSA
  Accounts and Contacts 190
  Leads 191, 192, 193
  Opportunities 191, 192, 193
  Quotes 191, 192, 193
custom entities
  about 57, 330, 331
  versus business entities 329
Customer Service Manager Dashboard 145
Customer Service Performance Dashboard 144
Customer Service Representative Social
  Dashboard 143
Customer Service Representatives (CSRs) 51

D

Dashboards
  about 354, 355, 356
  types 355
Data management area, administration settings
  Auto-Numbering area 590
  Automatic record creation policies area 590

Data import wizard area 592
  Data Maps area 592
  Duplicate Detection Rules area 593, 594
  Duplicate Detection Settings area 594, 596
data source
  defining 469, 471
Data Warehouse (DW) 63
data
  Charts 352, 354
  Dashboards 354, 355, 356
  presenting, to user 347
  Views 348, 350, 351
default solution 317
dialog
  about 392
  alternatives, using 391, 392
  reference link 393
  replacing, with Business Process Flows 392
  replacing, with Canvas Apps 392
document generation template 423, 424, 425
document templates 421, 423
domain name
  configuring, for environment 28, 30, 31
Dynamics 365 App for Outlook
  configuring 445, 446, 447, 448, 449
  features 446
Dynamics 365 application elements
  about 56
  dashboards 61, 62
  entities 56, 57
  modular design 56
  processes 57
  reports 62, 63
Dynamics 365 Customer Service dashboards
  about 138, 140
  interacting, with Streams 140, 142
  interacting, with Tiles 140, 142
  standard dashboards 142, 143
Dynamics 365 Customer Service entities
  cases 125, 126, 127
  knowledge articles 132, 133, 134, 135, 136
  queues 128
  scheduling 131
  services 129, 130
Dynamics 365 Customer Service Processes 136

W

X

Made in the USA
Columbia, SC
06 July 2023

20104796R00352